Bernard Shaw and the Art of Drama

CHARLES A. BERST

Bernard Shaw and
the Art of Drama

UNIVERSITY OF ILLINOIS PRESS   Urbana   Chicago   London

CARL A. RUDISILL LIBRARY
LENOIR RHYNE COLLEGE

© 1973 by the Board of Trustees of the University of Illinois
Manufactured in the United States of America
Library of Congress Catalog Card No. 72–93625
ISBN 0–252–00258–x

822.912

B46b

90752

Nov.1974

*To My Mother
And in Memory of My Father*

ACKNOWLEDGMENTS

A great pleasure in writing this book has come not only from the challenge itself but also from the kind help, good talk, and rigorous teaching it generated. I feel initially grateful to the late James Hall of the University of Washington, who directed my dissertation on Shaw eight years ago, and to William Matchett, who, as editor of *Modern Language Quarterly*, gave me a psychic boost by publishing my first Shaw article. Subsequently a friend at the University of Alberta, Barbara DeLuna, helped unmix my metaphors, only to be followed by a friend at UCLA, Edward Condren, who had me mixing them once again as we charged, lances poised, into aesthetic matters.

In addition to many colleagues at UCLA who have happily prodded me this way and that, the numerous Shavians I encounter in the course of the following pages have my thanks. Special credit and appreciation go to Arthur H. Nethercot for valuable suggestions regarding the manuscript, and to Louis Crompton for a perceptive, generous reading. Students who have been most diligent in matters of research and manuscript preparation are Janet Bloom, Beverly Gray Bienstock, and Geoffrey Harpham.

Four chapters, in slightly different form, have been published as articles. The discussion of *Arms and the Man* appeared in *Modern Language Quarterly* (June 1966), followed by discussions of

Mrs Warren's Profession in *A Journal of English Literary History* (September 1966), *Major Barbara* in *PMLA* (March 1968), and *Caesar and Cleopatra* in *Journal of English and Germanic Philology* (January 1969). My thanks to these journals for their permission to reprint the respective material.

Most deeply, this work is indebted to my wife Roelina, who sustained me with constant understanding and care, and to my daughters Nelina and Caroline, who enriched my compound, quirky cogitations with moments of joy.

CONTENTS

PREFACE

A Need to Explore the Plays

One remarkable fact about the plethora of books on Shaw is that very few have undertaken a close critical analysis of his plays as separate works of art. Good biographies, critical surveys, source studies, and specialized critiques abound, but those achievements of Shaw which are likely to be most enduring—his individual plays —have been sorely neglected. Ironically, this neglect is partly the result of an abundance of riches. The multiplicity of Shaw's masks and talents contributes to intriguing deflections and troubling complications in the study of either the man or his work. On the one hand, biographies unfold his art and philosophy in a context of multifold personal details; on the other hand, philosophical studies are bothered by his aesthetics, and aesthetic studies are haunted by his philosophy. Personality, philosophy, and aesthetics are so profoundly intermixed in Shaw that critics have moved toward approaches which are either sweepingly eclectic or carefully delimiting. While many of these approaches have been valuable in the building of a total image or a particular theme, they have frequently obscured Shaw's most distinctive greatness as a writer of specific plays. The result has been a minor critical paradox, since it is probably through his best plays that we can most deeply understand the man and his philosophy, rather than vice versa. And as it may be plausibly argued that Shaw is the greatest English playwright after Shakespeare, the paradox grows. A more thorough analysis of his outstanding works seems long overdue.

What I am saying is, of course, not new. In 1938 Edmund Wilson sounded a keynote for modern Shaw criticism, suggesting that it move away from personality and philosophy: "It used always to be said of Shaw that he was primarily not an artist, but a promulgator of certain ideas. The truth is, I think, that he is a considerable artist, but that his ideas—that is, his social philosophy proper —have always been confused and uncertain. . . . With Voltaire, it *is* the crusader that counts; with Shaw, it is the dramatic poet."[1] But Wilson's keynote sounded in an empty chamber, and eleven years later, one year before Shaw's death, Stephen Spender could remark about Shaw: "His works have scarcely been discussed by modern critics. The various essays devoted to him have been by enthusiasts of his biography and his personality rather than of his works. Apart from one interesting essay by Edmund Wilson, I can think of no serious criticism of his many volumes."[2]

Both Wilson and Spender oversimplify. From early in the century there have been studies of Shaw's art, climaxing in the third chapter of Eric Bentley's notable book in 1947.[3] And, conversely, while criticism of Shaw as more philosopher than playwright was particularly rampant at the turn of the century, Shaw's ideas have been the focus of numerous anthologies and critical works since the 1930's.

The central point which Wilson and Spender make, however, bears reiterating, especially in 1973. As time passes and Shaw's personality has become more a fond memory than a persistent barb, his ideas and the age that produced them have become correspondingly less challenging and pertinent. Indeed, apart from his plays, Shaw the iconoclast, Fabian spokesman, and Life Force religionist slowly but continually waned ever since the second

1. Edmund Wilson, "Bernard Shaw at Eighty," in *George Bernard Shaw: A Critical Survey*, ed. Louis Kronenberger (Cleveland, 1953), pp. 131–32.

2. Stephen Spender, "The Riddle of Shaw," in Kronenberger, *Shaw: A Critical Survey*, p. 236.

3. Eric Bentley, *Bernard Shaw* (New York, 1947); amended as *Bernard Shaw 1856–1950* (New York, 1957).

decade of the century, along with the Victorian values which had originally excited his concern and hence contributed to his reputation. Shaw's appealing, contentious personality and notoriety long kept him in the public view as a venerable eccentric, a man who had achieved the distinction of becoming a classic in his own lifetime. But along with the classical tag came the public's amused and bemused detachment. Though he survived to the middle of the twentieth century, Shaw scarcely moved the conscience of mankind for the last thirty years of his life. His *avant-garde* spirit was either considered obsolete, disregarded, or absorbed into the amorphous sponge of popular toleration. As he was a character and caricature at once, his ideas might be piquant, slightly startling, or mildly shocking, but, after all, this was the way Shaw was supposed to be. What his admirers liked could be hailed as pithy wisdom; what irritated his detractors could be scorned as senility. With a fate akin to that of Bertrand Russell twenty years later, the nonagenarian died after having survived long in the afterglow of his own legend. The fact that he had survived so vitally was a marvel obscured by the more splendid brilliance of his past.

The mortality which shadows Shaw's personality and ideas has merely discriminated selectively regarding his art, and time has found that the personality and ideas gain immortality, depth, and pertinence as they are an integral element in his plays. This would not have surprised Shaw, who was ambivalent regarding his role as an artist-philosopher. Clearly, he felt that art without a philosophy was hollow. But he also felt that philosophy without art was unlikely to make much of an impression on the world. So he strained his philosophy through the spirit and talents of an artist, not merely explicating thought, but, in the process of giving it life, transmuting it into fine art, an art which not infrequently qualified, contradicted, or transcended his philosophy.

Shaw is so frequently quoted in his role of social critic, propagandist, and philosopher that his comments on the primacy of his art need forceful resurrection. Speaking of *Widowers' Houses*, his first and ostensibly one of his most didactic plays, he commanded: "You will please judge it not as a pamphlet in dialogue but as in intention a work of art as much as any comedy of Molière's is a work of art."[4] In a letter to Golding Bright dated 30 April 1894 he expressed his irritation regarding critics who were quick to react negatively to his unorthodox dramatic voice: "There is nothing that annoys me more than all this nonsense about new schools & the new drama & the rest of it. I suffer from it considerably, as it leads people to construe purely dramatic passages in my plays as interpolations of what are supposed to be my political views."[5] In his drama criticism of the 1890's he is even more sweeping: "In all the life that has energy enough to be interesting to me, subjective volition, passion, will, make intellect the merest tool";[6] and later: "People's ideas . . . are not the true stuff of drama, which is always the naïve feeling underlying the ideas."[7] He touches on variants of this theme again and again, such as in *The Perfect Wagnerite*: "There is only one way of dramatizing an idea; and that is by putting on the stage a human being possessed by that idea, yet none the less a human being with all the human impulses which make him akin and therefore interesting to us."[8]

The heart of Shaw's craft involves more inspiration than calculation, more intuition than rationalism. Shaw anticipated Wilson by more than forty years, defining his own aesthetic subjectivity and poetic spontaneity—aspects of his art which too many critics have overlooked. His emphasis was repeatedly on the creative, instinctive, and dramatic. Observe the following comments, which span his entire playwriting career. In a letter to Henry Arthur Jones, 2 December 1894:

> Like you, I write plays because I like it, and because I cannot remember any period in my life when I could help inventing people and scenes. I am not a storyteller: things occur to me as

4. Quoted, ibid., p. 102.

5. George Bernard Shaw, *Advice to a Young Critic and Other Letters*, ed. E. J. West (New York, 1963), p. 4.

6. *The Works of Bernard Shaw*, XXIII: *Our Theatres in the Nineties* (London, 1931), I, 7.

7. *Works*, XXIV: *Our Theatres in the Nineties*, II, 201–2.

8. George Bernard Shaw, *The Perfect Wagnerite: A Commentary on the Niblung's Ring* (New York, 1916), pp. 30–31.

scenes, with action and dialogue—as moments, developing themselves out of their own vitality.[9]

In a letter to the *New York Times*, 2 June 1912:

> I am not governed by principles; I am inspired, how or why I cannot explain, because I do not know; but inspiration it must be; for it comes to me without any reference to my own ends or interest.
>
> I find myself possessed of a theme in the following manner. I am pushed by a natural need to set to work to write down the conversations that come into my head unaccountably. At first I hardly know the speakers, and cannot find names for them. Then they become more and more familiar, and I learn their names. Finally I come to know them very well, and discover what it is they are driving at, and why they have said and done the things I have been moved to set down.[10]

In a letter to Alexander Bakshy, 24 May 1923:

> A live play constructs itself with a subtlety, and often with a mechanical ingenuity, that often deludes critics into holding the author up as the most crafty of artificers when he has never, in writing his play, known what one of his characters would say until another character gave the cue.
>
> I am not a Rationalist.[11]

And in his postscript to *Back to Methuselah*, 1944:

> When I am writing a play I never invent a plot: I let the play write itself and shape itself, which it always does even when up to the last moment I do not foresee the way out. Sometimes I do not see what the play was driving at until quite a long time after I have finished it; and even then I may be wrong about it just as any critical third party may.[12]

9. *Bernard Shaw: Collected Letters 1874–1897*, ed. Dan H. Laurence (New York, 1965), pp. 461–62.
10. *Shaw on Theatre*, ed. E. J. West (New York, 1959), p. 116.
11. Ibid., p. 184.
12. *Complete Plays with Prefaces* (New York, 1963), II, xci.

This last comment should chasten those who turn to Shaw's prefaces for some final word on his plays. It reveals a critical modesty regarding his own works which one does not ordinarily associate with Shaw, but which runs as a minor motif through all his prefaces and commentaries. The final critical word on Shaw was by no means written by Shaw, and to a degree his commentaries partake of the art of his plays, being frequently more creative than derivative. Thus, while he had an answer to the poet's secret at the end of *Candida*, he observed, "It is only my way of looking at it; everybody who buys the book may fit it with an ending to suit his own taste."[13] For while Shaw could assert that "the quality of a play is the quality of its ideas,"[14] the assertion is deceptive, since in his art his finest ideas are less fixed than fluid, more stimulative than definitive—moving, turning, mutating, and evolving through shifting dramatic perspectives. The ideas in his plays are as frequently tied to emotion and aesthetics as to reason. At their best they concurrently inform and are informed by dynamic theater. In this light Shaw's critical abilities are transcended by the instinctive depths and poetic ambiguities of his dramatic consciousness.

The roots of Shaw's artistic idiom are notably traditional. Martin Meisel has aptly demonstrated Shaw's debt to the nineteenth-century stage,[15] and Shaw himself acknowledges his predecessors all the way back to the ancient Greeks. In his preface to the second volume of *Plays: Pleasant and Unpleasant*, he remarks, "I have always cast my plays in the ordinary practical comedy form in use at all the theatres"[16]—an observation he elaborates in his preface to *Three Plays for Puritans*:

> But my stories are the old stories; my characters are the familiar harlequin and columbine, clown and pantaloon . . . my stage tricks and suspenses and thrills and jests are the ones in vogue when I was a boy, by which time my grandfather was tired of them. . . .

13. Letter to Rugby schoolboys, 8 March 1920; quoted by George A. Riding in "The *Candida* Secret," *Spectator*, 17 Nov. 1950, p. 506; reprinted in *A Casebook on "Candida,"* ed. Stephen S. Stanton (New York, 1962), pp. 168–69.

14. West, ed., *Shaw on Theatre*, p. 290.

15. Martin Meisel, *Shaw and the Nineteenth-Century Theater* (Princeton, 1963).

16. *Complete Plays*, III, 113.

It is a dangerous thing to be hailed at once, as a few rash admirers have hailed me, as above all things original: what the world calls originality is only an unaccustomed method of tickling it.[17]

In his preface to *Back to Methuselah*, Shaw refers to all of his former plays as "a series of comedies of manners in the classic fashion,"[18] an overstatement which he reiterates at the end of his life in a commentary in *The New Statesman and Nation* of 6 May 1950: "The truth was that I was going back atavistically to Aristotle, to the tribune stage, to the circus, to the didactic Mysteries, to the word music of Shakespear, to the forms of my idol Mozart, and to the stage business of the great players whom I had actually seen acting . . . I was, and still am, the most old-fashioned playwright outside China and Japan."[19]

Shaw's distinctive infusion into the traditional genres offers more than a revolutionary spirit; it is a drive toward new levels of awareness, seeking through an artistic sensibility to cultivate, sensitize, and civilize the very quality of his audience's consciousness. It is a thrust in "the struggle of Life to become divinely conscious of itself instead of blindly stumbling hither and thither in the line of least resistance."[20] He remarks in his preface to the second volume of *Plays: Pleasant and Unpleasant* that his drama seeks to *humanize* a shallow society, rather than allowing a shallow society to dehumanize the drama.[21] In an interview appearing in the *Pall Mall Budget* of 19 April 1894 Shaw links this humanization to a classical view of art: "The labourer who has never seen a picture does not know that the scenery round his village is worth looking at. By looking at pictures one learns to appreciate nature. And by looking at plays—if they are reproductions of life as they ought to be—one learns to look intelligently at life."[22] And, more loftily, he extends this in "The Sanity of Art": "Art should refine our sense of character and conduct, of justice and sympathy, greatly

17. Ibid., lx–lxi.
18. Ibid., II, lxxxvii.
19. West, ed., *Shaw on Theatre*, p. 294.
20. *Complete Plays*, III, 500.
21. Ibid., 113.
22. "A Talk with Mr. Bernard Shaw about His New Play," reprinted in *Arms and the Man*, ed. Louis Crompton (New York, 1969), pp. 77–80; quotation, p. 80.

heightening our self-knowledge, self-control, precision of action, and considerateness, and making us intolerant of baseness, cruelty, injustice, and intellectual superficiality or vulgarity."[23] Thus Shaw asserts a profound didacticism which is inherent in the deeper reaches of most fine art. In such terms, his didacticism is less specific and socialistic than aesthetic and humanistic. It strives more for the understanding and sensitivity which underlie enlightened social, moral, and religious action than for detailed solutions. Aesthetics, melded with a nearly spiritual desire for illumination, bring drama and philosophy together, with the scale of reciprocal debt tilting strongly toward art. The intuitive dramatist gives both human dimension to philosophy and philosophy to the human dimension.

Shaw the playwright is thus primarily and admittedly an artist —in theory, inspiration, practice, criticism, and even in philosophy and didacticism. This fact is one which gives considerable trouble to studies which concentrate on his philosophy, his politics, or his historical sensibilities, all areas which his artistic sensibilities qualify. Eminent writers and critics who are favorable to Shaw have frequently described his talent in terms of poetry. Tolstoy commended his "great gift of original thought,"[24] but more notable are Pirandello, who spoke of "the most secret depths of poetry that exist in Shaw,"[25] Mann, who saw the plays in terms of "the winged wit of their poetic idiom,"[26] and Auden, who comments: "For all his theater about propaganda, his writing has an effect nearer to that of music than the work of any of the so-called pure writers."[27] Bentley stresses the primacy of art in Shaw, observing that "his thinking is at all points the thinking of an artist."[28] Meisel deals with Shaw's artistic heritage. Three sensi-

23. *Works*, XIX, 328–29.
24. Quoted in Archibald Henderson, *Bernard Shaw: Playboy and Prophet* (New York, 1932), p. 522.
25. Luigi Pirandello, "Bernard Shaw's *Saint Joan*," *New York Times Magazine*, 13 Jan. 1924; reprinted in *Shavian*, 2, no. 8 (1964), 6–12; quotation, 9.
26. Thomas Mann, " 'He Was Mankind's Friend'," in Kronenberger, *Shaw: A Critical Survey*, p. 254.
27. W. H. Auden, "The Fabian Figaro," in Kronenberger, *Shaw: A Critical Survey*, p. 156.
28. Bentley, *Bernard Shaw 1856–1950*, p. xxiii.

tive critics, discussing *Heartbreak House,* offer a chorus of agreement. Arthur Mizener emphasizes, "This is poetic drama of a very high order, because an imagination of great range and depth has found its expression completely within the conventions of its form";[29] Frederick P. W. McDowell finds, "In Shaw's greatest plays are those symbolic intonations, those spiritual resonances, that indefiniteness of suggestion we associate with greatness in literature";[30] and Robert Brustein speaks of Shaw's "highly charged dramatic poetry."[31]

My proliferation of quotations here may seem like overkill on a point which is entirely too obvious. But if the point is too obvious, one may well ask, then, why critics have neglected so major a playwright in the very capacity at which he excels. The critical surveys, source studies, and specialized critiques are helpful and often stimulating. Louis Crompton's recent book on the social, philosophical, and historical backgrounds of the major plays is a valuable contribution.[32] Good articles have appeared from time to time. But in-depth critical studies of the major plays are still few and far between. If Wilson, Bentley, and a score of writers are correct about Shaw's talents, such a sparsity is deplorable. Thus this book—not to fill a void, but to help counter a neglect, in hopes that others will join in enriching Shaw criticism by dealing critically, individually, and in detail with his major artistic achievements.

Approached as separate, distinctive works, the individual plays reveal the variety and flexibility of Shaw's art. Too many formulizers have tried to pigeonhole Shaw in several narrow dramatic categories, whereas his wide range and diversity are no less a mark

29. Arthur Mizener, "Poetic Drama and the Well-Made Play," *English Institute Essays: 1949* (New York, 1965), p. 54.

30. Frederick P. W. McDowell, "Technique, Symbol, and Theme in *Heartbreak House,*" *PMLA,* 68 (1953), 356.

31. Robert Brustein, *The Theatre of Revolt: An Approach to the Modern Drama* (Boston, 1962), p. 222.

32. Louis Crompton, *Shaw the Dramatist* (Lincoln, Nebr., 1969). Two later works which are welcome additions to the cause but which unfortunately arrived too late for reference here are Leon Hugo's *Bernard Shaw: Playwright and Preacher* (London, 1971), and Margery M. Morgan's *The Shavian Playground: An Exploration of the Art of George Bernard Shaw* (London, 1972).

of his genius than his clearly discernible common denominators. Such elements as his vitality, wit, social criticism, Life Force philosophy, and anticlimactic vision are but aspects of a complex and penetrating aesthetic sensibility. My approach attempts more to explore this sensibility than to categorize it, since the characteristics of Shaw's method are ultimately important according to the richness of their application, and Shaw's art by its nature irrepressibly qualifies and reaches beyond easy critical generalizations. Critical handles are convenient, but they must be employed with flexibility and discretion to grasp such diversity and creative energy. Aesthetically as well as organizationally, therefore, the immediate context of each play is given primary attention here, and while matters of general technique are observed, they are treated cumulatively so that they will achieve definition as they engage various materials. I hope this inductive, cumulative method will arrive at certain perceptions both in depth and breadth which will more fully grasp the genius which lies behind the all-too-easy and abused term, Shavianism.

For the most part I attempt to maintain a broad critical focus on each play I have selected, and to touch on all factors which seem aesthetically central and relevant. This involves considerable probing into new critical territory, an engagement with the best criticism to date, and an occasional playing of devil's advocate to right previous critical imbalances. My view is primarily positive, one which notes certain defects but leaves carping to others. Sources, background material, and much previous criticism are, by and large, relegated to the footnotes, unless they seem to contribute materially to the aesthetic quality or understanding of the given play. Admittedly, much is left unsaid, and ample room remains for future critics. My selection omits *Back to Methuselah*, a fascinating monster which may warrant a book in itself. Otherwise I have selected the major plays, along with a few minor ones which appeal to me for certain problems they pose. The number of good plays I have omitted causes me pain, and may be an incentive for renewed labor—if the Life Force so wills.

Bernard Shaw and the Art of Drama

CHAPTER ONE

MRS WARREN'S PROFESSION

Art over Didacticism

Since *Mrs Warren's Profession* is one of the most openly didactic of Shaw's plays, an examination of its achievement as art should prove helpful in assessing the extent to which Shaw's role as a dramatic propagandist limits his accomplishment as an artist. Few critics nowadays would agree with Percival P. Howe that the preface to *Mrs Warren's Profession* renders the play unnecessary,[1] or would go so far as Alick West and analyze it in terms of a Marxist tract,[2] but the decided tendency to generalize about Shaw's works first in terms of their message and only second in terms of their aesthetics is almost the rule with this early play. Commentators have made three major points, all having to do with the play's message: (1) Shaw's intention is to reveal that the guilt for prostitution lies more upon society than upon immoral women; (2) Shaw's premise, that prostitutes are forced into their profession by social deprivation and not by natural inclination, is inaccurate; and (3) contrary to scandalized contemporary reaction, the play is highly moral.

The first of these points is clear and self-evident from the preface, the play, and Shaw's socialistic background. In the preface

1. Percival P. Howe, *Bernard Shaw: A Critical Study* (New York, 1915), p. 114.
2. Alick West, "*A Good Man Fallen among Fabians*" (London, 1950), pp. 55–66.

Shaw emphasizes that Mrs. Warren's girlhood choice was between wretched poverty without prostitution or comfort and luxuries with it. The blame for the fact that she is offered such squalid alternatives falls squarely onto society: "Though it is quite natural and *right* for Mrs Warren to choose what is, according to her lights, the least immoral alternative, it is nonetheless infamous of society to offer such alternatives. For the alternatives offered are not morality and immorality, but two sorts of immorality."[3] In the play, the society which brooks Sir George Crofts is clearly the villain. It is the society of the well-to-do which derives its luxuries from the suppressed lower classes and maintains its self-respect because it "doesnt ask any inconvenient questions" (p. 84). The cure is implicit and obvious: change the society, raise the standard of living of the lower classes to give them greater freedom and opportunity; in short, turn to socialism.

The second recurring critical point seeks to refute Shaw's central premise, not on grounds that society is not corrupt, but because it is less responsible for prostitutes' corruption than the prostitutes themselves.[4] Shaw boldly begins his preface with a statement of his intention: "MRS WARREN'S PROFESSION was written in 1894 to draw attention to the truth that prostitution is caused, not by female depravity and male licentiousness, but simply by underpaying, undervaluing, and overworking women so shamefully that the poorest of them are forced to resort to prostitution to keep body and soul together" (p. 3). Such an assertion, say the skeptics, simply is not true—prostitution has survived into relatively affluent times, indicating that the motive behind it is at least as much personal as economic.

The third point, that the play is highly moral, is no doubt a critical counterreaction to the Victorian shock which greeted it in its early years. In Britain, censorship prevented its public performance for over three decades, and in New York the cast of the first

3. *Bernard Shaw: Complete Plays with Prefaces* (New York, 1963), III, 23. All citations and quotations from the preface and the play are from this volume.
4. See Maurice Colbourne, *The Real Bernard Shaw* (New York, 1949), p. 124; Joseph McCabe, *George Bernard Shaw: A Critical Study* (London, 1914), p. 175; and A. C. Ward, *Bernard Shaw* (London, 1951), pp. 59–60.

production was arrested, the press describing the play in such colorful terms as "illuminated gangrene," "gross sensation," and "wholly immoral and degenerate."[5] The Victorian conscience had been thumped on two of its most delicate spots: its purity and its sense of economic respectability. And so critics have gone out of their way to assert that the play is, to the contrary, quite moral, its motivation being to enlighten and reform a hypocritical, corrupt society.[6]

These three points are interesting but obvious, and though they contain elements of truth, they do not fully come to terms with the play. Shaw may be a propagandist, but in practice, if not always in admission, his emphasis in his plays is on fine art to achieve his ends, and certainly the complexity and ambiguity of fine art qualifies, modifies, and even at times contradicts simple, overarching propagandistic conclusions. An art form which grasps the vital realities of life has more potential as propaganda than a discourse which concentrates on intellectual verities. Thus Shaw remarks: "I am convinced that fine art is the subtlest, the most seductive, the most effective instrument of moral propaganda in the world . . ." (p. 7). However, the propaganda which emerges from fine art is certainly far different from propaganda of the journalistic variety which is too often glibly attributed to Shaw. Shaw comments: "Mrs Warren's Profession is an economic exposure of the White Slave traffic as well as a melodrama. . . . But would anyone but a buffleheaded idiot of a university professor, half crazy with correcting examination papers, infer that all my plays were written as economic essays, and not as plays of life, character, and human destiny like those of Shakespear or Euripides?"[7] So although it may appear in terms of the preface that Shaw puts the blame for prostitution on an economic basis, and although it may similarly seem that his motives are basically moral, when these attitudes are subjected to art they become

5. See George E. Wellwarth, "Mrs. Warren Comes to America; or, the Blue-Noses, the Politicians and the Procurers," *Shaw Review*, 2, no. 2 (1959), 12.

6. See St. John Ervine, *Bernard Shaw: His Life, Work and Friends* (New York, 1956), p. 253; also, Archibald Henderson, *George Bernard Shaw: His Life and Works* (Cincinnati, 1911), p. 308.

7. George Bernard Shaw, *Sixteen Self Sketches* (New York, 1949), p. 143.

qualified, and consequently considerably more real and effective. Thus in the play Mrs. Warren has an inner vitality and drive which keep her in the profession despite economic independence, and thus Shaw can throw back the question of morality with the remark: "It is a profoundly immoral play, exceedingly so; more so than many of the people who have written about it really imagine. . . . The play is a conscientiously immoral play."[8]

In sum, the preface is far less consequential regarding the play than critics have assumed it to be. It offers a fine display of Shavian style and conviction—it roundly blasts the censor, who actually had objected only to the suggestion of incestual interest between Vivie and Frank; it condemns society alone for prostitution, condemnation which the play reveals to be only half justified; and it comments on the irony of corrupt New York suppressing the play. But the real substance of the matter is left to the play itself, and here true dimension develops. The play evolves on three levels with a high degree of success. First, a moral allegory polarizes around Vivie, providing both thesis and action with much of the archetypal energy of a morality play. Second, a firm realistic level polarizes around Mrs. Warren, developing the problem of the individual's adjustment to society. And third, a deep-seated comic-ironic perspective emerges through the adventure of the morality play and beneath the tragedy of the realism, leavening both and putting them in greater touch with reality.

As a moral allegory, the play might well have been entitled *The Battle for the Soul of Vivie Warren*. Throughout, as in a morality, Vivie is confronted with successive temptations, to some of which she temporarily succumbs, but all of which she at last transcends, achieving ultimate salvation in the fervent pursuit of her particular religion. A correlation can be drawn between Vivie and Shaw: Vivie pursues independent habits in her cigars and whiskey, as did Shaw in his teetotalism and vegetarianism; Vivie hates holidays and wasters precisely as did Shaw; Vivie has Shaw's boundless energy, vehemence, and almost ascetic dedication to work. Though it is not explicit in the play, Vivie is much like a young

8. In Hesketh Pearson, *G. B. S.: A Full Length Portrait* (New York, 1942), p. 166.

Fabian socialist being tested by the vanities and vicissitudes of the wayward world. In fact, she had a Fabian counterpart, Arabella Susan Lawrence, a cigar-smoking, monocle-wearing Cambridge mathematics graduate who later was to become chairman of the Labour party.[9] Vivie is not Everywoman, but she is probably Every Woman who tries to make her intellectual talents and instinct for independence meaningful and remunerative in a man's world. As such, she is set upon by forces which seek to push her back into the more conventional role of womanhood. Repressive elements of Victorian society test her one by one.

The temptations which beset Vivie, like those of a morality play, appeal to the most basic human desires, each symbolized by one figure. That this is to be no conventional morality is established in the very beginning, however. The Reverend Samuel Gardner, as the voice of the Church, provides merely the plaintive bleat of atrophied religion and is immediately and almost incidentally thrown over as being too petty and inconsequential for serious consideration. The divine goal of the play is obviously not to be in terms of the Christian tradition. Vivie's rejection of it is implicit in Act I. The Church, in the image of Samuel Gardner, has capitulated to intellectual bankruptcy and social ambition. It has become a fit receptacle for the stupid sons of large families. Regarding Vivie, Frank remarks to his father: "Ever so intellectual. Took a higher degree than you did; so why should she go to hear you preach?" (p. 47). And Gardner's concern over social

9. See Geoffrey Bullough, "Literary Relations of Shaw's Mrs. Warren," *Philological Quarterly*, 41 (1962), 347. Shaw describes Vivie as "the daughter, in whom I have sought to put on the stage for the first time (as far as I know) the highly educated, capable, independent young woman of the governing class as we know her today, working, smoking, preferring the society of men to that of women simply because men talk about the questions that interest her and not about servants and babies, making no pretense of caring much about art or romance, respectable through sheer usefulness & strength, and playing the part of the charming woman only as the amusement of her life, not as the serious occupation" (*Advice to a Young Critic*, ed. E. J. West, Capricorn ed. [New York, 1963], p. 42). Stephen Grecco offers an autobiographical interpretation in "Vivie Warren's Profession: A New Look at *Mrs Warren's Profession*," *Shaw Review*, 10 (1967), 93–99. He links Frank to Shaw, Vivie to Shaw's sister Lucy, Mrs. Warren to Mrs. Shaw, and Sir George Crofts to George Vandeleur Lee. While interesting and provocative at points, this speculation has many obvious weaknesses.

position indicates that the world is dragging the Church behind it, rather than the Church offering dynamic leadership. The progressive modern woman, such as Vivie, has passed beyond the crustiness of conventional religion by the sheer power and advancement of her intellect. Religion need scarcely be thrown over, since it tends to drop of its own dead weight. A final blow is delivered in Act II when Mrs. Warren tells of her church-school training. The foolish clergyman of the church school had predicted that sister Liz, lost in sin, would jump off Waterloo Bridge. Instead, Liz prospered in prostitution. Rather than have the girls attain a good living and a respectable retirement, the clergyman, in the name of Church and society, would have had them scrubbing floors for one and sixpence a day, coming to their end in a workhouse infirmary. As a vital temptation for a truly intelligent person in the modern age the Church is thus represented as a negligible factor, and this theme fades out in Act III with Vivie scarcely considering it at all.

Sir George Crofts offers Vivie a more tangible, generally far more popular temptation than religion. He offers her an exalted social position, backed up by money. The price is also the reward—to become Lady Crofts. In a parody of Victorian marriage transactions, he seeks virtually to buy Vivie from Mrs. Warren, dangling not only money but his death and a wealthy widowhood as bait. As Gardner represents the emptiness, pompousness, and hypocrisy of a Church incapacitated by its worldly representatives, Crofts represents the immorality, avariciousness, and hypocrisy of a society which gilds its licentiousness, greed, and corruption with money and social prestige. Thus Crofts may equate himself with the most elite—with a duke whose rents are earned in odd ways, with the Archbishop of Canterbury, or with his brother, an M.P. and factory-owner who underpays his girl employees so that they are forced to supplement their income as best, or as questionably, as they can. All society from top to bottom is compromised in its unwillingness to ask embarrassing questions about its economic base and in its persecution of those who do. Mrs. Warren recognizes that the transition from irresponsible, promiscuous young spark to lecherous, dirty old man is merely one of age. Vivie, with more clarity, sees that to sell her soul to conventional Victorian prestige and monetary respectability would be to sell it far too cheaply. It would be to sell oneself to the fundamental corruption of an entire social system.

Far more subtle is the temptation of Mr. Praed, who offers Vivie the allurements of travel and aesthetics, or, as he specifically repeats, romance, beauty, and art. The offer is made all the more tempting by the attractiveness of Praed's character, which is gentlemanly in its responses, gently modulated, and perceptive. Similar to the other characters, and in true morality play fashion, he is a walking exemplification of the way of life he proposes. He is a believer in the eternal youth and creativity of art, feeling himself born a boy—in contrast with Crofts, the manifestation of aging society, who was born old. But Vivie rejects this temptation as basically foreign to her character. Three days of art in London, of the National Gallery, the Opera, and music hall were enough for her, causing her to fly to Honoria Fraser and actuarial calculations. A fundamental difference of temperament is involved. To Praed, aesthetics are the true reality; to Vivie, as her eyes are opened to the corruption of the world, aesthetics are merely a deceptive froth concealing the brothels of Ostend, Brussels, and Vienna. Praed at last explains that his is the Gospel of Art and Vivie's is the Gospel of Getting On. The situation is a precursor of the argument in "Don Juan in Hell," with Vivie foreshadowing Don Juan's part and Praed foreshadowing the Devil's. Vivie's character is one of action, of steering the ship; Praed's is one of inaction, of drifting. As attractive as the romance and beauty of the latter may be, there is implicit self-deception in it as far as Vivie is concerned, a constant danger that the ship may end on the rocks. The temptation of art, of Praed and Italy is overshadowed by the reality of social hypocrisy, of Crofts and Brussels, and it is consequently rejected as not substantial or effectual.

Love's young dream, conventionally the greatest temptation to an unmarried woman of twenty-two, is offered Vivie in the person of Frank Gardner. An affair has apparently been going on for some time; the jarring lover's baby-talk of Act III is but a retrogressive manifestation of it. Frank, however, has not the Gospel of Getting

On. He is a drifter, consciously immersed in the waywardness of society, too lazy to come to terms with it in any positive way. Vivie recognizes early in the play that she will eventually have to get rid of him. Without a disposition to work, he is potentially a Crofts. Significantly, the possibility that he is her half-brother is less important to Vivie than that he is intrinsically worthless, and though feminine instinct momentarily causes her to relapse into lover's cooing, her dynamic mental discipline tells her that romantic love is an illusive puff. It will not get the world's business done.

Mrs. Warren tempts Vivie with a life of independent luxury, a fulfillment of all the material and social desires of a young woman. This offer has the prime advantage that it is not encumbered by a Sir George Crofts. All it calls for is a nominal amount of filial affection, or at least filial endurance. But Vivie is not willing to pay even this price. At first she is willing to grant filial fondness, even slipping toward sentimentality, when she learns of her mother's dynamic, albeit unorthodox rise to economic security. Her mother's story appeals to her own instincts of work and enterprise. But what would have been for Vivie a means to an end of greater freedom has been for Mrs. Warren a fascinating occupation, an end in itself, and financial independence has led not to better things but only to further involvement in the corruption of society. The staunchness and vision required for the struggle up through the slime have not led to fresh air, but rather to a diving back into the filth.[10] At the discovery of her mother's continued involvement in the business, Vivie's admiration and daughterly compassion evaporate. Were she now to accept support, knowing its source, she herself would be tainted; further, her instincts are all for freedom unencumbered by the vanities her mother offers as bait. She must be an unnatural daughter in order to escape both the clinging Victorian bonds of duty to one's parent and the whole pollution of a society in which money can float brainless young creatures on a smooth river of vanity and luxury. As a saleswoman of such things, there could be no more effective advocate than an experienced procuress such as Mrs. Warren, but the wares she

10. Shaw describes Mrs. Warren as "much worse than a prostitute. She is an organism of prostitution" (*Advice to a Young Critic*, p. 41).

has to sell are too cheap for a third wrangler, idealist, and New Woman.

As the protagonist in a morality play, then, Vivie starts out in comparative ignorance of the world and progresses through a series of temptations which educate her, clarifying and purifying her vision, leaving her at the end in a state of self-knowledge, purgation, and peace with herself, constituting salvation. The religion of the philistines, encrusted with social servility, is rejected in the person of the Reverend Gardner. The traditional Victorian impulse to raise one's social standing through marriage is thrown over in the person of Crofts. The world of aesthetics and romance, with its inaction and passive concealment of foul reality, is allowed to go to Italy with Praed. Love's young dream, the idealism and passion of youthful marriage, is scrutinized by pragmatic intellect and dismissed, since Frank Gardner in his coasting, idle way is its advocate. Luxury and filial affection are resolutely rejected in the form of Mrs. Warren when their attachments to social corruption become clear. The common denominator of all the temptations is that they have become mired with the thoughtless, squalid, inactive, and hypocritical elements of worldly existence. Each in its way is a dodge from reality, and Reality is the goal of the morality play and of Vivie. The morality finds it in God; but God has vanished somewhere in the Industrial Revolution, the social revolution, and modern rationalism. Vivie finds it in as near a set of absolutes as she can determine—in facts, in hard, cold mind, and in work, work, work. The active mind dealing in tangibles becomes the basis of salvation.

Thus in morality terms *Mrs Warren's Profession* develops coherently and effectively, the action evolving into a spiritual triumph for the protagonist. On a realistic level, however, the ending amounts to a tragedy, and although temporal tragedy tends to be involved in many spiritual triumphs, the inevitable irony is especially strong here since the realism is heavily weighted and since Vivie's spiritual goal is a relatively modest one—infused with spiritual vigor, it is true, but diminished by an intrinsic mundanity. The moral allegory may be the structural idea behind the play, but each of the characters functions nearly as well in life as in allegory, and the two levels act as sounding-boards for each other, creating the greater depth and reality of a synthesis.

The element of greatest interest, revealing the highest dramaturgical skill on the realistic level, is the conflict between Vivie and her mother. On this level the focus shifts away from Vivie and onto the vital difficulties and ironies of the conflict in a manner which ultimately gains the sympathetic upper hand for Mrs. Warren. Obvious flaws elsewhere in the dramaturgy tend to fade out in the total kinetic effect.[11] Characters who have nearly equal independence and importance in an allegorical sense are, in their realistic sense, unevenly subordinated to the major conflict, although they still carry an echo of their allegorical significance. The Reverend Gardner is a puffy, foolish man, ineffectual as a father and a misfit as a clergyman, a pathetic picture of what twenty years of playing a clergyman's role will effect in a stupid gay young blade who was shunted into the Church for lack of a better place. Sir George Crofts's moral emptiness and greed are products of his younger days and are an indication of the society which endured him. In age this moral bankruptcy emerges in the form of a worn-out lecher, leeringly wanting to settle down with a young wife, offering the security of money as a substitute for the virility of youth. His lechery, cynicism, and temper are briefly and adroitly set forth in Act II in an exchange with Mrs. Warren regarding Vivie—"Theres no harm in looking at her, is there? . . . And a baronet isnt to be picked up every day. No other man in my position would put up with you for a mother-in-law. Why shouldnt she marry me? . . . If you want a cheque for yourself on the wedding day, you can name any figure you like—in reason"— all of which, when Mrs. Warren cuts him down, is erased with a savage "Damn you!" (pp. 58–59). Rotten respectability, sustained both by money and family, weave his character into the fabric of

---

11. The eating arrangements of Act II, used as a device to shuffle people on and off stage, are unnatural and clumsily handled; the Reverend Gardner's portrayal is too broad and obvious; Frank's melodrama with the gun in Act III is greatly overdrawn; and in Act IV Praed and Frank's seeming innocence and surprise at the full nature of Mrs. Warren's occupation do not ring true.

the social system, yet the leering, brutal bulldog has independent force.

Praed is less an individual than a representative of cultured society and a sounding-board for the other characters. As an architect he is naturally apprehensive about the Reverend Gardner's church restoration; he gets along famously, offstage, with cultured Mrs. Gardner, and he offers Vivie the broadening aesthetic opportunity of art and travel. He is more a gentle pressure than a positive force in the scene, respected by all but scarcely understood by them—the artist in a philistine world. Frank Gardner combines a chronic irresponsibility with a sensitive, flexible appreciation of his own and others' worth. His lack of self-deception, his insolent boldness, and his adaptability to circumstance create a vital character sketch deeper than that of a mere shallow youth, a category in which he could be easily dismissed. His poignant remark to his father about Vivie—"Took a higher degree than you did; so why should she go to hear you preach?" (p. 47)—would be insolent and shallow were it not so insolent and true. When at last Frank gives up Vivie, he does so with some genuine realism and nobility —"I shall be on short allowance for the next twenty years. No short allowance for Viv, if I can help it"—to which Praed responds— "But must you never see her again?"—and he piquantly answers: "Never see her again! Hang it all, be reasonable. I shall come along as often as possible, and be her brother. I can n o t understand the absurd consequences you romantic people expect from the most ordinary transactions" (p. 96). On three separate occasions Frank extols the virtue of character, a quality he has seemingly abrogated but one which he must by implication possess to some degree in order to be able properly to respect its superiority in others. His perception of Vivie's true relationship with her mother is instinctive, accurate, and penetrating.

It is the irony of Vivie's evolution and a special element of the effectiveness of the play that, as she ascends through illusion to reality on an allegorical level, she descends from ignorance to illusion on a realistic level. In the meantime, her mother's great vitality and unconventionality unfold with increasing emotional power throughout the play, forcing a collision of principles which approximates tragedy at the end. When early in Act I Praed admires Vivie's outstanding record in mathematics at Cambridge, she disclaims its value as "grind, grind, grind," asserting that it has left her ignorant of everything but mathematics. From this basis of ignorance she is suddenly thrust into a complex moral position which for any balanced judgment requires substantial knowledge of the world. Naturally she turns to the tools she has at hand, which are mental and analytical. In her emotional world she wavers into sentimentalism toward her mother and baby talk with Frank, but invariably she catches herself short, because to her stringent mental nature this is an area of retreat, of uncertainty, of hazardous loss of self-control. Since the various temptations she encounters all require that she give up pure rationalism and self-control to some extent, she repulses them through fear of a loss of reasonable order. She recoils from the worlds of religion, marriage, art, and her mother, less because she knows their nature truly and intrinsically than because they are foreign to her and she instinctively does not like them. Her antipathy is based on ignorance and temperament, not on knowledge. She can perceive them intellectually, and on these grounds she passes judgment, but she can in no sense trust herself to know them emotionally. She claims that she is prepared to take life as it is, as a woman of business, permanently single, unromantic, with no illusions. In truth, when the moral complexity of her mother confronts her, she finally falls in line with Victorian moral principles and rejects it. She denies herself emotional involvement with her mother or Frank, turning to work and mathematics as a young nun turns to devotion and God. Her Gospel of Getting On is a rejection of life as illusory, an avoidance of that sensitive immersion in life which is conducive to a knowledgeable absorption of it, of that first step which is necessary for a true transcendence.

Mrs. Warren says that Vivie has been taught wrong on purpose, that she has been instilled with a false view of life which is quite removed from reality. This is manifestly true, and Vivie's awakening is too abrupt for her to absorb the world, so she rejects the beauties of Ostend and Brussels merely because there are "private hotels" in those cities. The brothels of society distort her perspective. In facts, figures, and morals she can draw sure lines, but in affairs of the heart she is uncertain, weak, and distrustful of herself. Like Don Juan in *Man and Superman*, she equates the sentimental world with hell and illusion, seeking a purer life in the mind. But, less like Don Juan, there is a sterility and loss in her retreat, an evasion of the difficulties and ambiguities of existence. Whereas on an allegorical level she finds her soul in mind and work, on the level of the world she loses her soul to cold calculations and a negation of human emotion, inflicting ascetic contraction upon her own personality and cruelty upon others. She thus is a near saint and very foolish girl at the same time, interestingly (and ironically) not unlike Saint Joan, but without Joan's bold vision, warmth, strong compassion—and without Joan's God.

The passages in Acts II and IV in which Mrs. Warren reveals herself to Vivie are two of the most notable instances where Shaw transcends verisimilitude to powerful effect.[12] By giving Mrs. Warren heightened insight and eloquence, he achieves a brilliant and penetrating portrayal of a vital human character impressing itself upon the putty of society. Early in Act II Vivie had accused her mother of being among wasters and without character. This misconception is speedily demolished, and Mrs. Warren emerges as the most dynamic individual in the play, a true "career woman" antedating Vivie by at least twenty-five years. It would seem in Act II that Shaw's preface regarding the social causes of prostitution is borne out: rather than the whitelead factory, the scullery, the bar, or even a jump off Waterloo Bridge, the most sensible course for a poor and pretty woman is prostitution. There is more self-respect in selling oneself, saving the proceeds, and living to a comfortable old age than in starvation and slavery. But by Act IV the premise is modified if not quite refuted. It becomes apparent that Mrs. Warren *likes* her work and pursues it with much the same devotion and absorption with which Vivie pursues hers.

12. Richard Burton appraises the confrontation in Act IV as "one of the very few great serious scenes in English-speaking drama of our generation. . . . Nothing in the English theatre is better, for its purpose" (*Bernard Shaw: The Man and the Mask* [New York, 1916], p. 54).

Thus natural inclination emerges as nearly as much a motive as economics—perhaps less sexual than some commentators would have it, but surely as deeply tied to a psychological need.[13]

Vivie's shocked reaction to the discovery that her mother is still in the business, and her rejection of her, ultimately takes two courses. On the one hand, she claims not to object to the fact that Mrs. Warren must work in the line which destiny has thrown her way—each person has his own occupation to follow—but, on the other, Vivie would not have lived one life and believed in another. Her mother is conventional at heart, and that is why Vivie is leaving her. But both reasons are only half-truths, and they reveal Vivie's actual eclipse into irrationality. First, it is quite clear, when she learns from Crofts that her mother is still a procuress *par excellence*, that she experiences a revulsion close to Victorian priggishness. In Act IV she clearly *does* blame her mother for continuing the trade: "Tell me why you continue your business now that you are independent of it" (p. 102). There are all sorts of traditional moral compunctions vibrating on the fringes of her reasoning. Second, it is clear that indeed Mrs. Warren is not a conventional woman at heart. She does cluck over Vivie like a Victorian mother hen, worrying about sunburn, marriage prospects, and daughterly duty, but the foundation behind all this is scarcely conventionality. Mrs. Warren has beaten the Victorian system at its own game, and she knows it. She has chosen an anti-social, anti-religious path and has thrived on it in a "virtuous" society. The society, rather than repudiating her, sells itself to her—prestige, comfort, and luxury are all to be had for a price. And Mrs. Warren has bought them for Vivie. A mother's affection in this context is less conventional than biological. The woman conventional at heart may be Aunt Liz, who sold out and went into respectable retirement. Perceptively, Mrs. Warren likens Vivie to Liz—she has the air of a *lady* (p. 70). Certainly if anyone is conventional at heart it is Vivie. Mrs. Warren admits that she herself is too much

---

13. Bernard F. Dukore emphasizes natural inclination, discussing the relationship of prostitution to childhood emotional problems, specifically to the estrangement of the child from an immature mother. See "The Fabian and the Freudian," *Shavian*, 2, no. 4 (1961), 8–11.

of a vulgarian, too honest, too imbued with the excitement of her work—in essence, she admits that she is less able to play the hypocritical role which society demands as the price of respectability. Ultimately, on this realistic level, she triumphs over Vivie, calling the cards quite accurately, albeit overemotionally: "Oh, I know the sort you are . . . I can tell the pious, canting, hard, selfish woman when I meet her. . . . I was a good mother; and because I made my daughter a good woman she turns me out as if I was a leper" (pp. 103–4). Both emotionally and rationally the power of Mrs. Warren is felt after she has left the stage. The justice of the case, if not the triumph, has been hers.

Shaw has filled *Mrs Warren's Profession* with cohesive parallels and themes which give the fabric of the play artistic tightness. For example, the parallels between Mrs. Warren and Vivie tie the two together in a fine web of paradoxes and ironies. Both hate wasters, admire character, and have a compulsion to work; both have romantic illusions, Mrs. Warren in motherhood, Vivie at first in Frank, later in the purity of her work; both desire to tell the *truth* about prostitution; both condemn hypocrisy—and each sees it in the other. Recurrent themes of social and philosophical import reverberate throughout: the theme of who has character and who has not—Frank attributing it to Vivie, Vivie denying it to Mrs. Warren, Mrs. Warren denying it to common prostitutes; the theme of who has choice and who has not—Crofts corrupt because he had a choice to invest in the profession or not, Mrs. Warren exonerated because she had no choice; the theme of the profit of youth by the death of elders—Frank by the death of the Reverend Gardner, Vivie by the death of potential husband Sir George, then by the death of her mother; and, finally, the frequently recurring distinction between workers and wasters. Both the structural unity and intellectual and aesthetic harmony of the play are enhanced by Shaw's attention to such detail.

Permeating and subliminally compromising both the morality play and the realistic level is a strong comic element. G. K. Chesterton called the play "pure tragedy,"[14] but this is only a very par-

14. G. K. Chesterton, *George Bernard Shaw*, Dramabook ed. (New York, 1956), p. 102.

tial view. The comic potential of incongruity is rife throughout: the Reverend Gardner is the absurd contradiction of a mindless young blade grotesquely metamorphosed into an old clergyman; Crofts is a pathetic-comic representation of an old lecher seeking to retrieve vestiges of youth in a young bride, much like Chaucer's January in *The Merchant's Tale*; Mrs. Warren is a vigorous whore in the autumn of life pursuing the ideal of Victorian motherhood with as much tenacity as she pursues her lucrative business; and Aunt Liz, a wealthy procuress, is now a respected lady of Winchester, living near the cathedral, entrusted to chaperone girls at the county ball. The comic element of repetition occurs with wryness in a number of instances: Crofts is backed into cursing "Damn you" at Mrs. Warren in Act II and again at Vivie in Act III; on learning in Act III that Vivie knows about the business of the "private hotels" from her mother, Crofts mutters, "The old—," to which Vivie responds, "Just so," and the same pattern is repeated with Mrs. Warren and Vivie in Act IV. The bandying of the terms "wasters" and "character" in different contexts, achieving fine ironic ramifications, has been noted, and Vivie's perception that her mother is trying to entice her into a life of luxury with the same arguments she uses to allure young girls as a procuress produces a lethal sense of contrast, incongruity, wry humor, and horror all at the same time. Humor also appears when humans are likened to animals or inanimate objects, such as in the repeated references to Crofts's dog-like appearance, to Mrs. Warren as a sparrow, and to Vivie as a steam-roller. The sparrow, it will be remembered, carries connotations of lechery.

Most comically telling and important is a sense of the humorous which revolves around Vivie, compromising the seriousness of her quest. Vivie is comical in a Bergsonian manner as she avoids a full, flexible contact with life and takes on the qualities of an automaton. Vivie has vitality, and in this there is a degree of growth and seriousness. But her quest is ultimately more one of mental fixation than of spiritual expansion, and this fixation tends to reduce her image with comic aspects throughout the play, permitting the dynamic emotional transcendence of her mother at the end. From the first she is the New Woman with a vengeance, loving nothing better than a chair, whiskey, cigars, and a detective story for her leisure, when she is not ardently engaged in actuarial calculations. Her hard handshake and her tough, uncompromising, unaesthetic attitudes make Frank's Act IV image of her as a steam-roller seem remarkably apt. In writing a novel as a sequel to *Mrs Warren's Profession*, Sir Harry Johnston felt it necessary to make Vivie more human by repudiating her whiskey and cigars for tea and cigarettes.[15] And if a steam-roller can roll over Crofts, Frank, and Praed, what chance has a poor lecherous little sparrow? Mrs. Warren is comical in adopting the ill-fitting convention of a Victorian parent, but there are warmth, frailty, and humanity in her which tremble in the end at the rumble of the mighty machine. Vivie rolls on to the conclusion with her mental integrity scarcely bruised and her emotional integrity remarkably insular. In one sense this makes her the victor. But it is a machine-like victory, and fundamentally absurd in a young lady. Mrs. Warren, with her more flexible and adaptable vitality, ultimately evokes the greatest sympathy, her dynamics being more human and more relevant to life.

Each of the three levels of moral allegory, realism, and comedy in *Mrs Warren's Profession* has its own integrity and consistency while it compromises and qualifies the others. The nobility and purity of the morality element elevates the realism and the comedy, giving allegorical scope to the action, while at the same time the realism and comedy pull it down to life. The tragedy on the realistic level gains a good part of its poignancy through the relatively blind triumph of the allegory, yet both are mollified and given perspective by contrapuntal comic sensitivity. The comedy has a life of its own, but it is given a considerable degree of pain by the pathos of the realism and by its contrast with the allegory—a pain which perhaps brings it closer to sympathy. The scope and depth of Shaw's artistic achievement, the play's final effect, lies in the aesthetic tension of these divergent forces.

15. Harry Johnston, *Mrs. Warren's Daughter: A Story of the Women's Movement* (New York, 1920), p. 7.

CHAPTER TWO

ARMS AND THE MAN

The Seriousness of Comedy

The tightly knit humor of incident and character in *Arms and the Man* has tended to obscure the more inclusive range of Shaw's artistic achievement in the play. At the first performance the audience reacted with uproarious laughter; it would seem that the play had been a triumph, but Shaw was seeking something more. Afterward, in a letter to Henry Arthur Jones, he remarked: "I had the curious experience of witnessing an apparently insane success, with the actors and actresses almost losing their heads with the intoxication of laugh after laugh, and of going before the curtain to tremendous applause, the only person in the theatre who knew that the whole affair was a ghastly failure."[1] Apparently someone in the audience was in accord with Shaw's at least half-sincere reservations. When he appeared at the end of the performance, there was a solitary boo from the gallery, which called forth Shaw's famous response: "My friend, I quite agree with you—but what are we two against so many?"[2] In this first play to follow his three

1. In Doris Arthur Jones, *Taking the Curtain Call: The Life and Letters of Henry Arthur Jones* (New York, 1930), p. 112.
2. In Archibald Henderson, *George Bernard Shaw: His Life and Works* (Cincinnati, 1911), p. 312. In Bernard Shaw, *Advice to a Young Critic and Other Letters*, Capricorn ed. (New York, 1963), p. 6, editor E. J. West confirms Hesketh Pearson's identification of the booer as Golding Bright, to whom Shaw later wrote the letters which West reproduces.

unsuccessful "Unpleasant Plays," Shaw was experiencing one of his first tastes of popularity based on an appreciation for his humor, a popularity which sublimated his more serious concerns. His desire to expose and castigate sentimentalism, hypocrisy, and social ills was as keen as ever, but from his awareness that Unpleasant Plays annihilate themselves through lack of a willing audience, and from his own natural disposition to comedy, he had turned to humor as a vehicle for thought. He now discovered that audiences were prone to take the humor and leave behind the thought, along with everything peripheral to it.[3]   *comic*

Shaw found it necessary to plead that *Arms and the Man* was "a classic comedy and not an opera bouffe without the music."[4] It was not a *Chocolate Soldier*. He expressed concern over the problem numerous times, most strikingly in commentaries on the characters of Sergius and Raina. Realizing that Sergius was likely to be overplayed and hence misinterpreted, he sought in vain to have Richard Mansfield play that role instead of Bluntschli in the American production. The danger was that the genuine subtlety and seriousness of Sergius, which render him truly high comedy

3. Both Arthur Bingham Walkley and William Archer considered the play, in Walkley's terms, "merely secondhand Gilbertism" (review of *Arms and the Man*, in *The Speaker*, 9 [1894], 471). Shaw defended himself in an article in *The New Review* of July 1894, entitled "A Dramatic Realist to His Critics" (reprinted in *Shaw on Theatre*, ed. E. J. West, Dramabook ed. [New York, 1959], pp. 18–41), where he substantiated, at great length, details in the play which had direct correspondences to real life. Such information, though it makes for a polemic tour de force, is not intrinsic to the artistic success or the essential philosophic perceptiveness of the play. Shaw's artistic approach to history is clearer in an earlier statement about his selection of a locale and his use of details in the play: "In the original MS, the names of the places were blank, and the characters were called simply The Father, The Daughter, The Stranger, The Heroic Lover, and so on. The incident of the machine-gun bound me to a recent war: that was all. My own historical information being rather confused, I asked Mr Sidney Webb to find out a good war for my purpose." Webb suggested the Servo-Bulgarian war, and Shaw *then* researched the background for *Arms and the Man*, adjusting his material accordingly. See *To-Day*, 28 April 1894, p. 373; quoted in Louis Crompton, *Shaw the Dramatist* (Lincoln, Nebr., 1969), p. 219. Also, see "A Talk with Mr. Bernard Shaw about His New Play" in the *Pall Mall Budget*, 19 April 1894; reprinted in *Arms and the Man*, ed. Louis Crompton (New York, 1969), pp. 77–80.

4. Quoted in Hesketh Pearson, *G. B. S.: A Full Length Portrait* (New York, 1942), p. 168.

and effect the most interesting contrast with Bluntschli, would be lost in an *opéra bouffe* interpretation. Shaw remarks:

> The whole difficulty was created by the fact that my Bulgarian hero, quite as much as Helmer in *A Doll's House*, was a hero shown from the modern woman's point of view. I complicated the psychology by making him catch glimpse after glimpse of his own aspect and conduct from this point of view himself, as all men are beginning to do more or less now, the result, of course, being the most horrible dubiety on his part as to whether he was really a brave and chivalrous gentleman, or a humbug and a moral coward. His actions, equally of course, were hopelessly irreconcilable with either theory. Need I add that if the straightforward Helmer, a very honest and ordinary middle-class man misled by false ideals of womanhood, bewildered the public, and was finally set down as a selfish cad by all the Helmers in the audience, *à fortiori* my introspective Bulgarian never had a chance, and was dismissed, with but moderately spontaneous laughter, as a swaggering impostor of the species for which contemporary slang has invented the term "bounder"?[5]

Notably, Shaw was seeking to portray not a bounder, but a "comedic Hamlet" awakening to a tentative consciousness of his own absurdity and tortured by it.[6] As such, Sergius is sensitive and reasonably complex, neither brave nor cowardly, neither a gentleman nor a humbug, but a confused soul seeking the meaning of life on the periphery of experience. He is comic in his uncertainty and childishness, but it is the comedy of the incongruity between a soul flying with noble impulses on the one hand and exploring itself dubiously on the other, the comedy of disparity between ideals and actions rather than the comedy of a bizarre, overstuffed character-type. Shaw felt that this distinction was lost in the laughter of his audience.

Similarly, subtlety was lost during the play's first run when

---

5. Preface to William Archer, *The Theatrical "World" of 1894*, pp. xxvii–xxviii.
6. For a discussion of Sergius as a "straight" role, see E. J. West, " 'Arma Virumque' Shaw Did Not Sing," *Colorado Quarterly*, 1 (1953), 267–80.

Alma Murray modulated the role of Raina from a straight, serious portrayal toward farce. In a letter to the actress Shaw expresses the anguish of a playwright at seeing his conception defiled:

> What—oh what has become of my Raina? How could you have the heart to play that way for me—to lacerate every fibre in my being? Where's the poetry gone—the tenderness—the sincerity of the noble attitude and the thrilling voice? Where is the beauty of the dream about Sergius, the genuine heart stir and sympathy of the attempt to encourage the strange man when he breaks down? Have you turned cynic, or have you been reading the papers and believing in them instead of believing in your part? . . . When you are right the play cannot fail: when you are wrong, it cannot succeed.[7]

If psychological complexity and earnestness were abandoned for the easy tricks of farce, the ironies and meaning of the play, as well as the real edge of its comedy, could be severely blunted.[8]

The critical consensus about *Arms and the Man* is epitomized in Archibald Henderson's comment that "the play has for its dramatic essence the collision of romantic illusion with prosaic reality."[9] This calls forth a rather simple formula, generally equating Raina and Sergius with romantic illusion and Bluntschli with prosaic reality. A close look at the play, however, shows that this formula is too generalized and simple. Shaw's artistic accomplishment is in fact highly subtle and complex, creating at its best a

7. 11 May 1894. *Bernard Shaw: Collected Letters 1874–1897*, ed. Dan H. Laurence (New York, 1965), p. 435.

8. In this light, Shaw remarked in 1904 that he was "startled to find what flimsy, fantastic, unsafe stuff it is . . . it really would not stand comparison with my later plays unless the company was very fascinating" (quoted in Pearson, *A Full Length Portrait*, p. 168). The point that, when well performed, it *can* stand comparison with his better plays mitigates this somewhat too harsh appraisal; and in 1927 Shaw did go so far as to call the play "a classic comedy." We shall note frequently that Shaw was not always his own best critic.

9. Henderson, *Life and Works*, p. 310. See also Augustin Hamon, *The Twentieth Century Molière: Bernard Shaw*, trans. Eden and Cedar Paul (New York, 1916), p. 171, and Maurice Colbourne, *The Real Bernard Shaw* (New York, 1949), p. 126.

high comedy which is a synthesis of psychological insight, tragicomedy, and penetrating social perception.

Rather than contrasting the fantastic with the prosaic, or portraying an evolution in Raina's perception from the romantic to the realistic, the play explores the interlocking relationship and mutual dependence of romanticism and realism. Through the three major characters it reveals the double standard of the human mind which is genuinely thrilled with absurd heroics, yet at the same time reserves a realistic level of awareness regarding its self-deception. It involves Coleridge's willing suspension of disbelief, translated into life. As usual in Shaw, simple absolutes are undercut by multifaceted qualifications and second thoughts. The play is thus a revelation of the psychology of romanticism and realism, projecting an inclusive, nonabsolutist approach which is the essence of Shavianism. Shaw expresses his principle clearly in the preface: "But the obvious conflicts of unmistakeable good with unmistakeable evil can only supply the crude drama of villain and hero, in which some absolute point of view is taken, and the dissentients are treated by the dramatist as enemies to be piously glorified or indignantly vilified. In such cheap wares I do not deal." [10] Although by comedic and philosophic nature Shaw had a disposition to cut through illusion to reality, he was too good a dramatist to develop them at length as distinct alternatives. Especially in *Arms and the Man*, through the interaction of character, temperament, and event, he achieves a subtle fusion of the fantastic and the prosaic which gives texture and depth to the surface elements of a comic situation.

Raina Petkoff would be too much a fool for dramatic credibility were it not for a leavening of skepticism with which Shaw provides her as early as the opening lines of Act I. In dashing terms, her mother recounts the success of the cavalry charge led by Sergius; her words are given a mock heroic ring which swings the moment into absurdity: "Cant you see it, Raina: our gallant splendid Bulgarians with their swords and eyes flashing, thundering down like an avalanche and scattering the wretched Serbs and their dandi-

10. *Bernard Shaw: Complete Plays with Prefaces* (New York, 1963), III, 111. All citations and quotations from the preface and the play are from this volume.

fied Austrian officers like chaff" (p. 126).[11] Raina catches her mother's enthusiasm, but not without a constant counterpoint of negation in terms of her former doubts: she had kept Sergius waiting a year before consenting to a betrothal, because Byron and Pushkin and the opera at Bucharest were too much like dreams. Now it would seem that a brave new world has opened before her.

But the artificiality of such a moment of enthusiasm cannot last long without being confronted with facts of life, and Shaw confronts it immediately with the inglorious sequel to glorious cavalry charges, the cruel pursuit and slaughter of fugitives. Within ten minutes the vision of the battle degenerates from the noble abstraction of a heroic victory to the reality of a tattered, dirty, bloody, exhausted fugitive standing starkly incongruous in the lady's bedroom. The prosaic human element is thus brought into immediate juxtaposition with the romantic heroic element, causing the latter to vaporize in its insubstantiality. The sequence of the total act deftly turns from the unreal romance of an absent hero's operatic victory, to the imminent danger of a pursued fugitive, and finally to a more real, "prosaic" romance of compassion and maternal affection.

Danger is the catalyst through which Raina's vague romantic dreams become a romance of life. Ironically, it is Aristotle's tragic components, pity and fear, which bring her into immediate psychological sympathy with Bluntschli. She conceals him partly out of romance, but more basically out of compassion for him and fear of the brutal bloodshed which will undoubtedly ensue if she does not. His obvious weakness and exhaustion, his childlike taste for chocolate, and his frightening admission that the slightest provocation will make him cry awaken in her the spontaneous womanly instinct of maternal affection. The psychology of her emotion is not unlike Candida's for Morell, though Raina has the awe and innocence of a younger woman. She can be temporarily indignant at Bluntschli's laughter about Sergius as Don Quixote, but his laughter reflects her own earlier doubts, now enforced by the greater reality of the present. All that is instinctive, vital, and

11. The tone, meter, and spirit of Catherine's words appropriately echo the first two stanzas of Byron's "Destruction of Sennacherib."

maternal in Raina confronts her romantic dreams of Sergius in this first act, and though she may not immediately recognize it, her servant Louka realizes the true nature of her affections. Already Shaw has brought his two antagonists, romance and reality, onto the battlefield, and there is no doubt as to which wins out. The question of victory is too inconsequential to occupy the serious attention of the play: what is interesting is the nature of the battle and its ability to reveal fully the strengths, weaknesses, and similarities of the contending qualities.

As Act I portrays the prosaic viewpoint of Bluntschli, Act II allows free play to the romantic world of Raina and Sergius, a world which meets restrictions and difficulties even in its simplest contacts with life. That the romantic disposition simply cannot sustain the burden of a normal existence is surely no new insight on Shaw's part, but what is valuable and effective here is his stark objectification of its difficulties, revealing how a basic folly in one's outlook toward life ramifies itself into dozens of little follies which incapacitate normal action and may end in boredom and fatigue. Since her romantic love is no instinctive part of her, Raina must stage manage it. "She always appears at the right moment," says her father. "Yes," says her mother, "she listens for it" (p. 152). The entrance on cue, the noble air, and the spying out of the window on Sergius, which Louka suspects, are all contrivances to support an artificial pattern. "Higher love" in a young lady of twenty-three is an adolescent hangover; it obviously tires Sergius very quickly—he turns to Louka for relief—while Raina herself is not slow to indicate her own rebellion: "I always feel a longing to do or say something dreadful to him—to shock his propriety—to scandalize the five senses out of him" (p. 161). This is one step beyond her previous skepticism: this is clear irreverence, indicating that the natural focus of a realistic perspective in her has sensed the foolishness all along.

By Act III Raina is merely clinging to the vestiges of her heroic romance with Sergius. Her remark, "My relation to him is the one really beautiful and noble part of my life" (pp. 172–73), is as false in her own mind as is her subsequent assertion that she has lied only twice in her life. This is obviously play-acting, and though she still may have some illusions about Sergius, she certainly has few about the fraudulence of her own pretensions. When Bluntschli comments that he finds it impossible to believe a single word she says, she collapses from the heroic into the familiar: "How did you find me out?" (p. 174).[12] She flatters herself that no one else has penetrated her façade, whereas Shaw has made it abundantly clear elsewhere that Louka, her mother, and her father all see through her. Only she and Sergius are fooled by her dream world, and even they cannot keep up with its demands. Recognizing the truth about herself, Raina can recognize the truth about Sergius as well; and when she discerns his flirtation with Louka, she tears him into little pieces of humiliation, laughing at herself at last in complete purgation, guessing Bluntschli's state of mind: "I daresay you think us a couple of grown-up babies, dont you?" (p. 187). In Act I she had concealed Bluntschli partly in the spirit of the romance of the situation, but more basically out of compassion and maternal affection, the two qualities of romance and reality being joined. This joining is never present in her relationship with Sergius, a relationship she instinctively mistrusts, but it reappears in Act III along with the realization that Bluntschli takes her as a woman, not as a tinsel goddess. Hence Raina's role may generally be an evolution from romance to reality, but it is by no means uncrossed by contradictory currents. She undergoes an education under the influence of Bluntschli, but it involves an awakening of her latent impulses and insights more than an alteration of her basic disposition.

The character of Bluntschli reverses the order of the romance-reality evolution. In Act I he appears to be the antithesis of a romantic hero. He introduces, with a shock of contrast, the grisly proximity of war. His uniform is torn and splattered with mud and blood. He is prepared to fight to the death only because he knows that, if caught, he will either be slaughtered like a pig or taken into the street for vengeful amusement. Stuffing himself with chocolate and tending to cry and sleep, he is more like a help-

12. Fred Mayne observes that, as a resolution of tension, this is both the anticlimax of the passage and the climax of the play. See *The Wit and Satire of Bernard Shaw* (New York, 1967), p. 25.

27

less child than a man. What there is of the man seems hopelessly antiheroic—his fear of death, his laughter at Sergius, and his description of a cavalry charge in terms of a handful of peas thrown at a window pane. In exhaustion, the prosaic soldier is almost schizophrenic: in his coolness, professionalism, and laughter he is a subtle cynic of warfare, yet at odds with this cynicism are the tastes and incapacities of a child. The final effect is to remove war from noble abstractions through the humanizing element of one who has no illusions about it and who is, in fact, a walking negation of it.

Bluntschli's character shifts and grows in Act II by verbal report. The prosaic and professionally pragmatic approach to war is deftly contrasted with the ineffectuality of romantic amateurs. Petkoff and Sergius reveal him as the highly experienced and competent captain who had the clear sight to advise Sergius to resign, had the best of them in a horse-soldier barter, and managed a miraculous escape while enjoying the company of a Bulgarian lady. Sergius disparages Bluntschli's competence in terms which reveal his own incapacity—the Swiss captain is a commercial traveler in uniform, a bourgeois. Several quick strokes render a remarkable class distinction. The gentleman is helpless in the hands of the tradesman; a consummate soldier and bourgeois can make a child of a gentleman. A basic social change of the nineteenth century is clarified briefly in passing—the genteel classes, adhering to their codes, are linked to custom and illusion. Their decline is inherent in the inefficacy of these illusions, which are taken full advantage of by the *bourgeoisie*, whose values and actions are based on practical experience and skills. Thus Sergius has only scorn to compensate for the fact that he was bested in the practical barter of war by a commercial traveler. This is a child's scorn, half-suppressing an uneasy sense of admiration for one whose ability is manifestly superior. Bluntschli's image consequently evolves, despite his absence, from one of ragged, inglorious defeat to one of keen military know-how and cunning—half-romantic in a prosaic genius which is most impressive when compared to the bumbling of his Bulgarian foes.

Paradoxically, the more Bluntschli's bourgeois shopkeeping

Arms and the Man

abilities become apparent, the more he grows in pseudo-romantic stature. In Act III he operates almost like a highly competent machine, first in disposing of the Bulgarian regiments, then in his choice of a machine gun as his weapon for the proposed duel with Sergius. Sergius at last refuses to duel with him because "Youve no magnetism: youre not a man: youre a machine" (p. 186). Yet Bluntschli is not a Bergsonian automaton. Rather, efficiency and humdrum are clearly means to an end for him, and involve the most flexible mental contact with the realities of life. His very prosaicness, cutting through the automatism of convention and pretense, gives him the true freedom of action which is at the heart of all that is serious in life. When Raina collapses from her imperious acting, she remarks: "Do you know, you are the first man I ever met who did not take me seriously?" He responds very truthfully: "You mean, dont you, that I am the first man that has ever taken you quite seriously?" (p. 174).[13] This genuine serious-ness is the key to Bluntschli's humor. He has the true Shavian perspective of amusement at anything which is intrinsically false or absurd, from his own desperate plight in Act I to Raina's pre-tensions and her cat-and-mouse fight with Sergius in Act III. To the somber or romantic mind, the little melodramas of life are bloated with importance; to the truly serious mind, a sense of their comedy reduces them to proper proportions.

Thus in Act III it is Bluntschli who has that combination of prosaicness and imagination which is necessary to solve the prob-lem of the disposal of the Bulgarian cavalry; it is Sergius who is the machine, rubber-stamping the orders which come from Bluntsch-li's practical mind. The romantic image of Sergius deteriorates, not only in itself, but especially by contact and contrast with the efficiency of the Swiss captain. Bluntschli's ability and cool com-mon sense tend to assume a romantic aura: he grows in stature as some of the elements of a superman begin to radiate from him,

---

13. The intrinsic humaneness of Bluntschli's balloon-pricking, and of Shaw's humor in general, is that it attacks false ideals rather than individuals. Hence Raina, and later even Sergius, can laugh at their foolishness. See Charles A. Car-penter, *Bernard Shaw & the Art of Destroying Ideals: The Early Plays* (Madison, 1969), pp. 93–97.

the man who has the natural genius to succeed where others fail. The crowning union of romance with the prosaic temperament occurs when Bluntschli admits to "an incurably romantic disposition" (p. 193). Romantically he ran away from home as a boy, romantically he joined the army, romantically he climbed Raina's balcony instead of seeking her cellar, and romantically he has returned. It is clear at last that his relationship with Raina has all along been more truly romantic than Sergius's.[14] The point, however, is scarcely made before the Shavian brilliance juxtaposes it with Bluntschli's compromising misjudgment of Raina's age, followed by his prosaic proposal and the magnificently bourgeois attraction and encumbrance of a chain of Swiss hotels. The romantic and the prosaic end in a magician's shuffle, and Sergius's final exclamation and question—"What a man! Is he a man?" (p. 196)—come too fast for the ambiguous reflection that in his romance Bluntschli is quite human, while in his prosaicness he is to some degree a superman.

One critic interprets Bluntschli as a debased Falstaff, playing opposite Sergius's debased Hal, and therefore making an ironic comment on the shallow alternatives offered to nineteenth-century man.[15] But the facts and tone of the play belie this comparison. Sergius is more a Hotspur than a Hal. He finally offers no simple alternative to Bluntschli, because Bluntschli is concurrently humanized and exalted with the qualities of both Falstaff and Hal. And if, in the general emphasis of the action, Bluntschli progresses from an image of reality to one of romance, Raina evolves in the opposite direction, from romance to reality, the two characters creating an aesthetic tension in their development and interaction which reveals multifold aspects of both qualities. Both qualities have actually existed in each character from the beginning, but for dramatic effectiveness the most forceful indications of this do not come until late in the development of the play.

14. An observation also made by Martin Meisel, *Shaw and the Nineteenth-Century Theater* (Princeton, 1963), p. 194.

15. Robert C. Elliott, "Shaw's Captain Bluntschli: A Latter-Day Falstaff," *Modern Language Notes*, 67 (1952), 461–64.

In the character of Sergius, Shaw reveals a third element in the relationship of romance and reality—that of tortured self-consciousness, the tragedy and comedy of a man caught in bewilderment between his noble impulses and the ignominiousness of life. Even before Sergius appears, the daring heroism of his cavalry charge is pulverized by prosaic fact. First it is brought into question by the mock-heroic tone of Catherine Petkoff's description and by Raina's extravagant, foolish reaction. Then it is utterly demolished by Bluntschli's humorous perspective which typifies the entire action as the folly and ignorance of an operatic tenor or a Don Quixote, who in this case survived only by a bit of uncanny luck. G. K. Chesterton asserts that sentimentalism is necessary because it is one of the very practical incentives behind action.[16] Shaw would generally agree, but he indicates that this is a dangerous truth in warfare, where sentimentalism often leads to annihilation. When Sergius appears in Act II, he is uncomfortably trying to avoid this fact by retreating inside a new romanticism, that of Byronic cynicism. As would be expected of Shaw, Sergius is no mere romantic clown, which would be all too easy a target. Rather, he has "the physical hardihood, the high spirit, and the susceptible imagination of an untamed mountaineer chieftain" (p. 150). He is aware of the disparity between his own romantic disposition and the dull facts of the world. Heroic charges are out of place in the prosaicism of modern warfare, where soldiering is a coward's art of attacking when strong and retreating when weak. What he fails to see is that the disparity invalidates his romanticism—rather, he would have it invalidating reality. His outlook is distorted by confusion and cynicism resulting from the irony of his position: he remains a major because he won a battle in the wrong way, while others are promoted for losing battles in the right way. For consolation he turns to Byronic disillusionment and scorn, a romantic pose much more interesting and complex than that of a mere war hero.

The "higher love" is another aspect of the search for Truth above reality; but as war has an ingredient of cowardice, love has

16. G. K. Chesterton, *George Bernard Shaw*, Dramabook ed. (New York, 1956), p. 89.

an ingredient of biology, and nineteenth-century idealism lacked the medieval *savoir faire* that allowed Chrétien de Troyes to depict Lancelot genuflecting before Guinevere's bed, which he had just familiarly occupied. The strain of higher love necessitates a release for the lower, but the romanticism of Sergius as a late Victorian, albeit a Bulgarian, is not sophisticated enough to combine them in the same person. So he grabs Louka, and in doing so he merely adds to the doubts which nurture his schizophrenic split between illusion and reality. Like Hamlet, he is acutely aware of his many-sided personality, an awareness which is romantic but also true to life. Is he hero, buffoon, humbug, blackguard, or coward? Certainly he is all of these. But one thing he definitely is not: he is not a noble lover. The strain of higher love is too great because it has no meaningful contact with the true personalities of either Raina or Sergius. Since higher love involves the acting of a foreign role, it cannot be maintained with prolonged consistency. Sheer physical drives render its continuity impossible: Sergius is subject to lust on the one hand, Raina to her maternal-womanly instincts on the other. Both have visceral impulses which subvert their abstractions.

Just as Bluntschli's sense of humor gives him a considerable depth of seriousness, Sergius's intense seriousness makes him comical. His heroic propensities and subsequent doubts render him both a comic machine and tragicomic introvert, and it is a revelation of Shaw's skill that both elements deterministically converge, bringing Sergius to his fate. His tragicomic introspection in Act III, carrying over the self-analytical strain of the previous act, is highly active and varied. It is a soul-searching which, though seemingly at odds with romanticism, is highly romantic in its Byronism. First, he questions the concept of authority—who is *he* to give orders to the soldiers? Next, he goes to the very heart of his predicament: "Mockery! mockery everywhere! everything I think is mocked by everything I do" (p. 182). At last, he is convinced by Louka that true courage exists in such things as defying the whole world in order to marry the person you love, no matter how far beneath you that person may be. Louka takes advantage of his image of himself and traps him temperamentally. He agrees that if he touches her again, he will wed her.

Concurrently, the mechanical aspect of his nature guides his action. The stubbornness of the self-assured hero asserts itself first in Act II. When Catherine Petkoff suggests that he withdraw his resignation, he folds his arms and exclaims, "I never withdraw" (p. 152).[17] This mechanical pattern repeats itself in Act III. As an officer he mechanically signs Bluntschli's orders; as a gentleman he mechanically challenges Bluntschli to duel; and finally, after he has refused to withdraw or apologize in a number of situations, he at last touches Louka—and she dares him to keep his word: "You can withdraw if you like." To which, quite consistently, the conditioned man replies: "Withdraw! Never!" (p. 191). The trap has been sprung, psychologically consistent, according to the code of a gentleman's word, mechanically perfect, penetratingly comic. Significantly, this is the point of truth for Sergius, as realistic and illuminating as that for Bluntschli and Raina.

In Act III the horror and ludicrousness of war are brought into graphic focus through Bluntschli's account of his friend who was wounded and burned alive in a wood yard, and the true instincts of love are revealed in Raina's love for Bluntschli, active and vital, beneath her feigned love for Sergius. The truth converges upon Sergius, and although his reaction is strongly tinged with Byronic despair, he is caught in the essence of a reality which propels him toward Louka. He can now with an honest mind legalize his normal sexual drives toward a pretty wench, and at the same time he can fulfill his sense of courage. It is romantic in its prosaicness. Sergius is a notable advancement over the gull of Jonsonian and Restoration comedy: he both is duped and dupes himself into a lowly marriage, but in the process he is being true to his genuine nature, and he finds himself in spite of himself.

17. These words were famous for having been declared in Parliament by the flamboyant Cunninghame Graham. Crompton suggests Graham as a source for Sergius, and Sydney Webb as a source for Bluntschli—the swashbuckler versus the quartermaster. See *Shaw the Dramatist*, pp. 21–23.

The characters most in touch with reality are the two servants, Louka and Nicola. It is a necessity of their class that, though they may have romantic daydreams, these dreams should always be in touch with potentially profitable facts. Here again Shaw draws a telling contrast, differentiating between the strictly prosaic temperament and the prosaic temperament with romantic ambition. Nicola is the absolute realist; in his clarity of insight is etched the predicament of an entire social class. He remarks to Louka: "Child: you dont know the power such high people have over the like of you and me when we try to rise out of our poverty against them" (p. 146). His eyes are open to his dependence on the wealthy classes, and within this framework he operates with complete efficiency and cleverness, getting all he can out of it, planning to set up a shop in Sophia with the Petkoffs as his principal customers. In his pursuit of economic security he even forgoes marriage to Louka, since as Sergius's bride she will be a good customer rather than an expensive wife. Such clearheadedness attracts the admiration of Bluntschli, who remarks: "Never mind whether it's heroism or baseness. Nicola's the ablest man Ive met in Bulgaria. I'll make him manager of a hotel if he can speak French and German" (p. 191). Nicola is the prosaic ideal, and Bluntschli's prosaic side is naturally keenly attracted to him. Yet what makes Bluntschli rounded and human is that he also has a strong motivating romantic temperament. Lacking this balance, Nicola is more base than heroic. He would make an excellent hotel manager. There is something mundane, lifeless, and dehumanizing in his perspective. For a servant—or a hotel manager —its end is clever servility.

In contrast, Louka combines clear prosaic vision with imagination, ambition, and romance, and succeeds thereby in rising above servility. Between Nicola and Louka there is a Pygmalion-Galatea relationship foreshadowing Higgins and Eliza. Nicola has taught her not to overuse make-up like common Bulgarian girls, and to be clean and dainty like a lady. But, like Higgins, he has created a monster beyond his control—he has made a real woman out of a servant. His advice promotes social stratification: "The way to get on as a lady is the same as the way to get on as a servant: youve got to know your place" (p. 179). To Louka, this is but "cold-blooded wisdom," and one may anticipate Eliza's words: "The difference between a lady and a flower girl is not how she behaves, but how she's treated."[18] As Nicola introduces in a natural fashion a didactic element regarding the social and economic dependence of the servant class, Louka brings into question the superstructure of gentility. She sees clearly that Nicola has the soul of a servant and that the effect of such souls is to reinforce class distinctions. But she views such distinctions as not very flattering to the social elite. The moral laxity of the upper classes tends to put her on a par with them. This feeds her natural ambition. Thus she can say familiarly to Sergius: "Gentlefolk are all alike: you making love to me behind Miss Raina's back; and she doing the same behind yours" (p. 157). She has the insight all along that Raina will marry Bluntschli if she has the chance. Obviously, biological drives are more real than "higher love," and this fact encourages Louka's hope of climbing above her class to marry Sergius. In his abandoning higher love and in her marrying for social advancement, there is a sexual and economic honesty which is in accord with the play's dénouement. As with Raina and Bluntschli, the fairy-tale romance of the general situation is undergirded by natural and prosaic impulses.

The mixture of the romantic and the prosaic which Shaw achieves in his characters he carries further into a contrast between the characters and the events and setting. In Act I the pervasive prosaicness of Bluntschli is in contrast with the romantic setting of a lady's bedroom and with the melodramatic events of a heroic cavalry charge, a strange man at the window, and Raina's daring concealment of him. In Act II the romantic, Byronic Sergius is in contrast with the laundry on the fruit bushes and the after-breakfast atmosphere. The servants are quarreling, an ignominious peace has been established—it is a time for flirting with the servant girl, disposing of troops, and telling vulgar stories about the war. Act III offers a fusion of the prosaic and the romantic,

18. *Complete Plays*, I, 270.

[handwritten margin note at top: genteel belongings are suited to polite society]

with troop dispersion, the plotting of servants, flirting, the domestic comedy of Petkoff's coat, and practical concerns over eligibility in betrothal all offering a constant counterpoint to the threat of a duel over a lady, the development of romantic love between the two couples, and the romance of a double marriage in the offing. By constantly juxtaposing the prosaic and romantic in such ways, Shaw achieves a maximum reflection of their many facets and interrelationships. His ideas on the matter, which are more an intuitive grasp of multifold ironic interplays between romance and reality than straight-line logical conclusions, are thus given full expression and pertinence in a dramatic situation.

The play develops three major themes. First, there is the satire on war, its heroics represented by Sergius, its prosaicness by Bluntschli. This brings into focus both the nature of the individual soldier and the tactics and psychology of warfare. Second, there is the satire on the nature of the genteel classes, on what comprises a lady, a gentleman, and a servant. Third, there is an exploration of the spectrum of human disposition which ranges from the romantic to the prosaic, the two elements being not just opposites, but, paradoxically, capable of appearing in life as shadings of each other. All the characters serve an illuminating function in this area. The themes run concurrently, coalescing at last in Act III in terms of paradox.

The war theme is brought to a head when Bluntschli tells about his wounded friend being burned alive in a wood yard. Raina exclaims on its horror; Sergius remarks on its ridiculousness. In fact it is both, just as Sergius's charge was both brave and ridiculous and Bluntschli's preference for chocolates over ammunition is both realistic and foolhardy. The tragedy and humor of war may ironically coexist. The theme satirizing the genteel classes is brought to a conclusion in the betrothal of Sergius and Louka. The common concept that a gentleman is a gentleman only if he behaves like one is subjected to the inquiry—but what does a gentleman behave like? By seeking consistently to maintain genteel love with Raina in Act II, Sergius is both noble and idiotic; by sticking to his gentlemanly code of honor regarding Louka in Act III, he is both honorable and ridiculous. To descend below one's class is to be both courageous and self-indulgent; to climb the social ladder is to be both ingenious and conceited. The theme regarding the romantic and prosaic in life quickly destroys the simple abstraction of "higher love" in Act II, and in Act III achieves a more nearly lifelike resolution in ambivalence. Prosaic Louka marries romantic Sergius; romantic Raina marries prosaic Bluntschli. Yet in her social elevation Louka attains romance, and in following his biological instincts Sergius capitulates to prosaic impulse. In the same vein Raina pursues her natural maternal-sexual drives, and Bluntschli culminates his romantic act of climbing to a lady's balcony with the romantic conclusion of marrying the lady.

The ending of the play consequently involves a fusion of disparate elements, from prosaic fact to romance, resolving themselves on a pragmatic biological level and evoking from all the characters concerned a higher degree of honesty and self-awareness than they had possessed at the beginning. It was Shaw's hope as artist-philosopher that some of this heightened awareness would rub off on his audiences. But, in making his art popular, he made his point obscure. The increase in perception he sought tended to be drowned in laughter. Further, his ideas are less subject to strict analysis than to intuition; consequently the deceptively easy single-line approach, which asserts that "Shaw says this" or "Shaw says that," simply is not accurate, since it fails to grasp the complexities and ambivalences of Shaw's artistic thought and method. Yet it is these complexities and ambivalences that give depth and subtlety to his art. In *Arms and the Man* he wishes to reveal the blindness of the romantic element in life more than he desires to satirize romantic characters. All life is a mixture of the romantic and the prosaic; what is important is that the prosaic temperament properly assimilate and control the romantic element. Life simply cannot support sustained romance. By its very dreamlike nature, romance must be essentially discontinuous, and hence out of touch with what Bergson called "the fluid continuity of the real."[19] Illusions about war, gentility, and love are ultimately given

19. Henri Bergson, *Creative Evolution*, trans. Arthur Mitchell (New York, 1911), p. 302.

their true perspective through prosaic awareness, but at the same time Shaw reveals with artistic sensitivity that such awareness is most vitally attached to life when it is combined with the incentive power of romance.

CHAPTER THREE

CANDIDA

The Poetry of Characterization

After reading Shaw's novel, *Cashel Byron's Profession*, Robert Louis Stevenson wrote to the critic William Archer: "I say, Archer, my God, what women!"[1] The wife of the Reverend James Morell has elicited a similar response from critics and audiences for the past seventy years—all the shades of meaning that Stevenson's exclamation can imply, from complimentary to pejorative, have been expressed. Initially Candida was interpreted as a feminine ideal, and in the popular consciousness she has perhaps remained so; but over the years sensitive critics have responded to some of the less noble aspects of her character, and the charm which a leading lady may give her has been qualified by contradictory observations. The diversity of response is curious, since many have referred to *Candida* as Shaw's most perfect play (frequently for different reasons), and of all Shaw's works this one has passed through the critical wringer more than any other except *Saint Joan*.[2]

1. Quoted in Archibald Henderson, *George Bernard Shaw: Man of the Century* (New York, 1956), p. 128.
2. Some of those remarking on its technical excellence are Joseph McCabe, *George Bernard Shaw: A Critical Study* (London, 1914), p. 180; Archibald Henderson, *Bernard Shaw: Playboy and Prophet* (New York, 1932), p. 476; Maurice Colbourne, *The Real Bernard Shaw* (New York, 1949), p. 129; Homer Woodbridge, *George Bernard Shaw: Creative Artist* (Carbondale, 1963), p. 37.

The confusion has been partially engendered by Shaw's own reactions to his creation. At first his attitude was favorable, nearly adulatory, but he eventually qualified it and later expressed wry skepticism. He wrote to Ellen Terry in 1896: "But one does not get tired of adoring the Virgin Mother. Bless me! you will say, the man is a Roman Catholic. Not at all: the man is the author of Candida; and Candida, between you and me, is the Virgin Mother and nobody else." And later that year, he added: "I *have* written THE Mother Play—Candida—and I cannot repeat a master-piece."[3] Clearly, a Virgin Mother worthy of Shavian worship and presented in a masterpiece is likely to be a character of some stature. Shaw's description of her in the play as possessing *"large-ness of mind and dignity of character"*[4] tends to bear out this original estimate. But in 1908 Shaw qualified his stand in a letter to James Huneker. He was notably ambiguous. On the one hand, he likened Candida's immorality and unscrupulousness to Sieg-fried, which was a veiled compliment on the independent side of her nature; on the other hand, he described her as "a woman with-out 'character' in the conventional sense. Without brains and strength of mind she would be a wretched slattern or voluptuary. [She has] freedom from emotional slop [and] unerring wisdom on the domestic plane"—but her world is a "greasy fool's paradise."[5] To which he added, "As I should certainly be lynched by the in-furiated Candidamaniacs if this view of the case were made known, I confide it to your discretion"—whereupon Huneker pub-lished it. By 1920 Shaw had reduced Candida even more, down to small beer, dearness, and niceness: "What business has a man with the great destiny of a poet with the small beer of domestic

---

3. In *Ellen Terry and Bernard Shaw: A Correspondence*, ed. Christopher St. John (New York, 1932), pp. 23, 29.

4. *Bernard Shaw: Complete Plays with Prefaces* (New York, 1963), III, 213. All citations and quotations from the play are from this volume.

5. Quoted by James Huneker, "The Quintessence of Shaw," in *George Bernard Shaw: A Critical Survey*, ed. Louis Kronenberger (Cleveland, 1953), pp. 18–19. In *The Perfect Wagnerite*, Shaw described Siegfried as "a type of healthy man raised to perfect confidence in his own impulses by an intense and joyous vitality" ([New York, 1916], p. 65).

comfort and cuddling and petting at the apron-string of some dear nice woman?"[6] And in 1944 he lowered her further, implying that she is a female counterpart of Torvald Helmer: "The play is a counterblast to Ibsen's *Doll's House*, showing that in the real typical doll's house it is the man who is the doll."[7]

Shaw's changing attitude toward Candida indicates a personal ambivalence which reflects a dramatic ambivalence in the play. Both ambivalences have led to critical contention. The primary aesthetic problem of *Candida* results from the dynamics of characters being at odds with a rational and moral estimate of their development. Eric Bentley seems to have been the first to appreciate this fact: dynamically Candida triumphs through charm, whereas dialectically she displays thoughtless cruelty.[8] Similarly, he recognizes (as does William Irvine) that Marchbanks may be effective dramatically while he is unsatisfactory as a psychological portrayal.[9] When charisma in characters deviates from their more objective reality, critical estimates are bound to be a matter of dispute, depending upon the mixture of susceptibility and sensibility in each observer.

However, Bentley and Irvine have barely touched upon a problem which has further ramifications. The central critical issue has to do not only with the feminine lead, or with Marchbanks, but with basic considerations of viewpoint regarding all the major characters. The aesthetic essence of the play involves a conflict of three perspectives. From one viewpoint, which is still predom-

6. Quoted in George A. Riding, "The *Candida* Secret," *Spectator*, 17 Nov. 1950, p. 506. Reprinted in *A Casebook on "Candida,"* ed. Stephen S. Stanton (New York, 1962), pp. 166–69.

7. From *The Evening Standard*, reproduced in the *Radio Times*, 12 April 1946. Quoted in Robert Rattray, *Bernard Shaw: A Chronicle* (London, 1951), p. 102.

8. Eric Bentley, *The Playwright as Thinker*, Meridian Books ed. (New York, 1955), p. 134. Part of Candida's magnetism and success may be attributed to the expectations of romantically conditioned audiences. Shaw's conscientious violation of such expectations is discussed by Paul Lauter in "*Candida* and *Pygmalion*: Shaw's Subversion of Stereotypes," *Shaw Review*, 3, no. 3 (1960), 14–19.

9. Stanton, ed., *Casebook*, p. 156; reprinted from "The Making of a Dramatist (1892–1903)," foreword to *Plays by Bernard Shaw*, ed. Eric Bentley (New York, 1960), pp. xx–xxiv. William Irvine, *The Universe of G. B. S.* (New York, 1949), p. 178.

inant among critics, the play's dramatic resolution results from the insights of Candida, who serves as a catalyst resolving a bizarre love duel between her unenlightened husband and her immature but imaginative poet-lover. The triangle is shattered by the maternal wisdom of a mother-woman teaching marital realities to the husband and common sense to the poet.[10] A second viewpoint derives from Shaw's intellectualization of the characters and their meaning, both in his comments on the play and in other writings. From this view Morell is unenlightened, but so is Candida. They are both philistines, Morell with an idealistic bent, Candida with a domestic bent. Marchbanks is the catalyst who illumines the sociodomestic shallowness of the Morell parsonage and at last goes off into the night, seeking a greater world of poetic insight and philosophic reality.[11]

A third viewpoint, neglected in most discussions of the play, is essential to the total conceptualization. In contrast to the play's charismatic epicenter in Candida, or its imaginative-philosophical epicenter in Marchbanks, is the less dramatic moral epicenter in Morell, reflecting a social integrity and personal humaneness which the other two characters lack. Critics have sensed these qualities in Morell, but, in the face of the inherent power of Candida's charm and Marchbanks's iconoclasm, have failed to give them full definition.[12] This oversight is especially serious, since it

10. This approach is maintained by such critics as Augustin Hamon, *The Twentieth Century Molière: Bernard Shaw*, trans. Eden and Cedar Paul (New York, 1916), pp. 186–96; Henry C. Duffin, *The Quintessence of Bernard Shaw* (London, 1920), pp. 53, 77; Louis Kronenberger, *The Thread of Laughter* (New York, 1952), p. 230; and Martin Meisel, *Shaw and the Nineteenth-Century Theater* (Princeton, 1963), p. 230. See also the perceptive work of Elsie B. Adams, "Bernard Shaw's Pre-Raphaelite Drama," *PMLA*, 81 (1966), 433–37; Charles A. Carpenter, *Bernard Shaw & the Art of Destroying Ideals* (Madison, 1969), pp. 98–123; and Louis Crompton, *Shaw the Dramatist* (Lincoln, Nebr., 1969), pp. 29–44.

11. Bentley asserts Marchbanks's strength and his ability to live without illusion (*The Playwright as Thinker*, p. 133); but Arthur H. Nethercot formulates the theory most completely by using Shaw's *Quintessence* to categorize "Marchbanks as the developing realist, Morell as the wavering idealist and Candida . . . as the static Philistine." See "The Truth about *Candida*," *PMLA*, 64 (1949), 641.

12. Several who mention Morell favorably are Joseph Wood Krutch, "A Review of *Candida*," in Stanton, ed., *Casebook*, p. 213 (reprinted from *The Nation*, 20 April 1946, p. 487); Alick West, "*A Good Man Fallen among Fabians*" (London,

is through Morell that the limitations of Candida and Marchbanks are dramatically realized. Morell's viewpoint will therefore
be stressed here, with a minor sort of devil's advocacy, in an attempt to restore balance to what has become a rather lopsided
critical approach to the play.

Shaw's usual artistic position encompasses a multiplicity of
perspectives, such as the above, and the vitality of his dramaturgy
lies in the vigorous dramatic and intellectual interaction of these
perspectives.[13] The final reality is frequently a Hegelian synthesis,
a tension of opposites which have been given meaning through a
two-fold exploration—concretely through the vicissitudes of the
action, and abstractly as a dialectic rises out of the action. *Candida*
follows this pattern. Its basic assertion is not in any one of the
approaches to love—maternal-wifely love, conventional husbandly
love, or idealized love—but in what survives after their interaction.
Morell's world view, based on the oratory and altruism of a Christian social consciousness; Candida's view, based on a domestic
consciousness; and Marchbanks's view, based on the poetry and
iconoclasm of idealistic youth, are all facets of a flawed prism,
revealed first in terms of life, which remains contentious and
fragmented, then in terms of thought, which assimilates and
synthesizes.

It is especially important to Shaw's method that the vital integrity of each character be dramatically sustained. This puts a
special burden upon the actors. Each must command a considerable degree of power and charisma to enable him to maintain
both the human depth of the drama and the significance of the
dialectic. Hence a real warmth should enhance the vain female
and philistine woman in Candida, the power of idealism and
iconoclasm should offset the physical insignificance of Marchbanks, and nobility of mind and the best of intentions should

1950), p. 107; A. N. Gilkes, "Candour about Candida," *Fortnightly*, NS 171
(1952), 122; Arland Ussher, *Three Great Irishmen: Shaw, Yeats, Joyce* (New
York, 1953), p. 37; and St. John Ervine, *Bernard Shaw: His Life, Work and
Friends* (London, 1956), pp. 280–81.

13. In his "Preface to the Second Volume of *Plays: Pleasant and Unpleasant*,"
Shaw remarks: "Even in my unpleasant propagandist plays I have allowed every
person his or her own point of view" (*Complete Plays*, III, 111).

undergird the pompous rhetoric of Morell. The aesthetic and intellectual substance of the play is unusually dependent upon these compensating qualities being projected with dramatic force and proper balance. An entirely effeminate Marchbanks and pompous Morell in relation to an entirely charming Candida will do as much to distort the total picture as would a powerful Marchbanks, a tragic Morell, and a cruel Candida. The alternate possibilities are within the script, however, and fidelity to the total conception consequently calls for a careful assessment and portrayal of the special ambiguities of character which give the play its subtlety and distinction.

The magnetism of Candida the Mother prevails throughout the play. The power of her self-confidence, the warmth of her maternal affection toward her husband and poet-lover, and the charm of her geniality all project a forceful and humane image. But these elements, strong as they may be, are set in a context which qualifies and at times contradicts them. In Act I we may excusably miss the hints of fallibility in Candida's self-assurance, sense of humor, and sensitivity to emotional and aesthetic realities; but by Act II her deficiencies are manifest—her assertiveness can be brazenly shallow, her humor cruel, and her sensibilities banal. Act III reiterates these failings, underlining Candida's insensitivity and magnifying her pathetic, oppressive egocentricity. Both positive and negative elements coexist in her character to a cumulatively ironic effect, providing her with dramatic vitality and psychological depth and further contributing to the complexity of the dialectic. Whether Candida should be analyzed in terms of the flaws in her virtues or the virtues in her flaws is a matter of personal disposition, but in either case one element is given a perversity by the other, and the result is perceptive and dynamic characterization.

With typical adroitness Shaw at first builds Candida's character through the reports of a number of biased characters. She actually plays a very minor role in Act I, and the audience is led into a view of her more through the partialities of those commenting on her than through immediate observation. From her husband we hear that marriage to a good woman like Candida is a foretaste of the

Kingdom of Heaven on earth. This Elysian view is subsequently countered by Prossy, who is impatient with such foolishness over a woman possessing "good hair and a tolerable figure" (p. 205). Lexy, in turn, praises Candida's beauty and fine eyes; but Prossy responds with the critical mind of one woman observing another. In admitting that Mrs. Morell is very nice and good-hearted, Prossy in effect delimits her through praise, and there is a hint that Prossy's estimate is far less starry-eyed than that of the men, albeit the dowdy secretary is probably not impartial. Thus Shaw dramatically sets up an assertion and a rebuttal which provide that slight mystique to Candida's character which clings to those who are contentiously praised. The disparity between the undefined but "real" Candida which Prossy sees and the paragon which Morell and Lexy perceive becomes a matter of sexual differentiation, dialectical viewpoint, and psychological disposition. Dramatic anticipation augments the heroine's fascination.

And what does Candida actually amount to when we see her? Her opening line—"Say yes, James"—is as simply and poignantly representative of her as is Ann Whitefield's first "Mamma" in *Man and Superman*. It is a coaxing command, a conciliatory gesture, and a positive assertion. Good nature combined with a strong will characterize Candida's maternal indulgence. But her "largeness of mind" described by Shaw, and conveyed by certain actresses, clearly has its limitations. When Candida, touched that Marchbanks did not laugh at her father, remarks, "You are a very nice boy, Eugene, with all your queerness" (p. 217), she reveals a condescension laced with ignorance which typifies her. To Candida not only is Eugene a "great baby," but this appellative may loosely be attached to all men. We become aware that what may be good-humored cajoling in one sense is narrow-minded managing in another. Her use of "queerness" to describe Marchbanks's poetic temperament indicates her lack of understanding regarding his aesthetic and intellectual nature, a lack which she disguises under maternal coddling and a rather supercilious, callous sense of humor. Candida tends to enjoy herself at the wrong times and usually at the expense of others, such as when she makes fun of Eugene's naïveté in offering the cabman ten shillings. Morell is

45

charitable regarding Eugene's mistake, but the insecure and doting young man can only remark, "Mrs Morell's quite right." Candida's response—"Of course she is" (p. 218)—has both the positiveness and egocentricity that underlie most of her assumptions. Thus, although she may be considerate toward her husband in not inviting Eugene to lunch, she may also be seen as arranging her homecoming according to her own desires.

Candida is on the stage only briefly at her first appearance, and the positiveness of her character tends to obscure her limitations. In the light of her short appearance it is still possible for Marchbanks's account of her to be credible, when he refers to "the love she inspires" and speaks admiringly of her as "a woman, with a great soul, craving for reality, truth, freedom" (p. 223). But Shaw does hint at the true state of affairs. In a refrain which gains in irony as the play progresses, Marchbanks asserts that "she will understand me." Almost immediately thereafter Candida, observing his half-throttled state and echoing her comment on his "queerness," remarks, "You a r e a poet, certainly" (p. 225). Obviously, Marchbanks is talking about his innermost nature, while Candida is reacting only to his rumpled clothes. As Marchbanks's mind works in grandiloquent abstractions, hers deals with detail. She tidies him up as though he were a small boy and bustles him off to set the table.

A house is run on detail, and Act II picks up appropriately at this point, with Candida's concern over "my own particular pet scrubbing brush" (p. 236). Marchbanks's "horror" at this defilement of his pure ideal has all the absurdity of its excess and irrelevance. Candida has the good sense of a home economist and a proper awareness of her responsibility to keep the domestic machinery functioning. What *is* possibly a "horror" is that this scrub-brush pragmatism controls her view of the world. In certain ways she is like her father, sure of herself as genial and kind at heart, while running her small show with self-righteous cunning and an exaggerated sense of self-importance. Shaw suggests a hereditary link between the Burgess Candida and the bourgeois Candida in her father's comment on Marchbanks: "He talks very pretty. I awlus had a turn for a bit of poetry. Candy takes arter me that-away" (p. 237). The implication is not very covert. As careless dress and queerness make the poet, "pretty talk" makes poetry, and Candida's "turn" for a "bit" of poetry seems just as deep as those words indicate. A common bond of prosaicism ties the daughter to the father, giving Burgess a coherent place in the play, despite the incongruities of his dialect.[14] As with Nicola in *Arms and the Man*, the purely prosaic viewpoint is a limited one. The observation is implicit that while the wheels of the world may be greased by attention to detail, the volition of the world requires imagination, and one without the other is likely to run into trouble. Thus Candida, with her domestic vision, blunders at many points where she feels most wise.

What little imagination Candida actually possesses reveals itself in her estimate of her husband's public role. It quickly becomes clear that, just as she does not understand Eugene's profession of poetry, she has a sadly uncharitable and incomplete view of the poetry of Morell's profession. There is an implication that she is partly prejudiced by a touch of jealousy as she comments, "Why must you go out every night lecturing and talking? I hardly have one evening a week with you" (p. 239). Her assertions that Morell's parishioners "dont mind what you say to them one little bit" (p. 239) and that his sermons are "mere phrases that you cheat yourself and others with every day" (p. 242) are not only cuttingly harsh and demoralizing, coming from one who is ostensibly loving and supposedly a helpmate, but they also have the ring of sophomoric truisms, aggressively iconoclastic, perceptibly biased. Her comment that the women all have Prossy's complaint indeed touches upon one of the aspects of a popular preacher's appeal, but in this dramatic context it is a perverse echo of Marchbanks's assertion in Act I that Morell whips the men into an enthusiasm resembling drunkenness. Probably Candida's ego is bolstered in having a desirable male and in feeling superior to

14. The criticism that Burgess is overdrawn is valid, however. Whether he is aesthetically disruptive or not depends on the disposition of the actor—and of the auditor. See McCabe, *Shaw: A Critical Study*, p. 180; Ervine, *Shaw: His Life, Work and Friends*, pp. 181–82; and Richard Burton, *Bernard Shaw: The Man and the Mask* (New York, 1916), pp. 72–73.

that commodity, just as Marchbanks's ego grows through disparaging the popular preacher as a demagogue for fools, with both fools and demagogue being despised by their wives. While Marchbanks portrays the men as deluded, so that he may build up his image of Candida, Candida portrays the women as deluded, in order to build up her image of herself; both views represent Morell as blind and foolish for not perceiving their conception of the truth. The tone of the two disparagements is distinctly similar, and there is implicit feeling that Candida's derives from Marchbanks's. Her attack is too close to that of the previous act not to suggest a common source—possibly that sojourn in the country with Marchbanks, mentioned in Act I. As Morell remarks later, "He said nothing that you did not say far better yourself" (p. 264).[15] Candida, of course, interprets Marchbanks's iconoclasm in her own light, but it is more than happenstance that, in this conversation about her husband's profession, she suddenly turns the subject to unloved Eugene, and repeats twice that "Eugene's always right" (pp. 241, 243).

Regarding love, Candida reveals the same good sense combined with vacuity which typifies her elsewhere. Inconsistent with her "choice" at the end of the play, she claims that Eugene needs love more than Morell does—which indicates that either she is carried away by the compassion of the moment, changes her mind later, or is reflecting something Eugene has impressed upon her. Her greatest misjudgment, however, is in assuming that Marchbanks has no suspicion that he is about to fall in love with her. This is especially important because of its dramatic force, impressing upon the audience in a poignant manner (especially upon those who have missed it thus far) that this supremely self-confident woman *is* fallible, and that she is either ridiculous or ominous to the extent that her smugness transcends her intelligence. Her subsequent impulse, to teach Marchbanks about love, is further undercut by her continuing shallow sense of poetry and poets: "But suppose he learns it from a bad woman, as so many men do, especially poetic men, who imagine all women are angels!" (p.

15. Candida's debt to Marchbanks is noted by Judith B. Spink, "The Image of the Artist in the Plays of Bernard Shaw," *Shaw Review*, 6 (1963), 85.

242). Neglecting to define a "bad" woman, and with the comfortable assumption that Candida is a "good" one, this observation is both platitudinous and inaccurate. The opinion that poets are prone to imagine all women as angels is the notion of one who has not read Chaucer, Shakespeare, Donne, or Milton.[16]

So Candida's "shawl" speech is built on a foolish foundation, and it should hardly be necessary to observe that while she speaks unconventionally, she is (vastly more than Mrs. Warren) a conventional woman at heart. Her actions at no time challenge propriety. Her admonition to Morell—"Trust in my love for you, James, not in my goodness and purity"—is well taken, but only verbally adventuresome. In its best sense it is an affirmation of genuine affection and should be comforting. In its harshest sense it dangles the specter of infidelity before a well-meaning, faithful, albeit conventional husband. When Morell shows anguish, Candida taunts him with having taught her to think for herself—an ironic assertion, since her thoughts are mostly Marchbanks's. Candida's good humor here, repeatedly indicated by Shaw in the acting instructions, adds poignantly to the impression of her lack of taste, her insensibility, and, as Marchbanks aptly emphasizes, her cruelty. Her final bewilderment in the act—"I cant understand"—is a refreshing reversal of her iron-bound self-confidence. It appropriately emphasizes and punctuates the fallibility which Shaw has been displaying all along.

The tableau which opens Act III is a visual comment on intrinsic human relationships and on the ensuing scene. Marchbanks is in the small chair (the child's chair) reading poetry—a striking indication of his innocence and of his relationship to Candida. By contrast, Candida is in the easy chair, and here the image is as graphically and suggestively sexual as anything in Shaw: "*The poker, a light brass one, is upright in her hand. Leaning back and looking intently at the point of it, with her feet stretched towards the blaze, she is in a waking dream*" (p. 249).[17] One may wonder

16. This may be a debased reflection of Shaw's questionable assertion that the attitude of artists toward women is both more romantic and less sexual than that of ordinary men. See Epistle Dedicatory to *Man and Superman, Complete Plays*, III, 498–99.

17. The phallic symbol here has been alluded to briefly by one critic—Charles L.

how conscious Shaw was of his implications here, but the passage calls for attention since the entire following scene reinforces it with recurring puns and allusions. Indeed, it has central significance, not only in this scene but in the entire play. Candida has not been listening, and she awakens from her reverie *"with a guilty excess of politeness,"* remarking, "I'm longing to hear what happens to the angel," a comment which further reflects her aesthetic limitations. First, she finds poetry dull, and second, it must have a story line to be tolerable. Candida, whose conception of love obviously involves a consciousness far more earthbound than that of Marchbanks, admits to having been "hypnotized" by the poker—a singularly appropriate admission to come at this specific, private time with her young poet-lover. The implication is that she has ambivalent longings, since the attraction and very existence of husband, family, and home—the elements which prove to be her entire world—are clearly indebted to sexual bonds. The phallic symbol is evocative of two alternatives—most likely it suggests, in this barren moment, Candida's subconscious desire for the virility of the absent Morell, especially on this "sacred" first night at home after three weeks in the country; or, less likely, it symbolizes, in these romantic surroundings, her even more subliminal desire for physical satisfaction from the vital boy-poet. Either alternative would represent a greater fulfillment of Candida's nature than the reading of poetry which her limited imagination finds sterile. And in either case it is tempting to suggest that "boring" is a sexual pun, since it applies so well to the symbolic nature of the scene: Marchbanks remarks, "I beg your pardon for boring you"; to which Candida replies, "But you are not boring me."

In this context it is apparent why the poker makes Eugene "horribly uneasy." He says: "It looked as if it were a weapon. If I were a hero of old I should have laid my drawn sword between us." The covert connotations of "weapon" and "drawn sword" assume compound humor through being utterly unintentional *double-*

Holt, *"Candida*: The Music of Ideas," *Shaw Review*, 9 (1966), 12. Holt deals with the musical structuring of Candida—this type of approach proves rewarding as it helps to explain the rhetorical and dramatic power of many Shaw plays.

entendres. Typically, Eugene converts the poker into a sword, consciously turning from a vulgar modern object to a romantic one. Unconsciously, and more significantly, he converts the fertility symbol into a symbol for maintaining chastity and moves metaphorically from the sensual love of one into the platonic love of the other. Of course, the sword is also a fertility symbol, but here Marchbanks uses it as a defensive device. One might well ask whose chastity is being protected. Is the aesthete not in danger of being psychically raped by the mundane woman? Almost like a temptress (still, of course, on a plane of subliminal *double-entendre*), she urges him on, first onto the hearthrug at her knees, then with the alluring words—"You may say anything you really and truly feel. Anything at all, no matter what it is"; to which all the poet can respond is "Candida, Candida, Candida, Candida, Candida" (p. 251). The name and its repetition extend the platonic/earthly doubleness of the scene. It is almost a substitute for "Hail Mary" (as Candida is to him the Virgin of the Assumption), or, more mundanely, for orgasm (a one-sided substitute)—had the evening come to a passionate conclusion, this would have been about time (as Morell suggests later [p. 254]). Such happiness is the answer to Marchbanks's prayer. Candida's understanding may be equaled by an element of disappointment as she now asks, "Do you want anything more?" No. Marchbanks has come into his heaven, which is clearly *not* Candida's heaven.

Thus Shaw with remarkable economy symbolizes and dramatizes the essential relationship between the two. This is their most intimate point of contact, the climax of their relationship, and it is bogus, surrogate, and incomplete, since they are existing on two different levels. It can hardly be accidental that so many sexual allusions occur at this precise moment in the play, because at this moment they are most appropriate.[18] But, despite their obviousness, Shaw carries the scene concurrently on a high platonic level. Candida transcends Marchbanks in her fuller vision and instinc-

18. Such extensive and pointed sexual innuendo is unique in Shaw. One would like to speculate that Shaw, still burning over the censor's rejection of *Mrs Warren's Profession*, is, incidentally, mocking that man's obtuseness, sailing by him with a smile.

tive desires; Marchbanks transcends Candida in his nobler vision and intuitive longings. Candida is tender here, and to some degree sympathetic toward the young man, but the instinctive aspect of her nature cannot be satisfied by the aesthetic airiness of his.

By this time the full implications of Titian's "Virgin of the Assumption," which has been hanging over the fireplace throughout the play, become apparent. The picture presents a visual irony, an implicit comment on the action, and is a type of device Shaw was to use with subtle effectiveness throughout his playwriting career. As Marchbanks's gift to the Morells, it reveals his platonic idealization of Candida, an idealization which, by their nature, neither Candida nor Morell appreciates very deeply. At Candida's first entrance Shaw comments: *"A wise-hearted observer, looking at her, would at once guess that whoever had placed the Virgin of the Assumption over her hearth did so because he fancied some spiritual resemblance between them, and yet would not suspect either her husband or herself of any such idea, or indeed of any concern with the art of Titian"* (p. 213). What is for Marchbanks a spiritual analogy is for the Morells, in Burgess's terms, "a 'igh class fust rate work of ort" (p. 215). They are both too philistine and too aware of earthly realities to draw the comparison. Thus the picture is a constant reminder not only of the disparity between Marchbanks's aesthetic sensitivity and theirs, but of the high-flying falseness of his ideal when set against the mundane reality of Candida. Elsewhere Shaw describes this painting as uniting flesh and spirit, being both voluptuous and devotional.[19] In the scene just past we have observed exactly these two qualities, dramatized in juxtaposition and interaction.

Although Candida again grows by report near the end of the play, being given more credit than she deserves by Marchbanks, the conclusion reveals the full perversity of her strength: as her power emerges most forcefully, so does her domineering short-sightedness. Her quiet anger and stern vehemence appear at this point and are among her most attractive qualities. Her remark

19. "The Living Pictures" (6 April 1895), in George Bernard Shaw, *Our Theatres in the Nineties* (London, 1948), I, 82. Referred to by Crompton, *Shaw the Dramatist*, p. 42.

regarding Eugene—"Two men! Do you call that a man? [*To Eugene*] You bad boy!" (p. 257)—perhaps reflects her disappointment in him earlier in the act; but of course she treats all men as boys, and has completely undercut the false climax of the "choice" by her antecedent comment regarding James: "My boy shall not be worried: I will protect him" (p. 256). Does she really "choose" James because he is the weaker of the two men? Certainly not entirely. First, he is her husband, and she loves him—on the two grounds of convention and affection, he is the winner. Second, as indicated above, he is *her* boy, and she will *protect* him—her maternal nature is involved, as toward a son, and Marchbanks is at best only a stepchild. It is symbolically and dramatically important in the final scene that Morell is in the child's chair while Marchbanks is in the visitor's chair. Third, she can manage him and feel important as the executive behind the figurehead. And, most important, it is clear that Morell offers her *both* physical virility, to which she can respond as a wife, and dependence, to which she can respond as a mother. Since Eugene's aesthetics are meaningless to her, he is only half a male: the boy, not the man.

These reasons are, of course, not the ones she gives. Candida ennobles her motives in terms of the self-sacrifice involved in being the power behind the throne, the support of the domestic social structure. She neglects to mention the benefits of the union to her—she loves details and she loves to manage things, as she loves to be a mother to all and a mate to a virile, admired man. Further, since she is her own advocate here, she certainly cannot pretend modesty. The fact that keeping the home fires burning does not necessarily make a man, is a fact she chooses not to see, probably because it would diminish her sense of importance. It is consequently clear in retrospect that she must disparage Morell's public role, as she does in Act II, in order to exalt her domestic role. And when she has emasculated him to the degree that he humbly drivels, "What I am you have made me" (p. 267), her triumph is complete, her egocentric and mundane view of the world is vindicated. In her moment of glory she ignores the fact that marital debts are generally reciprocal.

Candida has the strength of her ignorance. Caught in the details of life, she is insensitive to the poetry of its great abstractions, such as are involved in Morell's career and Marchbanks's idealism. She is too self-confident and egocentric to understand Morell, and too philistine to understand Marchbanks. Candida is tied to a finite wheel of time which both the pastor and the poet seek to transcend. She has none of the doubts, humility, and sensitivity which beset her husband, or the poetic horrors and poetic love which obsess Marchbanks. Her greatest poetry is motherhood, and in this she flourishes with dramatic force, forgetting that motherhood is at last inhibitive to growing boys and that masculine fulfillment lies beyond weaning.

Beneath the charm and maternal power of Candida, then, runs a strong countercurrent. She is comparable more to Laura, the forthrightly antifeminist target of Strindberg's *The Father*, than to Ibsen's Torvald Helmer. As Laura ignorantly disparages the value of her husband's scientific research, Candida short-sightedly criticizes Morell's ministry. Laura taunts her husband with the possibility of the illegitimacy of their child; Candida dangles the possibility of her infidelity before Morell. Laura at last reduces her husband to madness and utter dependence; Candida at last reduces Morell to the child's chair and professions of gratitude for being managed so well. But it is in part a measure of Shaw's art that this current flows subliminally to other dynamic concerns, specifically to the problem and challenge of Marchbanks. The point is made without being intrusive or melodramatic; indeed, it is cloaked in its seeming opposite—the virtue of a good woman—and in this it gains ironic, dramatic, and human force.

The more we realize the essential mundanity of Candida, the more we can define the limitations and subjectivity of Eugene's insights. It is highly ironic that the philistine is elevated dramatically by the accolades of the iconoclast. But Marchbanks's views, faulty as they are, carry persuasive weight, and one must discriminate between his rhetorical effectiveness and his illusions. Eugene is an insecure young man, eagerly seeking affection, who loses his heart when he finds a sympathetic response in a congenial, attractive older woman. His susceptible state of mind is suggested in his comment to Prossy: "I know. You feel you could love anybody that offered" (p. 230). To him Candida is convenient, and Candida offers. Much of her appeal is that of a protective and ordered maternal force, although Eugene violently rejects it as such at the end of the play. Like Mrs. Higgins in *Pygmalion*, maturity has worn off some of the rough corners which may be found in younger women—Candida has a little of the sophistication and softness which render her a slight enigma and subtly attractive to the sensitive, immature idealist. The eventual growth of the artist involves a breaking away from this juvenile emotional tie. Shaw dramatizes this at the end by having Marchbanks reject Candida as mother, reject happiness, refer to his love in the past tense, and transcend Candida's finite sense of time: "In a hundred years, we shall be the same age" (p. 268). Thus the greatest obstacle Marchbanks has to overcome is not his "rival" Morell but his own apotheosis of a motherly and engaging thirty-three-year-old woman, an apotheosis which is tied to confused affections and errant poetic enthusiasm.

These latter elements in his character have in large part alienated critics, whose comments on Marchbanks run a gamut of abuse from "snivelling little beast" to "an example of how an inadequate idea is reflected in inadequate art."[20] The most prevalent criticism questions Shaw's portrayal of a poet. Marchbanks, viewed as an effeminate pipsqueak spouting purple passages and insolent opinions, does not seem adequate for the role. Equally germane, but generally unstated, is the objection of inconsistency—Marchbanks appears to understand Morell with a penetrating sensibility, while he is blind to manifest defects in Candida. Criticism is generally based on the rather hazardous assumption that Shaw intends Marchbanks to represent in some complete sense "the poet" and, further, that Marchbanks indeed functions in this capacity in the play. The first assumption involves the intentional fallacy; the second, though more impersonal, is generally derived from the first. To support such a premise one has merely to cite Shaw's admiration for Shelley, Marchbanks's Shelleyan temperament, and the play's frequent references to Marchbanks as a

20. Patrick Braybrooke, *The Subtlety of Bernard Shaw* (London, 1930), p. 32; Reuben A. Brower, *Major British Writers II* (New York, 1959), p. 689.

poet. Further, there are Shaw's subsequent comments to Huneker and the Rugby boys regarding Marchbanks's poetic insight and noble destiny.[21]

In spite of all this evidence, the casual identification of Marchbanks with a poet's role is a misleading one. Shaw admired Shelley, having read his complete works at an early age, deriving both revolutionary principles and vegetarianism from them. In *The Quintessence of Ibsenism*, written before *Candida*, Shaw typified Shelley as a realist—one who tears away the masks of empty traditions which idealists maintain.[22] In his Epistle Dedicatory to *Man and Superman* he includes Shelley in a list of writers "whose peculiar sense of the world I recognize as more or less akin to my own."[23] Marchbanks's personal characteristics in the play are Shelleyan, as are his iconoclasm and his history of an unsympathetic aristocratic family, unhappiness at Eton, and his desertion of Oxford. The identification was borne out in an early production of *Candida*, in which Marchbanks was made up as Shelley and read a snatch of that poet's work at the beginning of Act III.[24]

Shaw's admiration of Shelley was not unqualified, however, and his reservations may be nowhere more apparent than in the play itself. His portrayal of Marchbanks emphasizes numerous deficiencies. In the Epistle Dedicatory to *Man and Superman*, Shaw speaks of the value of the prosaic qualities of the English as opposed to the vanity of the poetic qualities of the Irish, and he goes on to refer to Shelley's "amoristic superstition."[25] Shelley's weakness is reflected in Marchbanks, who is indeed a victim of amoristic superstition and of ideals suggested by "half-satisfied passions" such as Shaw had criticized in his preface to *Plays Pleasant*.[26] Such passions are inherently uncritical, insipid, and debili-

21. In Kronenberger, *Critical Survey*, p. 18; and Riding, "The 'Candida' Secret," p. 169.

22. George Bernard Shaw, *The Quintessence of Ibsenism*, Dramabook ed. (New York, 1957), p. 42.

23. *Complete Plays*, III, 507.

24. Archibald Henderson, *George Bernard Shaw: His Life and Works* (Cincinnati, 1911), p. 346.

25. *Complete Plays*, III, 495, 512.

26. Ibid., 121.

tating. Clearly Marchbanks has certain attributes of genius, but he is as yet only an incipient poet. Shaw describes him as a sensitive youth *"before the character has grown to its full strength"* (p. 215). His spirit is more poetic than his talents. His terrible passages about marble floors washed by the rain, the south wind dusting green and purple carpets, wreaths of stars, and beautiful archangels with beautiful wings (pp. 236, 255, 256), are altogether too purple; they presage Shaw's later comment on Shelley as one "who could not write a big poem without smothering it under a universe of winds and clouds, mountains and fountains, glories and promontories . . . until its theme was lost like a roseleaf in a splendid sunset."[27] Further, according to Hesketh Pearson, Shaw "denounced Shelley's *Epipsychidion* as the worst love poem in the world because no woman could possibly believe that she was a bit like its obviously imaginary subject."[28] This is apropos to Marchbanks's appraisal of Candida. Shaw was by temperament poetic in drama but not in verse, and such bad attempts as Marchbanks makes may be attributed to Shaw's deficiency.[29] But in terms of Marchbanks's aberrations such saccharine stuff is consistent and is probably an example of Shavian parody, a conscious delimiting of character. Certainly it plays this way.

Tidy and interesting as it may be, therefore, to place Eugene as a realist at the right angle of the triangle and to relegate Morell as idealist and Candida as philistine to a mere forty-five degrees each (in keeping with Shaw's definition of varying senses of reality in *The Quintessence of Ibsenism*),[30] the geometry of vital forces in the play is far more complex. The weak points of Marchbanks/

27. "An Aside" (May 1933), in *Shaw on Theatre*, ed. E. J. West, Dramabook ed. (New York, 1959), p. 223. Shaw's relationship to Shelley is dealt with by Roland A. Duerkson, "Shelley and Shaw," *PMLA*, 78 (1963), 114–27.

28. Hesketh Pearson, *George Bernard Shaw: His Life and Personality*, Atheneum ed. (New York, 1963), p. 119.

29. Such a suggestion is made by C. E. M. Joad, who deals with Shaw's prosaic limitations in *Shaw* (London, 1949), pp. 52–54. This is countered somewhat by Shaw's hint to Huneker: "The language of the poet, *for those who have not the clew to it*, is mysterious and bewildering and therefore worshipful" (p. 19; my italics). Shaw's sensitivity to what *is* poetic may in part be observed in Caesar's opening soliloquy in *Caesar and Cleopatra*.

30. See Nethercot, "The Truth about *Candida*," pp. 639–47.

Shelley come through as decisively as the strong points, not only because Shaw mistrusted poetic romanticism as much as he admired courageous iconoclasm, but also because the artist in Shaw sees to it that the dramatic situation in *Candida* takes on a life of its own. The Shavian dialectic again becomes subject to the ambivalence of Shavian art. Marchbanks has a lively sense of reality, but it is conditioned by his own wayward though brilliant, immature though perceptive, insights; and the greatest value of his sense of reality lies more in the vigor with which he pursues its promptings than in its absolute grasp of fact.

Thus, not being entirely "psychologically unsatisfactory" as William Irvine and others suggest, Marchbanks develops throughout the play in terms of intriguing ambiguities. These offer a sensitive rendering of his youth as well as of his peculiar genius and its limitations. In Act I his plight on the Embankment and his introduction to Burgess reveal painful shyness, while his desperate challenge of Morell bursts forth with a contrary assertiveness. Likewise, his naïveté and worship of Candida run counter to his knowledgeability and scorn of Morell; further, his pathetic physical weakness and cowardice are offset by his argumentative strength and bravery. Ironically, it is Morell who gives respectability to Marchbanks's erratic brilliance: "You will be one of the makers of the Kingdom of Heaven on earth; and—who knows?— you may be a master builder where I am only a humble journeyman . . . the heavy burthen and great gift of a poet may be laid upon you" (p. 222). Most of this encomium is speculative and born of tact, but it does grant Marchbanks dignity by giving his sharp and impassioned eccentricity the reputable title of "poet." With youthful impetuosity thus given weight, the evolving triangle becomes less lopsided, and Marchbanks gains dramatic power, his words being precognitive of the end of the play: "You think yourself stronger than I am; but I shall stagger you" (p. 220). Marchbanks's assertiveness and Morell's shaken self-confidence tend to carry the act. In retrospect, however, the myopia of youth is apparent—Eugene's inordinate praise of Candida as "a woman with a great soul, craving for reality, truth, freedom," builds her dramatically at first, but later compromises Eugene as we realize its romanticism; and his conflict with Morell, physical as well as intellectual, he converts into desperate melodrama, revealing an aberration of his will to dramatize life.

Marchbanks's limitations become clearer in his dialogue with Prossy at the beginning of Act II. He senses the partial truth that shyness thwarts the love of the world, but this perceptive view is obviously an extension of his adolescence, reflecting the adolescent tendency to overgeneralize from limited personal experience. His subjective flaw is manifest elsewhere, in such little things as his assumption that business people must be "clever," since he himself is no good at details, and in such major things as his exorbitant estimate of Candida's character, resulting from her kindness to him. What he intellectualizes or feels as his own truth must be Absolute Truth. His instinctive sensitivity gives him an aura of precocious insight, but this is qualified by the immaturity with which he leaps at conclusions only half-considered and half-true.

Lacking the perspective of age and experience, Marchbanks is his own worst judge, being unable to qualify his feelings in the fuller contexts of love and marriage which Candida and Morell take for granted. Most revealingly, he comments, "I go about in search of love" (p. 228), aptly indicating his adolescent need; and, regarding Morell, he pleads, "Tell me: is it really and truly possible for a woman to love him?" (p. 230). An emotional hunger complements an emotional naïveté. The pathos and humor of his plight are most poignantly emphasized in his excessive reaction to the incongruity of his angel and a scrubbing brush. Lacking both poetic and practical maturity, he sees the ideal as divorced from the mundane, rather than sensing an instrinsic relationship of the two. He is unable to appreciate spiritual love coexisting with physical love. The essence of romance which he seeks has no practical correspondence in earthly terms—to try to find it on earth is to begrime it with earth, and this compromise Marchbanks is unwilling to make. Therefore, while in one sense his love is spiritual and transcendent, in another sense it is priggish and naïve. His response to Morell's remonstrance regarding such poetic escapism is most revealing: "Yes, to be idle, selfish, and useless: that is, to be beautiful and free and happy . . . thats my ideal: whats yours, and that of all the dreadful people who live in these hideous rows of houses? Sermons and scrubbing brushes!" (pp. 236–37). This sounds at first like the romantic Devil of *Man and Superman*, and at last like the snobbery of T. S. Eliot. Both are clearly inimical to the Shavian spirit and raise further doubts about too closely identifying Marchbanks with Shaw.[31]

Candida, aesthetically dull though she may be, hits upon a half-truth in Act III when she remarks to Marchbanks, "Talk moonshine as you usually do" (p. 250), for obviously Marchbanks's poetry, so disastrously displayed in Act II, is more moonshine than truth. But generations of philistines have seen genuine truth as moonshine, and Candida gives no evidence of being sensitive to distinctions. Similarly, Marchbanks, whose finer sense of truth is closely linked to "moonshine," is only half accurate in his comment, "Take care. I'm ever so much older than you." He means that his sensitivity and comprehension are more mature, which is true in a sense of precocity, but false in terms of the juvenile world lying beneath precocity. Half-truths such as these are common in the play, being most frequently typical of Candida and Marchbanks. It is such partial vision which leads to the recurrent theme of misunderstanding and its comically exploited counterpart, "madness." Marchbanks's platonic vision is both his greatest self-realization and his limitation. It has the glory of being happily fulfilled and the flaw of incompleteness. This is dramatized by the disparity of consciousness between Marchbanks and Candida: he is caught up in ecstasy at the satisfaction of his platonic affection, while she, who is aesthetically so much more obtuse than he, can look down upon his childish happiness from her philistine sphere, knowing so much more while intuiting so much less.

The limits of Marchbanks's sophistication as opposed to the scope of his intuition are strikingly implied in his description of his emotional climax with Candida: "I was standing outside the gate of Heaven, and refusing to go in. . . . Then she became an angel; and there was a flaming sword that turned every way, so that I couldnt go in; for I saw that that gate was really the gate

31. As Bentley does in *The Playwright as Thinker*, p. 133.

of Hell" (pp. 252–53). Again poetic enthusiasm naïvely cloaks sexual symbolism, and, also again, it comes at precisely the appropriate dramatic moment—the lover's confrontation with the husband, after the evening of bliss. Marchbanks's observation, while conveying his extravagant romanticism, further captures his fastidious disposition to mutate physiological fact into poetic fancy, as well as his rhetorical instinct to mimic the clergyman's idiom. There is an implicit iconoclasm in joining sex and heaven in a common context, but he seems hardly aware of it. The gate and the flaming sword, when reflected against the earlier "love scene," suggest a sexual metaphor. Marchbanks's "refusing to go in" indicates his reticence to debase his platonic idealism by physical action—to violate his Virgin of the Assumption would be profoundest sacrilege. The flaming sword guarding the gate has a twofold significance, previously noted. In Marchbanks's poetic sense it becomes the sword of chastity, while in a more subliminal sense it is phallic, indicating Morell's virility. Both are powerful forces keeping him from physical involvement with Candida. The sword of chastity, appropriately romantic, deters him, while Morell's virility, appropriately sexual, deters Candida.

On a more sublime level, no doubt that which Marchbanks primarily intends, the allusion is biblical, recalling that "flaming sword which turned every way" (Genesis 3:24) to bar Adam and Eve from Paradise. Marchbanks's observation that "that gate was really the gate of Hell" is fraught with amusing paradox and ambiguity. Sexually the meaning is obvious, since, to Marchbanks, physical consummation would debase his spiritual communion with Candida and create all sorts of social problems as well. Philosophically the comment is a rejection of the primal innocence—ignorance, in Shavian terms—of the Garden of Eden, since in the Garden there is no knowledge of good or evil, and surrender to its enticements would be an escape and regression, both antithetic to the poetic spirit. Thus Shaw metaphorically alludes to one of his major points: Candida's little paradise would be Marchbanks's hell.

Although at this moment Marchbanks poetically intuits his relationship with Candida, there is subtle irony in the fact that he does not grasp the full implications of his symbols. He continues to romanticize—"A woman like that has divine insight: she loves our souls"—and to ponder the obvious—"What I want to know is how you got past the flaming sword that stopped me" (p. 254). He consciously avoids clear evidence of Candida's mundanity, failing to appreciate her sexual-maternal-conventional ties to Morell. And his sensitivity is decisively anti-Shavian when he insists that man can dwell forever on the highest summits.[32] By this time it is clear that Marchbanks is guilty of the same "gift of gab" which he disparaged in Morell in Act I. His rhetoric, though more "poetic" than Morell's, is just as windy.[33] To say that Candida offered him "her shawl, her wings, the wreath of stars on her head, the lilies in her hand, the crescent moon beneath her feet" (p. 255) displays nothing but Rossettian froth, with a subject matter and style even more hollow than Morell's rhetorical platitudes. No doubt Shaw intends to convey this, since he has Marchbanks remark, "All the words I know belong to some attitude or other" (p. 251), and, later: "James and I are having a preaching match" (p. 256). Marchbanks, trotting and dancing throughout this scene, can scarcely be calculated to engage our affections. The sensitive young man is in many ways confirmed as very much a fool. He can react with tender compassion to Candida's torturing of Morell on the one hand, but on the other he can be blindly supercilious as he remarks from his ignorance, "You dont understand what a woman is" (p. 256).

The obvious conclusion is that Marchbanks is hardly a poet. He may be an incipient poet, but now he is merely a pretender. He is an unstable, sensitive young man, full of impetuosity and romantic illusions, who aspires to poetry; he seems to have some of the potential for incisive insight which might enable him to become first-rate (or second-rate) later on, but he is only third-rate (or worse) at present. His mediocrity or excellence cannot be accu-

32. Shaw characterized the modern hero as "touching the summits only at rare moments . . . instead of ridiculously persisting in rising to them all on the principle that a hero must always soar, in season or out of season." Quoted in Henderson, *Playboy and Prophet*, p. 493. See my chapter on *Caesar and Cleopatra*.

33. A point also made by Walter N. King, "The Rhetoric of *Candida*," *Modern Drama*, 2 (1959), 75.

rately judged by the Morells. He has vitality, magnetism, and a distinctive hint of genius, but he is now making his mistakes: his idol suffers by comparison to Titian's Virgin; his love is puppy love, as Morell says; and his poetry is even more vacuous than his idealism. His youth and naïve exuberance limit his perspective, but his natural perceptiveness reveals intrinsic insight which may well amount to something once it is disciplined and educated. In this light, the most aesthetically workable one, Eugene is not an imperfectly drawn character. We are falling into the trap of his rhetoric and the Morells' high appraisals of him if we expect more. Nor is he a Shavian. While his iconoclasm no doubt appealed to his creator, his aestheticism, his love of love for love's sake and of art for art's sake are qualities Shaw frequently and vociferously deplored.

Just as Marchbanks grotesquely romanticizes Candida, he perversely misunderstands Morell. His judgment is flawed even where it seems sharpest. His iconoclasm can be as brash and sophomoric as his romanticism is vague and empty. He may be somewhat of a realist in his ability to tear away conventional masks, but this seeming realism is founded on his immature estimate of life. Shaw's critical comments on "the poet's secret" must therefore be qualified, like so many of his second thoughts and afterviews. Marchbanks appears to have a minor epiphany at the end, but one which is scarcely as convincing as Shaw would have it when he comments that in rejecting Candida's greasy fool's paradise Marchbanks "is really a god going back to his heaven, proud, unspeakably contemptuous of the 'happiness' he envied in the days of his blindness, clearly seeing that he has higher business on hand than Candida." Nor does Marchbanks necessarily seem to be "a man with the great destiny of a poet" who avoids petty domesticity by going out proudly "into the majestic and beautiful kingdom of the starry night."[34]

Marchbanks's "strength" at the end does not logically or emotionally emerge from a sensitive touch with reality, but from a consistent rejection of reality on his own romantic terms. Like

34. Huneker, "The Quintessence of Shaw," p. 18; Riding, "The *Candida* Secret," p. 169.

Sergius Saranoff of *Arms and the Man*, when the world does not fit his romantic conception of it, he rejects the world, not his romantic conception. His ideal love, which bears a striking kinship to the "higher love" of Sergius and Raina, is invalidated. He flees into the night as a Byronic figure, like Sergius, caught more in the romance of his disillusionment than in a realistic rejection of Candida's greasy fool's paradise. Life is *not* "nobler" than this mundanity, and to change life one must first come to terms with it. To Shaw, art and ideals must face life, not flee it.[35] Hence the night seems to be less Tristan's holy night than the darkness of Marchbanks's own romance, and the star he is seeking is elusive because it probably does not exist. Shaw expresses some ambivalence toward this dramatic situation as he describes the instinctive promptings of the artist, with specific reference to Marchbanks: "Here, then, was the higher but vaguer and timider vision, the incoherent, mischievous, and even ridiculous unpracticalness, which offered me a dramatic antagonist for the clear, bold, sure, sensible, benevolent, salutarily shortsighted Christian Socialist idealism."[36] Through such qualifications Marchbanks is nearly disqualified—and these are what survive most strongly in the play. His poetic vision seems flawed, obscure, and irrelevant when subjected to a worldly test. On the other hand, Morell may be myopic, but his prosaicism reflects virtues which transcend the ineffectuality of Marchbanks's abstractions. Finally, the logical and dramatic conclusion of the play is, in very Shavian terms, at odds with Shaw's commentaries on it. The fulcrum of reality shifts away from Marchbanks, much as the fulcrum of ideal womanhood slips awry in Candida.

The result is a double paradox. Shaw stated its most obvious level in a letter to Siegfried Trebitsch: "Now the whole point of the play is the revelation of the weakness of this strong and manly man, and the terrible strength of the febrile and effeminate

35. Note Caesar's coalescence of art with peace, war, government, and civilization; also Shaw's comment: "But 'for art's sake' alone I would not face the toil of writing a single sentence" (*Complete Plays*, III, 466, 513–14).

36. "Preface to the second volume of *Plays: Pleasant and Unpleasant*," *Complete Plays*, III, 112.

one."[37] In terms of the dramatic story line and the rhetorical pyrotechnics, this observation is correct. But it does not go far enough, since there is an ambiguity which, while it does not turn the paradox upside down, nonetheless evolves with it concurrently, in a topsy-turvy relationship. While the strong man is being proved weak, and the weak man gains strength, a counterrefrain is at work, reaffirming, on more fully revealed grounds, the true strength of the strong man and the romantic incapacity of the weak one. The man may become a "boy" in the child's chair, and the boy may become a "man" in the starry night, but the inversion dramatizes a strange reality: the man who recognizes the boy in himself is ultimately nearer to a true grasp on life than the boy who boldly (and romantically) takes on the attitudes of manhood. In Act I Marchbanks scornfully labels as "cant" Morell's admonition to "be a man" (p. 221), but by Act III their roles are reversed when Marchbanks speaks *"with the ring of a man's voice"* (p. 267)—and with a heroic cant all his very own.

Although the play offers a threefold perspective in terms of its three major characters, Morell is at its most significant dramatic and dialectic epicenter. Candida with her charm and Marchbanks with his vigor tend to divert attention toward themselves, but it is Morell and his values which undergo the most sustained attack and analysis, and it is as a result of this attack that Candida's mother-woman role is revealed as egocentric and philistine, and Marchbanks's poetic vision, so acutely critical, is revealed as myopically romantic. Morell, ostensibly the beaten one, is remarkably resilient. Through having his weaknesses ruthlessly revealed and in acknowledging them, his strengths are all the more apparent. His conceptions about himself, his marriage, and his profession are at stake. Marchbanks attacks his personal role in Act I, and Candida disparages his public role in Act II. But in the process it becomes clear that his sins are venial, while his virtues are outstanding. He has, in fact, a whole set of admirable qualities which are distinctly Shavian: personal dynamics, a proclivity for

37. 9 January 1903. Quoted in Meisel, *Shaw and the Nineteenth-Century Theater*, p. 231.

work, a sound sense of humor, and, above all, an active social consciousness.

Some measure of Morell as an effective character may be taken by comparing him to Pastor Manders in Ibsen's *Ghosts*.[38] Both men are full of platitudes and both have a conventional moral sense, but in Ibsen these qualities flatten the clergyman, while in Shaw they are reflected against a congenial and forceful personality. Shaw is portraying a first-rate clergyman, a leader, not a sad reflection of respectability and the status quo; Shaw sought "a really powerful and brilliant Morell."[39] Like so many admirable Shavian men (i.e., Caesar, Tanner, Higgins), Morell has an element of the child in him, being *"a great baby, pardonably vain"* (p. 201), combined with the quality of a responsible adult in his dedication to "hard unselfish work" (p. 204). In a thoroughly Shavian manner, his principles combine personal integrity with enlightened social awareness, such as in his remark, "We have no more right to consume happiness without producing it than to consume wealth without producing it" (p. 204)—a statement which is rescued from mere rhetoric by evidences of Morell's desire to fulfill his role on both counts. He is as carefully and considerately attentive to Lexy, Prossy, and Eugene as he is to socialist causes. His personal charity toward them has its corollary in his social concern over his women parishioners, whom Burgess was going to underpay and overwork. He craves the honesty of recognizing Burgess as a scoundrel, as he himself may be a fool—and more than in the sense of a doddering Polonius (who is echoed in "I like a man to be true to himself" [p. 212]), since he pursues all of his convictions with meaningful action. The effective social power of Morell is most graphically attested to by his father-in-law—"You and your crew are gittin hinfluential" (p. 213)—as his personal virtues are extolled by Lexy: "What a good man! What a thorough loving soul he is!" (p. 205). This essential link between the social man and the

38. Huneker does this very briefly ("The Quintessence of Shaw," p. 16). Jacob H. Adler compares *Candida* to *The Wild Duck* in "Ibsen, Shaw and *Candida*," *Journal of English and Germanic Philology*, 59 (1960), 50–58.

39. See *Florence Farr, Bernard Shaw, W. B. Yeats: Letters*, ed. Clifford Bax (New York, 1942), p. 31. Cited by Carpenter, *Shaw & the Art of Destroying Ideals*, p. 103.

personal man points up a central problem of the play. Eugene does not appreciate the personal man, and Candida does not appreciate the social man—each discredits Morell in proportion to an inability to understand him fully. Meanwhile, in a conscientious and forthright manner, both privately and publicly, Morell is devoting all his forces toward the fulfillment of a faith which is markedly Shavian in its tone: "God has given us a world that nothing but our own folly keeps from being a paradise" (p. 222).

Shaw introduces themes and insights at the very beginning of the play which serve as a commentary on its development and outcome. Morell may seem overly exuberant about the virtues of Candida in the opening scene, but his comments are consistent with his vigorous, uncritical, kindly nature. His idolization of marriage may be naïve, but it is hardly ignoble, and when it is turned against him by a sharp-tongued young man and a thoughtless wife, the fault seems scarcely his own. His gratitude and frank admission of dependence on Candida in Act I—"Get a wife like my Candida; and youll always be in arrear with your repayment" (p. 204)—is a healthy precursor of the pathetic abjection to which his wife forces him in Act III. It anticipates and undercuts Candida's final clincher, rendering her little version of marital realities superfluous and anticlimactic. Clearly, her concluding purpose, though only half-conscious, is to reduce this gracious acknowledgement, and its implicit counterpart in Morell's behavior, to her own terms. Far from not recognizing his debt to her, Morell fails, if anything, in being too uxorious, a shortcoming which Prossy is quick to point out. The problem with Candida is indirectly but sharply expressed in this opening scene, as Lexy parrots Morell: "Ah, if you women only had the same clue to Man's strength that you have to his weakness, Miss Prossy, there would be no Woman Question" (p. 206). Candida's clue to the weakness of her husband blinds her to his strength. Morell's marital enthusiasm has in fact a genuineness and charity in comparison to which her marital picture seems petty and self-centered. His spontaneous good will expresses itself in an instinctive ability to put precept into practice, typified by his simple offer of a silk handkerchief to Lexy, to protect the curate's throat from a cold wind. In contrast, Candida does not venture beyond precept, though she asserts, with proud daring, that she would give her goodness and purity to Eugene "as willingly as I would give my shawl to a beggar dying of cold" (p. 242).

Marchbanks's frontal attack on Morell's conception of his marriage elicits a defense which is touching in its incongruities. The self-confident preacher, with his built-in penchant for pulpit rhetoric, is thrown into a struggle between the pride of his public humility and a genuine personal humility. His rhetorical style both floats over and represents a very real world of personal insecurity and doubt. Dramatically, Marchbanks strikes a sympathetic chord in his remark that people make fools of themselves over things which may well be more true than things they behave sensibly about. This comment touches a tender spot because it parallels Morell's own acute and heartfelt observation to Burgess earlier in the act. Morell's doubts about his faith in himself and about his faith in his marriage reveal a sensitivity in his character which counterbalances the bold façade of the "moralist and windbag." The rhetoric of the following does not preclude its sincere feeling: "I will help you to believe that your wife loves you and is happy in her home. We need such help, Marchbanks; we need it greatly and always. There are so many things to make us doubt, if once we let our understanding be troubled. Even at home, we sit as if in camp, encompassed by a hostile army of doubts. Will you play the traitor and let them in on me?" (p. 223). Against this, Marchbanks's appraisal of Morell seems too facile, and, by comparison, Candida's smugness seems shallow.

The metaphors, sermons, and stale perorations are in Morell. But they are not "mere rhetoric," nor are they only the "gift of gab" (p. 223), and Marchbanks in claiming this reveals the insensitivity of his youth. In suggesting that Morell, like King David, is an entertainer despised by his wife, Marchbanks seems motivated in part by jealousy of the successful man. Morell has both repute and Candida. To disparage the first in terms of the second is to effect general demolition. The fact that he succeeds so well, despite Morell's accurate diagnosis of Marchbanks's obsession as calf love, indicates that Morell has all along harbored a double vision which qualifies his platform personality with his human weaknesses, the image with the reality; and he has perhaps sensed the truth that Candida lacks the charity and understanding to fully reconcile the clerical mask with the flawed man. Thus Morell's doubts about himself and his marriage, which Marchbanks so easily stirs up, are given poignancy by what must be his vague personal doubts about his wife.

Morell is taken advantage of in proportion to his kindness. His gentle and thoughtful sense of humor reveals much about his character and may be contrasted with Candida's humor, which tends to be derisive and thoughtless. Marchbanks, on the other hand, remarks that "I never can see a joke" (p. 217)—a limitation which renders him more the Shavian fool than the Shavian hero, since absurdity in Shaw (and in life) usually rests with those who take themselves too seriously. While Candida mocks Marchbanks's social ignorance when he nearly overpays the cabman, Morell gently rejoins that the overpaying instinct is a generous and uncommon one. Later, when Prossy calls Burgess a silly old fathead, Morell's reaction is as understandingly good-humored as his reprisal is low-keyed. Morell's good nature and considerateness are abundantly evident in his instinctive willingness to treat Marchbanks as an adult, a charity which Marchbanks exploits ruthlessly and childishly. While this attitude may be a failing in Morell, leading him into taking Marchbanks too seriously, at least it is founded in a nobler and more sensitive nature than that of Candida, whose attitude maintains an implicit maternal superiority and at times an explicit condescension. Morell naturally allows for the dignity of those with whom he deals—Lexy, Prossy, Eugene, and Candida—and while the first two reward him with admiration, the latter repay him with insults. Only when he is relentlessly pressed and insulted does Morell lose his equanimity, and even then it is frequently in terms of penetrating insight, such as his observation that Marchbanks does not even know how many servants his father has. His social awareness suspects immediately the irresponsibility and superficiality of a poetic idealism which shunts all the dirty work of the world onto others. Morell is most accurate and Shavian when he refers to such an attitude as idle, selfish, and useless, and Marchbanks is rhetorically evasive and escapist as he twists this into beauty, freedom, and happiness.

Candida is as much a philistine regarding Morell's Christian and social effectiveness as she is regarding Marchbanks's poetry.[40] Still very much her father's daughter, her attitude toward Morell's mission combines Burgess's sense of it as "foolishness," and Marchbanks's view of it as a sideshow, with her own jealous observation that it disrupts her evenings and amounts to little more than a romance between James and his female admirers. Thus the dialectic ammunition of Act I is refired, with a bonus, and Morell is not slow to draw parallels. Marchbanks likens him to King David; Candida likens him to a performer; and Marchbanks's "mere rhetoric" has been transmuted into Candida's "mere phrases that you cheat yourself and others with every day." Morell's great mistake is that he assumes conventional standards for the marriage bond. When pressed, he confuses Candida's fidelity with conventional virtues rather than with love alone, and this slip is played against him with a bantering callousness. His ideal of purity and goodness in his wife, phrased as a tender compliment, is taken out of context as a moral issue. Such conventional assumptions are mocked, cruelly in any case, but especially so when one considers that he has had little reason to doubt Candida's love.

Morell's view of marriage, pat though it may be, has no doubt been conventionalized by Candida herself. He naturally interprets love and happiness in the context of marriage, as in Act I, where he sought to teach Marchbanks love's meaning: "I should like you to see for yourself what a happy thing it is to be married as I am. . . . I will help you to believe that your wife loves you and is happy in her home" (pp. 219, 223). Against this tender though simplistic sentiment Candida suddenly sets her nebulous desire to teach Marchbanks "what love really is," presumably outside of "conventional" bonds. But her unconventionality does not materialize. Instead, the teaching seems to be the other way around, with

40. This corresponds to a point which Alick West makes most vociferously ("A Good Man Fallen among Fabians," pp. 107–11). Unfortunately, a slight Marxist hysteria confuses West's interesting perspective.

Candida absorbing many of Marchbanks's assumptions—so many, in fact, that Morell's words canceling his speaking engagement might also be addressed to his two critics: "These people forget that I am a man: they think I am a talking machine" (p. 245). Thus his final decision to speak is both a test of Candida and an assertion that the clergyman, man, and husband are one.

G. K. Chesterton found the scene of Candida's "choice" one of the two finest moments in Shaw.[41] To the contrary, it is contrived and melodramatic. But it comes across well because the contrivance and the melodrama derive naturally from the instincts of the characters. For Marchbanks it is a poetic climax, the romantic confrontation of false love with true love which will force to light his conception of the Truth of the matter. For Candida it provides a stage for the assertion of her feminine prerogatives and for the display of her indispensability. Morell, whose rhetoric is tied closely to a sense of the stage, falls naturally into the melodramatic mode. His response to the crisis of Act I—"Leave my house. . . . You are never going to cross our threshold again . . . You have behaved like a blackguard" (pp. 223–24)—reveals a personality whose most intense personal feelings are fused with melodrama, just as his convictions are fused with rhetoric. All of his instincts, therefore, are to push this moment to a crisis.[42] He has led himself into the confrontation by granting Marchbanks more than his due, mistaking Marchbanks's dialectical sharpness for maturity, and therefore overestimating him as a man and poet. This leads to his assumption of Marchbanks's melodramatic frame of reference here, which, when combined with his own proclivities, renders the act somewhat fanciful, in part a dramatic extension of Marchbanks's illusions.

The climax is anticipated early in the scene when Morell, with

41. G. K. Chesterton, *Bernard Shaw*, Dramabook ed. (New York, 1956), p. 91.

42. In his preface to *Getting Married*, Shaw is on Morell's side: "What an honorable and sensible man does when his household is invaded is what the Reverend James Mavor Morell does in my play. He recognizes that just as there is not room for two women in that sacredly intimate relation of sentimental domesticity which is what marriage means to him, so there is no room for two men in that relation with his wife" (*Complete Plays*, IV, 367).

his usual combination of unselfishness and rhetorical style, asks, "Who will protect her?" Marchbanks responds, "It is she who wants somebody to protect." Whereupon Candida enters, and soon hurries to Morell with the words we have noted previously: "My boy shall not be worried: I will protect him" (p. 256). Her real choice has been clear all along, but this makes it doubly clear. Similarly, when Candida remarks that "James is master here," and Morell responds, "I dont know of any right that makes me master. I assert no such right" (p. 262), Candida is profoundly reproachful. In her light this is an unwitting slight on *her*, since Morell is her abstraction, her creation—as she says at the end: "I make him master here" (p. 267). The final confrontation, therefore, may be dramatically effective, but it is logically superfluous.

By the end it becomes apparent that Morell is a different person to each character in the play, and it is through the composite of these persons that Shaw draws his character. To himself he is the earnest, effective Christian Socialist pastor and loving husband— his motives are liberal and charitable, and he translates them into action with integrity, forcefulness, and effectiveness. To Marchbanks he is a do-gooder with a gift of gab, a self-righteous and selfish windbag, constitutionally insensitive to the truly noble and exalted character of his wife. To Candida he is a child doing his best, and, as his best is not as good or effectual as he thinks it is, he needs maternal support and insulation. To maintain the clerical illusion there must be a base of domestic equanimity, and because the man is her mate he must fill the role of master and father—a carefully stage-managed role, of which she is the director. To Prossy, Morell is the ideal of manhood, too noble and desirable to be foolish over an average woman like Candida. To Lexy he is the ideal servant of God—a kindly man and forceful leader. And to Burgess he is a fool to be reckoned with both publicly and privately; doctrinally unsound, temperamentally "mad." Shaw's skill is apparent in the fact that Morell emerges with both the complexity of all and the simplicity of each of these viewpoints.

Notably, Candida represents her relationship to James as mother, sisters, wife, and mother to his children, in that order. Morell, on the other hand, acknowledges his debt to her in a different sequence—that of wife, mother, and sisters. Their respective orderings signify their different views. Candida is right that she insulates Morell from the petty nuisances and shocks of domestic existence. Her discretion is indicated in the masculinity of his drawing-room study, hardly the decoration of a woman who forces her femininity on her husband. But what she denigrates about Morell in her own mind, because she does not understand it, is his distinctive role as a man, as a spiritual and political leader of considerable talents and significant influence. From her practical domestic sphere she sees only the human foibles which lie alongside his idealism and public service. She misses the special social value of Morell because his influence lies in abstractions and many intangibles; she does not understand that the fact of the world not listening to him (as it did not listen to Caesar or Saint Joan or Christ) only partially limits his value. His voice is one of a chorus sounding out moral awareness and social consciousness, a chorus without which both the physical and spiritual progress of society would be even slower than it is. Shaw asserts this small value, which is great compared with that of others, in the concrete good of Morell shaming local authorities into demanding more humane working conditions for his parishioners. As Shaw indicates in *Major Barbara*, only from a base of physical well-being can there be any great hope of true spiritual growth. Marchbanks's ideals are, by contrast, adolescent and insubstantial—as he does not care about his father's servants and neglects the mundane in a search for the spiritual, he is operating in a poetic vacuum. The vitality of Marchbanks confronts the system of Morell, but ironically this is a vitality which reflects a romantic system, while Morell's system is founded on the vitality of pragmatic altruism.

As Candida keeps the domestic machinery going, and as this domestic machinery is about all she really understands, she quite naturally feels herself indispensable. It hardly seems an accident in Act III, however, when Morell returns home to face his domestic crisis, that he remarks on how well he lectured—"I have never spoken better in my life" (p. 252)—a fact which is vociferously affirmed by Lexy. Clearly, in his public life—his most significant life—Morell can do very well without Candida. The implication is that perhaps all he needs is *any* good woman obsessed by domestic details so that he may pursue his more important business. Morell's dependence on Candida is certainly a matter of a tender personal relationship, but it scarcely involves his primary *raison d'être*. So, at last, his confession—"What I am you have made me" (p. 267)—expresses less his own case than a capitulation to Candida's view of things. Though he may indeed believe it, its relevance to the facts is manifestly oblique. It will serve for the moment by keeping Candida happy in her static, unimaginative little circle, while he goes on to get the work of the world done.

Were Morell not so resilient, the ending might well have tragic implications à la Strindberg; indeed, one French production made the play into a tragedy.[43] However, a cruelly emasculated husband and a disillusioned and desperately disappointed poet, scarcely humorous stuff, are transmuted by the volition of the comedy, and by an implicit projection into the future which suggests Morell carrying on his mission and Marchbanks progressing to new romantic glories from new embankments. What Morell and Marchbanks have learned may be disillusioning but it is not debilitating, if only because Candida is not quite worth the fuss. As for Candida, she has learned very little, which is perfectly satisfactory since she is cozy in her self-confidence, and ignorance is bliss. The dramatic theme of lack of understanding, and its comic counterpart "madness," prevail to the end. Shaw's greatest accomplishment is that he has given vital illumination to several divergent views—Candida's domestic vision, warm and maternal on one hand, but narrow and egocentric on the other; Marchbanks's poetic vision, incisive and iconoclastic, but irresponsible and romantic; and Morell's social vision, kindly and humanitarian, but rhetorical and melodramatic. Their ambiguity gives these views artistic complexity and depth, their interaction gives them dramatic vigor, and both the ambiguity and interaction provide food for critical controversy.

43. Hamon, *The Twentieth Century Molière*, p. 203.

CHAPTER FOUR

CAESAR AND CLEOPATRA

An Anatomy of Greatness

The vital greatness of Shaw's Caesar has been much admired by critics, but the grounds on which they base their approval are notably vague. It is a critical commonplace to assert that Shaw has made Caesar effective by making him antiheroic, largely through the device of portraying him from the viewpoint of a valet—out of battle dress, in off moments, an aging, somewhat vain man beneath a mantle of glory.[1] In this context his kindliness and magnanimity seem even greater because they are quietly genuine and are in marked contrast to the melodramatic heroics of conventional stage conquerors. Shaw bears out this observation in his frequently quoted comment on the subject:

> Our conception of heroism has changed of late years. . . . The demand now is for heroes in whom we can recognize our own humanity, and who, instead of walking, talking, eating, drinking,

---

1. See Archibald Henderson, George Bernard Shaw: His Life and Works (Cincinnati, 1911), pp. 337–38; William Irvine, The Universe of G. B. S. (New York, 1949), p. 230; Gordon W. Couchman, "Here Was a Caesar: Shaw's Comedy Today," PMLA, 62 (1957), 284–85; J. I. M. Stewart, Eight Modern Writers (Oxford, 1963), p. 142. C. E. M. Joad goes further, defining Caesar's special qualities as (1) realism, (2) certainty of aim, (3) sustained power of work, and (4) "special quality of mind" (Shaw [London, 1949], pp. 116–23). This is useful, but a more inclusive frame of reference is needed to fully explore both the greatness and the dramaturgical effect of greatness.

making love and fighting single combats in a monotonous ecstasy of continuous heroism, are heroic in the true human fashion: that is, touching the summits only at rare moments, and finding the proper level of all occasions, condescending with humor and good sense to the prosaic ones as well as rising to the noble ones, instead of ridiculously persisting in rising to them all on the principle that a hero must always soar, in season or out of season.[2]

Thus Caesar appears all the greater because his nobility is couched in obvious humanity, a humanity reflecting the humor and good sense of a truly rounded and admirable character.

But this appraisal is surely far too simple to account for the full dimensions, one might almost say the magic, of Caesar's role in the play. It is too incomplete to explain the paradoxical effectiveness of the valet perspective, and it neglects the equally significant external and dramaturgical elements which work toward the fullest artistic development of the play. How does the valet's view work? What does it reveal? Certainly Caesar's humor and good sense gently modulate his character toward greatness, but equally important are the ironic counterpoint of opposite extremes in the same man, the flux in his nature which baffles and intrigues us, and his sensitive, keenly active immersion in life as an art. And reflecting significantly upon Caesar are the carefully worked elements of mystery in both setting and character, the epic conflict of cultures, the pessimistic reflection on his inability to truly inform and enlighten his environment, the tragic ironies of the vengeance theme, and, finally, the curious historical relevance that artistic nonhistory can achieve. Only in these profounder terms can the full artistic significance of his portrayal be realized.

What is just as important as the valet viewpoint is the audience's perspective regarding Caesar's influence on his "valets." Those closest to him are bothered by his original sense of values, yet they appear to love him in proportion to their being frustrated by him, and not just for his inherent kindness. Rufio and Britannus are caught in the ironic position of being willing to follow

2. Quoted in Archibald Henderson, *Bernard Shaw: Playboy and Prophet* (New York, 1932), p. 493.

Caesar to the death precisely because of that heroic nature which shocks their sense of propriety and expediency. In Act II Caesar cannily challenges their conservatism: "Rufio: if I take Lucius Septimius for my model, and become exactly like him, ceasing to be Caesar, will you serve me still?"[3] The answer is obvious. Rufio balks at Caesar's clemency and Britannus is astonished at his imprudence, but their fondness and admiration for him are tied closely to the ambiguous feelings he thus engenders. They experience both paternal affection, as for a boy who innocently violates the ways of the world, and childlike bewilderment, in the suspicion that his seeming naïveté probably conceals superior insight. This bewilderment creates much of the sense of fantasy in the play, and ultimately what may seem to be a valet's view becomes a child's view, epitomized in Cleopatra.[4] As a kitten, or later as a cat in relation to Caesar's mystical sphinx, Cleopatra may seek to understand; but after she seems most to have attained perceptive queenship, she regresses, revealing how childish both her morality and her pragmatism are in comparison to Caesar's. When the others enter into moral agreement with her regarding the killing of Pothinus, and catastrophe subsequently stalks them, their deep reliance on Caesar is all the clearer, and they look to him for protection from the ravages of their folly. That part of the audience's sympathy which is bound to Rufio, Britannus, and Cleopatra consequently moves into a perplexed yet admiring relationship to Caesar, particularly as he seems to confound common sense or expediency with a supernal wisdom and capability. The effect is one of children viewing a very real adult world which they do not understand.

The intimate focus on Caesar also provides insight as it contrasts his public image with the private reality. To the Egyptians of the alternate prologue he is a prosaic barbarian of diabolical

3. *Bernard Shaw: Complete Plays with Prefaces* (New York, 1963), III, 399. All citations and quotations from the play are from this volume.
4. See John Mason Brown, "*Caesar and Cleopatra*," in *George Bernard Shaw: A Critical Survey*, ed. Louis Kronenberger (Cleveland, 1953), p. 248. Brown observes that Caesar is "humanized by being seen through the irreverent eyes of a child," which is true. But just as important is the *reverence* which Cleopatra holds regarding Caesar.

strength. To Ptolemy's court he is the audacious conqueror. To the Sentinel and Centurion in Act III he is the strict taskmaster, demanding absolute adherence to duty. Finally, to his army he is the noble general, the ruler of the civilized world. Contrasted with these views are those of personal intimacy. Shaw structures the play to take full advantage of the contrast. After Caesar's public monstrousness in the alternate prologue and his private humanity with Cleopatra in Act I, he ascends to full public glory in the rousing acclaim of his soldiers at the end of Act I.[5] The same pattern is repeated in the rest of the play, as Caesar shocks the Egyptian court by his audacity in Act II, becomes intensely human in Acts III and IV, ascends in personal stature by the end of Act IV, and triumphs in public stature with the "Hail, Caesar!" at the end of Act V. The nonplussed indignation of the Egyptians and the enthusiastic acclaim by his legions could amount to shallow stage-craft, but in terms of the revealed vitality and humanity of Caesar's private life these public reactions resound with full and profound intensity.

Probably the most striking aspect of Caesar's portrayal is the remarkable number of opposite traits which are revealed in the same man. The dynamic effect of these opposites and their subtle influence in building the complexity and power of his character have not been fully appreciated by commentators on the play. The few who have sensed a certain bloodless and manufactured element in Caesar are probably intuitively grasping at this point, but they fail to come to terms with the artistic and psychological implications which are involved.[6] In one sense Caesar may be intellectually contrived and hence somewhat mechanical in execution, but this is a pejorative explanation which fails to account for the striking synthesis which Shaw effects. It is in the tension and

5. G. K. Chesterton found this to be one of the two truly inspired moments in Shaw (*George Bernard Shaw* [New York, 1956], p. 91). I would suggest that Shaw's brilliant use of contrast—light against darkness, public life against private life, sound against silence—makes it so.

6. See Henry L. Mencken, *George Bernard Shaw: His Plays* (Boston and London, 1905), pp. 42–43; Maurice Colbourne, *The Real Bernard Shaw* (New York, 1949), p. 134; Irvine, *The Universe of G. B. S.*, p. 231.

interaction of disparate qualities that the character achieves the vitality and depth which comprise its special greatness.

Most telling of the seeming contradictions in Caesar's character are those between his mythical age, his temporal age, his spiritual maturity, and his youthful spirit. As Caesar speaks to the sphinx in Act I he takes on the aura of its agelessness. He identifies with its centuries, and its centuries tend to carry him beyond time. The effect is furthered by the audience's association of both the sphinx and Caesar in nearly mythical as well as historical terms: in a very special sense, the two have immortality in their shared legendary status. This effect may be punctured by Cleopatra's small voice tagging Caesar as "old gentleman," but in the contrast between Cleopatra's youth and naïveté and Caesar's maturity and wisdom, the impression of Caesar's age is given a new dimension. He becomes more temporal, but he gains the earthly years of a fatherly sage who can make a queen of a young girl. All of this changes in Acts II and III. Although his wisdom and superiority shine through these acts, we see him observing the Egyptian architecture with a child's curiosity, an attitude reflecting back softly upon his seemingly more mature contemplation of the sphinx. He handles Ptolemy's court with both the quiet confidence of age and the boldness of youth. Certainly it is as a youth that he springs into action at the end of both Acts II and III, and he is something like an old man but more like a small boy when, in Act III, his dejection over the Romans' unfavorable military position evaporates as his appetite is satisfied by a handful of dates. Caesar as the father figure reappears in Act IV when we see the maturing effect he has had on Cleopatra, and by the end of the act, when the entire company throws itself into his subtle, powerful hands, their concepts of vengeance having failed them, the impression of his mythical age, couched in wisdom, reemerges. At this point, upon the news of reinforcements, Caesar again leaps into action, but there is a notable difference now in the effect of his enthusiasm. His vigor seems no longer to be that of a boy, but carries with it the accretion of his wisdom and power as they have been revealed throughout the play, and especially as they have had such telling emotional effect in the immediately preceding scene. By Act V he is the ageless conqueror in complete triumph and control. His youth and age have coalesced in terms of commanding vigor and vital insight.

Thus, though Caesar compromises the mythical hero with boyishness, he qualifies youthfulness with age and at last emerges as a spiritual father. In Acts II and III he is admonished for his imprudence by Rufio and Britannus, but in Acts IV and V he is the admonisher, frequently referring to Rufio as "my son." Cleopatra remarks in Act IV that Caesar is a god, "we are all Caesar's slaves" (p. 439), and in Act V Britannus chooses the noble freedom of being Caesar's slave rather than the status of a free man. This last gains power through being reminiscent of the Christian's relationship to God's providence: true freedom is in submission to divine will, not in the pursuit of one's own flawed judgment. It reflects the Christian analogy which is inherent in Cleopatra's comment to Pothinus—"he will put on this land of Egypt as a shepherd puts on his garment" (p. 440)—and recalls the implications of Caesar's words to his vengeful disciples: "If one man in all the world can be found, now or forever, to k n o w that you did wrong, that man will have either to conquer the world as I have, or be crucified by it" (pp. 456–57). Caesar's gods, like Christ's God, are irresistible, and Caesar is referred to by Pothinus as "a worker of miracles" (p. 445). As a miracle-worker Caesar achieves a certain degree of moral success which complements his temporal victory over the Egyptians. The grace of spiritual wisdom emerges briefly over the blindness of worldly expediency; but the triumph is as temporary as the god is mortal.

The effect of this spiritual ascendency is made richer as it is linked to the most subliminal comic level of the play. As Rufio and Britannus at first assume the mantle of cautious age, the opposition of Caesar's vital youthfulness creates a classic comic conflict between the conservatism of the traditional father figure and the subversion of youthful unconventionality. When youth triumphs and reconciliation is effected in the end, the conflict is resolved with archetypal comic consistency. The audience is carried into the basically amusing and satisfying realm where vigorous subversion, with its intense life, flexibility, and vitally new perspective, boldly transcends the mundanity of traditional ethics and values. The comic fabric is woven even tighter by the fact of Caesar's actual age and wisdom. As Shaw was later to do with Undershaft and his son Stephen, the usual comic subversion is paradoxically reversed, and it is the vital brilliance of age which triumphs over the obtuse conventionalism of youth. Even further, Caesar himself represents both entrenched authority and subversion. On the one hand he must be the statesman, while on the other he deplores his role, most pointedly in his lament regarding the "statesmanship" of killing Vercingetorix and severing the right hands of the Gauls. In attacking Pompey he was a rebel; in defeating Pompey he is a statesman. At this point the comic undertone turns toward irony, and Caesar's victory is also his torment, since it becomes so profoundly intermixed with the crass expediency of the world.

Complementing the subtle interplay of age and youth in Caesar is the constant tension between his greatness and his insignificance. In the temporal realm he stands for the immense power of Roman authority. The magic and strength of this power are revealed most forcefully in the alternate prologue and in Act V. At the beginning Caesar's power is represented as that of a thousand-armed monster, and at the end, more solidly, as a consensus backed by armed might, to which gods and the populace fall in submission. But for much of the play this temporal power is an abstraction only, and it clearly relies upon Caesar's wits and luck. Caesar may be the victor over Pompey, but he is in imminent peril of being vanquished at the hands of the Egyptians. The specter of the great Pompey's ignominious death hangs over the action, alleviated only by the audience's historical perspective as to the outcome, and given ironic validity even in this historical view, since it is obvious that the fate which Caesar escapes in Egypt he will face in Rome. He is in the tenuous state of being almost a victor and almost vanquished at the same time. This tenuousness, reflecting Caesar's finite manhood, is graphically objectified by the stage sets. Shaw considered the settings an integral element of the play, and he went into considerable detail regarding them, even sketching out his ideas for a proposed German production.[7] Their magnificence dwarfs the humanity which dwells against them. Caesar, as a slight, aging man, is puny and ephemeral by contrast, although he may be the Voice of Rome. It is in abstractions that his influence lies, in moral strength and in the power of leadership.[8] Thus he is revealed as existing in the perilous opposition between his magnificence as a god, a sphinx, a conqueror, and his insignificance as a mortal, an almost laughable vain old man, a species facing extinction. His greatness, emerging at the end, is more remarkable and spiritual to the extent that it suppresses this irony. As the irony is negated, the play offers hope; as it survives, the play is a tragedy.

Caesar is both dreamer and realist, an advocate both of repose and of action. All of Act I has a dreamlike quality. The darkness, the silence, the moonlight, and the mystery offer a congenial background to the dreamlike soliloquy of the conqueror as he confronts his spiritual symbol in the sphinx. The mood is so pervasive that the elfin Cleopatra causes Caesar to doubt his wakefulness. The situation drifts gently into the absurd until Cleopatra pricks him with a pin, but even this drift carries with it a suggestion of somnambulance. In Act IV Cleopatra calls him a dreamer, implying that he is out of touch with many obvious realities. And certainly his diversions with the young queen frequently stall ostensibly significant action. His explicit ideal in Act IV would seem to be inimical to a man of action—"Oh, this military life! this tedious, brutal life of action! That is the worst of us Romans: we are mere doers and drudgers: a swarm of bees turned into men. Give me a good talker—one with wit and imagination enough to live without continually doing something!" (p. 443)—yet, as Rufio suggests, this ejaculation is notable as a half truth. Although Caesar refers to "this tedious, brutal life of action," it is clear that he is kinetically vitalized by action, as is revealed in his leap from the lighthouse parapet and later in his vigorous plans to join Mith-

7. See Martin Meisel, *Shaw and the Nineteenth-Century Theater* (Princeton, 1963), pp. 361–63. In a letter to Siegfried Trebitsch dated 16 August 1903, Shaw commented that "the staging is just as much a part of the play as the dialogue" (quoted by Meisel, p. 361).

8. This is akin to a point made by Meisel; ibid., p. 364.

ridates' attack against Achillas. He enjoys his diversion with Cleopatra in Act III, but when she urges her precedence over his soldiers, he bluntly informs her that her head is not worth a hand of one of his men. Caesar's aesthetics and his pragmatism tell him two different things. His statement reveals a mind which respects the value of well-spent repose, yet implies the necessity of an opposite in order to make repose meaningful. Ideally, one complements the other—one enriches and the other revitalizes. Caesar may be a dreamer, but his actions have made his dreams important; and he is a man of action, but one whose dreams have given action meaning. The significance of the action is in proportion to the nobility of the dream.

By representing so many opposites in Caesar, opposites in constant tension and interaction, Shaw gives vital dimension to his character. Caesar's youth in age is exploited in terms of a vibrant dichotomy, fused in a vigorous spiritual fulfillment and leavened by rich comic undertones. In the opposites of greatness and insignificance Shaw relates the inner strength of Caesar to the outer glory of his achievement, the magnificence of his environment, and his obvious mortality. A perceptive and ironic sense of historical perspective as opposed to spiritual significance is consequently developed. His stature grows as a synthesis of extremes, never as a simple abstraction, and it retains all the vital assertion of those extremes while tempering and balancing them with their opposites. By presenting these opposites in flux, Shaw foils the observer's tendency to stereotype, rounding out the character in terms of humanity on the one hand while elevating it with spiritual power on the other.

Complementing this subtle development of character is a structural element of anticlimax. The Caesarean monster of the alternate prologue becomes the solitary, lonely man in front of the sphinx; the conqueror who establishes a spiritual affinity with the sphinx becomes an old man with an arched nose; the sorcerer who creates a queen and is hailed tumultuously as Caesar, is laughed at as powerless by the Egyptian court. When this court is vanquished with magnanimous mercy, and Caesar leaps into action, dressing in his armor, he is laughed at for being bald. Even in Act V, at the height of success and glory, Caesar is compromised by his observation that he is old and fit for the knife. The greatest anticlimax of all, death, hangs over his moment of victory. Anticlimax can be scaled from humor to pathos, and in Shaw's Caesar the entire scale is covered. However, whereas anticlimax tends to deflate the conventional hero, being inimical to grand effects, Shaw turns it into a force which not only humanizes but also exalts Caesar—first because of the equanimity and realism with which he meets its tests, and second because it ties him closer to life than were he blown up to a relatively static "heroic" state. Caesar may wince at his age, responding wryly when Cleopatra discovers his baldness, but he is ready to send Antony to her and he is above the fear of death. He deflates the power of Egyptian laughter at the numerical weakness of his forces by admitting that his forces are indeed limited. And further, his dignity collapses, but in full good humor, when Rufio calls him down for starting to repeat his favorite "sermon" about life and death. Significantly in these latter cases Cleopatra either is not amused or is outrightly furious, revealing a key difference in the balance and maturity of their characters. Caesar's spiritual dimensions actually grow through anticlimax, because they anticipate, absorb, and undercut all artificial ballooning. In peril he thinks of action and life; in victory he thinks of death.

Caesar's sense of humor is a measure of his sophistication. It reveals his candor, his kindness, and his realistic set of values. George Meredith once remarked, "Sensitiveness to the comic laugh is a step in civilization. . . . We know the degree of refinement in men by the matter they will laugh at, and the ring of the laugh."[9] So it is with Caesar. A sphinxlike laughter is inherent in Act I as Caesar calls his Roman nose to Cleopatra's attention and gently, slyly instructs her in the ways of queenship. In Act II it is partially his quiet humor, founded on a base of mastery and daring, which renders him so superior to the Egyptians. Achillas, as Roman *and* Egyptian general, has it both ways, an ironic and human advantage which tickles Caesar's sense of the absurd

9. George Meredith, "An Essay on Comedy," in *Comedy*, ed. Wylie Sypher (New York, 1956), p. 50.

though it places him in a dangerous position. Caesar's proposal for settling the royal succession question here is in tune with his reported settlement of the Jewish question later—it is a maneuver founded on a quick assessment of the realities, an attempt to resolve in minutes what courts would take years to accomplish. Though it does violence to complexities, it offers the shortcut of common sense and evokes a Bergsonian smile at the machinery of society, humor being implicit in the court's confusion and indignation. Britannus is dismayed that Caesar will not regard life seriously, and Apollodorus incredulously asks, "Is Caesar serious?" (pp. 426–27). The answer is that at heart Caesar is highly serious, but his sense of what is important differs widely from the norm. Thus he responds to Theodotus, "My life! Is that all?" and later observes that "he who has never hoped can never despair" (pp. 396, 459).[10] A tacit stoicism underlies his temperament. His humor is based on an accurate appraisal of the facts and is tickled by the facts bobbing to the surface, upsetting those who live lives of illusion. Thus he is not upset when Pothinus reveals Cleopatra's treachery, because he is fully cognizant of the facts of her nature.

As the portrait of a nearly archetypal civilized man, Caesar is, not surprisingly, strikingly reminiscent of his creator. The broad-mindedness and capacities of a world conqueror are combined with a puritan proclivity for work and barley water. Caesar's sense of humor, his several masks, his contradictions, vanity, values, asceticism, and kindness are quite Shavian.[11] In *Sixteen Self Sketches* Shaw describes himself in the third person. It is curious that he might well be describing Caesar:

> He has in an extreme degree the mercurial mind that recognizes the inevitable instantly and faces it and adapts itself to it accordingly. . . . He knows much sooner and better than most people when he is in danger and when out of it; and this gives him an

10. With typical diabolism, Shaw commented that this passage "is imposing; but who can feel sure that its inspiration is not infernal rather than divine?" (*Sixteen Self Sketches* [New York, 1949], p. 133).

11. Briefly noted by Colbourne, *The Real Bernard Shaw*, p. 134, and implied by H. Lüdeke, "Some Remarks on Shaw's History Plays," *English Studies*, 36 (1955), 243, and Stewart, *Eight Modern Writers*, p. 176.

appearance of courage when he is really running no risk. He has the same advantage in his sense of the value of money, knowing when it is worth spending and when it is worth keeping; and here again he often appears generous when he is driving a very good bargain. When we stand amazed at his boldness and liberality, it is doubtful how far he is capable of facing a real danger or making a real sacrifice.[12]

This last doubt is what gives interest and poignancy to our observations of noble genius, be it Shaw's or Caesar's. The intrinsic nature of a superior spirit is elusive, but genius is tied to earth by the mistakes and foibles of its involvement with humanity, if not by the lusts of the world. Insofar as the audience may have difficulty accepting Caesar's essential spiritual superiority and his subordination of his flesh-and-blood humanity, he gains authenticity as a character. Through the suspicion of weakness rises a more realistic appraisal of strength. The fact that Caesar wonders at the Egyptian architecture like a child, and like a boy is revitalized by a stomach full of dates, renders his greatness more vivid and credible by contrast. We can believe more in Shaw's genius when we can laugh at Shaw's vanity, smile at his childishness, suspect his altruism, and feel superior to his asceticism. So it is with his portrayal of Caesar. In these terms the Shaw in Caesar or the Caesar in Shaw is less important than the fact that in each case the character has vital and moving reality.

Like Shaw, Caesar is not afraid of seeming contradictions in character; in fact he temperamentally appears to court them for the varying perspectives they afford his genius. One can learn more and live more vividly if one sees the world not only from the viewpoint of a man, but also from that of a woman, a beast, a god, a boy, and an emperor. Though one may lose distinctive manliness in the process, one gains in wisdom and compassion; Caesar's universal kindness, which renders him so much better than human that Cleopatra calls him a god, is no doubt partially a result of his sensitive capacity to live fully in terms of the diverse demands of each moment. Life is a supernal art, and to him art which is most

12. Shaw, *Sixteen Self Sketches*, pp. 131–32.

meaningful will most poignantly express life. Caesar appreciates Apollodorus not because he mouths "Art for Art's sake" but because he plunges into life as an aesthetic experience—"Who says artist, says duellist" (pp. 413, 418). Let the library burn; its contents are dreams and shameful memories. Cleopatra puts the music master in his place in brutal imitation of Caesar putting down Theodotus. Such pedants destroy the effervescence which is at the heart of life. The trinkets of Egypt pale beside the achievements of Rome: "What! Rome produce no art! Is peace not an art? is war not an art? is government not an art? is civilization not an art? All these we give you in exchange for a few ornaments" (p. 466). Seven birthdays in ten months are not only politic, they are enjoyable; good talk is an antidote to the burdens of war, and one finds fulfillment in both repose and action. Ftatateeta must be taught how to be a servant, but Pothinus deserves decorous treatment as a guest.[13] Over Rufio's objections Caesar takes time out to play with the kitten queen at the Pharos. Thus in many ways life is a game to Caesar, to be played for all its vibrations, tender, deep, and violent. Cleopatra—youthful, various, vital, spontaneous—attracts his instincts for fun, which offset his instincts for work. It is this spirit in Caesar that prompts Apollodorus to call him a "creative poet-artist" (p. 451), and in this context both art and life are rendered resonant and purposeful.

Caesar's conflict with man's corruption is given dramatic extension in the conflict between the Roman culture and the Egyptian culture. At issue are different concepts of civilization, and as Shaw emphasizes Caesar's humanity through the settings, he provides a sense of the difference in cultures through stagecraft. Egyptian superstition, mystery, and remoteness are revealed explicitly by the dialogue but even more effectively through an evocative use of sets, lighting, and fantastic situations. In the first prologue the strange Egyptian god Ra, albeit a Shavian anachronism, appears in the gloom of a temple. In the alternate prologue darkness, su-

13. Caesar's insistence on this latter is reminiscent of Raina in *Arms and the Man*, who adheres to the romance of *Ernani* that one's enemy in one's home becomes a noble trust. What is humorous in one play is serious in another, indicating that Shaw is more interested in immediate dramatic effect than in consistency.

perstition, and fear pervade the scene. In the night of Act I the immortal, mysterious sphinx is contrasted with the kittenish Cleopatra, herself much like a fanciful vision, and the black transition to the dark palace, with its great moving shadows and idols, is that of a dream. In Act III the magic is of a more mundane variety, but it is quite fanciful in its charm and piquancy. Apollodorus is the artist-conjurer, and the young queen's emergence from the carpet, reminiscent of *The Arabian Nights*, is the height of trickery and art, surprise and delight. The calling-up of Father Nile in Act IV is set against a strange magenta purple sunset. In play, fancy, and imagination Caesar and the company are seeking out the mysterious, otherworldly roots of Egyptian myth, and the cry of Pothinus murdered becomes impressionistically the voice of Father Nile, founded deeply in blood sacrifice and spiritual darkness.

Set against this Egyptian magic of night are the Roman marvels of daylight, of military pragmatism, temporal rule, and, most important, of the supernal common sense and vision of Caesar, which attract to him overtones of godlike power. The Egyptian night of Act I is broken first by Caesar's torch in the palace and is followed by the Roman daylight of taxes and business in Act II. In Act III Egyptian romance coalesces briefly with Roman play, but Egyptian darkness reappears late in Act IV and is punctuated by the murder of Ftatateeta at the hands of Rufio. In Ftatateeta's death, the power of Egyptian magic is symbolically slain on its own altar by Roman pragmatism. Clearly a new dispensation is at hand, and the theme is significantly resolved in the Roman daylight of Act V, with Caesar receiving obeisance from the Egyptian priests, who are willing to sell their ineffectual idols to the prosaic conquering god.

The darkness of Egyptian ignorance gives poetic force to Caesar's confrontation with the blindness of society.[14] As the Egyptians are impressionistically associated with night and the Romans with daylight, the hyper-"civilization" of the Egyptian culture is revealed as caught in its own inefficient abstractions, manifestly

14. The Bergsonian implications of this confrontation are discussed by Daniel J. Leary, "The Moral Dialectic in *Caesar and Cleopatra*," *Shaw Review*, 5 (1962), 42–53.

corrupt, unrealistic, and curiously barbaric in contrast to the boy-
ish vitality, enthusiasm, and vulgarity of the Romans. Here again
is the comic pattern of age and youth—an old society versus a
young society, the expedient versus the spontaneous, rigidity versus flexibility, pompous somberness versus disarming candor. The
Egyptian society is paralyzed by tradition and myth. Those Egyptian soldiers who cling to their feelings of inherent superiority as
descendants of the gods are slaughtered on the brutal reality of
the battlefield; Ptolemy is a faulty little machine, wound up by his
mentors to recite his claim of royal precedence, and as the Egyptian court rests on him, it rests on the most fragile of foundations.
As Cleopatra receives knowledge of life from her involuntary bap-
tism in the Roman sea, Ptolemy finds death in the murky waters
of the Nile, his ancestor. The Egyptian civilization is feline—
treacherous and decadently subtle. Cleopatra is descended from
a cat, at one point is portrayed as prowling to and fro like a cat, and
her power is in the "tigress" Ftatateeta. In contrast, the Roman
society cuts through decorum and superstition in terms of a practical awareness of power and its uses. The Romans are canine; dog
references recur frequently in the play—blunt, open, noisy. Ptolemy spontaneously likens Rufio to a jackal. With symbolic and
precognitive accuracy Rufio remarks that he kills "as a dog kills a
cat" (p. 458); and so he does, the Roman jackal killing the Egyptian tigress. Caesar, significantly, has elements of both cultures in
his character, with a sense of civilization that embodies the best
qualities of the two, transcending them both. He is sphinxlike,
described by Ptolemy as a lion and by Cleopatra as a cat who eats
up enemy mice; at the same time he is frank and pragmatic, using
a sacred tripod as a stool. His personal integrity transcends cultural limitations, and he holds power partly through evoking in-
credulity, baffling his opponents so that their normal, culturally
ordered modes of action become disoriented and cannot deal coherently with such a unique and independent phenomenon.

Extraneous as Britannus may seem to be to the play's primary
movement, he is a significant parenthesis to this theme of conflicting cultures. He is a joke, but not merely a diverting, irrelevant
one. He projects a limited view of prudence and respectability

upon the action which is certainly more anachronistic caricature than cultural psychology, but which has the wry effect of subjecting modern British moral conservatism to the test of Caesar's greatness and to significant historical action.[15] The absurdity of such conservatism in meaningful affairs conveys Shaw's intended observation. Victorian morality is laughable froth, and only in the savagery of battle, when the Victorian loses himself to his more barbaric, more genuine emotions, does he seize onto the horse's tail of vital self-awareness and meaningful action. Significantly, it is Caesar's horse which pulls Britannus to glory. Britannus does not find life until he loses respectability; his final fealty to Caesar is made more genuine by the fact that he has realized the beast in himself, and this turns the social grace of subjection to Caesar's cause into a vital, personal commitment, founded not in the mere acceptance of an established social order, but in the immersion of all his instincts in a great cause.

The disparities between Egyptian and Roman interests are given overt expression in the stirring action of battle which surrounds the scenes and impressionistically echoes in upon the stage. This fighting is used to stimulate and clarify the stage action. Thus in the alternate prologue the advancing Roman army reveals the Egyptians through their reactions and panic, as it reveals Cleopatra in Act I. In Acts II and III the Romans and Egyptians are in open conflict, which is dramatically significant because it illumines the boyishness, policy, and skill of Caesar in action. Between Acts IV and V a grand battle takes place, its outcome revealing the triumph of inspired Roman prosaicism, which hones and unifies an army, over Egyptian pomp and superstition, which corrupt and incapacitate. The outer conflict is important, finally, as it instills a *sense* of action into the play, provoking the stage action and providing it with an enveloping tension, a pervasive aura of urgency and consequence.

To a great extent the offstage conflict is a reflection of Caesar's failure onstage. As Caesar fails with Cleopatra, he fails with the

15. Otto Reinert interprets the play as dramatizing that progress is a myth, and that consequently there can be no real anachronism ("Old History and New: Anachronism in *Caesar and Cleopatra*," *Modern Drama*, 3 [1961], 37–41).

world. Critics commonly refer to Caesar's role as a teacher, but few observe his notable lack of success. Cleopatra can be only superficially educated because instinctively she is a creature of her cultural heritage, and Shaw emphasizes that instincts, rather than reason, control man's behavior. It is in Caesar's nature to be the sphinx, a trinity of the conqueror-beast, compassionate woman, and transcendently moral god. But as Caesar is instinctively god-like, Cleopatra is instinctively the cat of her ancestors, Rufio is instinctively a faithful dog, Apollodorus is instinctively an artist, and Britannus is instinctively a prude. No amount of education or noble example will alter the basic pattern of their behavior: it may subtilize their attitudes, but it will not transform them. The Cleopatra of Act IV is obviously more subtle than before, but her undignified immersion has taught her to control her conceit and cruelty rather than to banish them. She may superciliously treat ladies as children, but Charmian is quite right in her observation that the queen is imitating Caesar and has merely turned "prosy." Cleopatra's maturity is in large part a façade which superficially conceals her natural savagery. She is clever in her treatment of the music master, but her cruel wit threatens him with the same death by whipping which she proposed for her lovers in Act I. She no longer wants to beat Ftatateeta, but she wants to kill Pothinus. Finally, she reverts to childishness when she is confronted by Caesar after Pothinus' death, and in the last act she is as willing as she was in the first to give up the godliness and wisdom of Caesar for the humanity and foolishness of Antony. The frequent animal appellatives throughout the play take their toll, implying that man, except for a few tricks, is carnal and unteachable.

Caesar's failure to educate society is accentuated by the vengeance theme. When Cleopatra urges Ftatateeta to "kill, kill, k i l l" Pothinus, she is a dramatic objectification of the barbarity of the society which later concurs in her action. The moral-political ethic of those who surround Caesar is dog eat dog. And Caesar, as a conqueror, cannot ultimately divorce himself from this barbarity. His initial impulse is to hide his face from Lucius Septimius because he realizes his inevitable worldly debt to the traitor, and he sees in Lucius a debasement of his own opportunistic spirit.

Vengeance may be contrary to his instincts, but the removal of Pompey was essential to Caesar's ambitions. In Lucius, Caesar's pragmatism is mocked, the difference between the two men being largely one of insight. Caesar takes a longer view, being consequently more subtle, and Caesar's opportunism tends to be creative and original, whereas Lucius' is imitative and subservient. But as they both are involved in worldly affairs, they have kinship. This kinship Caesar attempts to transcend through benevolence, but benevolence is contrary to survival in the world to which he has committed himself. It is scarcely trusted and generally scorned. Caesar's reputation for clemency is influential because it rests on the far more respected foundation of military and civil ability. Insofar as his benevolence and his wits coincide, he has rare strength; but ultimately they must rely on the scabbard of Rufio and the treachery of Lucius,[16] and in being dependent on these two Caesar is bound to an earthly wheel of fortune. The microcosm of Ftatateeta killing Pothinus, and of Rufio consequently killing Ftatateeta, complements the macrocosm of Roman politics, where Pompey is killed because of Caesar's power and Caesar must be killed because he is too powerful. A sense of this grand wheel holding Caesar in its spokes is maintained by the sequence of revenge within the play, in the frequent references to his mortality, and in his intuition of a violent end. Caesar's speech on vengeance is rendered ironic by his entanglements. Nobility of mind is of no avail.

The play thus evolves in pessimistic terms. Society, blind and corrupt, ensnares the potential reformer in its infinite complexities. It cannot be reformed unless it is willing to think differently, and it is too instinctively barbaric and has too great a vested interest in barbarism to desire change. True civilization, then, is possible only in terms of the individual who seeks to live according to high personal integrity and sensitivity. For Caesar life is not worth enduring on a level of treachery, intrigue, and vengeance, because such behavior is a negation of meaningful existence. Thus he cannot waste life digging for traitors in enemy correspondence,

16. A paradox noted also by Eric Bentley, *Bernard Shaw* (New York, 1957), p. 163.

especially when the enemies of today may be the friends of tomorrow. However, Caesar is saved from death more by his wits than by his beneficence, and ultimately the price of his fully *living* is death at the hands of the ambitious, the confused, and the treacherous. In mundane terms, the besieged soldier who takes time off to entertain a young girl is subject to surprise attack, and the conqueror who is so noble that he will not pry into enemy mail hazards death.

Despite his claims to the contrary, certainly it is not Shaw's purpose in *Caesar and Cleopatra* to reproduce history in any conventional sense. Rather, he *uses* history to achieve specific effects in art, effects which are then turned back upon their historical sources in a curiously revealing light. The Caesar of history appears in nearly all sources to be more worldly, more ambitious, and less ascetic than Shaw's portrayal of him. Pompey's death was a nasty political necessity; Caesar wanted to found a library, not burn one; Pothinus was a dangerous plotter, and it was probably Caesar who had him executed; Rufio was left to rule Egypt because his poor birth assured his subordination; and, most important, Cleopatra was twenty-one, not sixteen, and bore Caesar a son.[17] On the first program of *Caesar and Cleopatra* Shaw claimed, "The play follows history as closely as stage exigencies permit," whereupon, parodying the pretentious documentation on some nineteenth-century playbills, he provided a list of historical references. But he tipped his hand when he concluded: "Many of these authorities have consulted their imaginations, more or less. The author has done the same."[18] And later, with his usual penchant for inconsistency, he remarked: "I never collect authorities nor investigate conditions. I just deduce what happened and why it happened from my flair for human nature, knowing that if necessary I can find plenty of documents and witnesses to bear me out

17. These disparities are dealt with most thoroughly by Desmond MacCarthy, *Shaw's Plays in Review* (New York, 1951), pp. 95–100; Couchman, "Here Was a Caesar," pp. 272–85; and Stanley Weintraub, "Shaw's Mommsenite Caesar," *Anglo-German and American-German Crosscurrents*, II, ed. Philip A. Shelley and Arthur O. Lewis, Jr. (Chapel Hill, 1962), pp. 257–72.

18. Reproduced in Archibald Henderson, *George Bernard Shaw: Man of the Century* (New York, 1956), p. 555.

in any possible conclusion."[19] As a matter of fact, Shaw did collect one authority—the German historian Theodor Mommsen. As Mommsen sought to remove historical figures from their pedestals,[20] Shaw found him conveniently congenial, cited him, and then went further. Of course Shaw is imaginatively beyond the facts, and he is at the height of his audacity when he writes, "Given Caesar and a certain set of circumstances, I know what would happen, and when I have finished the play you will find I have written history."[21]

When Shaw refers to his "natural" history in the preface, then, he is referring to it more in terms of common human denominators than in terms of factual details. To Shaw, anachronisms may be impish and fun, but they have validity as they relate the past to the present. Further, they give a sense of life to the past, a sense which is probably nearer to the actual human factors than that derived from limited "historical" accounts. The critics who liken Cleopatra to a spoiled English girl may have considerable justification,[22] but this does not invalidate her in the play as a figure of both dramatic and historical reality. Her spontaneity, cruelty, and dreams have pertinence in both cases. Similarly, Caesar is all the more real and pertinent because some critics have found in him a kinship to Cecil Rhodes.[23] Shaw's attitude toward history is very near that which he has Caesar express regarding the library of Alexandria: books and the past are important only as they are meaningful in terms of the living. In working hard to prove his point, Shaw deviates from the facts of the past and turns from realism to fantasy,[24] but it is a fantasy with an organic truth

19. Quoted ibid., p. 335.
20. See Weintraub, "Shaw's Mommsenite Caesar," p. 259. For a reproduction of Shaw's notes on Mommsen, see Louis Crompton, *Shaw the Dramatist* (Lincoln, Nebr., 1969), pp. 231–34.
21. Quoted in Henderson, *Life and Works*, p. 335.
22. Joseph McCabe, *George Bernard Shaw: A Critical Study* (London, 1914), p. 191; Lüdeke, "Some Remarks on Shaw's History Plays," p. 242.
23. Arthur Baumann, quoted in Gordon W. Couchman, "Shaw, *Caesar*, and the Critics," *Speech Monographs*, 23 (1956), 266; and Irvine, *The Universe of G. B. S.*, p. 230.
24. As James Huneker and Henderson observe (quoted in Couchman, "Here Was Caesar," 273).

of its own which, though it may be idiosyncratic, sheds light on history and on history's relationship to modern ethics and humanity. We may lose some of the historical Caesar in the alteration of details, but conventional history at best renders him only vaguely accessible to us as a man, a personal reality. Shaw seeks his personal reality in terms of its hint of distinctive genius; as this is set against historical fact, the bitter ironies are clearer, and the play gains in both artistic and philosophical force.

The strength of Caesar's characterization thus arises from a complex of perspectives, the total effect of which is penetrating but ambiguous. Common sense undercuts foolishness, kindness undercuts cruelty, humor undercuts pomposity, and in the sum of these civilization confronts barbarism, but barbarism is tenacious. As a product of Shaw's imagination the play tends toward romance and fantasy. The romance is carried to some heights by the magnificent settings, the presence of two diverse cultures, and the outward drama of conflict. Fantasy is inherent in the myth of the sphinx, the relation of a kitten-queen and a sorcerer-emperor, the contrasting moods of darkness and daylight, and the frequent anachronisms. But all of this is leavened by the offhand, anticlimactic character of Caesar, couched in cunning, kindness, and humor, attracting poignancy through contrast to the spectacle while achieving power through a sense of constant purpose and high personal morality in a world of bloated abstractions and melodramatic motives. In the realm of fantasy Caesar is victorious, sailing off as the conqueror who, though he may not have illumined the world, has at least set it in order. However, the perspective of history counterbalances the fantasy with tragic irony.[25] From this view Caesar is defeated, and the daylight of Act V is but a prelude to the darkness of the future, the shadows of which are so obvious in the play. Levels of fantasy and history are thus played off against one another, revealing facets of each which would by themselves lie obscure, and contributing in total effect to a highly charged dramatic synthesis.

25. Here I concur with Louis Kronenberger, *The Thread of Laughter* (New York, 1952), p. 237.

CHAPTER FIVE

MAN AND SUPERMAN

The Art of Spiritual Autobiography

Man and Superman is a strange and puzzling conglomerate. The social comedy of Acts I, II, and IV, while lively and amusing, is not as great in its conception, characters, or thematic development as *Caesar and Cleopatra, Major Barbara,* or *Saint Joan,* and the philosophy of Act III, ostensibly one of the keys to Shaw's Life Force gospel, has gross philosophical weaknesses which offset Shaw's dialectical brilliance. But the total play is remarkably complex and effective, incorporating more quintessential Shaw than any other. The sum of its parts is, typical of Shaw, greater than the parts themselves, due to their subtle cross-fertilization and to the intensity of the Shavian spirit which broods quixotically but pervasively over the play. Shaw the comic playwright, dynamic dialectician, bemused husband, and philosophical artist fuse in what amounts to spiritual autobiography, both ironically capricious and deeply serious. His famous Life Force theory is not merely presented, but is parodied and run through a wringer of pessimism in the social comedy. While the Life Force underlies both the comic level of Tanner and Ann and the metaphysical level of Don Juan, each of these reflects upon the other in such a way as to ironically discipline the abstract concept. Thus any complete discussion of the play must account not only for the philosophy, with its background in the Epistle Dedicatory and elsewhere, but also for the social comedy, the hell scene, and the authorial presence, since all four of these factors qualify each other and transmute the whole into a very special sort of aesthetic and dramatic experience. Of all Shaw's thought, the Life Force concept is probably most frequently referred to. Ironically, Shaw's relationship to this theory and its relationship to the play are generally as misunderstood as they are assumed to be clear.[1] Readers have not only been too prone to start with the prefatory epistle—despite Shaw's pointed observation that most wise men will read the play first[2]—but apparently have also read the epistle too quickly or applied it too slavishly. It is deceptively easy to link Shaw's profession of a schoolmaster's temperament and a preacher's conscience with his comments on the sexual primacy of women, the independence of the male genius, the divinity of ascetic contemplation, and the necessity of having eugenic breeding to produce the superman. Ostensibly, these factors tie in neatly with the love chase of the play and the dialectical gyrations of the hell scene. Generally overlooked, however, are Shaw's own qualifications of his theory both dialectically and dramatically. When these qualifications are taken into account, we see Shaw less as schoolmaster, preacher, or prophet than as a poetic theorizer dealing metaphorically with a highly personal and tentative hypothesis.

In the epistle Shaw does indeed discuss his central theme, but he temporizes most uncharacteristically about his fitness as a judge. For a man to whom "effectiveness of assertion is the Alpha and Omega of style" (p. 514), he is remarkably modest. On the matter of sexual relations—ostensibly his primary concern—he admits with unwonted humility that his attitudes are likely to be distorted, and regarding his theories of the Life Force and eugenic

1. Responses range from G. K. Chesterton's comment that "this is the most serious play of the most serious man alive" (*George Bernard Shaw*, Dramabook ed. [New York, 1956], p. 157), to Reuben Brower's suggestion that one listen to *Don Giovanni* "to get into the right frame of mind for approaching the play, to be ready for something like comic opera" (*Major British Writers II* [New York, 1959], p. 695).

2. *Bernard Shaw: Complete Plays with Prefaces* (New York, 1963), III, 494. All citations and quotations from the Epistle Dedicatory and the play are from this volume.

breeding he is pointedly tentative, citing his own subjectivity and implying his own idiosyncrasy. He implicitly compromises himself by observing that, in sacrificing everyone for their work, creative geniuses (such as Shaw?) "are free from the otherwise universal dominion of the tyranny of sex"; thus, "Art, instead of being before all things the expression of the normal sexual situation, is really the only department in which sex is a superseded and secondary power" (p. 499). Further, Masters of the Arts are "patentees of highly questionable methods of thinking, and manufacturers of highly questionable, and for the majority but half valid representations of life" (p. 500). The irony is clear, and in his play Shaw is to develop it into the observation that while geniuses may steer the common herd toward a greater fulfillment of man's potential, genius is relative as insight is relative. The clear view in a myopic world may be highly useful in reassessing the status quo, but it may also be curiously unreal in a world controlled by the status quo, where standards of reality have strange foundations.

As the artist's view is atypical, his theories are likely to be atypical as well. Shaw applies the irony specifically to himself and his Life Force doctrine. He advances his philosophy in terms which compromise it, and he is still uniquely, repetitiously cautious:

> Every man who records his *illusions* is providing data for the genuinely scientific psychology which the world still waits for. I plank down *my* view of the existing relations of men to women *. . . for what it is worth. It is a view like any other view and no more,* neither true nor false, but, I hope, *a way of looking at the subject . . .* [The public] will take my books as read and my genius for granted *. . . So we may disport ourselves on our own plane to the top of our bent.* [p. 506]

My italicizing should adequately point up both the nonprophetic nature of Shaw's attitude, and the acknowledged idiosyncrasy— one might also infer the fun—of his doctrine. The statement compounds a confession of subjectivity with an admission of theoreticity. Therefore, Act III may have been, as Shaw wrote later, "a careful attempt to write a new Book of Genesis for the Bible of the

Evolutionists,"[3] but the mind behind it was not blind to the fact that evolutionists were unlikely to be tractable, since their bible is generally rational, not poetic or holy.

Given such a subjective and theoretical framework, what was *Man and Superman* to accomplish? Why all the words, the thought, the effort? Shaw is repeatedly condescending about his own forte: the world of books, whether professing gospels or philosophic systems, "is not the main world at all: it is only the self-consciousness of certain abnormal people who have the specific artistic talent and temperament" (p. 500). Accordingly, he mocks himself: "I first prove that anything I write on the relation of the sexes is sure to be misleading; and then I proceed to write a Don Juan play" (p. 505). There are contexts, however, in which the seemingly abnormal view may either be nearer to sanity or may be more provocative of sanity than any other. Hence, encompassing and transcending self-mockery, Shaw asserts himself less in terms of fact than in terms of personal audacity—the audacity (scarcely modest, now) of genius. His system, he indicates, being one of genius, is no doubt atypical. Therefore, beware: but since it comes from genius, its very processes are worth considering—the self-consciousness of the abnormal artist may be valuable in the very quality of that consciousness, and philosophy should be more a method than a sacred cow. Thus Shaw remarks in his postscript to *Back to Methuselah*: "We must have a hypothesis as a frame of reference before we can reason; and Creative Evolution, though the best we can devise so far, is basically as hypothetical and provisional as any of the creeds."[4] In this light, Creative Evolution is more a metaphor than a religion. As a metaphor it reflects Shaw the artist-thinker functioning as much in the realms of poetry and intuition as in the realms of philosophy or science.[5] In terms of

3. "A Foreword to the Popular Edition of *Man and Superman*" (22 March 1911), *Complete Plays*, III, 748.

4. "Postscript after Twentyfive Years," *Complete Plays*, II, cv.

5. William Irvine's comment that Shaw's Life Force metaphysics "now appear exaggerated and unreal" (*The Universe of G. B. S.* [New York, 1949], p. 239) reflects a feeling common from the beginning of the century. Shaw, by all indications presented here, might have generally agreed with this sentiment from the very first. Exaggeration and an artistic use of unreality are tools of his dialectic.

action, however, it seeks a very real movement away from the be-
leaguering limitations of the old orders. To improve the quality of
life and to give it a meaningful new direction, contemporary man
needs a vital, relevant spiritual context. The Life Force hypothesis
is a thrust in that direction.

Shaw's sources for the Life Force theory are well known. However, in his search for a personal metaphor his use of these sources
is highly impressionistic and intuitively eclectic, ordered to fit the
measure of his fundamentally optimistic nature. From a pragmatic, social, and philosophical point of view Shaw saw constant
negation as leading to nihilism, a self-defeating attitude, as sense-
less in a godless world as in a paradise. Optimism was the only
mode under which life might be endurable. Shaw's comment on
Don Juan could well be applied to himself: "His scepticism, once
his least tolerated quality, has now triumphed so completely that
he can no longer assert himself by witty negations, and must, to
save himself from cipherdom, find an affirmative position" (p.
492). Shaw faults Dickens and Shakespeare for their failure in
this regard. Their observations "are not co-ordinated into any
philosophy or religion . . . they are concerned with the diversities
of the world instead of with its unities"—in sum, they are irreli-
gious, anarchical, and "have no constructive ideas" (p. 508). The
world may stumble along in terms of interesting character types,
but it has no direction in such terms, and the metaphysical implication of art with such a focus, entertaining as that art may be, is
chaos. Shaw sensed order in the universe and felt that the philosophy behind art should include a reflection of that order. In his
preface to *Back to Methuselah* he remarks that the world "did not
look like a pure accident: it presented evidences of design in every
direction. There was mind and purpose behind it."[6] The problem
lay in defining the nature of that mind through the evidence of its
manifestations, and in affirming man's positive role in an ordered
cosmos.

6. *Complete Plays*, II, xxxvii. This statement, with its great and hazardous leap
in logic, exemplifies Richard Ohmann's observation that "the wish is for Shaw at
least stepfather to the thought" (*Shaw: The Style and the Man* [Middletown,
Conn., 1962], p. 27).

As Darwin was the major root and focus of nineteenth-century skepticism, his influence was basically inimical to the definition and affirmation Shaw sought. Natural selection resulting from biological and environmental chance was a denial of Shaw's optimism for a better world grounded on intelligence and will. Consequently he rejected Darwin and much of Darwin's evidence, gravitating to Lamarck, who had suggested the more positive hypothesis that organisms evolve by adapting to their surroundings, the individual organism having a self-determining volition. Lamarck's theory had been generally discredited, but no matter— it was nearer to Shaw's melioristic sympathies. Samuel Butler made the giant step beyond Lamarck which most appealed to Shaw: Butler theorized a force existing apart from the organism which *willed* its development, an independent spirit which controlled the matter it informed. Conveniently, certain aspects of Schopenhauer's *World as Will* corresponded to this assumption, except that Schopenhauer found the informing wills of different men working against one another, and consequently necessary to inhibit—a qualification which Shaw discarded, turning to Nietzsche. The German philosopher's *Übermensch* is notably ill-defined, being a dream about a leader above conventional morality, but the idea was appealing to Shaw as it imaginatively contemporized Carlyle's concept of the hero and provided the conceptualization of a Lamarckian-Butlerian evolutionary step beyond average man, a step on which Shaw could prop his theoretical cosmology in teleological terms. The superman hypothesis gave evidence of potential evolutionary perfectibility on a moral and spiritual plane, and it suggested a spirit informing the universe in general and men in particular which could find through man an avenue for self-realization.

Shaw thus delved into philosophy and biology on his own terms, fitting the material to his own notions less as a scientist than as an artist and mystic. Philosophically his theory gains most respectability by being akin to Henri Bergson's *élan vital*. Bergson is the great proponent of intuition, which he places in the province of art and philosophy—as opposed to analysis, which he places in the province of science. Bergson's *Creative Evolution*, first published

CARL A. RUDISILL LIBRARY
LENOIR RHYNE COLLEGE

in 1907, proposed that the *élan vital* (spirit of life, or vital impetus) permeates all living organisms, being the original source of life and manifesting itself through evolution in endless fragmentations, the most meaningful fragment at present being man. In lower forms of life it occurs as instinct, and in higher forms as intellect. The former responds directly to the world, while the latter has adjusted and developed through a process of analysis. Analysis has great evolutionary possibilities, but finally it is tied to symbols of language and logic, symbols which are highly effective in dealing with the material environment but which are ineffectual in understanding life itself or metaphysics, since the intrinsic nature of life is a vitality, a fluidity, a becoming. Hence scientific evolutionists, working with symbols and solids, have inappropriately reduced evolution to materialistic terms which are static and inflexible. These are inadequate to deal with the "fluid continuity of the real," the true nature of the evolution of life as opposed to the evolution of form. Bergson theorizes that true metaphysical comprehension can only occur when intellect turns its powers back to instinct in a process akin to sympathy, at which point intuition becomes operative: "So understood, philosophy is not only the turning of the mind homeward, the coincidence of human consciousness with the living principle whence it emanates, a contact with the creative effort: it is the study of becoming in general, it is true evolutionism and consequently the true continuation of science."[7] Since God in this cosmology is the *élan vital* or Life Force—both primal force and evolving spirit, manifesting more in a state of becoming than as an ultimate Goal—perfection and God are elusive, their very nature involving motion, change, and development. Were they constant, they would be stagnant, and consequently incapable of full realization. We may recall Blake's proverbs: "The cistern contains: the fountain overflows. . . . Expect poison from the standing water";[8] and, more

7. Henri Bergson, *Creative Evolution*, trans. Arthur Mitchell (New York, 1911), pp. 369–70. My references to Bergson are partially indebted to Albert William Levi, *Philosophy and the Modern World* (Bloomington, 1959), pp. 63–101.
8. William Blake, "The Marriage of Heaven and Hell," *A Collection of English Poems, 1660–1800*, ed. Ronald S. Crane (New York, 1932), p. 1024.

abstractly, Bergson: *"All reality, therefore, is tendency."*[9] Metaphysical truth lies less in absolutes than in flux which allows for ever increasing levels of awareness. For absolutes must change as awareness deepens, existing less in themselves than in their interpretation by the agent which perceives them.

Bergson's sense of reality is consequently highly compatible with Shaw's dramatic mode, where the characters "are all right from their several points of view; and their points of view are, for the dramatic moment, mine also" (p. 505). There are strong echoes in this of the Hegelian dialectic, which clearly had an influence on Shaw; but in combining intellect and instinct, testing logic against life and life against logic, Shaw moves beyond Hegel.[10] Most basically, his dialectical drama attains its truths through multifold perceptions of reality, overlaid by a sense of synthesis, an inherent reconciliation of opposites first intuited and then frequently dramatized. But, more subtly, a Bergsonian coalescence of intellect and instinct provides the metaphorical climax which lies behind Shaw's dramatic climax in *Man and Superman*. As Tanner represents intellect and Ann represents instinct, their union has the potential of an epiphany in the higher consciousness of intuition. Shaw suggests this union in his epistle, attributing it to the great artist who applies intellect to instinct in deciphering life: such men of genius are "men selected by Nature to carry on the work of building up an intellectual consciousness of her own instinctive purpose" (pp. 498–99); they are men who represent "the struggle of Life to become divinely conscious of itself" (p. 500).

Having developed such a kinship with Bergson, Shaw has trouble when his theories deviate from those of the philosopher. Nota-

9. Henri Bergson, *An Introduction to Metaphysics*, trans. T. E. Hulme (New York and London, 1912), p. 65.

10. Sidney Albert points out the Hegelian aspects of Shaw in "Bernard Shaw: The Artist as Philosopher," *Journal of Aesthetics and Art Criticism*, 14 (1956), 422–24. My summary of sources for Shaw's philosophical thought is highly abbreviated. His eclectic method of assimilating these sources seems more significant to his aesthetics than do specific points of indebtedness. For a more complete summary of Shaw's roots in nineteenth-century thought, see Julian B. Kaye, *Bernard Shaw and the Nineteenth-Century Tradition* (Norman, Okla., 1958).

bly, Bergson does not deal with eugenic breeding or the relations of the sexes. On these two issues, drawn in part from Schopenhauer, Shaw's metaphor is most vulnerable, perhaps in the fact that these issues tend to crystallize dramatically. Shaw's Life Force theory maintains vitality through its suggestiveness and tentativeness. It has the flexibility and spirit of Bergsonian intuition. When he pushes his hypothesis too doctrinally, however, as he did later in calling Act III "a revelation of the modern religion of evolution,"[11] he verges on absurdity and self-parody, for there is a stasis in religion incompatible with the dynamic art of Shaw's exploratory dialectic. In having the female chase the male and in offering eugenic breeding as a possible means of accelerating evolution, Shaw is dramatically and dialectically concrete. He has tied himself to symbols and logic which compromise the poetry of his drama and the sense of his philosophy.

The inversion of the love chase is a stock comic device. It appears frequently not only in Shakespeare, as Shaw observes, but also in nineteenth-century drama. As a device it has a certain comic and dramatic potential, despite its artificiality. But Shaw's intellectualization of it as an archetypal pattern is idiosyncratic, an example of his deliberately maintaining a perverse position for the new thought which may arise from dialectical sparks. It is barely a half-truth, making a partial psycho-physiological point, operating from a comic cliché. In tweaking biology with humor, it seems a harmless diversion; in being posed as something universal, on the other hand, it throws the play's cosmological picture out of focus.

The suggestion of eugenic breeding is a greater flaw. Eugenic breeding is not only socially unworkable, but also biologically and philosophically impracticable.[12] Nonetheless, while Shaw may not

11. "Foreword to the Popular Edition," p. 747.

12. Oddly, Shaw's notion has not come in for much criticism. Chesterton is the most outspoken: "Its practical difficulties; its moral difficulties, or rather impossibilities, for any animal fit to be called a man need scarcely be discussed" (p. 156). Medical science has only recently approached the possibility: "Boston—A team of Harvard scientists has isolated a pure gene from a living organism for the first time, thereby advancing the day when man will be able to manipulate his own genetic makeup" (Los Angeles Times, 23 Nov. 1969, sec. A., p. 1).

be entirely serious about it, he is not capricious, and the context in which he introduces it reveals his personal involvement and earnestness. He claims that his discussion of politics in the epistle is a digression, but at this point he deals with breeding at considerable length and reflects a lively, intense concern. His tone is sardonic and his attitude is pessimistic, both in striking contrast to his optimism elsewhere. He negates education and progress: "I do not know whether you have any illusions left on the subject of education, progress, and so forth. I have none" (p. 503). He negates democracy in bitter terms: "The multitude thus pronounces judgment on its own units: it admits itself unfit to govern" (p. 502). He asserts breeding as a desperate step to avoid impending political decomposition: "Our political experiment of democracy, the last refuge of cheap misgovernment, will ruin us if our citizens are ill bred" (p. 501), which he repeats with grim emphasis: "We must either breed political capacity or be ruined by Democracy, which was forced on us by the failure of the older alternatives" (p. 503).

Shaw uses "breeding" not only in a eugenic, physiological sense, but to imply a general cultural sense as well, his skepticism of man's political capacities having its counterpart in a strong disillusionment regarding man's aesthetic capacities. His animus, perhaps even more than that of the socialist, is that of the poet, the aristocrat, the genius, who is impatient with the insularity, sloth, vulgarity, and incompetence of the common herd. It is startling to see Shaw aligning himself with someone as conservative as Edmund Burke: "For remember: what our voters are in the pit and gallery they are also in the polling booth. We are all now under what Burke called 'the hoofs of the swinish multitude' " (p. 502). This comment can be inverted, of course, and the inversion is clearly in Shaw's mind. Certainly what the voters are in the polling booth they are also in the pit and gallery. For this multitude Shaw had turned cynically from writing "Plays Unpleasant" to "Plays Pleasant," his aesthetic and dialectic sensitivities having to compromise with mediocrity or disappear in a vacuum of neglect. At the time of writing *Man and Superman*, ten years after *Widowers' Houses*, his plays were still unpopular in England, and he muses, "What I have always wanted is a pit of philosophers" (p. 506). The proposition of eugenic breeding gives specific vent to this deep-seated feeling: may the swinish multitude be damned. *Breed* them out of existence; breed into existence a pit of philosophers. The feeling is irrational and inconstant, for certainly he did try to please the multitude. But in espousing eugenic breeding he gave this feeling a form, and this form suffers the weakness of its origin.

The political and aesthetic motive behind Shavian eugenics points up a sharp conflict in Shaw between theory and fact, optimism and pessimism, faith and disillusionment. Opposing his positive philosophy of the Life Force is his bitter observation of an unevolving, corrupt, ignorant world. The gap between the genius and the common man, a matter of intelligence and sensitivity, seemed to him no less in the twentieth century than in the tenth. Noting that the evolutionary potential has been historically unplumbed, Shaw maintains his Life Force theory in the face of its pragmatic improbability. Bogged down by the stubbornly incompetent masses and the cyclic, nonprogressive nature of history, just how is the race to improve? He meets this enigma with the proposition of eugenic breeding, which has the elements of a stopgap just short of despair, a trial balloon filled with hot air. He advances it boldly, not unlike a sensitive Christian trying to shore up faith against a sea of doubts.[13] But with its logical and practical weaknesses this hypothesis was bound to fail him. Significantly, he seldom deals with it after *Man and Superman*.

The practical difficulty of Shaw's evolutionary Life Force theory is thus manifest: it lacks a method of fulfillment. In the confrontation of optimistic faith with cynical reason Shaw was once again

13. Eric Bentley claims that eugenic breeding is a Shavian *suggestion*, thrown forth via Tanner to point up the problem of how to make democracy and society effective (*Bernard Shaw*, Amended ed. [New York, 1957], p. 57). Considering Shaw's own tentativeness in the epistle, which we have noted, this is no doubt largely true. But what is aesthetically interesting about Shaw's suggestion is the sense of personal animus which gives his expression an aura of bitter conviction and renders the drama more poignant. Emil Strauss touches on this latter, finding less seriousness in Shaw's proposition than a frustration regarding the general intransigence which met his social philosophy (*Bernard Shaw: Art and Socialism* [London, 1942], p. 81).

to propose an unlikely solution, in the Ancients' elongated life spans of *Back to Methuselah*. But such answers are those of the poet, not of the philosopher, and reflect a retreat into fancy as either an evasion of despair or a prelude to it. Imagination serves as a salve for anguish. More frankly, his disillusionment was to find expression in the pessimism, nihilism, and despair of *Heartbreak House*.[14]

In sum, the optimism of *Man and Superman* covers its opposite with a glass shield. Politically, Shaw's desires were bound to meet frustration, and the only ordered movement from his impasse was to be away from democracy toward the authoritarianism of a (hopefully) benevolent despot, the superman as a mythical ideal. Shaw hints at his future course in commenting, "Despotism failed only for want of a capable benevolent despot" (p. 503). This was to grow into the notion that only by the inspiring example and wise guidance of an exceptional leader or oligarchy could the race advance. Under these terms the Life Force philosophy could retain coherence and seem workable. The ideal is in Caesar or Saint Joan, and to a lesser degree in many other Shavian individualists, such as Juan, who has "a sense of reality that disables convention" (p. 497). The twentieth-century confutation was yet to occur.

Aesthetically and culturally on the other hand, there might be a more realistic hope for the Life Force. If a pit of philosophers could not be bred by eugenics, possibly they could be bred from a significant number in the swinish multitude through thought, iconoclasm, and persuasion. A cultural breeding, rendering the common herd more sophisticated and civilized, would hold at least the little promise that eugenic breeding did not. In this context Shaw himself assumed the role of a minor superman, a benevolent despot of intellect, and did not entirely abandon education as hopeless. Were it well managed, he could plant the seeds of an expansion of consciousness, not only political and social, but aesthetic and even spiritual, to further that keynote of his philosoph-

14. Irvine traces Shaw's disillusionment through four plays, each increasingly pessimistic: *Mrs Warren's Profession, Man and Superman, Major Barbara,* and *Heartbreak House* (*The Universe of G. B. S.*, pp. 235–36). Though this is a trifle artificial in particulars, its general outline does indeed reveal an underlying pessimism and deepening despair.

ical hypothesis on which we have already touched, "the struggle of Life to become divinely conscious of itself instead of blindly stumbling hither and thither in the line of least resistance" (p. 500). In this sense his Life Force theory meaningfully complements his optimism by providing the motivation to more fully develop what little potential actually exists. Cultural breeding may have a poor historical record, but it offers the only alternative.

So works the schoolmaster and preacher in Shaw—as an evocative dialectician and artist with nearly mystic convictions, seeking order out of chaos, divinity out of mundanity, and a positive pragmatic route in fulfillment of a noble cosmology. In such a role he is kindred to the prophets, except that his assumptions are more humble, his assertions more tentative, and his sense of humor more balanced. Most uniquely, however, he undercuts criticism by projecting his philosophy into drama, where it is subject to life and laughter, and he projects himself into caricature so that his own absurdities may be manifest. The laughter serves a paradoxical function—rather than negating the assertions, it chastizes them, purging them of pretentiousness while preparing them for popular consumption. Tolstoy objected to Shaw's levity, writing, "The first defect in [Man and Superman] is that you are not sufficiently serious. One should not speak jestingly of such a subject as the purpose of human life, the causes of its perversion, and the evil that fills the life of humanity today." [15] But to Shaw somberness was the other side of pompousness and tragedy the other side of pessimism. Both put psychic blocks in the way of perceiving life as he did, and neither could be as effective a philosophical tool as the heightened intellect which is alive in good comedy. And as an artist Shaw was not afraid of error, since error may be more dialectically and aesthetically purposeful in the discovery of new levels of perception than are safe platitudes. Thus he remarks, "Now if I am to be no mere copper wire amateur but a luminous author, I must also be a most intensely refractory person, liable to go out and to go wrong at inconvenient moments, and with incendiary possibilities. These are the faults of my qualities" (p.

15. Quoted in Archibald Henderson, George Bernard Shaw: Man of the Century (New York, 1956), p. 583.

515). His theory of the Life Force, therefore, attended by its illegitimate children (the love-chase inversion and eugenic breeding), moves into the play with more enthusiasm than infallibility, stronger in poetic suggestiveness than in metaphysical verities. The play's most essential faith is in the role of the playwright himself to inform where facts may fail, and to civilize where hope of civilization is running dry.

It is curious how obliquely the Life Force philosophy applies to the play itself. Without the hell scene, which Shaw misleadingly calls "totally extraneous" (p. 494), the weight of the metaphysics which have been attributed to *Man and Superman* seems excessive. Shaw proposes a philosophy which he then sublimates. In his epistle he dodges the full implications of Act III—"But this pleasantry is not the essence of the play"—and takes a highly artistic stance, asserting the independence and internal volition of a work of art: "Over this essence I have no control. You propound a certain social substance, sexual attraction to wit, for dramatic distillation; and I distil it for you. . . . You must therefore . . . prepare yourself to face a trumpery story of modern London life" (p. 494). He thereupon deals with his ideas further, only to again proffer the disclaimer of an artist: "But I hear you asking me in alarm whether I have actually put all this tub thumping into a Don Juan comedy. I have not" (p. 505). Obviously, however, his play is not off the dialectical hook. Trumpery story it may most superficially seem to be, but its aesthetics involve much more than the simple comic level. The distillation is all-important, and over this Shaw exercises considerable control, as he later admits: "I cannot be a bellettrist. . . . 'For art's sake' alone I would not face the toil of writing a single sentence" (pp. 513–14). The essence of the play, with its intertwining of fun, sociology, and metaphysical overtones, is most briefly and with greatest balance expressed in Shaw's subtitle for it: "A Comedy (and a Philosophy)."

The parenthetical philosophy of this comedy carries an impressive range of implications—personal, romantic, social, political, moral, mythical, and cosmic—all complexly reverberating in an echo-chamber of humor, and toned from subtle irony to farce.

Most simply, the trumpery story has a vigorous life of its own, romantic and light-hearted, the comedy of young love between a determined female and a recalcitrant male. Impressed upon this are social and political references, enriching the comedy, and moved with a moral instinct toward moral illuminations which underlie the seemingly frivolous plot. Finally, metaphysical implications act upon the comedy and, simultaneously, are acted upon by the comedy. As they are poetically suggested by mythical and archetypal allusions, they provide an imaginative foundation which evokes a sense of spiritual truth; as they are explicitly proposed by Tanner, on the other hand, they fall subject to the limitations of character, concept, and language, being compromised by the fallibility and absurdity of his overzealous explanations. Thus comedy is given dignity by an active moral consciousness, and metaphysics unfold in poetry and humor.

For sheer vigor the trumpery story can well hold its own. Vital characters, situations, and dramatic structuring propel the play on a level of lively social comedy. The men's differing views of Ann which are so widely contradictory, picturing her simultaneously as an innocent and dutiful girl, a feminine ideal, and a predatory animal, charge her entry with a suspense and interest similar to that of Candida's first appearance. In addition, the contentious guardianship dilemma, the scandal of Violet's apparently vulnerable virtue, and the childhood reminiscences of Tanner and Ann carry the first act through the interest and variety of sharp shifts of context. These fully reveal the characters by forcing them to react to various challenging situations. Dramaturgically impressive is the enjambment of incident which is so tight yet flows so smoothly, shining less for its ingeniousness than for its incisive revelations.

This surface energy is rendered more complex and profound as Shaw develops a vital, flexible relationship between the various characters' personal, social, and archetypal roles. Each character acts somewhat differently in each role, and the composite scene involves not only the confrontation of different personalities, but also the interaction of their varying symbolic levels. Ramsden's personal role is that of a kindly man fulfilling his duty; his social role is that of a well-meaning liberal in decay, suffering the atrophy of middle-aged respectability; and his archetypal role is that of age, of the father figure trapped in institutional attitudes and habit patterns. He has a heart and will which render him human, but his age, beliefs, and station make him also a social phenomenon, and as this phenomenon touches universal human relationships he takes on an archetypal aspect. Each role overlaps the others, but each has enough individuality to render the composite figure vibrantly alive with minor incongruities. Ramsden has piquant personal dimension in numerous refractory ironies. He is sure of himself as an advanced man who grows more advanced every day, while with Victorian righteousness he condemns a book he has not read and considers Violet's apparent transgression as a fate worse than death. His liberalism is symbolized by the bust of Herbert Spencer to which Shaw draws frequent attention: it embodies out-of-date convictions, philosophy turned to icon, life turned to stone. At the same time, as he is a representative of the past impinging upon the present, of the liberalism of yesterday which is irrelevant today, he is also precognitive of what may be Tanner's fate.

Tanner's part has similar complexities. In one aspect Tanner functions in the archetypal role of iconoclastic youth confronting the conservatism of age, while in another his unique vigor, talent, and shortcomings infuse the archetype with comic life and a highly charged personal dimension. He is both myth and personality. As Shaw describes him, he is a Jupiter, a big man with a beard, Olympian in majesty, mythical in figure, energy, and imagination. Yet when this Jupiter opens his mouth, he functions socially as Prometheus and personally as a divine fool and windbag. The god is compromised by the man who is, as Octavius observes, "so desperately afraid of Ann" (p. 523). Ironically, however, the man in part transcends himself through his very fear and obsessive vitality, which seem to underlie some of his theory and much of his talk. Tanner is rendered both noble and comic by the disparity between his grandiose abstractions and his personal blindness.

On a romantic level Shaw makes it patently clear that Tanner, while not admitting it to himself, is succumbing to Ann. Tanner's true inclinations are revealed in his bachelor's panic, his desperate comment that "I might as well be her husband" (p. 525), the "fascination" he finds in her, and the nostalgic reminiscence of the vicissitudes of a childhood crush. Little has changed in the Ann who bullied little girls with her virtue, was insatiably curious about her boyfriend, coyly led him on, and ruthlessly vanquished a rival. And the boy who loved to talk, impress his girlfriend, and make a romance of life is now the man who has converted his aims by a moral passion, but who is obviously still under the spell of his adolescent affections as he naïvely remarks, "Yes, Ann: the old childish compact between us was an unconscious love compact" (p. 551). The reminiscence scene, concluded with metaphoric aptness by a boa embrace, reveals the fullness of the romance which Tanner abstracts. While Ann uses her mother as a scapegoat, Tanner, in a pagan's perversion of vicarious atonement, skirts the implicit love which hovers throughout the act by offering Octavius to Venus as the sacrificial lamb. Though one of Shaw's limitations may be that he is no flesh painter, certainly this "love scene" is as adroit, ironic, and light-handed as the situation demands.[16] The manner is notably subtle in dealing with the obvious matter, and the playful art of the dramaturgy is splendidly consistent with the social artifice of the characters.

16. The "flesh painter" observation comes from Henderson. He goes on to say, "Inability to portray sexual passion convincingly is a limitation of Shaw's art" (p. 580). The same type of qualification is made by Joseph McCabe, who refers to the love episode as "love-making seen through Shaw's academic spectacles" (*George Bernard Shaw: A Critical Study* [London, 1914], p. 197). Henderson and McCabe are right in the sense that Shaw avoids getting thick about love. His grand passions are reserved not for romantic display, which he considered intrinsically mundane, but for man's more unique aspirations. His concentration in matters of love is consequently less on the sexual appetite than on evolutionary patterns underlying it which are in conflict with the inhibiting patterns of society. The mode here is thus akin to the comedy of manners, with the basic qualification that Shaw's underlying purpose is to change manners through providing new rationales. Hot love is certainly not appropriate to the *Man and Superman* context. Given the talkative, elusive nature of Tanner, the calculating nature of Ann, and the suspended aspect of their relationship, their particular type of verbal love-making fits the dramatic situation.

Since Tanner is so fallible in his recognition of personal realities, it is not surprising that he also trips over his social convictions. His moral passion may give him the incentive to seek a more just social and political order, but his moral sense is partly undercut and led astray by its intensity and obsessiveness. He fails to consider that liberal social idealism frequently does not fit the irrationality of society. He is on very good ground in compassionate, theoretical, and human terms when he defends Violet's supposed transgression. He ennobles the birth of a child as it reflects intense personal reality and the fulfillment of feminine destiny. Indirectly he extols Ann as he remarks, "You were right to follow your instinct; that vitality and bravery are the greatest qualities a woman can have" (p. 558). But, in addition to his unconventionality, his tone is too self-consciously iconoclastic, and in defying the sanctity of convention he is too strong in apotheosizing a natural function. Consequently, when convention undercuts him in the fact of Violet's marriage, both his assumption, and the exuberance with which he displayed it, backfire. His abstraction based on human compassion does not fit the social fact, and that fact wreaks indignant revenge. The abstraction which counts is neither compassion nor social idealism—it is the wedding ring, and this beats him into submission. Society operates in terms of generalizations and symbols for morality, mores, and conventions, which may be illusory and ephemeral in one sense but which form a stubborn, pragmatic order. Clearly, there are two realities—that of moral enlightenment, and that of social consensus. The clever man might weave his way between the two to the welfare of both, but Tanner, in trying to strike one with the other, throws a boomerang instead of a club. Even though he may be right, he is socially awry.

Being personally so myopic and socially so naïve, Tanner may well be suspected when he espouses his own metaphysics. His social miscalculations give a hint of his philosophical weakness: his theories may have a consistency within themselves, but they are flawed in the inconsistent, irrational contexts of life. He gains credibility when his appraisal of Ann as a guileful female is borne out by her initial entrance—obviously, he is more sensitive to her true nature than is either Ramsden or Octavius—but in his intensity he overstates his case, and through his exaggeration he opens a credibility gap between Ann and his representation of her, between the aptness of his observation and the conclusions he draws. This gap is most apparent in his metaphysical assertions of her significance. To say that Ann is a vital genius is one thing—forceful language to describe an ingenious and determined woman— and to describe her as a lioness swallowing Octavius bite by bite tags her feline propensities with an apt metaphor. But Tanner's philosophical generalizations clearly transcend Ann: "Vitality in a woman is a blind fury of creation. She sacrifices herself to it: do you think she will hesitate to sacrifice you? . . . Because they have a purpose which is not their own purpose, but that of the whole universe, a man is nothing to them but an instrument of that purpose" (p. 537). Interesting, but unsound in terms of what we have viewed. In the disparity between Ann and this assertion we feel the extravagance and error of Tanner's judgment. Further, to prop his metaphysics he gives Octavius a role which is entirely disproportionate to the ineffectual, untalented, romantic stripling which Shaw has portrayed: "But you, Tavy, are an artist: that is, you have a purpose as absorbing and as unscrupulous as a woman's purpose. . . . The artist's work is to shew us ourselves as we really are. . . . In the rage of that creation he is as ruthless as the woman, as dangerous to her as she to him, and as horribly fascinating" (pp. 537–38).

Tanner's metaphysics thus fall apart in the face of fact, being bloated beyond all human correlatives. Neither Ann nor Tavy nor their relationship rises to Tanner's grandiloquent picture. The epic struggle depicted by his imagination is mocked by the dramatic scene. It becomes necessary, of course, to replace Octavius with Tanner in the role of the artist, if this cosmic scheme is to work at all. But in the very necessity of substitution Tanner's perspicacity is admittedly askew, throwing his qualifications for the epic struggle into doubt, and the humor which attends his confusion undercuts the persuasiveness of his theories. He is caught in a thoroughly comic complex of incongruity between an Olympian manner and social ineptitude, a noble philosophy and prag-matic irrelevance.[17]

This comic fallibility is further dramatized in Act II. Through the depiction of Straker, Shaw not only introduces a new social type to literature, but adroitly plays that type against the protag-onist for both personal and social revelations. He draws a sharp contrast between Tanner's theoretical realism and Straker's prac-tical realism, in the process reemphasizing the inherent weakness of all of Tanner's theorizings. To be outwitted by a fellow phi-losopher is one thing, but to be outwitted by your chauffeur, whose gods are motors and speed, is another. Where wit is relative, it is hazardous to operate by halves. A double irony is maintained throughout the act in Tanner being glib about the New Man and condescending in his advice to Octavius about Ann, while Straker is whistling knowingly about Tanner's ignorance of Ann's inten-tions. At various times Ann, Octavius, and Violet all indicate that they endure Tanner's volubility without really listening to him, and Straker is as indulgent as the rest: "He likes to talk. We know him, dont we?" (p. 565). Thus while Tanner's observations re-garding Henry's pride of class may be accurate, they are inconse-quential wind over the social landscape. Tanner's remark to Octavius might well be directed back toward himself: "Youre only a poetic Socialist, Tavy: he's a scientific one." From such an ab-straction Straker moves to tangible reality: "Yes. Well, this con-versation is very improvin; but Ive got to look after the car" (pp. 565–66).

Tanner's personal irrelevance at this point is a reflection of the incompetence of the entire leisured class in comparison to the working mechanic and engineer. In Act IV Violet stresses the dependence of the middle classes on their chauffeurs, and here

17. Thus Shaw's tentativeness and qualifications in the epistle are carried over into the play. Several critics have remarked briefly on the discrepancy between Tanner's ideals and life. Most pointed are Strauss, *Shaw: Art and Socialism*, p. 65; Bentley, *Bernard Shaw*, pp. 156–57; and Robert Brustein, *The Theatre of Revolt* (Boston, 1964), p. 219. Louis Crompton observes perceptively that our laughter at Tanner is not corrective, but is that of "good fellowship"—recognizing his per-sonal virtues despite his social imprudence. See *Shaw the Dramatist* (Lincoln, Nebr., 1969), pp. 80–81.

Tanner remarks, "I am Enry's slave" (p. 570). With fine economy Shaw reveals both the evolution of a social relationship and
the relative perception of one man over the other:

> TANNER. Well, if you . . . leave Mr. Robinson a good deal occupied
> with Miss Whitefield, he will be deeply grateful to you.
> STRAKER. [Looking round at him] Evidently.
> TANNER. 'Evidently'! Your grandfather would have simply
> winked.
> STRAKER. My grandfather would have touched his at.
> TANNER. And I should have given your good nice respectful
> grandfather a sovereign.
> STRAKER. Five shillins, more likely. [p. 582]

The education of Eton and Oxford falters before such exquisite
one-upmanship, as it does later when the chauffeur corrects his
master's allusion to Beaumarchais.

Tanner is in part rendered foolish by an automatism which is
humorous in a Bergsonian sense. He is too vital and thoughtful to
be completely mechanical and too iconoclastic to have entirely
surrendered his will to a system, but in some respects a machine-
like impetus carries him past reality. He can admit that he is in
love with Ann, but at the same time dodge the consequences by
abstracting reality and transferring to Octavius his own role in the
Life Force scheme. In a reflection of Act I Ann is caught in a
double lie, maneuvering her sister Rhoda out of the way; but
before the second lie is discovered, Tanner has blindly and ver-
bosely talked his way into her way—a trip to Marseilles together.
The effect is that of pomposity slipping twice on the same banana
peel. Tanner's convictions about the need for independence in
youth, which are noble but irrelevant to the true facts of the
present situation, lead him into the immediate danger of his own
independence being compromised. With graphic dramatic emphasis a theory talks itself into its practical opposite, and a noble
impulse leads directly to its own contradiction. The mechanics of
Tanner's philosophy are obviously too inflexible for the infinite
complexities of life, and the final comic stroke is that this advocate
of social realism must be informed by his chauffeur about the most

obvious reality of all. So the chase is on—notably, in an automobile. Shaw dramatizes society's dependence on the mechanical age by the presence of a machine on stage. The psychic automatism of Tanner has its physical equivalent, which he employs with poetic appropriateness as love's pursuit takes on an automated and spatial dimension in twentieth-century terms.

Ann, being less pretentious and less philosophical than Tanner, is less comic. Her vitality is as great as Tanner's, but it is manifest on a plane of instinct, guile, and pragmatism which both opposes and complements his intellect, naïveté, and idealism.[18] Contrary to Tanner's claim that a woman seeks a man largely for the sake of children, Ann pursues Tanner for himself. Clearly, she sees in him qualities which she admires, in part because they are the opposite of qualities she possesses. The nostalgic reminiscence of childhood love reveals that Ann is a willful, cunning, and infatuated little girl who has merely put on some subtlety and a few years. Her veneer is notably pierced at one point when she reacts to Jack's childhood mischievousness: "[*flashing out*] I never wanted you to do those dull, disappointing, brutal, stupid, vulgar things. I always hoped that it would be something really heroic at last" (p. 547). This emotional outburst propels the past abruptly into the present. Clearly Ann is still very much involved emotionally, and the childhood crush is translated into an adult sense of hurt, indignation, and a keen desire for an ideal. Octavius bemoans the fact that he is not ambitious enough for Ann, and clearly this is true, for though she may not pay much attention to what Jack says, she loves to hear Jack talk. Obviously, this big man with a beard is going somewhere, and Ann is instinctively attracted to Tanner's sense of purpose.

In encountering outdated social strictures Ann has, oddly enough, a certain affinity with Tanner; but while he fronts society and is roundly beaten, she works her will through society and tri-

18. Much critical reaction to Ann has been too simplistic, from Irvine, who refers to her as not human, an idea (*Universe of G. B. S.*, p. 245), to Chesterton, who calls her a liar and bully (*George Bernard Shaw*, p. 158), to A. C. Ward, who admiringly says that she is "as various as Shakespeare's Cleopatra" (*Bernard Shaw* [London, 1951], p. 92).

umphs. In his epistle Shaw claims that *Man and Superman* has a profound sexual base, as opposed to most Victorian dramas which deal with sex relations in terms of a social problem (p. 487). He is only partially accurate, for although the drive of a woman's Life Force may be primally sexual, and Ann gives every sign of normalcy in this regard, Ann's specific problem is how to satisfy this urge in the face of propriety-ridden Victorian society. She is obviously in pursuit of her man, and almost everyone recognizes the fact, but the rigors of the chase must be balanced against Victorian decorum and the recalcitrance of the male. Thus Ann maneuvers Tanner into guardianship, attributes the responsibility for her motives to others, and utilizes Octavius as a temporarily useful foil. By using rather than challenging the hypocrisy of society, Ann works her own ends; were she not to be a hypocrite, she would be a fool, like Tanner.[19] Marriage is the social convenience which will ensnare the elusive man she admires and allow for fulfillment of both her and his potential. Consequently, any reasonable means to this end, such as social hypocrisy, is pragmatically justified.

The woman in love and social conniver in Ann are given additional dramatic power through archetypal overtones which are developed in a number of ingenious ways. Most obviously, Tanner's speculations about the Life Force woman give Ann a place in a cosmic framework. Tanner's theories, despite their qualification by the drama, tend to project her significance far beyond the immediate pragmatic concerns and render the joke of an inverted love chase susceptible to Olympian laughter. When Tanner asserts "the whole purpose of Nature embodied in a woman" (p. 537) he may not be accurate, he may be absurd, but his absurdity, in terms of Ann's vitality and perseverance, is poetically and dramatically evocative. Contributing to this poetic impetus is a prevailing metaphor for Ann which is built up most strongly in Act I—the image of woman as the predator and man as the prey,

19. Other critics have observed that Ann is forced into hypocrisy by society. More significant in terms of her character is the impression that she does not suffer in the role. Rather, she almost thrives in it, with an enthusiasm nearly amounting to enjoyment. See McCabe (*Shaw: A Critical Study*, p. 199), and Frederick P. W. McDowell, "Heaven, Hell, and Turn-of-the-Century London: Reflections upon Shaw's *Man and Superman*," *Drama Survey*, 2 (1963), 265.

developed through a reiteration of bestial appellatives. Tanner refers to Ann as a cat, a lioness, a grizzly bear, a Bengal tiger, and a boa constrictor. Although again Tanner misses the mark, the accretion of these images is as suggestive as it is humorous, moving Ann toward the mythical realm of Medusa and Grendel's dam. In addition, the images are given weight through dramatic extension. The lioness who swallows Tavy in three gulps has her correspondence in the girl who reduces the men by pet names to Annie's Granny, Ricky Ticky Tavy, and Jack the Giant Killer—diminuted forms in which they may more easily be managed and played with, as a cat might play with mice. The boa placed about Jack's neck is but a physical objectification of the predator who takes feline delight in observing the painful moral dance of the others regarding Violet. On one hand, Ann plays society's game in professing shock about Violet (whose aims are similar to her own), while on the other she is playing a personal game, watching the foolish mice tread the social maze. The revelation at the very end of the act that Ann knew of Violet's marriage all the while not only allows for a sensational drop of the curtain, but also evokes a flurry of afterthoughts which retrospectively haunt the scene with the image of Ann as the cat who is about to swallow its victim. The prey seems helpless before such feline duplicity.

Hector and Violet add further perspective to the social and dramatic scheme, primarily by serving as a comic variant and debased complement of the central romance. Hector exemplifies that American inferiority complex of the nineteenth century which turned toward foreign culture and foreign social respectability, a complex which found notable expression in Henry James and T. S. Eliot. Shaw gives this impulse social dimension by complicating it with the crossing snobbery of American wealth and English tradition. But, more important, while Hector is a counterpart of Octavius in idealizing love, he functions significantly as a clownish reflection of Tanner, harboring hazy illusions about the nobility of work, illusions founded on his actual incapacity and inexperience. His disregard of social realities and his propensity to go into idealistic clouds of his own offer a comic complement to similar qualities in the Revolutionist, and reveal, by simplification, how basically romantic many of Tanner's impulses are.

Violet offers a hardened reflection of Ann, an indication of what the heroine might be without natural charm and an idealistic spirit. Both Violet and Ann use society for their ends, but Violet's genius is bounded by social convention, while Ann operates with a personal freedom which is willing to stretch convention in terms of personal desires. Violet admires Hector's money, what it will buy, and his potential as a genteel male companion; Ann admires Tanner's ambition, vitality, and sense of higher values. Violet's consciousness is circumscribed and repressive, Ann's is open and expansive, but both are more keenly in touch with mundane reality than are their male counterparts. Thus Violet remarks, "You can be as romantic as you please about love, Hector; but you mustnt be romantic about money" (p. 581). The dead bird in Violet's hat at the end of Act I is a poignant detail, a precursor of Juan's image in Act III of man as a bird caught in the marital net, and of Ann's observation in Act IV that Octavius is like a bird who sings by pressing its breast against a thorn. Here the bird is Hector, wryly symbolized. This cat has already caught *her* bird.

The trumpery story, passing by the elaborate dialectic of Act III, bursts dynamically into Act IV. Dramatic economy matches dramatic vigor in resolving a doubly complex climactic problem. Not only must Mr. Malone be brought into line, but Tanner must capitulate as well. Typically, Shaw increases his problem by including abrasive social contentions between the characters, but as the personal difficulties are thereby compounded, the social context gains depth, and the resolution achieves dialectical significance as well as dramatic brilliance. The chauffeur Straker, detecting Irish derivation in the speech of the millionaire Malone, condescendingly remarks that he needs polish. The socially uneasy businessman Malone, scorning Straker's cockney origins and still rankling over the fact that his peasant father was starved by the English, has had the offer of two English ancestral homes. With a combined sense of revenge, profit, and romance he wishes to purchase a titled English wife for his son. Untitled, middle-class, pragmatic Violet, aware of the social stigma of marrying a descendant of Irish peasantry, seeks the obvious practical compensation:

"Hector must have money" (p. 660). But idealistic Hector berates his father for having the boorish audacity to open another's mail, and rejects the money. Incongruously, he seeks to be a worker, to attain manhood, and to be socially respectable in Violet's circle all at the same time.

The slice of social history and analysis which Shaw presents here is especially effective as it arises naturally from the characters, actually contributing to their individuality and depth by revealing their divergent social motivations. Issues which germinate in social abstractions grow in terms of deep personal convictions, and the comedy thereby gains the sociology of the abstractions, the psychology of the convictions, and the dramatic vigor of their contention. Malone's capitulation is thus unusually poignant as it is both acutely personal and profoundly social. Hector's rejection of his father's money cuts at Malone's expression of paternal love and evokes the father's deep awareness of what poverty means. Malone is broken in terms of his affection and his experience, and he rallies through both personal and social pride when others offer to support his son. Violet is at last the only means through which the situation may be salvaged, and she grasps her leverage with cool feminine instinct, exploiting her position for all it is worth. As Ann remarks, "Violet's hard as nails" (p. 673).

The sharpness and complexity of social confrontations in the first half of Act IV give way to the central theme in the last half as Tanner's metaphysics meet social realities in a climactic moment of truth. His theories at last come home to roost, but not according to his intellectual compartments. Ann indeed has qualities of the liar, the coquette, the bully, and the hypocrite, as he says, but these are almost as much social amenities as flaws. Her hypocrisy, though indulged in with a hint of personal delight, is primarily social and superficial. At its base is a hunger for reality as strong as Tanner's, and certainly nearer the facts. One reason she turns Octavius down is that she realizes the falseness of his illusions about her. She could never live up to his ideal, and would not want to try. Being so romantically naïve, Octavius is not quite a man, and this emptiness, combined with his lack of ambition, is no doubt behind her instinctive distaste at the impulse to kiss him.

In contrast, Ann can idealize, respect, and live with Jack because "he has no illusions about me." The reality of life offers far more excitement—and love—than the myth of romance: "I shall surprise Jack the other way. Getting over an unfavorable impression is ever so much easier than living up to an ideal. Oh, I shall enrapture Jack sometimes!" (p. 672). He is attractive because he is a Giant Killer, not susceptible to being swallowed in three gulps like Ricky Ticky Tavy. He may be absurd at times, but his is a noble absurdity, coadjutant to the mystique of manliness, and attended by sexual attraction. In short, Ann is clearly motivated by Jack's sense of reality about her, his ambition, and the Jupiter in him—all qualities which put him slightly beyond her control and consequently would add to the fascination, flexibility, and rich fulfillment of a marital relationship. The Life Force, if it is involved at all, is subliminal.

Tanner's true relationship to the Life Force is correspondingly oblique. Notably, in terms of the overt action it is less the Life Force which finally traps Tanner than Ann's feminine persistence, his own suppressed love for her, and accumulated social pressures. From early in Act I, as we have noted, he talks of her in terms of love and marriage but dodges the reasonable implication by transferring these categories onto Octavius's shoulders. His Life Force theory is partly an escape from personal realities via philosophical abstraction. In Act IV, however, Tanner becomes increasingly aware that he is not entirely a free agent. Society maneuvers and is maneuvered against him—Ann, Octavius, Mrs. Whitefield, Violet, Ramsden, and Straker all expect his marriage. He remarks on this a number of times, finally concluding, "We do the world's will, not our own. I have a frightful feeling that I shall let myself be married because it is the world's will that you should have a husband" (p. 680). He is again abstracting, for clearly his own affection is leading him on more than the world's will, and it is his friends, not quite the world, who see that Ann should have Jack, not just any husband. Compared with these immediate forces of mutual affection and common social expectations, the Life Force becomes Tanner's own pale rationalization, fit for play and bad punning, such as Ann's comment: "I dont understand it in the least: it sounds like the Life Guards" (p. 681). Tanner's awakening to personal reality is brought about by Ann near the end: "Men like you always get married"—a generalization too extreme to be accurate, but one which appeals to Tanner's actual emotions so poignantly that he responds, "How frightfully, horribly true! It has been staring me in the face all my life; and I never saw it before" (p. 681).

Thus Tanner is propelled into an elementary level of emotional and social consciousness which his theorizing mind had avoided. He is, however, but momentarily enlightened. He realizes a flaw in his facts, but not in his method. The manifestation of world of mind being blind to world of sense, of theory being out of touch with reality, remains to the end of the play. Earlier in the act Tanner fell precipitously into a social *faux pas* similar to those of Act I by urging that marriage laws are not morality—only to be once again undercut by the actual fact of Hector's marriage; and at the very end of the act he is off on further streams of talk. In the practical world his sense of philosophical reality is continually compromised by his psychological evasions and compulsive verbosity. The Life Force theory seems to be a superfluous hypothesis for what can be more readily explained in terms of sex, personality, and society. It may be interesting regarding evolutionary ends, but the end which Tanner faces is Marriage, and this is his dramatic, inexorable reality.

Throughout the play, then, the Life Force functions more as poetry than as philosophy. Ann as the archetypal predatory female is built up largely through Tanner's imagination; her deceptiveness as an artful, mildly sadistic and determined young lady is bloated into cosmic significance by his penchant for exaggeration. The most overt romantic movement of Act I—the boa embrace— is as boldly flirtatious as the action becomes until the final scene. A perceptible cosmic force is not displayed in the trumpery story (excluding Act III) until the moment late in Act IV when Tanner "*makes an irresolute movement towards the gate; but some magnetism in her draws him to her, a broken man*" (p. 679). At this point Tanner begins talking about the world's will, Ann throws away caution, and Tanner feels drawn on, exclaiming,

"The Life Force. I am in the grip of the Life Force" (p. 681). The archetypal echo which Ann sensed earlier when talking to Octavius occurs in Tanner's bewilderment: "When did this all happen to me before? Are we two dreaming?" (p. 683). With Tanner groaning and Ann panting, the two are drawn together. It is notable that while Tanner's resistance and Ann's aggressiveness build the scene dramatically into a grand contest, the cosmic context is counterpointed by the humor of Ann's comment about the Life Guards, her wily frankness, and the absurd sense of sexual melodrama wherein a commonplace biological attraction is grotesquely inflated. Ann uses every ploy of the Direct Approach, but, when this teeters toward inconclusiveness, she turns to a romantic Victorian convention—The Faint—which carries the day.

The melodrama of the climax is consequently fraught with humor, and the cosmic overtones remain just that, being profoundly qualified by the personal realities of the situation. Ann's magnetism and Tanner's helplessness most obviously reflect a commonplace sexual attraction. Tanner states it simply: "I love you." The fact that he cannot leave it at that, but must go on to make it metaphysical, mixing his philosophical abstraction with a romantic cliché, indicates his personal proclivities more than his philosophical accuracy: "The Life Force enchants me: I have the whole world in my arms when I clasp you" (p. 683). This comment is doubly revealing. In one sense he means that Ann enchants him; in another sense he is enchanted by his own abstraction. He is propelled on an ambivalent level where both count, and the world in his arms reflects a personal fulfillment regarding both Ann and his philosophizing. That this may all be an elaborate rationalization for sexual impulse does not occur to him, as it would not likely occur very strongly to anyone with such a basically romantic disposition. Shaw thus has his cosmic implications by suggestion, but in committing Tanner to them in no final sense commits his drama to them, since they function largely as tools of poetic effect. Tanner's capitulation has the richness of multifold causes, ranging from Ann's persistence and social determinism to his own compulsion and metaphysical rationale. As such,

Shaw elevates a romantic mundanity to a dramatically forceful conclusion.

In such comic-cosmic terms, trumpery story and philosophy coexist. The comedy tugs at the myth, and the myth augments the comedy. In metaphorical terms, meanwhile, Tanner's theory is integral, his intellect providing the context while Ann's instinct provides the action. Intellect, instinct, and society, all powerfully deterministic, struggle in a mutual confrontation which is resolved at the end of the play when each has its particular victory: intellectually, the metaphorical scheme is fulfilled as intellect unites with instinct; biologically, the man and woman are mated; socially, a respectable marriage is in the offing. Apart from Tanner's frequently bizarre conceptualization of them, these elements take on a life of their own as ghosts which can materialize quite differently in fact than in theory, appearing usually not as absolutes but as mutations run through the strainers of individual egos.[20] As such, their theoretical nature is qualified, but they gain dramatic reality.

In sum, as the characters sift and are sifted by metaphysical, biological, social, and personal forces, each element is compromised, qualified, and vitalized by the others. Ann is metaphysically a potential mother for the superman, biologically a predatory female, socially a guileful hypocrite, and personally a grown-up, determined little girl with a crush. Tanner is a noble Prometheus, a reluctant bachelor, a tolerated social clown, and a young man shouting forth his ideals. Similarly, though less precisely, Violet is ruthless womanhood, young love, ambitious snob, and self-centered female; Hector is victimized male, naïve husband, social idealist, and idle youth; Ramsden is conservative age, decaying liberal, and kindly friend; Straker is the genius of the new age, hotrodder, and knowledgeable servant; Malone is hard-nosed businessman, social climber, and pliable father; Mendoza is pragmatic leader, brigand, and romantic fool; Mrs. Whitefield is dear old

---

20. The play consequently limits the Calvinistic determinism of the Life Force as noted by McCabe (*Shaw: A Critical Study*, p. 201), and St. John Ervine, *Bernard Shaw: His Life, Work and Friends* (New York, 1956), p. 388.

mother, helpless scapegoat, and squeaky protestor. Contradictions between such diverse characteristics, instead of demolishing characterizations, are used to build them. The fabric of ideas is thus woven with fine art, since each character is not unitary, or a mere collection of masks, but a complex tension of forces and façades, within which lies the individual personality. As the façades of each interact with the façades of others, and as force plays against force, the dialectic becomes more intuitive than rational, and the drama gains complexity, scope, and energy. Shaw's distinction is that his sense of objective reality complements such poetic ambiguity by reflecting it against a social and philosophical context so that the two are mutually informing. The scene gains in total dimension and understanding as its idiosyncrasies are subject to an implicit frame of reference, while the frame of reference is qualified and jolted to life by the lively ambiguity of contentious characters.

Since Shaw wrote more in the tradition of the well-made play than he would have cared to admit, Act III of *Man and Superman* is exceptional, being as pure a play of ideas as he was to produce. The setting, *"omnipresent nothing . . . utter void"* (p. 600), and the sense of timelessness are forerunners of expressionist theater, as are the central concerns regarding the nature of reality and man's relationship to the universe. Paradoxically, the act is both extraneous and central to the drama which surrounds it. It can be dispensed with, and usually is, on grounds that it is just too long to include in an already full-length play. More significantly, it is in some aspects a digression, operates in a different mode from the rest of the material, delays the immediate well-made story line, and much of its subject matter is already implicit in the rest of the play. The play performs well without it. However, the scene does have a greatness and power which contribute strongly to the proximate action. It works as a variation on a theme, an intellectualization, a reflection on issues pertinent to the total context, and also promotes a sense of metaphysical, archetypal, and universal dimensions which stir up, point up, and broaden the implications of the play.[21] In one sense it elevates the action by relating it to myth and cosmology; in a further sense it chastens the action by subjecting it to a dialectic.

The most artful aspect of Act III is that it presents a reality inverse from that of the rest of the play. On earth, reality is the social game of the trumpery story, and as Tanner's abstractions run at cross purposes to omnipresent social assumptions he appears ridiculous and irrelevant. Social values are the *sine qua non* of life. In the hell scene, conversely, Tanner's contemplative ambitions (as represented by Don Juan) are the reality, while the social pursuits of hell are illusion. The society of earth has been consigned to hell, presumably below the stage trap and represented here by a sentimental Devil and a hedonistic Statue. Juan is triumphant over those same social attitudes which render Tanner foolish. The trumpery story is consequently given a new context which alters our appreciation of its nature and the significance of its characters. As the difference between heaven and hell is objectified by the difference between the contemplative spirit seeking self-understanding and the hedonistic spirit seeking happiness, Tanner is put on the side of the angels. He represents all that is positive and evolutionary, while society represents that which is stagnant, illusory, and self-destructive. His theories of the philosopher man versus the Life Force woman are given cosmic respectability, and the resulting inversion of fundamental assumptions as to what is real, realistic, and desirable gives the entire play a complex moral ambiguity. Ironic cross-currents serve to cross-fertilize aesthetics and thought. The comedy of Tanner is both leavened and deepened by allowing his philosophical notions free development, while Juan's metaphysics are made immanent through being parodied in the action. As sober second thoughts underlie the comedy, a smile attends the philosophy.

This smile is the result of a triple level of cross reference, Act III being linked to the rest of the play thematically as well as dramati-

21. The cosmic relevance of the act has been observed by McDowell ("Reflections upon *Man and Superman*," p. 267), and Martin Meisel, *Shaw and the Nineteenth-Century Theater* (Princeton, 1963), p. 181.

cally and psychologically. References in the first two acts to the diabolic, the Promethean aspect of Tanner, the Everywoman aspect of Ann, and Don Juan as Tanner's ancestor, followed by the Spanish Sierra environment and the novel band of brigands in Act III, function as dramatic steps in an increasing aura of fantasy which moves both the audience and Tanner into the dream world. The characters and ideas in hell are extensions of those in the play. There are images in common with other acts (man as bird caught in a net), character traits in common (the protagonist talks too much), and kindred speeches (in Act IV, Octavius romantically repeats the Statue's words regarding love in age). Most important, the hell scene unfolds as a reasonable projection of Tanner's subconscious. He is, after all, in Don Juan's country, and the Devil as Mendoza-sentimentalist, the Statue as Ramsden-hypocrite bound for hell, Doña Ana as Ann's Life Force threat, and Don Juan as Tanner-reformer-philosopher headed for heaven are all consistent with what might well be Tanner's metaphysical and metaphorical characterizations of them. He falls asleep disapproving of Mendoza's maundering over Louisa—the man is a monomaniac, the very devil of a sentimentalist; he sees Ramsden as a stony Statue, at last aware of reality—"Juan is a sound thinker, Ana. . . . I was a hypocrite" (pp. 609, 611). His Juan is a refined, ascetic idealization of himself, and Ana is his own naïve version of Ann—conventional, hypocritical, seeking at last a father for the superman. There is, in addition, fine implicit comic effect in the audacity which presumes to define the bounds of heaven and hell, an audacity and self-confidence quite like Tanner's. The scene, thus developed dramatically and psychologically as Tanner's, is second cousin to Strindberg's dream plays, implicitly centered, as they are, in a single dreaming consciousness, and developed in large part through the rambling associations of that consciousness.

However, as a dream play or a harbinger of expressionist drama, Act III is imperfect. The dreaming consciousness has a split personality which operates on two markedly different levels. Most cogently the dream is Tanner's, and serves to bind the play together in terms of his character. As an extension of his mind, its metaphysics and mode deriving from his preconceptions, prejudices, and forensic temperament, it offers more a tour de force of characterization than a coherent philosophy. Consistent with Tanner's insights, the dialectic and the myth are more immediately imaginative than ultimately convincing. The ideas are carried on streams of Tanneresque rhetoric, and the floating abstractions, vigorously but perversely applied to life, are related to his role in the play. Even the ends, bizarre, exaggerated, cosmologized, are Tanner's in substance, temper, and spirit.

But clearly, as effective as this character development is, it is only part of the essence of the act. Combined with it is the overriding consciousness of Shaw. While the dreaming Tanner confers a brisk and poignant immediacy to the dream, his fundamental naïveté becomes a subject for humor. In his exuberance his convictions approach the truth but suffer from his unique obfuscations. Consequently, set against this intemperance is a clearer view which serves to balance the philosophy by straightening its assumptions, perceptions, and directions. Explicitly, this authorial presence is indicated in Shaw's dramatic instinct to assign the dream also to Mendoza, a note which does not alter the scene's intrinsic Tanneresque character but does give the Devil's role more dialectical individuality. Implicitly, and more important, the playwright is apparent in several key aspects—first, in a sense of dramatic sharpness, in which the scene glows for its rhetorical brilliance, its contentious voices, and its inversions; second, in a pervasive sense of irony, notably removed from Tanner, irony scarcely being his forte; finally, in a sense of an overview which gives the scene a poetic frame of reference and binds it integrally to the play as a whole.

These two levels of consciousness serve as a subliminal complement to the vigorous dialectical voices in the scene itself. The one provides a comic link which connects the scene directly to the trumpery story, giving abstractions dramatic immediacy, while the other provides an oversoul which exploits the ironies between the drama and life, and searches more seriously for a direction between the ironies. In nearly every respect except the last, the act is a brilliant success. The extension of Tanner's consciousness in Juan, and less directly in the other hell personalities, gives the surface wit a substratum effectively founded in character. The ironic vision of the oversoul tempers all sorts of social and cosmic pomposities with a sensitive view of ignominious realities. But although this latter contributes a poetic, sardonic richness to the whole, it moves the play more toward ambiguity than resolution. Shaw's pervasive ironic-dramatic sensibility tends to undercut its own philosophic base, developing ambivalences which (similar to those in the trumpery story) make for effective art but poor philosophy. Those insights which are highly sensitive in rendering life as it is are erratic in projections regarding life as it ought to be. The playwright's wit feeds upon itself, energizing the drama at the expense of evolving a convincing thesis.

The short-range potential of this Shavian wit is impressive. Act III, despite its elaborate intellectual content, is infused with dramatic vigor through rhetorical power, diverse characters, dialectical pyrotechnics, and an imaginative, cosmic frame of reference. Such elements transcend the stigma of so much talk and so little action, giving the ideas a dynamic context or directly vitalizing the ideas themselves. On the most obvious level, witty details sustain the vigor both of the dialectic and of the drama. These are ubiquitous, from the highly facetious to the cuttingly apt. They leap forth in brief, sharp exchanges:

> THE OLD WOMAN. Happy! here! where I am nothing! where I am nobody!
> DON JUAN. Not at all: you are a lady; and wherever ladies are is hell. . . .
> THE OLD WOMAN. My servants will be devils!
> DON JUAN. Have you ever had servants who were not devils?
> [p. 604]

They emerge in droll observations, such as the Devil's comment on Milton:

> The Englishman described me as being expelled from Heaven by cannons and gunpowder; and to this day every Briton believes that the whole of his silly story is in the Bible. What else he says

I do not know; for it is all in a long poem which neither I nor anyone else ever succeeded in wading through. [p. 620]

Or they recur in thematic patterns, such as those which playfully and subtly effect the demolition of conventional moral attitudes:

> THE OLD WOMAN [on finding herself in hell] Oh! and I might have been so much wickeder! All my good deeds wasted! [p. 602]
> . . . Why am *I* here? I, who sacrificed all my inclinations to womanly virtue and propriety! [p. 604]

> THE DEVIL . . . But the English really do not seem to know when they are thoroughly miserable. An Englishman thinks he is moral when he is only uncomfortable. [p. 615]

> DON JUAN. [Marriage is] the most licentious of human institutions: that is the secret of its popularity. . . . The confusion of marriage with morality has done more to destroy the conscience of the human race than any other single error. [p. 633]
> . . . Nature, my dear lady, is what you call immoral. I blush for it; but I cannot help it. [p. 639]

More basic and effective in vitalizing thought are Shaw's inversions. By upsetting our expectations they are both dramatically startling and dialectically forceful. This he does on multifold levels. He inverts the moral significance of words and concepts—"Hell is the home of honor, duty, justice, and the rest of the seven deadly virtues" (p. 604); he inverts the traditional roles of characters, turning the usual versions of Juan and the Commander topsy-turvy (as the love chase is inverted in the play); and he inverts the significance of moral and spiritual platitudes by toppling to hell most mundane notions of heaven. The result is a disorientation of conventional assumptions, the shattering of old forms to make room for new.

Finally, the cerebral level moves with dramatic vitality through vigorous shifts of thought, allusion, emotion, and rhetoric which derive from the characters' marked differences in personality and viewpoint. For example, near the beginning of the hell scene the Devil recalls Juan's singing, and he breaks into "Vivan le fem-

mine!/Viva il buon vino!"—which the Statue takes up—"Sostegno
e gloria/D'umanità," and the following dialogue ensues:

DON JUAN. . . . Hell is full of musical amateurs: music is the
brandy of the damned. May not one lost soul be permitted to
abstain?
THE DEVIL. You dare blaspheme against the sublimest of the arts!
DON JUAN [*with cold disgust*] You talk like a hysterical woman
fawning on a fiddler.
THE DEVIL. I am not angry. I merely pity you. You have no soul;
and you are unconscious of all that you lose. Now you, Señor Commander, are a born musician. How well you sing! Mozart would
be delighted if he were still here; but he moped and went to
heaven. . . .
DON JUAN. I'll take refuge, as usual, in solitude.
THE DEVIL. Why not take refuge in Heaven? Thats the proper
place for you. [*To Ana*] Come, Señora! could you not persuade
him for his own good to try a change of air?
ANA. But can he go to Heaven if he wants to?
THE DEVIL. Whats to prevent him?
ANA. Can anybody—can *I* go to Heaven if I want to?
THE DEVIL [*rather contemptuously*] Certainly, if your taste lies
that way.
ANA. But why doesnt everybody go to Heaven, then?
THE STATUE [*chuckling*] I can tell you that, my dear. It's because
heaven is the most angelically dull place in all creation: thats why.
[pp. 612–13]

The dramatic vigor, suggestiveness, and cohesiveness of this
exchange reflects Shaw's aesthetic control. The implicit idea is carried by the explicit burst of song and by the contentious discussion, with its successive emotions of cynicism (Juan), indignation
(the Devil), disgust (Juan), irritation (the Devil), bewilderment
(Ana), contemptuousness (the Devil), and amusement (the
Statue). These emotions, besides stimulating the dialectic, help
to characterize the speakers—Juan, cynical, solitary, misanthropic;
the Devil, romantic, hedonistic; Ana, ignorant, confused, conventional; the Statue, spontaneous, good-humored, shallow. The na-

ture of hell is boisterously dramatized as vino, femmine, and song, and the level of intellectual development begins with Juan's reflection on this. His comment that hell is full of musical amateurs needs but a latinate turn to read "musical *amators*"—not lovers of music, but musical lovers, to whom music is intoxicating brandy, not, presumably, an aesthetic pleasure. The Devil is consequently twisting a bromide when he implies that *his* music is the sublimest of the arts, a bromide rendered doubly invalid by the sanctity in which he cloaks it. Juan's response to such rhetoric is withering, for obviously such talk is hysterically banal and irrelevant to the true nature of music. And equally indiscriminate is the Devil's dilettantish comment, "You have no soul," for Juan is borne out— Mozart went to heaven, clearly not delighted by the soul music of hell. Heaven, then, is the way of the moping Mozart, who is good and appropriate company for the misanthropic Juan. The Devil remarks that heaven is a matter of taste, which has been exemplified: the taste of the sensitive spiritual temperament as opposed to the taste of the flesh-bound soul. Ana, who assumes that conventionality and popularity go together with goodness and heaven, naturally misses the point. What is conventional is not, of course, necessarily good, and wine, women, and song are manifestly more popular than heaven. The Statue, who opened this brief exchange by singing of fleshly delights, appropriately ends it as a philistine chortling over the dullness of heaven. The metaphysics have progressed from hell to heaven, the dramatic context sharply illuminating a distinct impression of both, the conceptual unit closing with a sardonic, ironic chuckle. In the process, Shaw has rapidly and poignantly effected his definition.

A paradox of Shaw's method is that in this very wit and dramatic control he ultimately compromises his argument. While the wit and drama render the cosmology vital, the philosophy seems more dramatic than sound, the beauty of the rhetorical pyrotechnics more satisfying than the logic of the discourse. Indeed, the dramatic effectiveness of the dialectic goes hand in hand with its logical difficulties. The ingenious inversions of words, characters, and concepts make for startling dialectical effects, but their artistic virtues of vitality, uniqueness, new perspectives, and sharp insights are in large part due to their violation of coherent, readily accessible associations. Major trends of thought are frequently so qualified and twisted by rhetoric that inner conviction gives way to a succession of clever points. The unsophisticated audience may well be dazzled or impressed, yet come away from the performance with a most fragmentary sense of the central meaning. Such, at least, has been the case with not a few critics.[22]

In terms of Tanner's psychology, or in the mode of the dream play, the suprarationality of Act III is artistically appropriate. Even the irony, which is primarily artistic and witty, as frequently challenging as confirming logic, is highly successful within its particular range. But in terms of his central argument Shaw overindulges in iconoclasm, capricious wrong-headedness, and inconsistency. By so doing he loses some of the potential for a greater art which might have arisen out of his philosophy. Thus we have Juan's doubtful proposition of eugenic breeding and, reflecting Tanner, his incomplete view of women: "To her, Man is only a means to the end of getting children and rearing them" (p. 624). Equally distorted is his shallow, romantically oriented view of art: "The romantic man, the Artist, with his love songs and his paintings and his poems . . . led me at last into the worship of Woman" (pp. 628–29). And even more confusing is his shifting, superficial grasp of love and beauty. In one context they are physical and naïve, superior in birds over humans (pp. 626–27); in another context love is transcendent—"How do you know that it is not the greatest of all human relations? far too great to be a personal matter" (p. 638); and in yet a third context both are romantic—"Here there is nothing but love and beauty. Ugh! it is

22. Maurice Colbourne carelessly refers to Act III as coherent and lucid (*The Real Bernard Shaw* [New York, 1949] p. 156), and Ward cites its "clear argument" (*Bernard Shaw*, p. 96). Others have been more frank and accurate. Edmund Fuller refers to "over-abundant thought" (*G. B. S.: Critic of Western Morale* [New York, 1950], p. 43); Louis Kronenberger refers to "the scene's defects of logic, its perversities of argument" (*The Thread of Laughter* [New York, 1952], p. 247); and Brower speaks of lost meaning (*Major British Writers II*, p. 697). Shaw himself is aware of the problem when he mentions *Man and Superman* in his preface to *Back to Methuselah*: "The effect was so vertiginous, apparently, that nobody noticed the new religion in the centre of the intellectual whirlpool" (*Complete Plays*, III, lxxxviii–lxxxix).

like sitting for all eternity at the first act of a fashionable play" (p. 644). In all instances Juan is treading surfaces for the sake of making an allied dialectical point. Most obviously, he does the same sort of thing in closely proximate speeches regarding old age. He remarks, "In hell old age is not tolerated. It is too real," soon following with, "You see, Señora, the look was only an illusion. Your wrinkles lied . . . we can appear to one another at what age we choose" (p. 605), and later, "The humbug of death and age and change is dropped because here we are all dead and all eternal" (p. 607). The result is a combination of three maxims: old age is inevitable, none escape it; you are only as old as you think you are; and, age is meaningless in the context of immortality and eternity. All three are expressed by Juan as fact, whereas the first is canceled by the latter two, and fact truly lies in their ironic qualification of each other.

There is further confusion in an occasional inconsistency or misplacement of dialectical voices, and in weak, inadequate rejoinders by Juan which are left as definitive. Again, these may be excused as aberrations of the dreaming Tanner, but a dramatic and logical problem exists as the Shavian voice is an aesthetic factor. An early speech by the Statue, which includes, "For what is hope? A form of moral responsibility" (p. 610), sounds like Juan in both subject matter and rhetorical style. On similar grounds the Devil reflects Juan when he mentions "Justice, duty, patriotism, and all the other isms" (p. 621), and when he concludes, regarding the superman: "The 20th century will run after this newest of the old crazes, when it gets tired of the world, the flesh, and your humble servant" (p. 648). Juan is guilty of gross oversimplification in his response to the Devil's strong argument regarding the power of death over life on earth. He merely asserts that man overvalues himself as bold and bad, while in reality man is only a coward (p. 621). And when the Devil remarks, "You think, because you have a purpose, Nature must have one. You might as well expect it to have fingers and toes because you have them," Juan's response is woefully inadequate: "But I should not have them if they served no purpose" (p. 645). Further, when the Devil predicts that Juan, like all reformers, will experience "vain regrets for that worst and silliest of wastes and sacrifices, the waste and sacrifice of the power of enjoyment: in a word, the punishment of the fool who pursues the better before he has secured the good," Juan answers this penetrating, fundamental argument with a mere "But at least I shall not be bored" (p. 647). In sum, the dialectical dice are loaded, and while Shaw delights in strong antitheses, he sometimes dodges their implications. Had he maintained the act as a pure dream, its imbalances might have merely added to Tanner's character, but as it assumes greater pretensions, its lapses become flaws. Like Milton, Shaw is not really on the Devil's side, but his arguments against the Devil occasionally lack both balance and substance.

If we are sensitive to these lapses, we are perhaps less surprised by the greatest paradox of Shaw's entire Life Force philosophy—its fundamental conservatism. In expanding biological impulse into the Life Force, in interpreting the prophets as imperfect supermen, and in transmuting Jehovah into God in the Becoming, Shaw may convince the unwary that *Man and Superman* is "a revelation of the modern religion of evolution," but such a tag obscures the fact that this religion is as much a new dress as a new faith—more daring and contemporary than the old, but only thinly covering many attitudes basic to conventional Christian thought. Shaw is definitely not Christian in a doctrinal sense; his cosmology does not fit the slots of orthodox theology. But while Shaw's absolutes are not traditional, they have many aspects which are, and most of the moral implications he derives from them are decidedly Christian. Shaw's skeptical and rebellious stance has the virtue of subjecting old forms to irreverent scrutiny and a modern viewpoint, but finally it produces less an assertion of that which is truly revolutionary than an affirmation of old spiritual values, values revitalized and reemphasized by being shaken.

One key to the nature of a particular religion may be found in those souls it finds worthy of its heaven. In his heaven Shaw quaintly deposits that dwindling minority, "the saints, the fathers, the elect of long ago" (p. 615). These are the realists of Shaw's cosmos, for, as Juan remarks, "Heaven is the home of the masters of reality" (p. 616). Similarly, Shaw's moral base is remarkably old-fashioned. He provides a brief clue in his epistle: "The moral is a monkish one: repent and reform now; for tomorrow it may be too late" (p. 489). Thus Shaw's Don Juan story represents not a linear evolution from Tirso de Molina's *El Burlador de Sevilla*, as he claims elsewhere in the epistle; rather, it has many of the same morality play convictions and is preponderantly the last stage of a circular evolution. The central character may indeed appear quite different in the evolving versions: Tirso's rake of one thousand and three conquests was transmuted by the Romantic Age into a rebellious, freedom-seeking hero, and perverted by Shaw into a moralist and philosopher; the impetuosity and sensualism of Tirso's Juan are a far cry from the deliberateness and asceticism of Shaw's. But the moral theses of the two playwrights have much in common, both asserting that a life of sensuality, thoughtlessness, and irresponsibility will end in physical and spiritual destruction. Shaw has, most simply, merely switched the moral position of Tirso's Juan and the Commander—Juan is the moralist, as was Tirso's Commander; the Commander is the hedonist, as was Tirso's Juan. Shaw's Juan, from the vantage point of the hereafter, is more self-conscious and subtle than Tirso's Commander; his sense of social hypocrisy is keener, and he does not quite think in terms of sin and damnation, but the spiritual role of the two characters is similar. They are both on the side of God, and since Tirso is on the side of the Commander, and Shaw is on the side of Juan, the moral implications of the legend have come almost full circle.[23]

This hint of Shaw's conservatism opens medieval doors. As both he and Tirso oppose the epicurean, the self-indulgent, and the physical to the ascetic, the altruistic, and the spiritual, they are in a traditional vein. Shaw even more clearly than Tirso pur-

23. Thus I would qualify Bentley's observation that Shaw's Juan is similar to the original (*Bernard Shaw*, p. 51). Carl Henry Mills, in "*Man and Superman* and the Don Juan Legend," *Comparative Literature*, 19 (1967), 216–25, presents the most balanced view of the subject to date. In agreeing with Bentley, however, he does not allow for the self-conscious complexity of Shaw's characterization. For a more traditional approach, asserting that Shaw inverts the archetypal myth, see Robert J. Blanch, "The Myth of Don Juan in *Man and Superman*," *Revue des Langues Vivantes*, 33 (1967), 158–63. One might argue that Shaw's Juan is conceivably Tirso's Juan grown old and wise. But the aesthetic, perceptual, and philosophical quality of the two are so different that this seems most unlikely.

sues the medieval Christian dichotomies of flesh and spirit, *cupiditas* and *caritas*, reality and illusion, heaven and hell. He differs from the tradition, as we have noted, largely in his modernization of certain absolutes. For God he substitutes "Life," for Divine Providence he substitutes "Life Force." God as Life is evolving, seeking brains, self-consciousness, self-understanding. Divinity is thus more immanent than transcendent, and individual commitment to spiritual principles is more earth-oriented than in conventional doctrine, though one's mode of action should be motivated by the highest spirit. A by-product of spiritual self-consciousness is clear social vision, a vision cutting through the shallowness of ideals which rest on rhetorical symbols. In Tirso's play society offers moral direction, steering under implicit authority from God, while in Shaw only the vital and spiritual individual can steer, society being lost in moral aimlessness, drifting on its own foolish illusions.

Generally Shaw's modernism serves to stir up old spiritual distinctions. "Life" as Shaw's metaphor for God is in a long tradition of poetic and mystic attempts to delineate or symbolize the Absolute, and while Shaw allows deity considerable imperfection, treating it as a vital force in the process of evolution, his view of this force's ultimate, all-informing, ethereal nature verges on medieval mystic sensibility. Similarly, as Shaw's Life Force objectifies Divine Providence, it elicits the same Christan paradox: true free will is experienced in submitting oneself to the Life Force, as to the will of God. The man who rushes off on a tangent of his own under the guise of free will suffers extinction through irrelevance, as the sinner of Christianity suffers extinction through countering the reality of God.[24] Shaw gives this observation dramatic dimension through revealing that only in the role of Don Juan, in contemplative consciousness, can Tanner find true free-

24. Shaw's attraction to this paradox has been noted previously, in Britannus's desire for the greater freedom of slavery to Caesar above the nebulous freedom of being personally liberated. In the last year of his life Shaw briefly suggested the parallel I propose here, referring to "the mysterious activity I call the Life Force, and pious people call Providence" (*New Statesman and Nation*, 6 May 1950; reprinted in *Shaw on Theatre*, ed. E. J. West, Dramabook ed. [New York, 1959], p. 291).

dom as a spirit rising above society's thoughtless symbols and generalizations, a spirit presumably in accord with the Life Force and consequently free. Finally, Shaw's social distinctions, through being more sophisticated than those of Tirso's play, are actually more sensitively orthodox. Personal, social, and spiritual hypocrisy, all so frequently engendered by social pressures and aspirations, cloak subtle strains of *cupiditas*—a sure route to damnation, whether in Shaw or in Christianity.

With the talents of a modern playwright and the convictions of a socialist, then, Shaw blends morality play devices and the sensibility of a religious tradition. As he observes in his preface to *Saint Joan*, his dramatic technique and outlook are medieval when compared with Shakespeare's,[25] and his comment in the epistle that his conscience is the genuine pulpit article (p. 486) is frankly set in a context of religious commitment which informs (or transforms) his socialism. Thus Shaw's Devil, who diverts men from their real purpose into drifters (p. 642), resembles the Tempter of Mankind in the morality plays, and the Devil's comment that "I cannot keep these Life Worshippers" (p. 648) gains antiquarian poignancy in sounding like a morality play Satan foiled by the faithful of God. Conceptually, the Bergsonian metaphor of Tanner as intellect and Ann as instinct synthesizing in intuition is matched hauntingly by the suggestion of a more cosmic metaphor of the spiritual Father joining with the immortalized Mother to produce the incarnate Son. Shaw affirms this grander analogue in commenting on Ana: "For though by her death she is done with the bearing of men to mortal fathers, she may yet, as Woman Immortal, bear the Superman to the Eternal Father."[26]

25. *Complete Plays*, II, 311–12.

26. "Program Note [to] Don Juan in Hell," *Complete Plays*, III, 746. My application of the Bergsonian dialectic as a metaphorical base for the play is a variant of the interpretations of four critics who, remarkably, all had kindred epiphanies published in 1963. Meisel delineates the Life Force dichotomy as "projective intellectual aspiration" and "generative vital impulse" (*Shaw and the Nineteenth-Century Theater*, pp. 182–83); McDowell delineates it as "radical intelligence" and "primordial energy" ("Reflections upon *Man and Superman*," pp. 259–60). More simply, Daniel J. Leary interprets it as spirit in conflict with matter ("Shaw's Use of Stylized Characters and Speech in *Man and Superman*," *Modern Drama*, 5

The hope which resides in this ultimate analogue is tentative, and its power depends in large part upon faith, whether one be Christian or Shavian. For Shaw has many of the same difficulties in defining his God as had the Middle Ages. Appropriately Juan comments, "Heaven cannot be described by metaphor" (p. 617). How can one make infinite spirit and ultimate ends intelligible to finite imagination? How is the playwright to render them dramatically, and how is the philosopher to make them comprehensible? Shaw starts by shaking the platitudes which a mundane society creates, in its poverty of language and thought, to express its ill-defined ideals. Thus joy, love, happiness, and beauty are espoused by the Devil (p. 611), and thus Juan speaks of hell as "the home of honor, duty, justice, and the rest of the seven deadly virtues" (p. 604). The point is, as Juan observes later, that beauty, purity, respectability, religion, and so forth "are nothing but words which I or anybody else can turn inside out like a glove" (p. 643). And this is precisely what Shaw does, to destroy the sacredness of these false gods. To properly assess reality, or to approach God, one must distinguish between the symbol and the fact. Shaw's psychic inversion of the roles of Juan and the Commander is a forceful, dramatic extension of this observation. But once the point is acknowledged and we are refreshed by a freedom from the tyranny of symbols, where are we? Our minds may have been cleared of cant, but surely this is only the first step toward a higher consciousness. At this juncture we may object that earlier Juan remarked regarding heaven, "You live and work instead of playing and pretending" (p. 617)—an assertion which rings with a good sound, but which, according to Shaw's own iconoclasm, may be questioned. Are living and working any more meaningful or sacrosanct than love and beauty? May they not just as easily be turned inside out by a relentless nihilist? Similarly, Juan speaks of the realities learned from toil and poverty (p. 618), but he does not define these realities, and we suspect that were they defined

---

[1963], 478); and John G. Demaray analyzes it as a tension between mind and body ("Bernard Shaw and C. E. M. Joad: The Adventures of Two Puritans in Their Search for God," PMLA, 78 [1963], 263).

they would likely be idiosyncratic to Shaw's social views. The assumption that toil and poverty are somehow a key is one which confines reality more than defining it. Clearly, once Shaw enters topsy-turvydom, all abstractions are subject to the game, and Juan's arguments are self-defeating in a world of infinite convolutions and relativities. His convictions, the foundation of his dialectic, ultimately become a faith in the transcendence of some qualities over others, and, like all faiths, his can be granted only a degree of possible truth, being confined by the limitations and aberrations of his consciousness.

Juan's faith, quite predictably, seems to emerge as a blend of metaphysics and socialism, the vagueness of the first compromised by and compromising a melodrama of the second. His sense of reality leads to notions of social revolution and then transcends social goals as it transcends humanity into a mysterious land of spiritual perfection. The suprarational (or irrational, in a pejorative sense) thrust of Juan's argument is expressed in his remark that man "can only be enslaved whilst he is spiritually weak enough to listen to reason" (p. 623). Intellectually, with symbols inverted and reason subverted, the dialectic moves toward chaos. While Juan denies being a spiritual hypochondriac (p. 628), we suspect that to some extent Shaw is one. Thus Shaw falters, and his metaphysical ends become even vaguer than those of conventional Christianity. He has undoubtedly overreached himself, and we may realize parenthetically that Christian symbols have more value as hooks on which we can hang our imagination than danger as snares which snag us. The problem, of course, is less in the symbols than in our use of them.

In sum, Juan speaks of contemplating reality while Shaw renders his reality relative. Since in practice Shaw ultimately sacrifices logic for intuition, it seems ironic that he typifies heaven as primarily mental. Shaw's hell is easy to comprehend: it is the world, with its vanities, hypocrisies, and illusions. As Juan says, "Hell is a city much like Seville" (p. 604). But his heaven, deprived of hell's symbols, is incomprehensible, and Juan's denial of the flesh for the Greater Glory sounds much like Christianity's divine excuse for inhumanity: there'll be pie in the sky by and by.[27] In abnegating flesh and the world, Juan abnegates the most immediate realities of life, delimiting his character to its cerebral essence in which spirituality is no more than vaguely implicit. As such, he is but a fragment, and the play requires living correlatives in Tanner to gain dramatic fullness and credibility. And Juan's ill-defined absolute is but an extension of his own spiritual austerity, etherealized out of human relevance. Is this the goal toward which man must steer? The Ancients in the last part of *Back to Methuselah* objectify the cerebral sterility of Shaw's conceptualization.[28]

Compensating for the weakness of details in Shaw's argument and for the vagueness of his ends are the scope of his artistic conception and the vigor of its execution. Shaw's drama and spiritual quest are energized more by the power of iconoclastic probing and the creation of imaginative new contexts than by fully consistent or fully developed ideas. Shaw the vitalist may be caught in the dramatic impetus of his dialectic, and vitality may at times become more important than logic, but as his basic contribution involves a revitalization process, such means are inextricably bound to his ends. Thus he plugs his own genius and the twentieth century into the old metaphors of Christianity, charging Act III with a mental energy which complements the dramatic energies of the trumpery story. The roll of the rhetoric, the inventiveness of the dialectic, and the keenness of the wit are no doubt more impressive than sound, but here these qualities have a special poetry which reaches through philosophy to music and

27. McDowell likens Shaw's hell to a West End drawing room ("Reflections upon *Man and Superman*," p. 251). Desmond MacCarthy, no doubt like many of us, is apparently fond of West End drawing rooms, and would prefer their sort of hell to Shaw's astringent heaven (*Shaw's Plays in Review* [New York, 1951], p. 36). Such a view represents a mundane problem which Shaw does not overcome. It merely confirms his basic premise: most in the audience are damned.

28. C. E. M. Joad is most devastating, describing it as "a philosophy of Life arising from a nothingness and developing in a vacuum in pursuit of a purpose which is left undefined" ("Shaw the Philosopher," in *Shaw and Society: An Anthology and a Symposium*, ed. C. E. M. Joad [London, 1951], p. 243). While Joad is not precisely accurate on the first two counts, his frustration with the third tends to justify the whole. Similar sentiments occur to Kronenberger (*George Bernard Shaw*, p. 246) and Ervine (*Bernard Shaw*, p. 392).

delight. A deeper didacticism is perhaps served as intellect is or-
chestrated, with its movements producing an aesthetic experience
in and of themselves. Most important, by presenting a reality
inverse from that of the rest of the play, Act III provides a rich
cross-reference between philosophy and life, abstraction and fact,
caritas and *cupiditas*. As it is a dramatic, psychological, and metaphysical extension of the rest, it elevates the total play on multifold levels while unifying it with a broad frame of reference. Thus
despite (and partly because of) its imperfect philosophy, *Man
and Superman* evolves as fine art.

A factor which is to some degree inherent in the discussion of
any Shaw play, but which calls for special attention here, is Shaw's
authorial presence. This is most distinctive in Act III, but it is also
strongly implicit in the trumpery story, and one cannot speak of
the aesthetics of the play without being sensitive to aspects of the
playwright's ubiquitous ghost. In part, audiences attend a Shaw
play to hear it, and though Shaw is eminently successful both in
mutating and transfusing his presence into dramatic situations,
here it reverberates more noticeably and functions more intrinsically than in his other plays. We have observed, for instance, that
while Tanner's dream sequence may be dramatically and psychologically linked to his role in the rest of the play, its level of subconscious movement is counterpointed by Shavian dialectical
patterns and wit. The total consciousness has a multiplicity and
coherence which are something more than the sum of the dramatic parts. Thus, while Juan is a subconscious projection of
Tanner, he is also an alter ego of Shaw—dramatically an extension
of the play, dialectically suspended between characterization, abstraction, and author. Tanner, as society's divine fool, is in many
ways a caricature of Shaw; Juan, as Tanner's idealized abstraction,
is at times an adventuresome, gamesome Shavian mouthpiece.[29]

29. Although Bentley comments that Tanner is not Shaw (*Bernard Shaw*, pp.
55–56), and Crompton compares him in detail to H. M. Hyndman (*Shaw the
Dramatist* pp. 82–83), others have noted the autobiographical vein. See Hesketh
Pearson, *George Bernard Shaw: His Life and Personality*, Atheneum ed. (New
York, 1963), page references in subsequent notes; McCabe, *Shaw: A Critical Study*,
p. 197; Irvine, *The Universe of G. B. S.*, pp. 239–44; Brustein, *The Theatre of*

Evidence regarding this multiple consciousness abounds both inside and outside the play. At one point Juan begins with a Tanneresque social observation: "When the Spaniard learns at last that he is no better than the Saracen, and his prophet no better than Mohamet, he will arise, more Catholic than ever, and die on a barricade across the filthy slum he starves in, for universal liberty and equality." He then extends it to a metaphysical goal which is specifically his own: "Later on, Liberty will not be Catholic enough: men will die for human perfection, to which they will sacrifice all their liberty gladly" (p. 623). The first represents a somewhat too violent version of Shaw the socialist; the second represents an idealistic assertion, slightly beyond Shaw the visionary. Similarly, on a personal level, Juan remarks, "When the lady's instinct was set on me, there was nothing for it but lifelong servitude or flight. . . . It was not love for Woman that delivered me into her hands: it was fatigue, exhaustion" (pp. 640, 642). In terms of Tanner we see this as comic, since it is displayed with dramatic immediacy, and the panting, capitulating Tanner is not entirely the unwilling victim. In terms of Juan the immediacy has faded into introspective observation. It is an abstraction, a declaration of sexual and social fatalism. However, in terms of Shaw's own marriage Tanner's experience is a bizarre exaggeration, while Juan's account is a wry rationale, stretching the facts, but conceptually, cynically appealing. One of the Devil's final comments —"Beware the pursuit of the Superhuman: it leads to an indiscriminate contempt for the Human" (p. 648)—sounds like an admonishment echoing in Shaw's own mind. It applies to Tanner, who, blinded by ideals, fumbles in society. It is apropos to Juan, whose cerebral search unbalances his total view, rendering him uncharitable to emotional and social realities. But finally, it seems highly personal to the playwright, who was on the brink of disillusionment with democracy, being profoundly upset by mankind's persistent banality.

Such evidences of multiple consciousness contribute to and are

---

Revolt, p. 219; and McDowell, "Reflections upon *Man and Superman*," p. 263. Pearson is most detailed and Brustein most incisive, but none fully explores the unique aesthetics of this element.

augmented by an autobiographical aura which surrounds the play. Although Shaw asserted that Tanner was a caricature of the socialist H. M. Hyndman (whom in many distinctive qualities he indeed resembles), Granville-Barker assumed the more dramatic caricature and was made up as a youthful Shaw when he performed the role for the first production in 1905.[30] Much later, in *Sixteen Self Sketches,* Shaw admits, "In the final act . . . the scene in which the hero revolts from marriage and struggles against it without any hope of escape, is a poignantly sincere utterance which must have come from personal experience. . . . Tanner, with all his extravagances, is first hand: Shaw would probably not deny it and would not be believed if he did."[31] Numerous details bear this out. Like the young Tanner, Shaw had set fire to a field, and another boy was blamed; like Tanner he had thrilled in playing wicked roles, finding villains more interesting than heroes; and like Tanner he had awakened at an early age to a "moral passion," first through omitting his nightly prayers, and later through reading Henry George and Karl Marx.[32] The morality derived from this passion was, like Tanner's, of an Ibsenesque variety—questioning, inconoclastic, true to his own inner sense of integrity above the confusion and hypocrisy of society's norms. The socialism which woke out of this passion, also like Tanner's, was of a Fabian variety—genteel but fervent, revolutionary but scarcely violent. And finally Shaw found himself in Tanner's frustrating position, famed more as a great talker than as a great socialist—a celebrity of iconoclasm, amusing, challenging, but ultimately no prime mover when set against the preconceptions of a status quo world.

As a reluctant bachelor like Tanner, Shaw did not lose his virginity until he was twenty-nine, at which time he was "virtually raped" by an aggressive widow, Jenny Patterson. He did not marry Charlotte Payne-Townshend until he was forty-two. Jenny can in many ways be seen as Shaw's prototype for the sexually aggressive,

---

30. Pearson, *Shaw: His Life and Personality,* pp. 74n., 226.
31. George Bernard Shaw, *Sixteen Self Sketches* (New York, 1949), pp. 199–200.
32. Pearson, *Shaw: His Life and Personality,* pp. 43–45.

jealous female which emerges in Ann, and Shaw's procrastination about marrying Charlotte emerges in Tanner's reticence to be captured by Ann. As Shaw wrote to Ellen Terry a year after he met Charlotte and a year before his marriage: "I am at present scudding close reefed before a gale. Oh why wont women be content to leave their stars in the heavens and not want to tear them down and hang them around their necks with a gold ring!"[33] Shaw's early bachelor days, spent in self-education and one-pointed pursuit of socialistic and artistic ends, remind one of Tanner's declaration: "The true artist will let his wife starve, his children go barefoot, his mother drudge for his living at seventy, sooner than work at anything but his art" (pp. 537–38). Shaw avoided the starving wife by marrying a "millionairess"; he avoided the barefoot children by not imposing his sex on Charlotte; but in his many early London years he did shamelessly live off of his mother. In his words, "I did not throw myself into the struggle for life: I threw my mother into it."[34]

While there are obvious differences between Shaw's marriage and Tanner's, a number of similarities are striking. Charlotte was ostensibly more pursued than pursuer, but in Shaw's account of their two-year courtship one may sense in her a quiet duplicity, possibly unconscious, which is a gentle echo of Ann. Charlotte was very much a lady, and both Victorian propriety and feminine discretion dictated that she in no way present herself as the aggressor. We have observed that this is in large part Ann's problem. Regarding Charlotte, Shaw wrote to Ellen Terry: "Well, shall I marry my Irish millionairess? She . . . believes in freedom, and not in marriage; but I think I could prevail on her. . . . She knows the value of her unencumbered independence."[35] Circumspectly, Charlotte was quite possibly appealing to Shaw's preconceptions and vanity, since she was adapting herself to his picture of the independent woman in *The Quintessence of Ibsenism*, where,

33. 14 July 1897. *Ellen Terry and Bernard Shaw: A Correspondence*, ed. Christopher St. John (New York, 1932), p. 168.
34. Pearson, *Shaw: His Life and Personality*, p. 60.
35. 4 and 5 November 1896. St. John, ed., *Terry-Shaw Correspondence*, pp. 87, 88.

Shaw commented, "She found, as she thought, gospel, salvation, freedom, emancipation, self-respect and so on." What better way for a lady to entice a pretentiously confirmed bachelor? Render him unwary, render him doubtful, but appeal to his vanity and prejudices, and give him the hope that "I think I can prevail upon her." In this context the most notable thing is that Shaw procrastinated for two years.

The final forcing of the issue for Shaw was humorously close to that of the play. Prospects seemed so remote in 1898 that Charlotte left with the Webbs for a round-the-world tour. She got no farther than Rome when she received word that Shaw had broken down from exhaustion and was crippled by a diseased foot. Charlotte abruptly terminated her holiday and, like Ann, scurried across Europe to ensnare her man. Shaw, much like Tanner, was exhausted, weak, and cornered. He was as helpless physically as Tanner is psychically. To nurse him back to health, it seemed advisable that they go to the country together, an action which in those times could have definitely compromised a lady. So they decided to marry, more as a concession to propriety than as a romance, Shaw being surrounded by the same sort of social pressures that trap Tanner. For Charlotte the situation was even more opportune than Ann's: to Shaw she assumed the awesome triple powers of mother, nurse, and wife—like society and Ann's boa, a formidable combination. Though fame and wealth combined could have given them a grand wedding, the marriage took place at the West Strand Registry Office, the same sort of bleak environment in which Tanner insists he will be married to Ann. Writing to Beatrice Webb about it shortly afterward, Shaw remarked: "The thing being cleared thus of all such illusions as love interest, happiness interest, & all the rest of the vulgarities of marriage, I changed right about face on the subject and hopped down to the Registrar, who married me to her on one leg."[36] The words and situation are similar in tone to Tanner's last major speech: "What we have both done this afternoon is to renounce happiness, renounce freedom, renounce tranquility, above all, renounce the

36. 21 June 1898. Quoted in Henderson, *Shaw: Man of the Century*, p. 420.

romantic possibilities of an unknown future, for the cares of a household and a family" (p. 686). In neither Shaw's case nor Tanner's were the future prospects quite so grim, but the last gasps of assertive independence echo in both the living and the fictional situations.[37] Almost symbolically, Charlotte bought the ring and license, and on their honeymoon Shaw wrote a book.

And so Shaw was married, not entirely by accident, but under circumstances in which chance and female determination had laid urgent conditions and obligations upon free will. The daring genius and unconventional bachelor had now to admit to that mundane common denominator, the connubial parlor. No doubt a certain vacuum was apparent between the deed and a fully convincing rationale for the deed. Into this vacuum flowed Shaw's sense of the absurd, his Life Force conjectures, his moral vision, his social perceptions, and his dramatic talent, many of which did not exactly fit his case but most of which were proximate. *Man and Superman* provided an outlet and extension for personal musings upon the traditional pattern into which he had fallen. Shaw reveals a little of the domestic comedy of Socrates as well as of Tanner when he writes in his epistle, "I find in my own plays that Woman, projecting herself dramatically by my hands (a process over which I assure you I have no more real control than I have over my wife), behaves just as Woman did in the plays of Shakespear" (p. 496). One may recall a comment of Nietzsche to which Shaw was fond of referring, and which no doubt found its way implicitly into *Man and Superman*:

The philosopher abhors *wedlock* and all that would fain persuade to this state—as being an obstacle and fatality on his road to the

37. Thus I disagree with the arguments of Strauss (*Shaw: Art and Socialism*, p. 45) and Ivor Brown (*Shaw in His Time* [London, 1965], pp. 85–88) that Shaw does not analyze his own marriage in *Man and Superman*. Brown records a diary entry by Beatrice Webb in the summer of 1896: "Charlotte and G. B. S. have been scouring the country together and have been sitting up late at night. To all seeming she is in love with the brilliant Philanderer and he is taken in his cold sort of way" (pp. 84–85). If this is juxtaposed to Shaw's words regarding Charlotte on 5 November 1896—"And she doesnt really *love* me. The truth is, she is a clever woman" (St. John, ed., *Shaw-Terry Correspondence*, p. 88)—a slight disparity is clear. All hints are that tenuous realms of affection were indeed being exploited by a clever woman.

optimum. Who among the great philosophers is known to have been married? Heraclitus, Plato, Descartes, Spinoza, Leibniz, Kant, Schopenhauer—they were not; nay, we cannot even so much as conceive them as married. A married philosopher is a figure of *comedy*, this is my proposition; and that exception, Socrates, mischievous Socrates, married, it seems, *ironice*, with the express purpose of demonstrating *this very* proposition.[38]

Nietzsche's italics are curiously apropos to the central concerns both of Shaw's play and of Shaw's life at the turn of the century. Ellen Terry later expressed it just as bluntly and more personally: "I hope you and Charlotte are frightfully well and happy. Arent you funny, preaching against marriage, and marrying. Against other things, and doing 'em!"[39] Shaw must to some extent have agreed. So, in part, he had written *Man and Superman*.

Juan's aloof view glosses over the disparity between Tanner's marriage and Shaw's. To the Shaws, both in their forties, matrimony was more a matter of mutual convenience and comfort than a sexual relationship, and Life Force, superman, or even a string of little Shaws was hardly a consideration. Charlotte did not like children; Shaw thought sex impersonal, monstrous, and indecent.[40] In any modern middle-class terms they were in such matters neurotic. But the principle behind mating and its importance to the individual, the society, the race, and the cosmos were longstanding Shavian concerns, and his reflections on sex as related to these factors are revealed most fully through Juan, with whom he has a spiritual kinship. As early as 1887 he wrote a short narrative, "Don Giovanni Explains," in which his own experience and attitudes are clearly linked to the Don Juan legend.[41] Shaw represents

38. *The Works of Friedrich Nietzsche*, ed. Alexander Tille; vol. X: *A Genealogy of Morals*, trans. William A. Haussmann (New York, 1924), p. 144. Cited by Henderson, *Shaw: Man of the Century*, p. 580. Juan, of course, puts Nietzsche in heaven (p. 649).

39. 28 November 1906. St. John, ed., *Terry-Shaw Correspondence*, p. 315.

40. Pearson, *Shaw: His Life and Personality*, p. 109. Juan's comment on the impersonality of sex (p. 637) is typically Shavian.

41. *Works* (London, 1932), VI, 93–116. Quotations here are from p. 103. Both Pearson (*Shaw: His Life and Personality* p. 116) and Crompton (*Shaw the Dramatist*, pp. 92–94) note some of the autobiographical elements of this piece.

himself through Giovanni in a passage which anticipates Juan and Tanner: "In my youth and early manhood, my indifference to conventional opinions, and a humorously cynical touch in conversation, gained me from censorious people the names atheist and libertine; but I was in fact no worse than a studious and rather romantic freethinker." Jenny Patterson's assault is scarcely transmuted: "At last a widow lady at whose house I sometimes visited, and of whose sentiments towards me I had not the least suspicion, grew desperate at my stupidity, and one evening threw herself into my arms and confessed her passion for me." In a similar light we have Ann with her boa in Act I and her panting attack in Act IV tied together by Tanner's theories about the predatory woman and by Juan's reminiscences in Act III: "When the lady's instinct was set on me, there was nothing for it but lifelong servitude or flight" (p. 640).

Shaw's trouble with Jenny's fierce jealousies emerges in the romantic possessiveness of Giovanni's lady, in Tanner's desperation with Ann, and in Juan's ladies, who remarked in a proprietory tone: "When will you come again?" (p. 629). Finally, Giovanni's afterlife is a precursor of Juan's in *Man and Superman*, with a sentimental devil opposed to an intellectual heaven, the two being separated by a barrier of temperament. The fact that this material spanned sixteen years with so few substantive changes indicates something of its permanency in Shaw's mind. Shaw put Jenny's jealousy into *The Philanderer*, but that was autobiography only in terms of an embarrassing scene. Clearly, through Juan and Tanner, as grown out of Giovanni, he was working in a fuller spectrum, one which "was to put all intellectual goods in the shop window under the sign of Man and Superman."[42]

The net result in *Man and Superman* is a psychological-philosophical substratum, inherent in the tenuous link between caricature, abstraction, and playwright, which comprises perhaps the most subtle aesthetic level of the play. In its fullest sense this substratum represents spiritual autobiography, explored first on a level of self-parody and fun in Jack Tanner and second on a level

42. Preface to *Back to Methuselah, Complete Plays*, II, lxxxix.

of personal moral and spiritual analysis in Don Juan. In Tanner, Shaw evokes a number of aspects of his own personality and history, projecting them so that they may be more dispassionately examined, caricaturing himself so that both his virtues and his faults, his nobility and his absurdity, his truths and his confusions may be more accessible to both himself and his audience. Simple statement or understated characterization could in no such effective way achieve either the clarification of the issues involved or the context of poignant, meaningful fun that the character of Tanner achieves in its confrontation with the social milieu. Tanner is a personal objectification of the immediate agonies, absurdities, biological thwartings, and social capitulations which beset the idealist in his pursuit of noble principles. In contrast, Juan offers the philosophical perspective of looking back on all these pangs and arrows of fortune in retrospect, generalizing and abstracting the seeming caprices of life in terms of a sort of order, a personal philosophy. His virtues are Shaw's, extolling contemplation and work above thoughtlessness and play. His heaven is the Shavian heaven of impassioned thought, pure mind. Thus, as Tanner is parable and parody, Juan is commentary, the serious and the comic moving with a fine balance through these two characters, each qualifying the other. The sum evolves into a dramatic and poetic synthesis which is both effective art and a dramatic representation of the Shavian psyche of 1903.

The fullness of this expression and its aesthetic integrity not only survive its logical flaws but are also indebted to the foibled, idiosyncratic humanness of those flaws. A sense of personal freedom lies at the aesthetic heart of *Man and Superman* in terms akin to Bergson's: "In short, we are free when our acts spring from our whole personality, when they express it, when they have that indefinable resemblance to it which one sometimes finds between the artist and his work."[43] The freewheeling dialectic bears such a temperamental resemblance to Shaw in its vigor, humor, presumptions, and ends that autobiographical details which the

43. Henri Bergson, *Time and Free Will*, trans. F. L. Pogson (London, 1910), p. 172.

author drops into his work take on an active, personal significance, and the play is infused with the dynamic sense of an informing spirit unfolding and discovering itself.

Shaw's shop window contains more than Tanner and Juan. Autobiography and self-examination emerge elsewhere, such as in his satire of Mendoza's band of tag-end socialists and anarchists. Here are portrayed the simpler-minded aspects of socialism with which he so frequently contended, and the obsessiveness of political outsiders who clearly annihilate themselves in social irrelevance.[44] Roebuck Ramsden may also represent Shaw's personal apprehension regarding the tendency of individual liberalism to freeze as liberals grow old, removing them from the vanguard to the ice chest of reform. Shaw was already beginning to hear himself referred to as a "classic," and he sensed the partial paralysis that accompanies the reverence of such a term. A very few years earlier he had given up his series of weekly lectures on socialism, less because he lacked time than because he was becoming popular with the middle classes and inaccessible to the proletariat. His lectures made more money than converts. Like Ramsden, he had nearly been absorbed by that spongy monster, the Establishment; his platform oratory was admired as the idiosyncratic outpouring of genius, marvellous rhetoric, more to be listened to than heard. Shaw almost sputters (as much as he can sputter) in his epistle: "Why, even I, as I force myself, pen in hand, into recognition and civility, find all the force of my onslaught destroyed by a simple policy of non-resistance" (p. 512). And again, in a letter to Forbes-Robertson, dated 21 and 22 December 1903: "They used to laugh when I was serious; but now the fashion has changed: they take off their hats when I joke, which is still more trying."[45]

Thus Shaw, whose greatest fame as a spokesman for the *avant-garde* was truly just getting off the ground, at the incipience of the prominent intellectual role he was to play in the first decades

44. Alick West, Shaw's Marxist critic, was infuriated into calling this scene "a stupid, tasteless parody" (*"A Good Man Fallen among Fabians"* [London, 1950], p. 98). Once again, West reflects more the limitations of Marxism than of Shaw.

45. Quoted in Pearson, *Shaw: His Life and Personality*, p. 223.

of the twentieth century,[46] sensed the paradox which later was to make him old hat in a society of innumerable new hats. At a time when his influence was expanding, his psyche was turning inward in bemused frustration; the outgrowth of this ironic state of affairs was, in part, *Man and Superman*. In desperation over man's stupidity and recalcitrance regarding reform, Shaw asserts an essentially totalitarian social theory and melioristic metaphysical theory. But these are admittedly intuited, tentative, and metaphorical. When in Tanner they are tested against the vicissitudes of a dramatic situation, they falter—idealism scarcely triumphs in an indifferent society—and when in Juan they are expressed as faith, they seem imaginative but incredible. Act III universalizes the play, but at the same time has sufficient power to make the play seem trivial; the play in turn particularizes the generalizations of Act III, and in so doing mocks them. A fine ironic balance is thus achieved which ultimately reasserts Shaw's original dilemma. The obvious lack of resolution which results frustrates any clear socialistic or philosophical conclusion. But in the essence of their suspended juxtaposition the ironies are dramatically and aesthetically fruitful, providing ambiguities with which life and art are fraught. These ambiguities Shaw combines with an autobiographical reflection on his own marriage, its details and rationale, so that the social and philosophical is linked to a sense of the personal, all on a bizarre but penetrating comic-cosmic level. What we have is an exploration of reality and self in Bergsonian terms: "There is one reality, at least, which we all seize from within by intuition and not by simple analysis. It is our own personality in its flowing through time—our self which endures."[47] Or, in Juan's terms, we have an inversion of Descartes: "I am, therefore I think" (p. 631). This sense of an oversoul, combined with and undergirding the lively comedy and philosophy of *Man and Superman*, gives the play its greatest dimension and fullest sense of unity.

46. Pearson recounts his influence (ibid., p. 233), and Joad testifies to it personally in *Shaw* (London, 1949), pp. 8–18.

47. Henri Bergson, *An Introduction to Metaphysics*, trans. T. E. Hulme (New York and London, 1912), p. 9.

CHAPTER SIX

MAJOR BARBARA

Giving the Devil His Due

The approximate direction of Shaw's irony is generally not difficult to define if one takes into account his socialism, his puckish
humor, and his underlying philosophy of an evolving Life Force,
with its close correspondence to Samuel Butler's evolutionary
theories and to Bergson's *élan vital*. One critic has indicated that
in ironic method Shaw is far removed from Swift, whose devices
of indirection leave at least some doubt as to precisely where the
writer stands.[1] By stating one thing while implying another, irony
gains much of its effect through the possibility of being misunderstood. The less subtle it is, the more accessible it becomes to dull-
ards; the more subtle it is, the more it tests the refinement of the
reader's sensibilities, until finally it reaches a borderland of doubt
between seriousness and cynicism. Shaw, seeking clarity in his role
of proselytist as well as ironist, is seldom willing to operate for any
sustained period of time in this borderland. But there are instances when his convictions are double-edged, and when his
multi-dimensional artistic-philosophical vision plays havoc with
attempts to identify his ironic home base. *Major Barbara* offers
such an instance.

Since Shaw boldly asserts Undershaftian views in his preface,

1. Richard M. Ohmann, *Shaw: The Style and the Man* (Middletown, Conn.,
1962), pp. 99–100.

there has been a strong tendency to consider Undershaft's position and statements in the play as closely related to Shaw's.[2] Correspondences between the two are deceptively easy to draw. Undershaft unequivocally expresses his gospel in Act II as being "money and gunpowder; freedom and power; command of life and command of death."[3] Money to Undershaft is the source of freedom, a virtual giver of life because it overcomes the soul-shrinking effects of poverty. "Poverty," he remarks in Act III, "blights whole cities; spreads horrible pestilences; strikes dead the very souls of all who come within sight, sound or smell of it" (p. 434). And gunpowder, by giving power, the command of death, insures liberation from servitude: "Poverty and slavery have stood up for centuries to your sermons and leading articles: they will not stand up to my machine guns" (pp. 435–36). Governments ultimately remain in control through their power of death, their willingness to kill, which is also the ultimate threat of revolution, being "the final test of conviction, the only lever strong enough to overturn a social system, the only way of saying Must" (p. 436).

Such views are clearly repeated by Shaw in his preface, which was written after the play. Drawing upon Samuel Butler's sentiments regarding the importance of money, its absence being tantamount to a crime, Shaw remarks that Undershaft realizes "the irresistible natural truth which we all abhor and repudiate: to wit, that the greatest of our evils, and the worst of our crimes is poverty, and that our first duty, to which every other consideration

2. J. S. Collis makes the mistake of referring to Undershaft as an obvious mouthpiece (*Shaw* [London, 1925], p. 131). Joseph Frank, interpreting the play as a religious allegory akin to Dante's *Divine Comedy*, speaks of the munitions maker as Shaw's Virgilian spokesman, "the Christ and the Paul of this Shavian religion" ("*Major Barbara*—Shaw's 'Divine Comedy'," *PMLA*, 71 [1956], 64). Charles Frankel, in a perceptive philosophical analysis which finds Shaw synthesizing virtue with power in the tradition of Machiavelli, Hobbes, Nietzsche, and Marx, takes Shaw's seriousness in Undershaft as obvious, complete, and doctrinaire ("Efficient Power and Inefficient Virtue [Bernard Shaw: *Major Barbara*]," *Great Moral Dilemmas in Literature, Past and Present*, ed. Robert M. MacIver [New York, 1956], pp. 17–18). An early qualification which anticipates my thesis and which critics have neglected is made by Richard Burton in *Bernard Shaw: The Man and the Mask* (New York, 1916), pp. 125–26.

3. *Bernard Shaw: Complete Plays with Prefaces* (New York, 1963), I, 388. All citations and quotations from the preface and the play are from this volume.

should be sacrificed, is not to be poor" (p. 305). Shaw's comment on money could easily have come from Undershaft's lips, so unequivocal is it: "Money is the most important thing in the world. It represents health, strength, honor, generosity and beauty as conspicuously and undeniably as the want of it represents illness, weakness, disgrace, meanness and ugliness. Not the least of its virtues is that it destroys base people as certainly as it fortifies and dignifies noble people" (pp. 311–12).

The gunpowder part of Shaw not only reveals itself in his literary pyrotechnics, but in his conviction that it was ultimately men of action and violence, not Voltaire, Rousseau, and the Encyclopedists, who effected the French Revolution. He even indicts the negative potential of literary reformers: "The problem being to make heroes out of cowards, we paper apostles and artist-magicians have succeeded only in giving cowards all the sensations of heroes whilst they tolerate every abomination, accept every plunder, and submit to every oppression" (p. 319). This is a Shavian inversion, the sword being mightier than the pen, except insofar as the pen ironically deflects the sword, substituting the vicarious and illusory glory of rhetoric for the ruthless steel of action and the bombs of revolution. The case for Shaw as a theorist of violence, holding principles of the explosive Undershaftian variety, can be asserted by reference to a lecture he delivered to the Fabian Society in 1906, in which he said: "Revolutions, remember, can only be made by men and women with courage enough to meet the ferocity and pugnacity of the common soldier and vanquish it. Do not let us delude ourselves with any dreams of a peaceful evolution of Capitalism into Socialism, of automatic Liberal Progress . . . nothing is so constitutional as fighting."[4] So it would seem that Shaw and Undershaft are one in the admiration of money for the freedom it brings and the respect of gunpowder for its power to effect liberation and social change.

But how, then, is one to understand Shaw's Fabian views encouraging the constitutional reform of government, his history of anti-violence, and his anti-militarism? Are these elements, so basic

4. British Museum, MS. 50661, fol. 81–82. Quoted in Louis Crompton, *Shaw the Dramatist* (Lincoln, Nebr., 1969), pp. 119–20.

to his thought, thrown over in *Major Barbara?* Desmond Mac-
Carthy suggests that Shaw's attitudes underwent a fundamental
change, that, frustrated and impatient with the pacifistic powers
of persuasion, he turned from the evolutionary eugenics of *Man
and Superman* to the more direct revolutionary expedient of force
in *Major Barbara*.[5] But such a quick turnabout on Shaw's part
seems psychologically unlikely, and certainly this answer oversimplifies ambivalent elements in his political and philosophical
thought. More than twenty years after writing *Major Barbara*
Shaw expressed nonviolent Fabian principles in *The Intelligent
Woman's Guide to Socialism and Capitalism*, clearly stressing the
pragmatism behind a peaceful, economically sound progression
from capitalism to socialism. Shaw felt that property rights must
be respected, and that gains made under capitalism should not be
sacrificed to the undue haste of ignorant and destructive force.
Nationalization of property should be effected through compensating its owners rather than through expropriation, the revolutionary end being achieved by taxing the wealthy for the necessary
funds. This would result in a reasonably smooth transition with a
minimum of inhumanity and waste.[6] Further, in life Shaw was no
leader or advocate of overt socialist violence. He felt that the place
to exert power was more from within the government through
infiltration than from without. It is consistent that he once dis-
suaded a mob from a proposed window-breaking spree in the
West End.

There may be considerable similarity between some of Shaw's
views and some of Undershaft's, but critics have tended to interpret Shaw's intellectual fondness for the diabolism of the munitions maker, and a forceful portrayal of him, as indicating a closer
alignment between the two than actually exists. In a letter to actor
Louis Calvert, Shaw described Undershaft as "Broadbent and
[K]eegan rolled into one, with Mephistopheles thrown in,"[7] and

5. Desmond MacCarthy, *Shaw's Plays in Review* (New York, 1951), pp. 49–50.
6. George Bernard Shaw, *The Intelligent Woman's Guide to Socialism and
Capitalism* (New York, 1928), pp. 268–76. Referred to by Julian B. Kaye, *Bernard Shaw and the Nineteenth-Century Tradition* (Norman, Okla., 1958), pp.
146–47.
7. "George Bernard Shaw as a Man of Letters," *New York Times*, 5 Dec. 1915,

at another time he characterized him as having "a most terribly wicked religion of his own, believing only in money and gunpowder. . . ."[8] Shaw might have seen in himself an impertinent Mephistopheles in the face of nineteenth-century conservatism and blindness, but there was little of the bluntness, naïveté, and power of a Broadbent in him, and his Mephistopheleanism was more pert and quipping than that of Undershaft's heavy, diabolical Prince of Darkness. His reference to Undershaft's "most terribly wicked religion" has a tongue-in-cheek quality but is undoubtedly partly sincere. Militarism might occasionally achieve momentary virtue, but to claim general morality for it, an implication which Undershaft promotes under the guise of amorality, would have been contrary to common sense for the writer of *Arms and the Man*.

Similar in nature to Jack Tanner in *Man and Superman*, Undershaft exudes the Life Force, ingenuity, and his own gospel. Like Tanner, he maintains a personal philosophy consistent with the wellsprings of his spirit, a vital idealism enmeshed in the deepest sense of self and purpose. He is another manifestation in Shaw of Bergson's *élan vital*, a coherent self flowing through time, acting as much through time and space as acted upon. As such, he has his own personal moral values, much in the tradition of Nietzsche's superman; values which are a law unto themselves and tend to overwhelm and confuse the fragmentary, poorly formed moralities of conventional men. It is this profound inner consistency of his character which, more than the preface, gives a true feeling of identity between the author and his creation, a spiritual identity less personal but nearly as vital as that which exists between Shaw and Tanner. There is an important difference, however. Tanner's moral passion has the freedom and power which is open to the society of the idle rich; it is relatively unconditioned by repressive physical and social demands. As such, it can function more in the realm of pure thought than were it subject to constant friction

---

sec. VI, p. 6. Quoted in Martin Meisel, *Shaw and the Nineteenth-Century Theater* (Princeton, 1963), p. 33.
8. 4 July 1905. Quoted ibid., p. 296.

with the grossness of physical life, with the necessities of fighting
for survival and the struggle for status. Tanner functions glibly in
a poetic world of ideas, being cut down frequently by the inflexi-
bility of mundane society, but never truly facing the stark reality
of his own Life Force abstraction until it traps him into marriage
late in the play. Undershaft, on the other hand, bears the stamp of
a personality profoundly molded by stark reality from the very
beginning of his life, from a time when Tanner was still occupied
with the padded innocence of childhood love.

The brutal fact of poverty, with its correlatives of squalor and
suppression, confronted Undershaft as a foundling in East London. Shaw draws his character in terms of this background. In
Tanner the Life Force in its struggle upward had economic freedom to flower into a realm of untrammeled social benevolence
and philosophical idealism. In Undershaft the same vibrant spirit
of life was given a choice: repression and poverty in pacifism, or
fulfillment and wealth in the aggressive trade available to him.
Being a true manifestation of the Life Force, quite naturally he
chose the trade, and, expressing his Life Force through his trade,
quite understandably he made a religion of it. The choice was
clearly a moral one, the only one which he could make in good
conscience. As Shaw points out in the preface, "Undershaft, the
hero of Major Barbara, is simply a man who, having grasped the
fact that poverty is a crime, knows that when society offered him
the alternative of poverty or a lucrative trade in death and destruction, it offered him, not a choice between opulent villainy and
humble virtue, but between energetic enterprise and cowardly
infamy" (p. 308).

The situation is reminiscent of the one which confronted Mrs.
Warren as a girl. Shaw was mindful of the analogy, having at one
time remarked to Henderson, "Perhaps a more suitable title for
this play, save for the fact of repetition, would have been *Andrew
Undershaft's Profession*."[9] Such a title might well have been
better than the existing one, as it would with greater balance
shift the emphasis from Barbara's religious experience, her dis-

9. Report of a conversation, in Archibald Henderson, *George Bernard Shaw:
His Life and Works* (Cincinnati, 1911), p. 381.

illusionment and conversion, toward an expression in depth of Undershaft's religion. Critics who have found the third act a disappointment in terms of Barbara might then have perceived it more accurately as a fulfillment in terms of Undershaft.[10] Shaw's characteristic structural innovation of exposition, complication, and pointed discussion can in these terms be appreciated as a satisfying unity, the relatively varied movement of Act II being expanded conceptually in Act III, moving in a crescendo toward the intellectual, moral, and spiritual triumph of the Undershaftian religion.

Shaw's divergence from Undershaft, his intrinsic aesthetic distance, exists in his treatment of the munitions maker as an economic and sociological phenomenon, to a great degree conditioned by his environment even though he has a vision which rises splendidly through and above it. A distinction must be made between Shaw's basic sympathy and appreciation for a vital manifestation of the Life Force, and his approval or disapproval of the cruel alternatives and conditionings which society forces upon it and through which it must grow to express itself. Shaw asserts the moral correctness of Kitty Warren, who chooses a life of prostitution over an existence of "virtuous" poverty. Through prostitution she may express the true vital energy which makes her a vibrant human being, an individual living in the moral duration of Bergsonian reality, as opposed to a wretched, ridiculous, inhuman automaton, slaving in Christian righteousness as a servile drudge. In prostitution she has hope, economic security, and the not inconsequential modicum of social respectability which money can

10. Gilbert Murray, to whom Shaw read the play from manuscript, was the first to object to the weakness of Barbara and Cusins in Act III. Shaw consequently revised the act, but wrote the following qualification to Murray on 7 Oct. 1905: "As to the triumph of Undershaft, that is inevitable because I am in the mind that Undershaft is in the right, and that Barbara and Adolphus, with a great deal of his natural insight and cleverness, are very young, very romantic, very academic, very ignorant of the world. I think it would be unnatural if they were able to cope with him." Regarding the interesting Shaw-Murray correspondence on this matter, see Sidney P. Albert, " 'In More Ways Than One': *Major Barbara's* Debt to Gilbert Murray," *Educational Theatre Journal*, 20 (1968), 123–40. Cusins is modeled after Murray, and Barbara and Lady Britomart after Murray's wife and imperious mother-in-law (ibid., pp. 123–24).

buy; in poverty she would have had squalor, illness, overwork, and death in the poorhouse as payment for being a "good" woman. But Shaw is in no sense defending the morality of prostitution; rather, he is revealing that society offers Kitty no other choice. So it is, to a large degree, with Undershaft. As Kitty Warren's *élan vital* pushes her into the most creative and fulfilling work at hand, she makes the greatest thing of it she can, and in her very whole-hearted involvement it becomes a pseudo-religion. As Undershaft's *élan vital* pushes him into armaments, armaments become a part of his soul and emerge informed by religious spirit. The motto of both the prostitute and the armorer may consequently quite naturally be "UNASHAMED."[11]

Obviously, Shaw is promoting neither prostitution nor arms manufacture *per se*. He is, rather, struck with the near-religious implications which both of these professions may have when informed by a vital creative spirit, as well as with the guilt of a society which will allow its natural geniuses no better outlet. Even though Kitty and Undershaft may turn victimization into victory, the fact remains that they are still basically victims, their environments having influenced both their conduct and their social acceptability. Thus Shaw observes in his preface:

> What a man is depends on his character; but what he does, and what we think of what he does, depends on his circumstances. . . . The faults of the burglar are the qualities of the financier: the manners and habits of a duke would cost a city clerk his situation. In short, though character is independent of circumstances, conduct is not; and our moral judgments of character are not: both are circumstantial [p. 325].

This distinction between character and conduct is highly important. To clarify the issue, one need only consider Shaw's portrayal of another captain of industry, Boss Mangan of *Heartbreak House*. Mangan is very like Undershaft in his complete devotion

11. Bernard F. Dukore proposes an integral dramatic function for the mottoes of the Undershaft inheritors, in "The Undershaft Maxims," *Modern Drama*, 9 (1966), 90–100. Barbara Bellow Watson suggests that "UNASHAMED" forcefully reveals the corruption and unabashed evil of capitalism, in "Sainthood for Millionaires: *Major Barbara*," *Modern Drama*, 11 (1968), 231.

to the great abstraction of Industry, in his seeming power, in his clever manipulation of subordinates for his own profit, and finally in his awareness of his own actual powerlessness. Regarding the town of Percivale St. Andrews, Undershaft remarks: "It does not belong to me. I belong to it" (p. 425), and to Cusins he says, "From the moment when you become Andrew Undershaft, you will never do as you please again. Dont come here lusting for power, young man" (p. 431). The Mangan side of Undershaft, the mere role of an arms maker, is hence in itself spiritless and ignoble. It is the reduction of a man of genius to the pathetic-comic Bergsonian automaton, more acted upon than acting. Were it for this role alone, Undershaft's fate would be as absurd as Mangan's. His nobility lies almost entirely in his character.

G. K. Chesterton is clearly oversimplifying when he asserts that *Major Barbara* is an inversion of Shaw's faith, since it reveals the triumph of environment over will.[12] Chesterton is either looking too exclusively at Barbara or too narrowly at the philosophy of money as a foundation for spirituality. Undershaft is a synthesis of two roles—one public, the other private. As arms maker, he is a social, political, and economic fact; he provides much of the power which moves the world. Shaw's analysis of him in this role is highly perceptive and illuminating—but here, to repeat, Shaw is *not* by any means intrinsically sympathetic. As Undershaft the foundling, on the other hand, as a vital force transforming the brutality, amorality, and inherent cynicism of a war plant into a viable philosophy of life and hope for social betterment, he is for Shaw sympathetic, fascinating, and finally almost overpowering. Eric Bentley observes that Undershaft takes over the philosophical action perversely, overwhelming Shaw's attempt to achieve at the end a synthesis in Cusins of Barbara's idealism and Undershaft's realism.[13] Rather, he emerges as the dynamic spirit of power and wealth which offers the true foundation for Barbara's and Cusins's visionary, less pragmatically oriented hopes. Money is a fact of life which obviously does influence Undershaft and the entire

12. G. K. Chesterton, *George Bernard Shaw*, Dramabook ed. (New York, 1956), p. 147.
13. Eric Bentley, *Bernard Shaw*, Amended ed. (New York, 1957), p. 167.

social system, but, like gunpowder, it becomes truly significant only as a tool, or as it provides a favorable environment for the spiritual evolution of the *élan vital.*

Shaw builds the aesthetics of his argument by successfully playing the devil's advocate. At one point Cusins remarks that "all the poet in me recoils from being a good man" (p. 438), and the real poetry of *Major Barbara* is in the diabolism of Undershaft imposing itself contrapuntally upon the angelic quality of Barbara. The concentrated vigor with which Shaw develops Undershaft as the devil achieves for him both the aesthetic distance of an archetypal monster and the psychological immediacy of a fascinating, cunning deceiver. Explicitly, it is Cusins who builds the image by a fertile range of appellatives, including Mephistopheles, Machiavelli, devil, demon, and Prince of Darkness. Implicitly, there is considerable symbolic interest even in his name. The Church of St. Andrew Undershaft in East London, where Andrew was born, was built in 1520–32 on the site of an earlier church of the same name. In medieval times this earlier church was in the shadow of a tall maypole which rose higher than the steeple—hence the designation "Undershaft." The pole was cut down and burned by the parishioners after a cleric, named Sir Stephen, preached against its profanity.[14] Thus the religion of Undershaft, dominated as it is by the profanity of a pagan mysticism, renders his name symbolically apropos. In conventional terms his religion is perverted by the diabolical. Reflecting historical chronicle, Andrew's son Stephen, so righteously confident of his ability to distinguish right from wrong, attacks his father's heterodoxy as profane. Andrew is a mystic in the shadow of a pagan ontology.

Sensing that poverty in itself is indeed not a crime, and that ends are not always worth the means, critics have found themselves in basic disagreement with what they interpret as fundamental Undershaft-Shavian theses.[15] There is a tendency to overlook two

14. See Stanley Weintraub, " 'Shaw's Divine Comedy': Addendum," *Shaw Bulletin,* 2, no. 2 (1958), 22. Further, Daniel J. Leary observes that St. Andrew was patron saint of the gunpowder-makers' guild, and, according to legend, was the author of a lost gospel. See "Dialectical Action in *Major Barbara,*" *Shaw Review,* 12 (1969), 49.

15. See Henderson, *Shaw: His Life and Works,* p. 383; Patrick Braybrooke,

factors. First, the Shavian technique of overstatement is used as a rhetorical device to startle his audiences into new modes of thought, seeking frequently to establish a general truth by shooting beyond it. By making a religion of money and gunpowder Shaw may not convince the auditor of their holiness, but he does establish a sense of their great social importance. Second, the social reality of Undershaft is deeply tied to his psychological perversity, and as society has battered his personality, so in turn does his personality boomerang upon society. This gives him both social significance and psychological validity. In the conventional Christian sense his gospel of money and power is certainly that of the devil. A reasonable extension of the philosophy of money expounded here would be avariciousness, and the lust for power is the lust of pride. These are devilish modes. Shaw was a fond reader of Bunyan, and in Bunyan's terms Undershaft's philosophy is that of Worldly Wiseman, scoffing at poverty, scoffing at turning the other cheek, extolling expedience and the brutal facts of worldly existence. His gospel is based on the ethics of the City of Destruction, treating the Bible of the Celestial City as an impractical myth, out-of-date, to be scrapped as unworkable in face of the contradicting realities of life.

Undershaft's frame of reference challenges the theological distinction which Shaw draws so clearly in *Man and Superman*—the distinction between cupidity and charity, love of self and of the world versus love of others and of God. The point that spirituality can only thrive on a basis of physical well-being is exaggerated, its weakness being concealed dramatically by the moral squalor of Snobby Price and Bill Walker. The fact that religion has often been used by the upper classes to pacify the poor in their physical wretchedness is used as a justification for cannons and gunpowder. The suggestion is offered that somehow the poor will come into possession of the cannons and gunpowder and blow up the rich, obliterating a corrupt society to make room for a superior one. Undershaft's arguments neglect the fact that cannons are generally used to keep the poor and weak in their squalor, and that the

The Genius of Bernard Shaw (Philadelphia, 1925), p. 110; and MacCarthy, *Shaw's Plays in Review*, p. 47.

blowing up of one government does not necessarily mean the institution of a better one. Freedom and power are intellectual abstractions of what money and gunpowder may give man—greed and cruel death are nearer the reality. The tendency of *some* wealthy men is to become beneficent, but the tendency of others is to pursue an ascending spiral of greed. Many of Undershaft's principles are obviously only half-truths, thrown forth vigorously for the effect of startling and upsetting status quo thinking. As devil, pragmatist, and mystic all in one, he may most effectively ignite new fires of thought, retaining his grasp on the earth and reaching for the heavens at the same time.

In Act III Undershaft's diabolism fully reveals itself as the evil of a good businessman, the faith of an armorer: "To give arms to all men who offer an honest price for them, without respect of persons or principles" (p. 430); and this reflects back upon his delight in horrifying Mrs. Baines in Act II: "Think of my business! think of the widows and orphans! the men and lads torn to pieces with shrapnel and poisoned with lyddite! . . . the oceans of blood, not one drop of which is shed in a really just cause!" (p. 400).[16] His pleasure is immense and satanic in the irony that he can buy the Salvation Army, and also blatantly attach to his check the immorality of human slaughter and still have it gratefully accepted. Barbara exclaims in agony, "The worst thing I have had to fight here is not the devil, but Bodger, Bodger, Bodger" (p. 399). The whiskey of Bodger anesthetizes the bodies which the explosives of Undershaft destroy, leaving little but mutilated souls for a scavenger devil. The Salvation Army's motto of "Blood and Fire" is ironically Undershaftian and diabolical, and at the end of Act II it seems an appropriate poetic and dramatic climax to have Undershaft join the Army's band—an army with an armorer's

---

16. In another letter to Louis Calvert, dated 18 Nov. 1905, Shaw indicates his intention here: "There is that frightful speech where Undershaft deliberately gives a horrible account of his business, sticking detail after detail of the horrors of war into poor bleeding Barbara to shew her what Mrs. Baines will stand for for £5000. Cusins, who sees it all, is driven into an ecstasy of irony by it: it is a sort of fantasia played on the nerves both of him and Barbara by Machiavelli-Mephistopheles." Quoted by Sidney P. Albert, "Shaw's Advice to the Players of *Major Barbara*," *Theatre Survey*, 10 (1969), 7.

motto, a devil's motto, and an army he has just bought. The world, religion, and the devil have joined forces, and together they strike up a vigorous march, departing in a frenzy of Dionysian exultation, a desertion of the soul by both body and spirit, leaving the soul crying in isolation: "My God: why hast thou forsaken me?" (p. 403).[17] Shaw presents the Christian tragedy in a unique context and with great poetic and ironic power. Regarding *Major Barbara* W. T. Stead remarked: "Since I saw the Passion Play at Oberammergau, I have not seen any play which represented so vividly the pathos of Gethsemane, the tragedy of Calvary."[18] But, just as Calvary was as much an end as a beginning, the world proceeding on its own old merry-cruel way, so Shaw's play is more Undershaft's than Barbara's.

Shaw develops Prince of Darkness imagery most compactly in Act III, boldly juxtaposing the emerging idealism with trenchant satanism. Cusins sets the tone, describing Undershaft at the Salvation Army rally: "The Prince of Darkness played his trombone like a madman: its brazen roarings were like the laughter of the damned" (p. 408). Later, Undershaft takes great delight in slaughter, quite impervious to human factors: "Which side wins does not concern us here. No: the good news is that the aerial battleship is a tremendous success. At the first trial it has wiped out a fort with three hundred soldiers in it" (p. 422). Undershaft "brutally" kicks a prostrate dummy out of his way, like a callous Mephistopheles in his own domain. The parapet setting is a remarkable reflection of the paradox in the diabolism of Undershaft and of his ambivalent relationship with society. On the one hand is the view over the model city of Percivale St. Andrews, with its thousands of well-fed bodies and hungry souls, while on the other hand mutilated dummy soldiers litter the emplacement, constantly before the audience's eyes as mute evidence of the havoc which sup-

17. The power of Undershaft's Dionysian music at the end of this act is a dramatic parallel and contrast to the feebleness of "Onward Christian Soldiers," played on the concertina at the end of Act I. Also, the vigor of this vital pseudo-religious force, as juxtaposed to the vapidity of orthodox beliefs, reflects Euripides' *The Bacchae*, from which Cusins quotes in the play. See Leary, "Dialectical Action in *Major Barbara*," pp. 50–51, and Crompton, *Shaw the Dramatist*, pp. 113–15.

18. Quoted in Henderson, *Shaw: His Life and Works*, p. 386.

ports this paradise. A cannon also overlooks the city, a multiple symbol of Percivale St. Andrews's prosperity, evil, and ultimate slavery to power beyond its control. The cannon and the dummies, one of which *"has fallen forward and lies, like a grotesque corpse, on the emplacement"* (p. 421), offer a satanic and earthly comment on Undershaft's religion and especially on his conversion of Cusins and Barbara. The implications of his words and the means to Cusins's and Barbara's idealistic ends are staring them starkly in the face, an ironic judgment and grim stabilizer regarding the hope for the future which lies through an armorer's trade. There is much talk of buying and selling souls, first Barbara's (via the Salvation Army), then Bill Walker's, then Cusins's. Idealism has considerable diabolism to overcome before the audience can swallow the pill. And certainly this is Shaw's intention.

Being a foundling, Undershaft is symbolically a social charge, especially meaningful as his anonymous source gives him roots in all of humanity. And as he fulfills a devil role, his roots go even deeper into social foundations. He is dramatically and allegorically powerful in his devil role because he is representative of social and political truth stripped of pretense and hypocrisy. He is a statement regarding the actual location of power in society, and of society's moral enslavement to that power. His money is entirely respectable as a prop of the social structure—Lady Britomart does not hesitate to call on him to support her daughters in marriage. His money underlies religion—the Salvation Army would have to close down for the winter were he not to finance it, and Barbara's evangelism rests on the cushioned existence his wealth has provided for her. His armaments are the power behind politics, a point he makes very clear to Stephen: "The government of your country! *I* am the government of your country: I, and Lazarus. Do you suppose that you and half a dozen amateurs like you, sitting in a row in that foolish gabble shop, can govern Undershaft and Lazarus? No, my friend: you will do what pays u s. You will make war when it suits us, and keep peace when it doesnt" (p. 416). Society, religion, and politics rest solidly on money and gunpowder, and the freedom and power of anyone in society are considerably relative to his control of both. Shaw does not make power a moral system, as one critic suggests;[19] rather, he clearly states it as a fact of life, a diabolical fact, but one which man must face up to and try to use correctly if he is to survive and evolve. Thus Barbara remarks near the end: "Undershaft and Bodger: . . . there is no getting away from them. Turning our backs on Bodger and Undershaft is turning our backs on life" (p. 443).[20]

Once Barbara has got rid of the bribes of bread and heaven in Undershaft's model city, she has but the bare foundations of salvation: necessary physical elements, but negligible and even corrupt spiritual ones. Her well-to-do, self-satisfied, socially stratified subjects are about as far from salvation as is the typical missile engineer. Two New Testament verses are so apropos at this point that they provide an implicit comment both on the central theme of the play and on this armaments utopia: "Men shall not live by bread alone," and "all who take to the sword will perish by the sword" (Matthew 4:04 and 26:52). The spiritual bankruptcy of Percivale St. Andrews is inherent in its blindness to its economic and social base. Religion may temporarily be founded on mutilated bodies—the dummies Shaw scatters so obviously about the stage in Act III—but ultimately it must be a self-conscious religion, because it will be viable only insofar as it maintains contact with life, and, spiritually, with death. Thus in his preface Shaw pleads, "Creeds must become intellectually honest" (p. 339), perceptively in touch with living reality, with a perspective which no present-day religion has managed to achieve.

It is this sensitivity to reality, combined with spiritual consistency and idealism, which Shaw seeks to portray in Undershaft. Undershaft the realist is diabolical and cynical, reflecting the diabolical, cynical, and hypocritical society which nurtured and supports him, and which he thoroughly understands. In Act I when Lomax platitudinizes that "the more destructive war becomes,

19. Frankel, "Efficient Power and Inefficient Virtue," p. 18.

20. Undershaft is partly derived from European arms manufacturers, notably the Krupps (see William Manchester, *The Arms of Krupp 1587–1968* [Boston, 1968], pp. 244–45), and possibly Alfred Nobel (see Crompton, *Shaw the Dramatist*, pp. 115–16). Bodger seems to be a conglomerate of English distillers and brewers (see Sidney P. Albert, " 'Letters of Fire against the Sky': Bodger's Soul and Shaw's Pub," *Shaw Review*, 11 [1968], 82–90).

the sooner it will be abolished, eh?" he is clearheaded as to social fact in his response: "Not at all. The more destructive war becomes the more fascinating we find it" (pp. 360–61). It is a devil's business, and he is honest about it. As long as war is society's way, he will express his natural genius through armaments, fulfilling his instincts for freedom and power. On the other hand, this does not restrict his intellectual awareness, or the vision of the Life Force within him, that power may be off-balanced by power, and the social structure may change. He recognizes that there is power which is beyond him, "a will of which I am a part" (p. 431), and it is in light of this power that he challenges the idealism of Cusins: "Dare you make war on war?" (p. 440).[21] Thus he is a capitalist with Marxist vision,[22] a devil in facing the world, but a mystic in realizing the potential of a deeper, self-conscious contact with reality.

Such an interpretation of Undershaft is clearly supported by other Shavian writings. In Act III of *Man and Superman* Don Juan emphasizes the uniqueness of man's brain and its effectiveness as an instrument of survival in carrying forward the work of the Life Force. The Devil scoffs in reply: "There is nothing in Man's industrial machinery but his greed and sloth: his heart is in his weapons. This marvellous force of Life of which you boast is a force of Death: Man measures his strength by his destructiveness."[23] Here is the negative aspect of Undershaft. In his preface to *Major Barbara* Shaw refers to such commercial millionaires as brigands and scoundrels, made beneficent when they are successful merely because society worships them in success as much as it abhors and punishes them in failure. Success reaps Christian respect, and men tend to live up to the treatment they receive (pp. 324–25), but their moral base is no sounder. Don Juan's answer to the Devil involves the answer which is inherent in Undershaft: the brain raises man above cowardice and pettiness by giving him

21. I hope that to some extent this clarifies the seeming contradiction in Undershaft noted by Ozy, "The Dramatist's Dilemma: An Interpretation of *Major Barbara*," *Shaw Bulletin*, 2, no. 1 (1958), 24.
22. A point made by William Irvine, *The Universe of G. B. S.* (New York, 1949), p. 261.
23. *Complete Plays*, III, 619.

ideals. Ideals, of course, are relative, as Undershaft recognizes in Act I—"There is only one true morality for every man; but every man has not the same true morality" (p. 361)—and as Don Juan recognizes in citing the clashing idealisms of the crusading Christians and the Mohammedans. A logical impasse is quickly reached when conflicting idealisms take arms against one another, with a likely result being the destruction of one idealism or the maiming of both. Any answer must obviously be relativistic, and in *Major Barbara*, as in the rest of Shaw, that answer lies in the greatest fulfillment of the Life Force, a fulfillment most practically effected in life by the doctrine that morality exists in the greatest good for the greatest number. The positive nature of this doctrine coincides with Shaw's optimism regarding man: "It is quite useless to declare that all men are born free if you deny that they are born good" (preface, p. 327). In the play such optimism exhibits itself in Undershaft's Marxist vision and in Cusins's concluding idealism: "The people must have power; and the people cannot have Greek. . . . I want a power simple enough for common men to use, yet strong enough to force the intellectual oligarchy to use its genius for the general good" (p. 442). And this power cannot be in abstractions alone—it must be in both weapons and ideals, because at the present stage of the world ideals may give men their ultimate nobility, but weapons are the practical tools of immediate power.

Barbara and Cusins inform the dialectic as they offer hope for a spiritual fulfillment in terms of this realism and idealism. Barbara's role provides a focal point for illuminating the central issues of Undershaft's religion. As she is the most sympathetic character in the play, her "education" by her father tends to carry the audience into his unorthodox frame of reference, the evolution of her moral awareness acting as a bridge between the simplicity of Stephen and the complexity of Undershaft. Stephen's morality is the epitome of thoughtless conventionalism: "Right is right; and wrong is wrong; and if a man cannot distinguish them properly, he is either a fool or a rascal: thats all" (p. 349). Thus unequivocally stated, categorical and dogmatic standards become absurd, and through Stephen simplistic morality is laughed away. In contrast, Undershaft is at first rather bewildering. Described by Lady Britomart as a man who doesn't *do* wrong things, but says them and thinks them (p. 349), he is too much an enigma in Act I and too cynical a monster in Act II to provide a point for moral identification. In the midst of this moral confusion Barbara's lively idealism seems most hopeful and imaginative. Despite the unorthodox and almost bizarre associations of the Salvation Army, her devotion is so vital and spontaneous that she quickly becomes a sympathetic figure. Her bold and sensitive handling of Bill Walker is amusing as well as highly admirable in its courage, good sense, and charity. For striking Jenny Hill, Bill is deftly placed in a position where only by reforming can he hope to regain self-esteem; he is not allowed such conventional sops as punishment or vicarious atonement. Barbara's instinct is to elevate morality above conventional wordly and religious platitudes by infusing it with personal, pragmatic meaning.

In such action Barbara is revealed as a true Undershaft. She is no easy tool, but has much of the "managing matron" quality of her mother combined with the individualistic spiritual consciousness of her father. Cusins remarks that "Barbara is quite original in her religion," to which Undershaft responds: "Aha! Barbara Undershaft would be. Her inspiration comes from within herself" (p. 388). Having the strength of an inner spiritual coherence, she has the insight to see through the static rigidity and myopia of religious and social structures. Undoubtedly she was attracted to the Salvation Army because it had a more vital, flexible approach to life than do formalized religions. Her father perceives this inner strength but is aware of the weakness beneath it. He has only to expose Barbara to the flaw in the Army's essential connection with reality: she is worshipping in a church with a false foundation. As an Undershaft, she sees this at once, and though she cannot condemn the simple souls who work conscientiously in their simple belief, her perspective is now too great to build a spiritual life on illusion. Consequently, she is ripe for her shift from a spiritual romance without a solid base, to a solid base from which she can build a spiritual reality.

Once she is educated, Barbara's spiritual potential is, ironically, greater than her father's. Although Undershaft has attained the freedom of wealth, his mysticism is ensnared in his past and his position. As his psychology has been molded by the ruthless economics of his rise through society, his vital coherence is linked to his vested commercial interests. In comparison, Barbara has genuine freedom. As an unfettered soul (albeit because of Undershaft wealth), she descends from a full expression of idealism, through disillusionment, to realism. Her capacity for idealism is contrapuntal to Undershaft's cynicism. She finds in the end product of her father's life a foundation for a spiritual beginning which he may dream of but cannot fulfill except through her. Their bases of spirit and power, usually incompatible in a mundane world, have the potential of fusing at the end in a personal concord of idealism and realism. Barbara must temporarily submit to the reality of Undershaft and Lazarus, but arms manufacture is to her no end in itself; it is a vehicle for spiritual growth. By all indications, the managing matron in her is not likely to be dormant. Much of the system to which Undershaft is so closely tied must eventually be subordinated, that part of him defeated. The suggestion is that beyond the limitations of the play the greater spiritual consciousness of Barbara's utopian society will enable that society properly to alter and control its source of power. But this remains visionary.

Like Barbara, Cusins is as much Undershaft's pupil and complement as he is an antagonist. Shaw draws him as more instinctive than rational, his mental acumen being more quixotic than impressive. His ready involvement with the Salvation Army is a front to win Barbara, and is also consistent with his genuine appreciation for the Army's positively directed vigor: "It is the army of joy, of love, of courage: it has banished the fear and remorse and despair of the old hell-ridden evangelical sects" (p. 385). Cusins marches off with Undershaft in Act II with spontaneous enthusiasm for the wild, diabolical irony of the moment, and he enters Act III having largely accepted the devil's vital gospel offstage: Undershaft has "completed the wreck of my moral basis, the rout of my convictions, the purchase of my soul" (p. 408). In Act III he plays a weak and floundering Faustus to Undershaft's skillful

Mephistopheles. Only in bargaining for his salary does he become effectively assertive. His acceptance of Undershaft's gods on the basis of their potential for social reform is a move less sound and philosophical than impulsive and ambitious. His arguments are scarcely the effective ones we should expect from a philosopher,[24] and his surrender to "reality and power" is frankly anti-intellectual (p. 442). The devil Undershaft, not without angelic hope, dangles before him the bait of Plato's philosopher-king—the prospect of combining philosophy with power—and Faustus Cusins snaps it up, after appropriately exclaiming, "Oh tempter, cunning tempter!" (p. 439). However, Cusins's ambitions are more dramatically daring than dialectically convincing, his revolutionary optimism exceeding his philosophical realism. The potential of a philosopher-king may be in him, and surely salvation on a fourfold foundation of philosophy, wealth, power, and spirit is a central aspect of Undershaft's religion. But in terms of the play the ideal is only tentatively grasped, being artistically subordinated to the coalescence of wealth, power, and spirit in Undershaft and Barbara.

Thus *Major Barbara* has an informing philosophy. It is no mere parlor game, offering intellectual gymnastics largely for therapeutic reasons, as Francis Fergusson suggests;[25] nor is its end merely anarchist and unreal, as Alick West claims it to be.[26] It is a search for a new religion based on social fact as well as on idealism. Shaw is not Undershaft, because he does not delight in the cruel facts as Undershaft does, and his Life Force is not enmeshed in death and destruction as is Undershaft's. Yet intellectually he can appreciate the truth of Undershaft as a sociological phenomenon, and he can utilize this reality as a starting-point, concomitant with idealism, for a new moral direction. The hope for social improvement via Barbara and Cusins lies in the intrinsically fluid nature of power. For the moment, power driven by altruistic Life Force idealism instead of selfish cynicism may be put to use to improve

24. The weakness of Cusins's responses to Undershaft is noted by Chesterton, *George Bernard Shaw*, pp. 130–31.

25. Francis Fergusson, *The Idea of a Theater*, Anchor Books ed. (New York, 1953), pp. 193–94.

26. Alick West, *"A Good Man Fallen among Fabians"* (New York, 1950), pp. 129–30.

man's physical well-being, since this is the most practical first step toward spiritual well-being. Beyond this, the ends become more hopeful and intuitive than pragmatically definable. They involve human evolution and fulfillment, a greater self-consciousness and spirituality. Since they are necessarily intuitive and ill-defined, they are less powerful dramatically than the concrete paradox of Undershaft, and the rationale and conclusion of *Major Barbara* have thus been open to debate.

In his social role Undershaft is quite like Milton's Satan, forced by circumstances to make a religion of his surroundings. He is a prose picture of the assertion that "The mind is its own place, and in itself / Can make a Heav'n of Hell, a Hell of Heav'n,"[27] sensing, as finally Satan does, that no matter how evil his acts may be, they will be turned by a superior Will toward ultimate good. And Barbara has much of the naïveté of a Blakean angel[28] corrupted into infernal-divine vision by the vital realism of a Blakean devil—"This Angel, who is now become a Devil, is my particular friend; we often read the Bible together in its infernal or diabolical sense. . . ."[29] Shaw evokes much of the sense of the antinomy of Blake, his characters frequently transcending their humanity, reaching with Bergsonian intuition and Blakean idealism toward a Marriage of Heaven and Hell, founded in essential earthly realities:

> CUSINS. Then the way of life lies through the factory of death?
> BARBARA. Yes, through the raising of hell to heaven and of man to God, through the unveiling of an eternal light in the Valley of The Shadow. [p. 445]

Once again, the poet in Shaw reaches beyond the philosopher.

27. John Milton, Paradise Lost, I, 254–55.
28. "CUSINS. My guardian angel! . . . I adored what was divine in her . . ." (pp. 420, 427).
29. William Blake, "The Marriage of Heaven and Hell," *A Collection of English Poems, 1660–1800*, ed. Ronald S. Crane (New York, 1932), p. 1030.

CHAPTER SEVEN

ANDROCLES AND THE LION

Christianity in Parable

When Gabriel Pascal produced the film of *Androcles and the Lion* in 1952, the publicity which promoted it bubbled with an adman's superlatives:

Gasp at its SPECTACLE!
Glow at its Romance!
Howl at its Laughs![1]

Fortunately for Pascal, and unfortunately for the film, Shaw was dead. The adman avoided mentioning the play's central concern—Christianity—as though such topics were out of vogue and not likely to attract large audiences. This is hardly credible, considering that in those times the average mind absorbed the Ten Commandments from Cecil B. DeMille, gained its thrills from *Quo Vadis,* and perused its scriptures à la CinemaScope in *The Bible.* Clearly, the adman avoided the religion of *Androcles* not because it would not sell, but because he did not understand it, or because he had reservations as to whether he could sell Shaw's version of it to the twelve-year-old viewing mind. To this average mind Shaw's views might still be revolutionary, and the publicist, pandering to complacency, emotions, and animal instincts, was far safer in promoting sensation over reality. As popular conviction

1. Quoted by E. J. West, "Hollywood and Mr. Shaw: Some Reflections on Shavian Drama-into-Cinema," *Educational Theatre Journal,* 5 (1953), 224.

lags decades or even centuries behind revolutionary thought, there was little reason to suppose that even in the 1950's it could accept the Christianity of *Androcles* with much more equanimity than did the London critics of 1913, who found the play offensive and sacrilegious.[2]

In fact, Shaw is indeed trying something new and subversive in *Androcles*. Through a counterpoint of disparate perspectives, his play reveals a very serious purpose. Fable, parody, and parable interact in *Androcles*, achieving religious and historical insights which are nearly as profound as they are bold and sweeping. The fable is the classic one of a man helping a beast, and the beast in gratitude saving the man. The parody satirizes a whole tradition of pompous religious drama. The parable is seriously concerned with man's religious conviction and subjects faith to a terrible test which objectifies spiritual commitment. Shaw combines these elements not only in a mood of impish glee, but also for the special light they cast upon one another, and for a comprehensiveness of vision which their juxtaposition may produce .Thus the fun and fancy of the Androcles fable vitalize the parody of religious melodrama, rendering the parody cutting by giving it an absurd context. Further, the fable leavens the spiritual parable, rendering it more real by giving it poignant humanity. The parody of pompous religiosity, in turn, provides satiric insight which gives sting to the gay fable and fun to the serious parable, increasing the play's total view by bringing into question the very genre of religious drama. And, finally, the spiritual parable, in its profound test of faith, gives weight to the Androcles fable and provides a positive stance behind the parody—it establishes a broad context of sensitive religious perception and gives life to historical Christianity by relating Christian faith to recurrent human realities.

As might be expected, the complex meaning of a play which combines such interpenetrating genres is likely to be misinterpreted, missed, or prove merely confusing to those who most need its message, and the few who understand the multifold implications may be precisely those who are not in need of their lessons.

2. See Hesketh Pearson, "The Origin of 'Androcles and the Lion,'" *Listener*, 48 (1952), 804.

In this light Shaw describes British playgoers' reaction to the first production:

And so it went on, getting more and more bewildering (always except to the serious people who held the thread) until the fun, the satire, the historical study of manners and character, and the deadly deep earnest, were all on the stage at the same moment, many of the audience being so torn one way by laughter and the other way by horror, besides being quite upset by pure shock, that they did not know where they were, and left the theatre rending their garments (metaphorically) and crying Blasphemy, whilst the deeper people for whom the play was written proclaimed that a great movement in religious drama had been inaugurated.[3]

As usual Shaw exaggerates, but his concern is clearly with audience involvement on a number of levels, most of which are certainly more complex than Pascal's laughs, love, and sensation. Rending of garments indicates a state of mind more healthy than complacency, and though fun may be the mode of *Androcles*, religion is clearly its matter. Thus Shaw wrote to his American agent: "Be very careful not to start public opinion on the notion that 'Androcles' is one of my larks. It will fail unless it is presented as a great religious drama—with leonine relief."[4] Obviously, to sensationalize the relief as Pascal did is to misrepresent the drama.

The fun of *Androcles* is inherent in the classic fable which Shaw uses as a frame for his serious concerns. The original Androcles may likely have been a lion trainer who was saved in the Colosseum by the good fortune of confronting one of his trained lions,[5] but the delight of the surviving story involves the fancy of a child's tale. It has both the gentle moral of kindness to animals and of virtue rewarded, and the charm of a beast fable wherein the beast is nearly human. As such, when staged, it takes on some of the bizarre qualities of an animated cartoon which, by represent-

3. From the program for the Granville-Barker production of 1915. Quoted in Archibald Henderson, *George Bernard Shaw: Man of the Century* (New York, 1956), p. 594n.
4. Quoted in Pearson, "Origin of 'Androcles,' " p. 804.
5. The origins of the fable are discussed at length by Arthur Brodeur in "Androcles and the Lion," *Gayley Anniversary Papers* (1922), pp. 195–213.

ing beasts as somewhat human, renders humans slightly beastlike, illuminating the special peculiarities of each world by contrast and comparison with the other. When beasts are not beasts and humans not quite human, virtually anything goes, and horror can be funny since humanity is abstracted. Shaw captures the delight of this fable/cartoon world by placing it in the convention of the English Christmas pantomime, adhering to the convention in mood, subject matter, and structure. The pantomime, anything but silent, generally featured a dark opening, spectacle, and concluding clowning or "harlequinade," all of which are evident in *Androcles*.[6] Most important for Shaw's purpose, however, was the pantomime animal, which was not genuine or realistic but was played as a clown. This half-animal, half-human caricature is utilized to a very special effect in *Androcles*. The lions to whom the Christians are to be thrown become much less terrible with the impression of the Prologue's Tommy so alive in the audience's minds—a lion which is a bizarre conglomerate, purring like a cat, wagging its tail like a dog, weeping and waltzing like a gentle damsel. By arranging the primary action according to the fable, and by providing the fable with so artificial a lion, Shaw offsets the serious concerns of his drama with a multiple sense of fantasy. The frivolity of pantomime and the charm of fable serve as a context which, ironically, clarifies the spiritual message. Thematically, the fable and the lion have little relevance to the spiritual subject matter of the play; aesthetically, they alter the entire tone of the central concerns, moving them away from melodrama and tragedy toward fantasy and comedy.[7] The result is an emotional tension

6. The influence of the English Christmas pantomime on *Androcles* is discussed by Martin Meisel, *Shaw and the Nineteenth-Century Theater* (Princeton, 1963), pp. 327–34.

7. This ambiguity has proven indigestible to some, such as Percivale P. Howe, who senses it as a failure of aesthetic unity (*Bernard Shaw: A Critical Study* [New York, 1915], pp. 133–34). But Shaw is consciously seeking an aesthetic tension. He wrote to Henderson (8 March 1918): "Here I take historical tragedy at its deepest: a point reached only by religious persecution. And the thing is done as if it were a *revue* or a Christmas pantomime, the chief figure being a pantomime lion." Quoted in Archibald Henderson, *Bernard Shaw: Playboy and Prophet* (New York, 1932), p. 617.

between the serious and the comic, with each being qualified by the other. In this tension exists an ambivalence which allows the inherent spiritual concerns a freedom of development.

As the irreverent fun of the fable frame lends a tone of absurdity to the action, it accentuates the play's parody of pompous Christian melodrama. Such melodrama became respectable and popular with the production of Wilson Barrett's *The Sign of the Cross* in 1896. It has popped up in all its dubious glory ever since, descending at last to Hollywood, which, in making the genre more extravagant than ever, has kept Shaw's satire alive and pertinent. In reviewing *The Sign of the Cross*, Shaw wrote: "[Barrett] has drawn a terrible contrast between the Romans . . . with their straightforward sensuality, and the strange, perverted voluptuousness of the Christians, with their shuddering exaltations of longing for the whip, the rack, the stake, and the lions."[8] In *Androcles* Shaw follows the outlines of the tradition but mocks it in his gay, individualized Christians, relegating masochism to Spintho— "beat me: kick me"[9]—who most thoroughly deserves to be a victim of Roman sadism. Shaw's basic message is too seriously religious to invert tradition by converting Lavinia to the Captain's paganism, but he scorns conventional patterns of the genre in having Ferrovius revert to Mars, and in leaving the Captain a pagan, unconverted by love. Major Barbara's integration of Mars and Christianity is not offered as a hope, no doubt because, without a guiding genius such as hers, the reconciliation of war and religion has too often provided a cruel rationale for the hypocrisy of both statesman and ecclesiastic.

In parodying such shallow shams as *The Sign of the Cross*, Shaw aims less at a theatrical convention than at prevailing attitudes which make religious melodrama popular—attitudes based on vague, sometimes anxious, sometimes comfortable feelings which support a worn-out, unrealistic, and perverse tradition. The sickness of the tradition was dismayingly objectified for him by

8. Quoted in Meisel, *Shaw and the Nineteenth-Century Theater*, p. 340.
9. *Bernard Shaw: Complete Plays with Prefaces* (New York, 1963), V, 448. Subsequent references to the preface and the play will be from this volume.

the numerous churchmen who enthusiastically endorsed such bubbles as Barrett's play.[10] Through setting Christian melodrama in the context of a Christmas pantomime and its clown lion, Shaw laughs away the melodrama while satirically jostling the tradition which supports it. The tradition, meanwhile, has a certain dramatic power in suggesting the horrors of martyrdom, horrors which Shaw symbolizes by the lion, by the characters' reactions to it, and by its off-stage meal of indigestible Spintho. Martyrdom is thus alive as an idea, but, because the terrible lion is a waltzing Tommy, it is not allowed to become emotionally traumatic. The underlying issues are made clear and healthy through elimination of an emotional haze. The effects of "realism," which in this case might well be distorted by macabre spectacle, are discarded as fancy mocks melodrama, with the disadvantage that the drama loses verisimilitude but the advantage that it gains perspective.

Fun as the fable may be, and playfully cynical as the parody is, Shaw is also seeking to illumine a sense of history and Christian ethics, a sense which transcends barriers of time. The Androcles fable-frame is finally subordinate to the remarkable parable it encloses. Shaw explores history on a number of levels, jamming epochs into a single symbolic situation. He fuses his dialectic with his aesthetics as he reveals, most basically, the eternal conflict of heterodoxy and orthodoxy, of new religion and old. More specifically, he presents concurrently numerous aspects of Christianity which were historically separated by many centuries. The seemingly simple tale ultimately becomes a critical and dramatic parable of Christianity past, present, and future. Shaw represents the Christianity of the early converts—fresh, inspired, and vital—in opposition to the Christianity of today—stale, codified, and sterile; further, he examines dramatically the power of the original Christ, as well as projecting forward in time the implications of this power.[11]

10. See Meisel, *Shaw and the Nineteenth-Century Theater*, pp. 337–38.
11. I disagree with those who find no real religious issue in *Androcles*. See S. C. Sen Gupta, *The Art of Bernard Shaw* (London, 1936), pp. 120–21, and Louis Kronenberger, *The Thread of Laughter* (New York, 1952), pp. 261–62.

In his postscript Shaw likens the Roman Empire to the British Empire, suggesting that the paganism of the Romans in *Androcles* is supported on much the same grounds as is Christianity today: it is the tool of the Establishment for maintaining self-respect and for controlling subversive social or religious forces. Thus the play presents two eras of Christianity in conflict—Christianity's vital youth (represented by the Christians) opposed by its own conservative age (represented by the Romans). The Christian paradox is graphically revealed as being kindred to that of all revolutionary movements grown old: instead of mellowing with age, such movements either atrophy or grow corrupt in oversubtlety, are appropriated by forces of the status quo, and, in losing the original spark which vitalized their doctrines, lose the true sense of the doctrines themselves.

Shaw's parable presents the real nature of the early Christians as a multiplicity. Typically, Shaw breaks apart any image of a noble stereotype for the early martyrs, and he reveals the seeds of highly personal religious enthusiasms which were subsequently to be manifested in various schisms of the church. Androcles is the gentle humanitarian Christian to whom doctrine is subordinate to kindliness and good will. Lavinia is the free-thinker with her feet on the ground and her ideals in the heavens, surviving doubt through intuitive optimism and allowing for a liberal definition of spirituality. Ferrovius is the stupid but well-meaning Pauline evangelist, mouthing religious platitudes which in faith he believes but which in practice he perverts to his own unimaginative and violent nature. Spintho is the spiritual freeloader, the sour note in a doctrine of grace which opens heaven to rogues and makes it disagreeable to skeptics.[12]

All are but fragments of perception and conviction in comparison to the Christ spirit which inspires them. Each character pursues a separate conviction with a separate psychology, each

---

12. Desmond MacCarthy mentions two types which Shaw neglects—the man who goes into martyrdom with a bad conscience, and the martyr who sacrifices himself for certain definite dogmas (*Shaw's Plays in Review* [New York, 1951], p. 106). Obviously there are even more, such as the ascetic martyr and the devout but masochistic martyr.

turning the influence of Christ into a justification of personal idiosyncrasy. Christ is thus an abstraction already, his image being molded according to the needs and preoccupations of each individual. Ironically, it is as such that he is meaningful and that his ideals may be revivified in terms of each generation. As his words are codified into "religious" rules, the vitality of what he had to say is lost in a formalism similar to that of the Roman religion, in which the Romans lose all personal integrity through reputable thoughtlessness and tacit acceptance of the status quo. "Truth" scarcely survives as an abstraction, because as such it does not touch the individual closely and vitally; rather, it survives in terms of the dynamic *effect* it has on the individual. Thus, in their common willingness to face a cruel death for their ideals, the idiosyncratic Christians are spiritually united at the final point of mortal reality.

In representing these early Christians as such distinct individuals, Shaw's parable stresses the heterodox nature of vital faith, and the necessity for such heterodoxy if faith is to remain meaningfully spiritual. Further, the implication that these characters are also prototypes gives them allegorical interest insofar as their descendants in history have frozen their spontaneity into schismatic sects or attitudes. These Christians are still following Christ's dictum to live life more abundantly (preface, pp. 342, 403), in the light of Psalm 82, which asserts the godlike aspect of humanity. The hope of attaining heaven becomes more imminent as they face martyrdom, but death is not easy because, as Lavinia observes, life has been made especially rich and meaningful through their faith. In contrast to later rationalizations of orthodox Christianity, which justified human suffering and squalor on the basis that such is the way of the sinful world and that misery here would have compensation in bliss hereafter, these Christians find the glory of God on both sides of the grave. Their songs, jests, and compassion are a measure of their immersion in the human world as well as of their faith in a divine one.

Androcles' divine side has the connotations of a simple St. Francis. His instinctive kindness and sense of kinship with all life prompt him to insist on heaven for animals, and to hope that he will provide the lion in the Colosseum with a good meal. Until Spintho's despicable example strengthens Androcles' resolve, he responds spontaneously to the Editor's compassion, and is willing to burn incense at the Roman altar entirely as a personal favor. His Christianity is instinctive, reaching in human terms what Lavinia seeks in spiritual terms. Yet while Androcles is a St. Francis, he is also a Charlie Chaplin, his instinctive spirituality counterpoised with absurd humanity.[13] The tension of these two elements gives him vitality and dimension. As his absurdity is given a quality of dignity through his quiet spirituality, his spirituality is weighted toward reality by his absurdity. This incongruous mixture takes on the delight and some of the magic of both worlds, but, most important, it kindles his Christianity with a human spark, making it sympathetic and communicable.

A more complex aspect of this link between spirit and human nature is revealed in Lavinia. She is the most steadfastly spiritual of all the prospective martyrs, precisely because she has come to terms with the stresses between spirit and matter. Her encounters with the Captain are mildly flirtatious, and her attitude toward Ferrovius' un-Christian ferocity is one of spontaneous approval and admiration. In candidly recognizing that "I am not good always: I have moments only" (p. 447), she undercuts pretension through admitting the obvious. But more important, though she steadfastly seeks spiritual enlightenment, her spontaneous involvement in life renders her spiritual experience meaningful. Faith must be tested, she remarks (p. 437). Since the metaphysical partakes of much of the abstraction of a fairy tale, it must be objectified in terms of mortal commitment. The prospect of a brutal death forces the faith of such as Spintho to the cellar of religious illusion, whereas it cleanses the convictions of the steadfast by its ruthless reality. Thus spirituality can be realized only in terms of humanity, and, by recognizing a vital relationship between the mundane and the sacred, Lavinia moves realistically from one to the other.

13. A. C. Ward analyzes Androcles' Charlie Chaplin humor as a combination of humor and pathos which approximates the cathartic power of tragedy. (*Bernard Shaw* [London, 1951], p. 125).

Ferrovius, on the other hand, cannot come to spiritual enlightenment because he is both afraid and too stupid to assess his mortal limitations. His simple Pauline faith, foreshadowing the obtuseness of so much of historical Christianity, provides the basic humor behind his "conversion" of Lentulus. Ferrovius' faith is at war with his natural instincts; in at first trying to compromise the two, he perverts them both. In pursuing something above humanity, he becomes something less than human. Since his religion has no foundation in life, he can only mouth it in generalities and platitudes. His speeches contain nine-tenths of the religious verbiage in the play, commonplaces which Shaw displays for all their foolishness by crowding them into one short sequence. Ferrovius intones, "My son . . . Has the good seed fallen in a fruitful place? Are your feet turning towards a better path? . . . God has greatly blessed my efforts . . . leave the rest to heaven," etc., etc. (pp. 445–46). Such language is divorced from human realities, and the scene with Lentulus grows in humor as the disparities between Ferrovius' vague, undefined spiritual feelings, his sanctimonious verbiage, and his threat of physical violence become clear. A grim echo of the rationale of the Inquisition is inherent in his comment, "I may hurt your body for a moment; but your soul will rejoice in the victory of the spirit over the flesh" (pp. 444–45). The hypocrisy of such an attitude loses its connotations of horror in this context, but the situation renders it no less obvious and real. The human pleasure of the observer in seeing Lentulus getting what he seems to deserve enhances rather than qualifies the irony that Ferrovius is engaging in a very effective sort of revenge. The audience does not identify with the horror of the victim, since poetic justice is being executed, but neither does it identify with Ferrovius, since the hypocrisy is almost as clear as the horror. Thus intellectual factors are alive, unobscured by emotion.

Ferrovius' great terror that he will fight in the Colosseum is not the terror of confronting martyrdom, but merely fear of facing up to his true nature. When he does face up to himself, his "fall" is not a defeat for Christianity but a defeat of hypocrisy. Lavinia senses this in wishing him to fight to glory: it is the glory of self-knowledge, of truth—and, albeit that the god is Mars, it consti- tutes Ferrovius' salvation, just as his perverse Christianity involved personal damnation. Thus the character of Ferrovius, by inverting the usual scheme of damnation and salvation, displays the honor involved in truly following a profane god, and in submitting self- consciously to instincts of the flesh, over the dishonor of falsely adhering to a more noble God through perversion and hypocrisy. Neither alternative may be attractive, but at least the first involves an honest confrontation of human limitations, and only from such a ground can true spirituality grow.

Spintho's hypocrisy is a variant of Ferrovius', a logical extension of Pauline salvationism. But while Ferrovius is bold and tor- mented, having too much conscience, Spintho is sniveling and petty, with no conscience at all. He does not come to terms with his own errant nature as does Ferrovius; instead, he seeks out Christianity because it offers him a scapegoat, and quick martyr- dom provides an escape from the consequences of his own roguery. Given the promise of salvation, the hypocrite may avoid the true spiritual effort of reforming his soul. The doctrine of vicarious atonement offers him a heaven-sent shortcut. Thus well-meant doctrine is defiled by those who seek out its loopholes, and roguery insinuates itself into the strictures and structures of religious movements. However, poetic justice may prevail where spiritual justice flounders. While Ferrovius triumphs ironically through failing the test of his Christian convictions, gaining not Christian martyrdom but self-knowledge, Spintho flees the test, gaining neither, and ironically loses the life which he has damned himself to save. He survives only as a symbol of those who have through the ages sought out religion as a cheap insurance policy against being called to really account for their sins. If a modicum of re- ligion can salve the conscience, present a good social image, and secure for the sinner at least a second-class ticket to eternal glory, he can beat the game of two worlds—the hypocrisy of this one and the reckoning of the next.

Thus Shaw's Christians are, above all, individuals, facing mar- tyrdom with varied states of mind. Beneath their bold front of jesting lies a complex of reactions, from meek to defiant, instinctive to meditative, sorrowful to joyful. The spirit which moves those of vital religious conviction is the spirit of distinct psyches, each of which finds external expression through an ideal which is broad enough to shelter diverse impulses, yet unified enough to give those impulses a coherence, nobility, and sense of direction. Martyrdom in Christ's name serves as a rallying point for various dispositions which seek affirmation through association with a divine cause, and which desire a sense of apotheosis through submitting to a death that reflects his sacrifice. In contrast, systems and authorities may seek to monopolize the power and prestige of Christianity, but what life they have is that of a monster—one with great limbs and gross instincts, controlled by finite intellect. As time passes, the corruption of fallible men brings about the estrangement of religion from its prophet, and the true religious impulse becomes increasingly a private, personal matter.

The inclination of unimaginative and unspiritual men is to seek a powerful abstraction under which they can nestle. Once they are nestled, they can use the abstraction to beat others into line, thus protecting their comfort, their sense of security, and their status. In the guise of guardians of sacred principles, such men can tyrannize those of greater imagination and deeper spirit. They can use holiness as a bludgeon, a tool and excuse for sadism, a means of fulfilling with pious cruelty the assumptions of righteousness. It is in this light that the Christians of *Androcles* represent a religion which is more vital because it is nearer its source, and, particularly in the person of Ferrovius, herald certain future tacks Christianity was to take as it crystallized. With a similar doubleness, the Romans represent that eternal religious conservatism which suppresses the outpourings of any new faith; further, they provide a dramatic picture of the end to which Christianity has degenerated. In the Prologue Androcles offers himself as a sacrifice to the lion in order to save his wife, much as a sacrificial lamb is offered to propitiate a wrathful god. In contrast, the Romans use death for sport. When a religion is new and persecuted, personal fortitude is needed to pursue it; hence the Christians are individualists. When a religion is old and established, it appeals to thoughtless conformity; hence the Romans are represented as a mob. As the

spiritual vitality of heterodoxy dies and a religion becomes orthodox, a different type of person is attracted to it, and the individual
adherent is likely to suffer a loss of personal integrity—first because
he submits himself to an abstraction which controls him, and
second because as that abstraction ages it becomes irrelevant to
his vital interests, and the only service he can truly pay it is lip
service.

Shaw's parable amply indicates, on numerous steps of the social
ladder, the simple-mindedness, confusion, and potential perni-
ciousness of those who slavishly follow the route of orthodoxy.
The bitterness of being an outcast is expressed by Megaera in the
Prologue, as she longs for respectability and urges Androcles to
return to duty. The all too possible ignorance and bigotry of conformity are reflected in her comical obtuseness, so reminiscent of
modern fundamentalism, when she refers to followers of the new
faith as "dirty disreputable blaspheming atheists" (p. 430). The
dubious truth of this observation has to do with point of view, not
with reality. The Centurion at the beginning of Act I is equally
dense, speaking from the comfortable confines of conformity. He
is not unlike an old-fashioned Calvinist, sternly reprimanding the
wayward ways of the irreverent: "No singing. Look respectful.
Look serious" (p. 434). His real god is the Captain, who might as
well be Jupiter (or Jehovah), and he threatens the captives with a
special hell—the Colosseum. Similar to eighteenth-century reli-
gionists who urged the young to think on death, he remarks:
"Think of that" (p. 434). The point is that the Christians are at
odds with Authority, and distinctions as to exactly what aspects of
power are being flouted are fuzzy in simple orthodox minds. The
fact that the prisoners are laughing and joking brings a puritan
condemnation: "Theyve no religion: thats how it is" (p. 435).
Further, as the Centurion refers to the Captain, so the Captain
refers to the Emperor. The Emperor is not only Defender of the
Faith, upholding the interests of religion in Rome, but he is reputedly divine, and criticism of him is sacrilege as well as treason.
Thus personal confusion regarding the nature of authority is given
official encouragement. The ironies of "Defender of the Faith"
are manifold both in its anachronism and in the implicit humor

of historical fact. The title was originally granted by the pope to the not-too-divine Henry VIII in 1521, when Henry was still upholding the Roman faith against the incursions of Luther. The Crown subsequently retained the title while turning against Rome, thus giving it a perverse twist. The implication that somehow the Crown had a superior insight into the true nature of Faith involved a presumptuous linking of temporal power and spiritual authority which all Establishments actively or nominally infer and most simple minds nominally accept. Hence the historical tenacity of the Divine Right of Kings. Clearly, the game that the Emperor is playing is age-old and is as full of little ironies as such games played successfully must be.

A measure of the Roman faith and a sense of its modern relevance lie in the shallowness of the sacrifice it exacts of its followers, and the matching shallowness of their belief. The Christians can escape martyrdom merely by following good form and offering a pinch of incense at the pagan altar. When backed into a corner on a question of faith, the Captain excuses his ignorance on grounds that "the military regulations provide no answer" (p. 437), which is an obvious echo of the present spiritual dilemma in which God's Word does not quite seem to fit the dynamic flux of the times. The Captain asserts that Lavinia should sacrifice because this is what "all wellbred Roman ladies do" (p. 438)—an indication, curiously current and recurrent, albeit covert, that breeding and taste have a relationship to faith. The Captain's concern over a receipt for the prisoners, a receipt which must be properly countersigned, offers a passing hint that bureaucracy and detail have become more a matter of concern for the religio-social machine than matters of metaphysics. The works of the world run on the oil of details, which are tangible as fact, while problems of the spirit, which are abstract and elusive, seem too difficult and unreal. On the one hand there is an elite segment of society, the educated, to whom deities are fairy stories (p. 462), handy largely as tools to control the masses. On the other there are the masses, who believe in the deities, perhaps even fiercely, but not with any profound desire to actually follow their dictates. The faith of the educated is eroded by thought and self-interest;

the conviction of the masses is sapped by stupidity and sloth. Great abstractions being uncongenial, the mob turns to sensation —in the Colosseum, or on television. The crowd is moved by instincts akin to those of the vilest voluptuaries, instincts which may either lust to see a woman torn to pieces by lions, or yearn for the violence of sadistic cinema.

Ultimately in question is the perennial superficiality, stupidity, hypocrisy, and cruelty of the respectable, nominally religious fold. Thus Lavinia condemns not the difference of the religion of the Romans, but their religious indifference and false pretensions. The power of Caesar is akin to that of a deity who can do no wrong, who holds the balance of life and death over those in the arena, a reflection of the injustice and cruelty which may result from foolish delegation of authority. The Romans, through a lack of true religious sensibility and intelligence, allow a measure of divinity to the only power they really understand—that of the state—a wry indication that power corrupts not only the powerful. The Emperor takes his advantage accordingly. As Defender of the Faith, recognizing that he is the real god of a spiritually infantile people, he promotes the divinity of his role because it gives nearly unbounded license to private whim. He is analogous to a self-indulgent Calvinist God, wreaking his will capriciously on an ignorant, blind, and weak humanity—a manifestation of the danger of confusing power with virtue.

Thus fallibilities in the conventional religious temperament of modern times are reflected in the spiritual vacuity of Shaw's Romans. The problem is how to rescue religion from the non-believers who use it to maintain the status quo, and from the nonthinkers who negate it in terms of their inanity. Hope for the future lies not in the established religion, which has lost both perspective and vitality, but in those few who, in the true spirit of Christ, violate old forms in terms of personal conviction. Representing such a minority, Shaw's Christians of the first century are subversives, analogous to modern agitator-idealists whom the conservative public views with mistrust, alarm, and hostility. One great irony is that the revolutionary Christian spirit must fight an ossified version of itself in a never-ending battle against its own dwindling vitality and arthritic spirituality. The spiritual goal by its very nature cannot be defined, since an aspect of its perfection is flux and the nature of its being is a becoming. The Christ which Shaw's Christians follow has already been transmuted and fragmented in their individual preconceptions and obsessions. He is wholly present only in their common consent to die for the ideal which he represents for each of them. In this consent they attain his measure of sacrifice both individually and collectively, and his spirit exists in the reality of their conviction. Reality is primarily subjective, and life and convictions can easily be fabricated from fairy stories; but death is an "inexorable reality" which transcends stories and dreams. To commit oneself to sure death is to appraise profoundly the value of life and the value of beliefs which make life worth living. Lavinia is not correct that "a man cannot die for a story and a dream" (p. 462), because men do die for such stories as national glory and such dreams as moral righteousness, but she does effectively intuit that it is in the act of idealistic self-sacrifice, even more than in the cause of that sacrifice, that God may be found. Hence Lavinia is not dying for "nothing," but for "no thing"—"something greater than dreams or stories" (p. 463) —something above finite knowledge, involving human conviction to the uttermost limit of human sacrifice, the sacrifice of life.[14] Intuition is forced to its ultimate test, gaining true spirituality through the extremity of commitment.

In this context the reaction of the audience is to some extent a measure of its spiritual health. As the Christians are tested in the parable, the parable tests the audience. The fact that audiences do not rend their garments or cry blasphemy at Androcles may well be an indication that their proclivity for romance befuddles their ability to reflect on the true implications of the action; or, indeed, it may indicate that they are no longer quite Christian. For the action subverts rather than supports any conventional Christian

14. This is counter to assertions such as those of William Irvine, that "Lavinia's Christianity drops from her bit by bit," and "she must die for no reason at all, simply to satisfy her pride and sense of integrity" (The Universe of G. B. S. [New York, 1949], p. 285). Rather, the implications are that Lavinia has a tenuous, intuitive grasp of a greater spiritual reality.

ethic by presenting that ethic not as a coherent reality (except as Spintho romances with it), but rather as a nebulous abstraction, one which attains life only as it is vitalized by neurotic, fanatic, or idiosyncratic human convictions. Consequently, one may identify with the Christians not as they uphold a common creed, but as they are the underdogs, as they face a common danger, and as they maintain personal integrity—all exciting, but not necessarily Christian, aspects of their predicament. As the Christians are human they are noble, but as they are doctrinal they are inconsistent and absurd. Strictly Christian nobility scarcely exists in the play, and the auditor who finds it may well be partaking of the spiritual fuzziness which self-righteousness draws from religious heroics.

By pointing up the discrepancy between complacent, conformist religion and spiritual individualism, Shaw moves sympathy away from conventional doctrine toward vital personal values. But further, and more important, he differentiates between ideals founded on personal integrity and those founded on romance. From its instinctive sympathies and allegiances in this regard, the audience may find where it truly stands. Having stated in his preface that belief is a matter of taste and that we believe what appeals to our imagination (pp. 365–66), Shaw explores in the play the quality of various tastes and imaginations. The debased imagination founds its spiritual convictions on a romantic, melodramatic consciousness. The refined imagination seeks spiritual truth in terms of hard realities. One builds on patterns and stereotypes; the other violates patterns and stereotypes. Lavinia counters romantic expectations in choosing religion over love and martyrdom over living happily ever after. But religion and martyrdom can be highly romantic in their own right, and it is finally most significant that she chooses personal integrity over the abstractions of a Christian creed. Hence she is a violation of two middle-class romances—young love is not fulfilled; Christianity is not triumphant. Her spiritual superiority and dedication put platitudes to the rack. In another way Androcles counters the romantic conception of noble martyrdom with the ignobility of meekness, and the irreverent suggestion is that the meek are meek because they are weak (p. 460). Androcles may seem admirable as St. Francis, but he is also ignominious as the Little Man—his pluck and absurdity are interdependent. The meek may be blessed, but their self-sacrifice arouses more pity than compassion, and Androcles as the henpecked husband is as foolish as he is brave. But his imagination is founded in love for all living things, rendering shallow the laughter which delights in the ridiculousness of his person. His tenderness seems bizarre only to those of limited sensibilities.

The nobility of Ferrovius resides in his conscience, which is grotesque and inhibiting as a Christian, strong and fulfilling as a pagan. He loses faith, but he does so heroically and honestly, not by default or indifference. He may be comic as he is a Christian, but he is noble as a Martian, and when Lavinia in spite of her higher convictions wishes him success in fighting, the melodramatic and temporal inclinations of a philistine audience are likely to wish the same. Any satisfaction we may gain at seeing him succeed as a Martian where he fails as a Christian is an indication of our commitment to pagan values.

The modern religious temper is no doubt closer to Spintho than to any other character. The rogueries of life—the violations of Christian principles—are clearly more congenial to man than the straight and narrow, and it is convenient to have a ritual scapegoat on whom one may finally ride to glory after a lifetime of transgressions. As the scapegoat for Spintho is Christ, the scapegoat of the play is Spintho. The comic irony of his death is not only that he has lost the salvation of martyrdom, but also that the observer may gain satisfaction at having this representative of his own roguery and weakness eaten up. Spintho carries man's sins on his back, and his destruction, so full of poetic justice, provides the spectator with a vicarious purgation of the consequences of his own lower impulses. The savageness of Spintho's death titillates sadism, humor, and self-righteousness all at the same time; the true horror of this should be that his soul is eternally damned, but the perverse humor is precisely in this fact. Humor exists to the extent that we dissociate ourselves from this representation of man's eternal spiritual weakness.

In such ironic tests of modern man's spiritual sensibilities lies the most poignant message of Shaw's parable. Clearly, the majority of mankind is not like Shaw's Christians; rather, like Spintho, it enjoys corruption while romancing with illusions, presumably to be gobbled up in the end somewhere short of spiritual salvation. The test facing the Christians offers the true challenge: Would *you* face the lions for your faith, or would you rather choose the prudent expedient of sprinkling a few ashes on an altar? As the test is brutal—and as the escape is contrastingly easy —it challenges conviction. There is great temptation in the simple Roman path, which is bland, comfortable, and self-righteous, requiring little thought and less spirit. Shaw implies that mankind, like Ferrovius, is caught between ideals and reality—but that unlike Ferrovius mankind avoids confrontation of the problem or compromises it hypocritically. The Christian convictions of Lavinia, toughly spiritual, opposed to romance; of Ferrovius, agonizingly introspective, opposed to the heroics of glorious victory in the arena; and of Androcles, pacifistic and gentle, are all too difficult and are contrary to philistine notions of romance, heroism, and manliness. So although a large part of the audience might instinctively like to identify with these characters, and in romantic delusion may do so, it is likely to find its true sentiments reflected most closely by the Romans and by Spintho. Besides, the exuberance of the Christians, attractive as it may be, lacks appropriate religious dignity when one considers their impending sacrifice for principles most Sacred and Holy.

In sum, while *Androcles* maintains a penetrating relevance and commentary on the present state of man's spiritual hollowness, it does not drown the point in a bath of emotion. This latter would be all too easy to do, considering the intrinsic pathos of the subject matter. The play's fable frame sets the mood of lightness and comedy, while its parable interior delivers the religious message. The tension between the two maintains delight yet allows for clear development of the theme. The Androcles fable and the pantomime lion remove imminent terror through the audience's foreknowledge that all turns out well. But the idea of terror and the fact that tragedy is only accidentally avoided qualify the laughter. The trappings of terror are here, clearly represented by

Spintho. Lavinia's speech on faith and death points this up and is the conceptual climax of the play. Conceptually, it does not matter whether the Christians are martyred or not. It is their spirit and willingness in the face of the ultimate test which count. The Christians are saved not by virtue but by temporarily pleasing the mob on its own violent and sensational level. They triumph for the wrong reasons, Androcles being saved by a lucky accident, the rest being rescued by Ferrovious' turning to an anti-Christian god. In a spiritual sense the happiness at the end is bogus: if the Christians' cause has gained ground, it has not gained on its own merit. Consequently, what we have is a Happy Ending and little more. There is poetic justice in the lion eating Spintho, but this is romance, not reality. In reality, the reformers are usually eaten, while the Spinthos escape—generally the Christians have not survived, but the Spinthos have. So on the one hand Shaw has the power of his parable in Lavinia and in the threat of tragedy, but on the other he has the comedy of his fable, and finally he has the ironic reflection of one on the other which objectifies both the foolishness of abstractions we would dream by and the potential of realities we avoid.

Thus, though the comedy and the issues of religious faith may conflict aesthetically, their combination produces a special effect.[15] Through their interaction religious melodrama is not merely avoided; it is attacked and exposed, with both the fable and the parable mocking its pompousness and sentimentality. The fable mocks through parody and laughter; the parable mocks through substituting true spiritual sensitivity for inflated spiritual romance. The most important target is less religious melodrama than the shallow, conventional, romantic mentality which supports it. By consciously anachronizing the pagan-Christian conflict, the parable scrutinizes the modern Christian mentality and finds that time has inverted its spiritual role. This mentality reveals its myopia insofar as it romantically identifies with Shaw's

15. While I disagree with Howe that there is a complete failure in aesthetic unity (*Shaw: A Critical Study*, p. 134), I cannot go as far as Meisel to assert a really satisfying unity in the play (*Shaw and the Nineteenth-Century Theater*, p. 325). The ironic interrelationship of divergent qualities does not allow a complete fusion.

vital Christians, while its true nature is escapist, conformist, and pagan. Shaw's new movement in religious drama has considerable justification in these terms. By using humor and satire to shake old forms of religious sanctimoniousness, and by universalizing key aspects of religion both old and new, he maintains an aesthetic and spiritual flexibility ingeniously apt for discriminating between the false and the genuine in man's perennial religious dilemma.

CHAPTER EIGHT

PYGMALION

A Potboiler as Art

Shaw called *Pygmalion* a potboiler, and subtitled it "A Romance." As such, he might well have predicted its popularity. But so many qualities of *Pygmalion* so far transcend such disparagement that the play has special interest as Shavian art at its unpretentious best. The central theme is indeed romantic; but as it evolves, its romance is more social than sexual, and fully as spiritual as social. With unselfconscious ease Shaw has combined pure fancy with a kaleidoscope of mythical associations, and, even more, with a keen social and spiritual sensibility which transmutes a romantic story into a modern myth and touching spiritual parable. Critics have overlooked most of these elements because they tend to approach the play piecemeal, isolating themselves on one strand of argument.[1] Except for a nod in the direction of Cinderella and the

1. For example, the question as to whether or not *Pygmalion* ends as a romance, with an implied union of Higgins and Eliza, has received inordinate attention. Milton Crane suggests the logic of a romantic conclusion in "*Pygmalion*: Bernard Shaw's Dramatic Theory and Practice," *PMLA*, 66 (1951), 883, as do A. C. Ward, *Bernard Shaw* (London, 1951), p. 132; Alan Jay Lerner, "*Pygmalion* and My Fair Lady," *Shaw Bulletin*, 1, no. 10 (1956), 6–7; and St. John Ervine, *Bernard Shaw: His Life, Work and Friends* (London, 1956), p. 460. Contrary logic is argued by Myron Matlaw, "Will Higgins Marry Eliza?" *Shavian*, 1, no. 12 (1958), 14–19; Eric Bentley, "My Fair Lady," *Shavian*, 1, no. 13 (1958), 3; Paul Lauter, "*Candida* and *Pygmalion*: Shaw's Subversion of Stereotypes," *Shaw Review*, 3, no. 3 (1960), 14–19; Stanley J. Solomon, "The Ending of *Pygmalion*: A

mythical Pygmalion, along with a brief concern regarding Eliza's transformation, they have largely failed to come to terms with the real aesthetics of the play, the varied inner tensions which account for its special effects and its artistic success.[2]

Pygmalion unfolds on numerous evocative levels. Most obvious is the imaginative, romantic, dramatic situation, with its lively characters and dialogue, a situation which becomes particularly keen and contentious in the brilliant portrayal of the two principals. Impressed upon this surface action are relatively clear poetic and romantic echoes of the Cinderella fairy tale and the Pygmalion legend. Somewhat more complex, but still immediately intelligible, a social lesson and conscience are projected into the comedy, first revealing the importance of phonetics in the social structure, and, more profoundly, examining the structure itself in relation to individual worth. Beyond this, Shaw becomes far more poetic and suggestive. He takes the elements of his romantic story, his myths, and his social didacticism, and he subjects them to stress in terms of poetic ambiguities and a spiritual parable. The fairy tale of Cinderella does not in fact complement the classical tale of Pygmalion; rather, one plays against the other most ironically. Further, both are counterpointed by minor but poignant themes of medieval morality and modern melodrama. Concurrently, these myths are subject to vigorous social tests. And finally, most powerfully, the action, settings, lighting, story, comedy, myths, and social commentary all aim at the expression of an archetypal pattern in which a soul awakens to true self-realization. Through successive stages of inspiration, purgation, illumination, despair, and final, brilliant personal fulfillment, Eliza progresses toward self-awareness as a human being. Most simply, hers is a movement from illusion to reality; most grandly, she undergoes a spiritual voyage from darkness to light. Thus romance, social didacticism, myth, and spiritual parable converge upon the play

Structural View," *Educational Theatre Journal*, 16 (1964), 59–63; and Louis Crompton, *Shaw the Dramatist* (Lincoln, Nebr., 1969), pp. 141–51.

2. Maurice Colbourne calls it "a lucky play," one which is neither perfect nor extraordinary, and he seems to be somewhat baffled that it nonetheless has a "star quality" (*The Real Bernard Shaw* [New York, 1949], pp. 173–74). St. John Ervine passes over it as "not a major play" (*Shaw: His Life, Work and Friends*, p. 460).

from their different spheres, their tension providing a mutual enrichment. And all the while the dramatic scene, vital in itself,
maintains a story light enough to be widely popular.

With typical assertiveness Shaw claims in his preface a didactic
purpose of making the public aware of the importance of phone-
ticians. He gloats over the play's success and leaps to a remarkable,
thoroughly Shavian conclusion: "It is so intensely and deliberately
didactic, and its subject is esteemed so dry, that I delight in throwing it at the heads of the wiseacres who repeat the parrot cry that
art should never be didactic. It goes to prove my contention that
art should never be anything else."[3] To make his point Shaw is
obviously turning the artistic and entertaining substance of the
play topsy-turvy, since phonetics are only incidentally its subject.
Clearly, great art *can* be intensely didactic, and didacticism need
not imply pedantry. The play does bring phonetics into public
view, but more imaginatively than dialectically. The importance
of language and its use emerges as a cumulative awareness, arising
more from the action than as a net result of Higgins's or Shaw's
comments. Our primary attention focuses on the human ramifications of Higgins's experiment rather than on the mechanics themselves, but the phonetician and his work are always on stage,
impressing their importance on the action. They convey a "message" in the best sense: to the extent that the audience is convinced by the transformation of Eliza, it may carry away some
conviction of the importance of phonetics in society, and of language's essential role in revealing and even in forming character.

But the phonetic lesson, alive as it may be, is merely a stepping-
stone to a more fundamental message beneath the action. The
major didactic achievement of the play is its pointed objectification of the hollowness of social distinctions, and its assertion of
the importance of the individual personality which such distinctions obscure. If a flower girl can to all appearances be made into
a duchess in six months, the only things which distinguish a duchess are inherited social prestige and money, neither of which she

3. *Bernard Shaw: Complete Plays with Prefaces* (New York, 1963), I, 194. All
quotations from the preface, play, and postscript are from this volume.

has earned.[4] The message is projected with unique clarity, confronting the perennial fairy-tale mentality which attaches some esoteric nobility or virtue to social eminence. Eliza's individual assertiveness is unquenchable, and the play gives insight into social generalities by reflecting a vitalist philosophy more than a socialist one. Not any flower girl can become a lady—only one with the appropriate drive and talents. As Candida was not held down by Burgess, Eliza is not held down by Doolittle. Clara, conversely, is scarcely a lady, but she is limited less by a lack of money than by a lack of intelligence. True gentility ultimately rests upon properly channeled personal genius, and the barriers between classes, though they provide protection for vested social interests, are vulnerable to the assault of hard work, common sense, and ability.

The didacticism of *Pygmalion* is thus important primarily as it informs the action, providing a ballast of social observation and giving further dimension to the characters. By themselves, the didactic message regarding phonetics may be interesting and the social didacticism may be true, but the phonetic lesson is scarcely world-shaking and the social implications are rather obvious. More influential in the total effect of the play are levels of myth which counterbalance and enhance its prosaic concerns. Shaw uses these imaginative levels richly and suggestively. In contrast to the coherent bones òf the plot, which bear a striking resemblance in detail, arrangement, and social application to the sketch of the poor girl in Chapter 87 of Smollett's *Peregrine Pickle*,[5] the

4. Regarding this essential level òf didacticism, I am in agreement with Desmond MacCarthy, *Shaw's Plays in Review* (New York, 1951), p. 112, and Martin Meisel, *Shaw and the Nineteenth-Century Theater* (Princeton, 1963), p. 176. Several critics outrightly deny the play's didacticism. Reuben A. Brower calls it Shaw's "least didactic play," in *Major British Writers II* (New York, 1959), p. 692; William Irvine calls it "shameless art for art's sake," *The Universe of G. B. S.* (New York, 1949), p. 289; and Crane classifies it as "satirical comedy" ("*Pygmalion*," p. 884).

5. Shaw at first denied that he had ever read *Peregrine Pickle*. See Archibald Henderson, *George Bernard Shaw: Man of the Century* (New York, 1956), p. 614, and E. S. Noyes, "A Note on *Peregrine Pickle* and *Pygmalion*," *Modern Language Notes*, 41 (1926), 327–30. Much later, however, he admitted the possibility. See

play's mythical overtones are impressionistic and are evoked by association and selection keyed to suit the dramatic context, not by any strict ordering.

Ever present is the classical myth of Pygmalion, with its idealism, magic, and sense of vital fulfillment. In Ovid's version Pygmalion, repelled by the faults of mortal women, resolves to live single. Yet he so desires a feminine ideal that he sculptures an incomparably beautiful maiden in ivory, whereupon he attires the statue in gay garments and adorns it with jewelry. Without breath, however, the beauty is incomplete and the ideal not fully realized; so he prays to the gods, and Venus instills life into his creation. The ivory maiden suddenly gains vision, and she sees the daylight and Pygmalion at once. Pygmalion's desires are thus fulfilled, and he is united in marriage with his living ideal.[6] A spiritual substratum beneath this tale is not difficult to discern. It appeals to the most basic yearnings of all who are to some degree disillusioned by the grossness of humanity and seek an ideal, one which might be simulated in earthly terms but which ultimately may be found only through the breath of spirit, the gift of deity.

The play offers a close parallel to this appealing level, and the associations of the myth instill a sense of magic into the play's action. But just as interesting are the points at which the two deviate. Like Pygmalion, Higgins harbors a degree of misogyny and seeks to create an ideal in Eliza. Though he is an artist in his sense of dedication, he is a cerebral one, quite Shavian, and his final proposed union is intellectual, not physical.[7] Parallel to the legend, he creates his ivory statue by Act III, decking it in fashionable clothes and jewels, and the god of Eliza's psyche (urged, in part,

Hesketh Pearson, "A Shavian Musical," *Shavian*, 1, no. 13 (1958), 5. This and other possible sources are noted in R. F. Rattray, "The Subconscious and Shaw," *Quarterly Review*, 291 (1953), 210–22.

6. The myth comes originally from Greece, being elaborated upon by Ovid. W. S. Gilbert adapted Ovid's version in his play *Pygmalion and Galatea*, which introduced Galatea as the maiden. For a modern translation, see *The Metamorphoses of Ovid*, trans. A. E. Watts (Berkeley, 1954), pp. 224–26.

7. The point that Higgins is temperamentally an artist is made by Emil Strauss, *Bernard Shaw: Art and Socialism* (London, 1942), p. 51, and MacCarthy, *Shaw's Plays in Review*, p. 110.

by Venus) breathes life into it by Act IV, giving her sudden, clear vision of her Pygmalion. However, the creator and the created are out of tune, one existing in a world of intellectual austerity, the other inhaling a vibrant sense of being and seeking emotional fulfillment. The attraction of opposites is held in suspension by the stubborn independence of each, and the play ends in tension, not in resolution.

Contrapuntal to the classical, mythical, and spiritual tones of the Pygmalion legend are the folk-tale, fairy-tale, fanciful associations of Cinderella. The ragged, dirty, mistreated but beautiful waif who is suddenly, magically elevated to high society is common to both the play and the story. A cruel stepmother, a coach, a midnight hour of reckoning, slippers, and a desperate deserted gentleman are integral details of both plots and provide both with the exuberance of romance. There is even a doubling of the "test" in the play, as in Perrault's original version of the tale.[8]

But again, although *Pygmalion* absorbs much of the romantic nimbus, it converts the legend to its own artistic ends. The incidents are jumbled chronologically, reapportioned, changed in context, and they involve variant emotions and significance. The golden coach is the taxi of Act I which Eliza hires in personal defiance of poverty and in assertion of her rights as a human being. The cruel stepmother is both Doolittle's mistress and, as suggested by Higgins, a monsterized Mrs. Pearce. The slippers are Higgins's, and as Cinderella's fortunes turn upon hers, these become the symbol of Eliza's break with the past, objectifying her rejection of Cinderella notions. The magic of the fairy godmother in *Pygmalion* is social and psychological, having little to do with dress and fine jewels, and the mystery of the fairy godmother is not that of a magic wand but of her collective nature: she is something of Higgins, something of Mrs. Pearce, and a great deal of Pickering and Mrs. Higgins. Most important, the key "ball" scene is omitted from the play, because the emphasis here is not on the fairy-tale climax of the triumphant "test"—this has been rendered anticli-

8. For a reproduction of the earliest English translation (1729) of Charles Perrault's tale, see Jacques Barchilon and Henry Pettit, eds., *The Authentic Mother Goose Fairy Tales and Nursery Rhymes* (Denver, 1960), pp. 73–91.

mactic by Act III—but on the social and personal ramifications of the real world to which Eliza must adjust after the test, not the least troublesome of which is a recalcitrant prince charming.

Thus the "reality" of the play is reflected against the romance of legend and fairy tale, and the ramifications are subtle and telling. But even further, one myth is played off against the other. If we see Eliza as Galatea, we see her much as Higgins does in the first three acts—as a statue, a doll, a creature of his own making. Conversely, viewed as Cinderella (which is her own point of view), she is vitally, personally motivated from the very beginning, and Higgins's conceit and blindness as Pygmalion become obvious. The interplay of these variants, of myth against the story and of myth against myth, redounds subtly to the complexity of the ironies and to the delight of the play.

Less obvious than the classical Pygmalion legend and the Cinderella fairy tale, but nearly as pervasive, is a medieval morality element. Eliza in Act I is breaking that little Chain of Being which assumes that flower girls do not hire taxis, and the presence of an Old Testament God may be implied in the lightning that flashes as she bumps into Freddy, as well as in the church bells which remind Higgins of charity. The profound morality test comes in Act II. Here Eliza is The Tempted, most notably in terms of innocent Eve—"I'm a good girl, I am" (p. 219)—suffering from the sins of curiosity and ambition, lured on by Satan Higgins. The symbol of the temptation is a chocolate, taken from a bowl of fruit, the implications of which are nearly biblical: here is a sweet from the tree of the knowledge of good and evil, a psychedelic goody leading to semi-divine worlds beyond the imagination, offered by a diabolically clever and seductive tempter whose intentions are entirely selfish. The combination of hesitancy and desire in Eliza suggests the contention of the good and evil angels in her simple soul, spirits like those of the moralities, one urging the salvation of retreat, the other urging the damnation of acceptance.

The temptation is also evocative of the Faust legend, first in the medieval sense of Marlowe's *Doctor Faustus*, which is correlative to the moral context of Eve's downfall. In desiring language lessons Eliza seeks the knowledge and power of the upper classes, a

presumptuous aim reminiscent of Faustus's similar but more ambitious goal. Eliza's inclination to cross a socially ordained barrier
is a winsome parody of Faustus's unholy inclination to cross a
divinely ordained barrier. Higgins becomes the artful spirit, the
Mephistopheles who has the power to make this possible and who
maneuvers through his own self-interest to render the prospect
enticing. Eliza forfeits her flower-girl's soul to visions of climbing
beyond her station, visions which are fully as profound to her as
Faustus's are to him. And her reward is the damnation of Acts IV
and V, when she comes into an awareness that her former values
were unreal, that heaven has eluded her, and she cries, "Whats to
become of me?" (p. 256). Faustus's final despair is scarcely more
poignant.

But once again there is a typically Shavian twist in *Pygmalion*.
The fear of Old Testament damnation in Act II and the despair of
the last two acts are overcome by the enlightenment at the end. As
opposed to Eve's, Eliza's soul is saved. It is at this point that the
context is shifted toward Goethe's Age of Reason *Faust*: there is
a salvation in the very search for transcendence above human
limitations. The status quo grows brittle as it crystallizes, it does
not fulfill the human spirit, and medieval patterns and inhibitions
are shattered as Eliza breaks free in an assertion of individual
genius and independence. As with Goethe's Faust, truth may be
elusive, but the individual who seeks it is ennobled by his search,
and it would have been true damnation for Eliza never to have
tried. Mephistopheles Higgins may taunt her and work on her
emotions in Act V, but she properly recognizes the devil for what
he is—"Oh, you a r e a devil" (p. 275)—and in this she reveals
her true state of grace.

The play alludes to a form of contemporary mythology as well.
From sentimental fiction comes the melodramatic consciousness
which Eliza and her father reflect in Act II. From Eliza's point of
view, as a poor good girl she is in dire danger of being compromised by a rich, unscrupulous gentleman, a vile seducer. She is a
Pamela, upholding her virtue against Squire B; a Pauline, confronted by an ultimate peril. Thus she remarks to Higgins, "I've
heard of girls being drugged by the like of you" (p. 219), and she

refuses the unreal lure of gold and diamonds—though perhaps chocolates and taxis are a different matter. Similarly, Doolittle enters as the melodramatic father of a ruined daughter, demanding satisfaction, anticipating the worst, and, in an ironic turn, deflated and disappointed that it has not occurred. In the very presentation of this consciousness Shaw laughs it away, but he makes a point in the process which is integral to his drama. If the audience can laugh at the melodrama of Eliza and at melodrama comically inverted in Doolittle, no doubt it should chuckle at the romance of Cinderella. The exposure of one should illumine the fantasy of the other. Eliza's fears are a reflection of the ignorance of the melodramatic state of mind which treats life in terms of absolutes and reality in terms of fiction.

As the mythology and didacticism provide an imaginative, provocative reference behind the scenes, there is an even deeper level which emerges from the action—that of Eliza's evolving consciousness. Commentators have observed that Eliza gains a soul in Acts IV and V,[9] but they have failed to delineate adequately the aesthetic and dramatic terms in which it develops. Eliza's soul grows by degrees, not just at the end. Ostensibly, the lessons and example of her numerous mentors provide the basis for growth. These Eliza absorbs in terms of her vitality and talent, her own essential qualities without which the lessons would prove futile and the transformation hopeless. She emerges as a synthesis of her education, her environment, and her special abilities, her incipient genius flowering in the broader horizons which are offered her by the relative sophistication and freedom of the upper classes. But this explanation only partially captures the poignant sense of real evolution which the play conveys. While the Cinderella and Pygmalion stories are tied irrevocably to myth by the magic of their heroines' abrupt transformation, the Eliza story evokes the overtones of a magic metamorphosis but also maintains a sense of reality through closely tracing a pilgrim's progress of the soul. Poetic realism results from the artistic and spiritual integrity with

9. Eric Bentley, *Bernard Shaw*, amended ed. (New York, 1957), p. 122; MacCarthy, *Shaw's Plays in Review*, p. 109. Bentley's brief treatment of the play (pp. 119–25) is probably the best to date, and I cross his argument at several points.

which Eliza follows an archetypal pattern! Shaw presents her spiritual growth act by act in carefully plotted, psychologically sensitive, progressive stages, and he complements these stages with special effects of setting, lighting, and timing. Thus Eliza evolves according to a soundly forceful archetypal poetry, augmented by the graphic powers of a theatrical dimension.

In Act I the darkness of the night, the rain, and the confusion of the scene reflect the darkness and confusion which envelop Eliza on multiple levels—physical, social, intellectual, and spiritual. Hers is a world of chaos, and she is swept along by it, oblivious to the suggestive portents of the lightning and the church bells. Eliza's ties to her class are apparent in her confrontation with Higgins, and the scene would be spiritually static but for the sudden inspiration of her soul by a few coins. This inspiration is pathetic and partial, but is as much as her consciousness is capable of at the moment. She howls with delight as she examines Higgins's money, which is incidental to him but the door to grand things for her; and with great exuberance and flair she indulges in the extravagance of a taxi, the symbol of a higher order of existence which is suddenly within her grasp.

Eliza enters Act II voluntarily, her ambition fired by the feeble spark of trivial good fortune. With flower-girl naïveté, she is seeking economic security and social respectability. What she scarcely realizes is that this deliberate step toward such goals sharply objectifies her initial impulse and constitutes a key second stage in a much grander quest, one leading toward spiritual emancipation. Although she is myopic as to ends, her goals seem most glorious to her, and her instincts as to the means are instinctively correct— she must have knowledge. Her immediate fate is appropriately purgatorial. The dimness and strangeness of Higgins's drawing-room laboratory offer a fit otherworldly background, an apt purgatory for a flower girl. The social battering Eliza goes through, the burning of her clothes, and the curious, hot, exotic bath amount to purifying rigors quite necessary to cleanse both soul and body: the soul, of childish notions and conceit; the body, of lice.

By Act III the body is clean but the soul still has more pretensions than depth. The light and airiness of the setting reflect the minor spiritual illumination of Eliza, which consists of a more sensitive perception of a higher state and some involvement in it. But she has adopted a new mask more than a new character, a mask which only imperfectly conceals lower-class values. In attempting to live up to the mask and in carrying it off her soul has grown, but in not reconciling the show with reality she is amusingly imperfect.

Act IV, significantly, starts at midnight. In the deflation after the party, beset by surrounding gloom, Eliza experiences the dark night of her soul, the despair of isolation and absence of meaning. But in her despair lies self-realization, since it involves an awakening to the disparity between her ambitions and her means. The values of society seem fragile when compared to her affection for Higgins, but both are frustrations when Eliza can see no hope of expressing herself through either. In this awareness her sophistication at last transcends her façade, and the soul which lays bare its realities to Higgins, causing him to lose his temper, is a soul sufficiently integrated with personality to be able to face social realities. Finally, in Act V, the daylight and the gentility of Mrs. Higgins's drawing room appropriately complement Eliza's union with the social order, now on a sophisticated plane of spiritual identification and self-knowledge. Her powers are certainly enhanced, and her sense of reality has so far advanced that now she is a match for the professor.

Thus Eliza evolves from confusion, ignorance, and illusion to coherence, knowledge, and reality. The inspiration in Act I, the quest and purgation in Act II, the minor illumination in Act III, and the purgation of the falseness in this illumination in Act IV all lead progressively toward the sophisticated unifying of spirit with personality and society in Act V. By tracing an archetypal pattern in these steps, and by richly complementing the pattern with dramatic effects, the play transcends fable on a plane of poetically endowed socio-spiritual parable.[10] The profoundest

10. Curiously, Eliza's development parallels, act by act, the five steps of mystical evolution which Evelyn Underhill explores in her book *Mysticism*, first published a year before *Pygmalion* was produced. Underhill outlines a "composite portrait" of the mystic path, including Awakening, Purgation, Illumination, the Dark Night

aesthetic level of *Pygmalion* exists in this parable, which qualifies the play's less serious aspects and serves as a substratum underlying the disparities, conflicts, and incompleteness of the didacticism and the myths.

Important as they may be, the evolution of Eliza's consciousness, the didacticism, and the myths all are made an integral part of the immediate vivacity of the dramatic scene, serving primarily to give it significance, richness, and depth. Act I, for example, is no doubt the most openly didactic part of the play in terms of Shaw's avowed intention. Yet it is managed with skillful dramaturgy, and the focus soon falls more upon Eliza than upon phonetics. The setting and the action, the darkness, the after-theater confusion, and Eliza's pathetic scramble for pennies are dramatically essential to provide a brief glimpse of the flower-girl's world so that her later transformation will be the more graphic. When Higgins is brought to Eliza's attention and she wails in fear of arrest, the crowd's observation, sympathetic to the girl, falls upon the professor. Shaw thus adroitly sets up his platform, and Higgins's performance is not unlike that of a sideshow artist, or, as Pickering suggests, a music-hall performer. The audience, along with the crowd, is given a brief illustrated lesson in the skills of a phonetician and in the remarkable role phonetics can play in society. But at the same time a lively human dimension is maintained through Eliza. As Higgins plays at his profession, Eliza is in agony, concerned about arrest, her rights, and her virtue. Thus the plight of the poor is contrasted with the privileges of gentility, gutter slang is contrasted with the king's English, ignorance with knowledge, humanity with science. As the phonetic message is exemplified, the social message is implicit, but both add to rather

of the Soul (anguish; a sense of isolation), and Union, all "involving the movement of consciousness from lower to higher levels of reality, the steady remaking of character" (Noonday Press ed. [New York, 1955], p. 169). Though Shaw's debt may not be directly to Underhill, it is to the tradition and its universal principles, implicitly expressed by the spiritual integrity of Eliza's portrayal. These stages of Eliza's evolution seem to offer as clear an explanation for the play's structure as do the more conventional elements of exposition, complication, catastrophe, and resolution, which prompt Milton Crane to agree with Shaw's estimate of himself as an "old-fashioned playwright" (*"Pygmalion,"* pp. 879–82).

than diminish the essential human dynamics of the scene. With her cleverness in extracting the maximum return from her violets, her insistence on her virtue, her assertion of the sacredness of her character, and her laughter at being mimicked by Higgins, Shaw reveals in Eliza an ambition, self-respect, pride, and sense of humor which are bound to triumph dramatically over the soapbox he has provided for the phonetician.

Numerous background elements are subliminally suggestive. The churchfront setting, the lightning and thunder at Eliza's collision with Freddy, Higgins's insistence on the divinity of speech, and the bells which remind Higgins of the voice of God all introduce a quizzical suggestion of divine presence, a morality note. But the real light of the scene comes as Eliza, amazed and thrilled with the relative fortune the gentleman has thrown her, audaciously takes her coach toward the strange glories of genteel life in Act II. This action is singularly vital on many levels, since this is Eliza's first minute step toward self-realization. The spontaneity of the moment, while seemingly trivial, reverberates romantically, socially, and spiritually, all at the same time. The structure of the act is so complete that it could stand by itself. The didactic point has been made, climaxed by a Cinderella triumph. However, the momentary triumph will obviously be squashed in terms of a grander pattern, because the life of *Pygmalion* and the ultimate significance of Eliza lie in anticlimax, and that soon follows.

Act II provides a lively exposition of character which is in itself an expression of the social problem. At the same time it maintains a tension between ignorance and knowledge, illusion and reality, fairyland and fact, which renders the scene a fanciful, whimsical one, wavering between humor and pathos. These incongruous elements are manifest in the different perspectives regarding Eliza. To herself Eliza is a virtuous young woman with worldly intelligence, dignity, and great expectations. To Higgins she is personally "baggage" and professionally a phonetic experiment. To Pickering she is a naïve young woman with feelings, and due the courtesy one displays toward anything feminine; to Mrs. Pearce she is poor, underprivileged, ignorant, and common, yet a human being;

to her father she is little more than the present opportunity for a good time which some quick extortion money will buy. As such views are in constant counterpoint, they provide a vibrant energy to Eliza's portrayal.

Eliza arrives in a Cinderella illusion, a taxi serving as her golden coach, an ostrich-feather hat and a shoddy coat serving as the garb of a fine lady. Her concepts of gentility are founded in the ignorance of her class, and they cling to easily observable surface elements—manners, money, and speech. With these preconceptions and a lower-class shrewdness as to the power of money, she confronts Higgins, obviously to be confounded when he does not fit her stereotype of a gentleman. As he does with her father later, Higgins completely disorients Eliza because she has no realistic context in which to judge him; the scene becomes purgatorial for her as she is reduced from haughtiness to a confusion of terror, weeping, bewilderment, and helplessness. The profane novice is scarcely prepared for *this* sort of initiation into the higher mysteries. She is only equipped to change illusions, from Cinderella to melodrama—she the poor innocent, Higgins the foul villain. It is not until Pickering suggests that she has feelings that Eliza takes up this refrain. She is manifestly incapable of expressing herself or of conceptualizing her state other than in simplistic alternatives, and, in turn, her feelings have shallow definition because she has neither the language in which to express them nor the perspective or experience to objectify them. Thus terror, rebelliousness, dismay, and indignation are all vented by a howl, through which she may reflect different emotions by intonation, but which obscures the expression of her emotion and probably obscures the emotion itself. Eliza is clearly not just a problem of phonetics, but of an entire orientation, and the humor of the scene, resulting from the wide gap in understanding between classes, is also its didactic message.

As Eliza misconstrues her predicament as a seduction peril, Higgins oversimplifies the situation as a fascinating experiment. The Cinderella dreams and Pamela fears have their counterpart in the Pygmalion obsession. By categorizing Eliza as a draggletailed guttersnipe and scarcely allowing that she has feelings, Higgins is dehumanizing her, viewing her with drastically less consideration than Pygmalion granted his ivory. He is indulging in a level of illusion as misguided and potentially more pernicious than hers. He abstracts her humanity in terms of inhuman generalizations. So Higgins becomes a devil in blindness and in method, and the action develops both as an interplay of ignorance with knowledge and of illusion with reality, and as a revelation of two kinds of oversimplification. One involves loss of individuality in dreams and ignorance; the other involves a loss of humanity in taking that ignorance for the person behind it. Eliza ironically lends herself to stereotyping, but Higgins violates his own assumed sophistication in accepting the abstraction. The courteous, considerate voice of Pickering and the prudent voice of Mrs. Pearce, much like the voices of good angels in a morality play, form a counterrefrain to Higgins's demonic, symphonic gust of enthusiasm. But, like the words of most good angels, their admonitions go unheeded.

The grand flourish with which Pygmalion Higgins ends his persuasion is typical of the vibrant associations which echo throughout the act, rendering the complex counterpoint of character, myth, and ideas so effervescent: Higgins begins as Mephistopheles, tempting Eliza with the comforts, riches, and prestige of the world—"If youre good and do whatever youre told, you shall sleep in a proper bedroom, and have lots to eat, and money to buy chocolates and take rides in taxis." He then threatens her with the plight of Cinderella—"If youre naughty and idle you will sleep in the back kitchen among the black beetles, and be walloped by Mrs Pearce with a broomstick"; he suggests the glory of Cinderella and a Happy Ending—"At the end of six months you shall go to Buckingham Palace in a carriage, beautifully dressed"; he evokes shades of Henry VIII, Bluebeard, and melodrama—"If the King finds out youre not a lady, you will be taken by the police to the Tower of London, where your head will be cut off as a warning to other presumptuous flower girls"; he then comes to earth on a pragmatic social level, appealing to Eliza's ambition—"If you are not found out, you shall have a present of seven-and-sixpence to start life with as a lady in a shop"; and at last he concludes with an imposition of personal obligation, plus an implication of spiritual import—"If you refuse this offer you will be a most ungrateful and wicked girl; and the angels will weep for you" (p. 220). The temptation is overwhelming. What chance has a guttersnipe against a professor, the ivory against Pygmalion, Cinderella against her prince, Pamela against Squire B., Eve against Satan, Faust against Mephistopheles, the initiate against the high priest? The devil—paradoxically, a savior—will have her soul.

In the character of Alfred Doolittle, Shaw offers a roguish counterstatement to Eliza's aspirations and reaffirms the potential of a vital personality, even one which has compromised with the status quo. Doolittle has considerable self-knowledge without the sophistication of social advantages. The melodrama which is real to Eliza is meaningless to him, except as he tries to use it for extortion. He is too busy living in the present to lose himself to such middle-class myths as Cinderella. To rise in society is to be trapped by society's inhibitions, and he exudes a preference for the freedom of poverty over the prudence of wealth. Without hypocrisy, Doolittle is willing to face the reality of his sloth and to appreciate the value of money not saved. Yet beneath his frank philosophy there is an element of making a virtue of necessity, and the humor of his candid complacency conceals the pathos of a man who can scarcely afford morals. Everyone may have a price, but the price of the destitute must by necessity be low; refined morality is an upper-class luxury, sustained by adequate bank accounts. Thus Doolittle's rights as a father are worth about five pounds, and the prospect of Eliza entering a "career" as a kept woman is not unpleasing to him—especially when considered in the light of her earlier query: "Whood marry me?" (p. 217). Doolittle has dramatic appeal in his refusal to romanticize his life, and he has comic and thematic soundness in his conscious violation of the bourgeois notions of success which Eliza holds dear.[11] His precipitant rise to the middle classes later in the play offers a comic parallel to Eliza's plight and provides delight as it tests his philosophy, revealing in the same man opposite sides of the problem of

11. Norbert F. O'Donnell posits that Eliza's freedom at the end involves her breaking away from an intimidation by middle-class morality. See "On the 'Unpleasantness' of *Pygmalion*," *Shaw Bulletin*, 1, no. 2 (1955), 7–10.

charity. As the dependent man turns independent, the social drag becomes society's crutch and develops a new compassion for the middle classes. He becomes trapped, besieged by hungry relatives, and intimidated by money, morality, and prudence. Eliza's success is the sensible man's doom. And ironically Doolittle, so aptly named, is more truly a Cinderella than Eliza, since his rise, unlike hers, comes suddenly, completely, and through no direct effort of his own. The true Cinderella is a freeloader whose success is a fairy-tale perversion of the Horatio Alger ideal. Through Doolittle, the motivation for Eliza's dreams becomes clearer, but the dreams themselves take on an additional tincture of the absurd.

In Act III myth is tested against reality, with Cinderella acting the part of a lady and Galatea submitting to critical scrutiny. Eliza has survived her preliminary purgation—the flower girl is at least superficially buried—and the bright, genteel, "at-home" setting serves to complement her budding spiritual illumination. But Eliza is thinking more in terms of Cinderella than of soul, and as Galatea she is a social success less in terms of her mythical perfection than because of her critics' stupidity. The disparity between the magic of the myth and the pretensions of the reality, added to the incongruity between the automatism of the mechanical lady-doll and her ill-concealed flower-girl psyche, account for both the humor and the meaning of the scene. Galatea, Cinderella, and Eliza do not mix. The fancily garbed, phonetically molded Galatea is an attempt to freeze Cinderella into an image of beauty and gentility, but the earthiness of Eliza's curbstone background and the vigor of her spirit are not to be confined. Consequently both myths fall apart, cracked by reality. But in her flower-girl ignorance and conceit Eliza does not see this, and in his enthusiasm Pygmalion is blind.

The only clear head in the scene is that of Mrs. Higgins, whose motherly candor and frankness toward her son cut sharply through his bluff and bluster, quietly yet clearly placing him in perspective. Mrs. Higgins quickly grasps the intrinsic reality of Eliza and sees the concomitant "problem," yet in so doing she is as gentle and kindly toward the girl as she is explicit and stern toward Higgins and Pickering. She is as capable of decorously handling the awkward experiment her son has foisted into her drawing room as she is sympathetic and delicate regarding the predicament of Mrs. Eynsford Hill. Personally, Mrs. Higgins is the ideal of candor, good manners, sophistication, and kindliness which are at the heart of true gentility, and, as such, she provides the standard against which Eliza's growth throughout the play may reasonably be measured. Parabolically, she is symbolic of the ultimate toward which Eliza strives, an all-knowing social goddess (or fairy godmother) who puts the large-talking, unmannerly devil in his place as though he were a small boy, and who reveals compassion toward a presumptuous, trespassing sinner.

The problem which Mrs. Higgins senses regarding Eliza is personified by the Eynsford Hills. Mrs. Eynsford Hill is plagued with manners and social pretensions beyond her means. She is a misfit, a social orphan, and her misfortune breeds misfortune, notably in her children. Freddy's good-hearted simplicity might be sustained by a sizeable bank account, but without financial backing he is adrift, socially above entering trade and economically below obtaining the gentleman's education which would qualify him for something better. Clara attempts to become fashionable by adopting the fads and small talk of sophisticated society, but like Eliza, whose colorful talk indicates the wretchedness of a flower-girl's existence, tinting comedy with pathos, Clara reveals through her uncouthness and abruptness the frustration of living impecuniously on the fringes of a moneyed class. Lacking Eliza's natural talents, she is involved in a life of social tag-ends, pathetic in the disparity between her means and her ambitions, and comic in her ignorance of the disparity.

The didacticism regarding phonetics reaches its peak at this point, with Higgins claiming the alteration of a soul through his science. He is only partially correct, and the limitations of phonetics are apparent in his success. Whereas Mrs. Higgins is limited only by her inability to read Henry's patent shorthand postcards, Eliza is limited by her inability to grasp the genteel mode which enables one to walk home instead of taking a taxi and which inhibits one from using such terms as "bloody."[12] As Mrs. Higgins observes, Eliza is a triumph of the art of phonetics and of the dressmaker, but she is *not* a lady. Her acquirements are superficial, and what she has in natural vigor and genius she lacks in restraint, sophistication, and true spiritual coherence. Thus the play pivots on this central act: the phonetic point has been made, and social implications take over; the myths tend to destroy each other, and Eliza's humanity becomes a problem. She has the manners but not the soul.

Act IV provides the greatest moment of truth for Eliza, revealing her transcendence beyond myth—myth which would, if this were a fairy tale, have rendered the party scene imperative. But any party scene could only display again the illusions of Act III, along with those gains in Eliza's social sophistication which can be better revealed in deeper personal terms here.[13] Shaw delves beyond the point at which most plays would prepare for a rapid conclusion. Prior to this act the primary attention of the characters is on Eliza, her training and her performance. Now that the test is over, the "play" finished, the time comes for plaudits and bows, and while Pickering is generous, Eliza is shoved into the wings by Higgins. The dream has been fulfilled, midnight has tolled for Cinderella, and morning reality is at hand. Eliza's efforts and her importance are denigrated, her ego is shaken, and she awakens to the facts behind her Cinderella illusion. Her despairing cry—"Whats to become of me?" (p. 255)—comes as a true climax to a crescendo of serious concern which has accompanied the comedy through Acts II and III, first voiced fretfully by Mrs.

12. This word was apparently enough of a shocker to the general public that no English newspaper review quoted it, though it was considered a comic highlight of the play. See Henderson, *Shaw: Man of the Century*, p. 615n.

13. Shaw commented that "the scene in which Eliza makes her successful début at the Ambassador's party was the root of the play at its inception. But when I got to work I left it to the imagination of the audience, as the theatre could not afford its expense and it made the play too long." Quoted in Meisel, *Shaw and the Nineteenth-Century Theater*, p. 172. Shaw added it to the film of *Pygmalion*, no doubt as a concession to the lack of imagination of motion picture audiences, just as he added a romantic element as a grudging concession to their fairy-tale expectations. See Pearson, "A Shavian Musical," p. 6.

stepmother further reveals that she is not yet fully a Mrs. Higgins. She is too close to her squalid roots to easily adopt the kindness, understanding, and integrity which transcend class distinctions.

Fairy-tale patterns are further violated when the talk turns to love and marriage, with Higgins avoiding direct personal confrontation of the issue by shifting it toward Pickering. Obliquely, the professor dodges. Less obliquely, the woman pursues (though denying it) under the guise of desiring kindness (which Pickering has amply given her), unsure of her feelings and, in striking contrast to her earlier poise, even more unsure of how to express herself. However, such comments as "You can twist the heart in a girl" (p. 275), "What did you do it for if you didnt care for me?" (p. 276), and "Every girl has a right to be loved" (p. 277) are strong hints as to where her disposition lies.[14] Eliza's snobbery and attitudes now being middle class, it seems likely that her affection toward Higgins would seek the middle-class goal of marriage. When she deals in genuine personal terms with him, as opposed to maintaining her social façade, she tends to slip into flower-girl vernacular which suggests the depth of her emotions. Her final declaration of independence would be more convincing were she not to gain such pleasure in provoking Higgins to wrath. She produces Freddy as Higgins's rival in love (Freddy is significant in this context as a vapid, middle-class, surrogate prince charming, primarily useful as a foil); then, vastly more infuriating for a person of Higgins's temperament, she promotes Professor Nepean as Higgins's professional rival. Eliza triumphs in the notion of Higgins striking her. In this outburst he reveals emotional involvement, and even hostile involvement implies a warmth of feeling, a sense of equality, and perhaps jealousy—a reaction which is not scientific, a reality which is not mental. The emphasis of the closing dialogue thus suggests that Eliza may have found financial freedom but not emotional freedom, and Higgins's final request that she order ham and cheese for him takes this into account. Notably, his request involves a contradiction of that independence he has just extolled in her.

14. The implications of the dialogue contradict Shaw's comment in his postscript that "Eliza's instinct tells her not to marry Higgins" (p. 282).

Higgins seems to be motivated by a desire for Eliza's companionship, not marriage. He admires her new strength of character as he admires his mother's strength of character,[15] but he values her primarily as she serves his ego and convenience. At the beginning of the act Higgins may have been searching for Eliza with all the desperation of Cinderella's prince, but certainly not with the same disposition. His distraction is scarcely that of Romeo: "But I cant find anything. I dont know what appointments Ive got" (p. 261). Through discovering the unique value of Eliza's soul and feelings, he has progressed beyond the shallowness of his early callous, categorical estimates of her, but he has not learned emotional maturity. Now, devil-like, he tries to keep her for her soul and for his self-satisfaction, little else. Thus Eliza's "Oh, you a r e a devil."

A close examination of Higgins's character and comments cannot support a romantic conclusion. He is by nature celibate and self-centered, slightly perverse in both respects. His reference to sensual love in terms of thick lips and thick boots reveals a confusion and revulsion which considers marital sensualism gross. And his justification of his social egalitarianism is equally distorted. His statement that he treats all people the same, as in heaven, where there are no third-class carriages, sounds impressive at first. But it seems less noble on the second thought that it provides him with a convenient excuse both for his callousness toward Eliza and for his self-indulgence in a lack of manners. He treats everyone the same, but this is hardly admirable when he behaves as though he were the aristocrat and they all flower girls. Pickering also treats all women the same, but he is more inclined to treat them as duchesses, since he has a sensitive respect for human dignity and feelings. As Higgins's vitality tends to run at right angles to society, Pickering's vitality runs parallel. One is consequently more startling, but the other is no less real. Pickering's charity and

15. Higgins's exclamation, "By George, Eliza, I said I'd make a woman of you; and I have" (p. 280), has been used (though incompletely explained) by critics to point up Eliza's evolution. Of course Higgins is incorrect—he has helped give Eliza only the façade of a lady and a means of expression. See Louis Kronenberger, *The Thread of Laughter* (New York, 1952), p. 264; Bentley, *Bernard Shaw*, pp. 123–24; and Meisel, *Shaw and the Nineteenth-Century Theater*, p. 177.

kindliness give society a moral meaning which Higgins, with in-
born egocentricity, ignores.

Higgins, finally, is a motor bus temperamentally, a Milton
mentally, and a confirmed bachelor emotionally—a well-drawn
composite which is, all told, a rather formidable nut to crack. He
is much like a precocious, headstrong young boy. He requires a
mother more than a wife and relishes the idea of an emancipated
Eliza being not a woman but a bachelor buddy. In avoiding social
trivia he is missing many of the details which, when considered
cumulatively, make life endurable and worthwhile; in pursuing
scientific truth he is pursuing obscurity, substituting mechanics
for intrinsic humanity. His science is tied to the expression of life,
but he is inclined to negate life for the expression. Insofar as Eliza
brings him to an awareness of his dependency as a human being
on other human beings, and to a perception of the limitations of
his science, Galatea transforms Pygmalion, and the myth undergoes an ironic extension. But Eliza's success is a limited one, and
the chance of a marriage between the two is, for anyone who
closely observes Act V, highly improbable. This bachelor is truly
confirmed, emotionally unsophisticated, hostile to sentiment. The
myths, of course, suggest an opposite conclusion: Pygmalion marries his Galatea, Cinderella marries her prince. Higgins's Oedipus
complex might even logically be channeled toward Eliza, since by
Act V she so closely resembles his mother in insight and sophistication.[16] Socially she is now a lady and eligible. But through Higgins's character Shaw counters the romantic expectations of the
final act, and he does so with psychological consistency, creating a
perverse tension between the anticipated and the actual.[17] Ulti-

16. Shaw's postscript observation (p. 283) that Mrs. Higgins has set so high a
feminine standard for her son that he cannot be content with women of lesser
quality is borne out by Higgins's comment to her in Act III (p. 237), but tends to
be nullified later in the play by Eliza being nearly comparable to Mrs. Higgins.
Shaw's further point that Higgins, through admiration for his mother, has divorced
love and aesthetics from sex may be fair psychoanalysis, and is hinted at in Higgins's repulsive picture of marital intimacy (p. 279), but is largely extrinsic to the
play. Henry B. Richardson classifies Higgins's complex as a "Pygmalion reaction"—
the suppression of love through aesthetics (*Psychoanalytic Review*, 43 [1956],
458–60).

17. In the first production Beerbohm Tree as Higgins sentimentalized the end-

mately, only the fairy-tale preconceptions of a sentimental audience can comfortably turn *Pygmalion* into *My Fair Lady*.

The play is thus comprised of divergent elements of character, myth, didacticism, and parable which are mutually enriching. Their interrelationship is in flux, but it is carefully worked to move the drama forward in terms of a metamorphosis founded in reality. Following variant patterns, the play progresses from ignorance to knowledge: the myths fade into the reality, the didacticism turns from phonetics to life, Eliza's spirit evolves from darkness to light. Even the comedy complements a rising sense of temporal and spiritual awareness, moving generally from a humor of confusion toward a humor which seeks order and understanding. Act I thrives in chaos, the delight of the sideshow. Act II plays levels of comprehension against each other, provoking a humor of misunderstanding, of fact versus fairy tale, of science versus melodrama. Act III is Bergsonian, Eliza being comic as she is mechanical, the decorous manner of her presence being sharply incongruous with the earthy matter of her speech. Act IV involves the humor of a lovers' quarrel, with a comic peripety occurring when the underdog triumphs and the master loses all dignity. And Act V carries this to greater personal depths through a humor of inversion, involving a psychological and spiritual search in which the total complex is sensitively analyzed. With humor, myth, didacticism, and spiritual evolution thus reflecting dynamically upon one another and incorporated vitally into the vigorous story, *Pygmalion* emerges as an effective synthesis of Shaw's careful dramaturgy, intrinsic fun, and thoughtful aesthetics.

---

ing by throwing a bouquet of flowers to Eliza just before the final curtain. Tree wrote to the disgusted Shaw: "My ending makes money: You ought to be grateful." Shaw responded: "Your ending is damnable: You ought to be shot" (quoted in Matlaw, "Will Higgins Marry Eliza?" p. 14). Shaw later remarked that he could not "conceive a less happy ending to the story of 'Pygmalion' than a love affair between the middle-aged, middle-class professor, a confirmed old bachelor with a mother fixation, and a flower girl of 18" (quoted in Lauter, "*Candida* and *Pygmalion*," p. 14).

CHAPTER NINE

HEARTBREAK HOUSE

Shavian Expressionism

Heartbreak House has the distinction among Shaw's major plays of being the one he was in many ways most proud of yet least inclined to discuss. Indeed, he was uncharacteristically reticent and evasive about the play, remarking that "I am not an explicable phenomenon; neither is *Heartbreak House.* . . . These things are not to be explained, and I am no more responsible for them than the audience."[1] This confession is especially remarkable considering the fact that he had subtitled his work "A Fantasia in the Russian Manner on English Themes," and had begun his long preface by explicating Heartbreak House as "cultured, leisured Europe before the war."[2] Apparently Shaw felt that in this case especially there was an artistic substance which transcended prefacing, a quality which was essentially more intuitive than rational. This quality has, not surprisingly, evoked dissension and confusion among the play's observers. While numerous critics have echoed Shaw's own high appraisal of the play, many of these are

---

1. Quoted in Archibald Henderson, *George Bernard Shaw: Man of the Century* (New York, 1956), p. 626. In a conversation with Paul Green he was only vaguely more helpful: "It has more of the miracle, more of the mystic belief in it than any of my others, and, too, it is a sort of national fable or a fable of nationalism" (Paul Green, *Dramatic Heritage* [New York, 1953], p. 127).

2. *Bernard Shaw: Complete Plays with Prefaces* (New York, 1963), I, 449. All citations and quotations from the preface and the play are from this volume.

almost as vague as he in defining its greatness, and there is a no-table handful of dissenters.[3] Clearly, *Heartbreak House* calls for both diligent and imaginative critical sensibilities.

Grasping at the obvious, critics have taken Shaw's prefatory reference to Chekhov as a touchstone to explain *Heartbreak House* and as a standard against which to judge the play's special poetry.[4] This approach is deceptively easy—so easy as to hint that Shaw must have been perverse not to merely point to the preface when he was asked to explain his work. The kinship of *Heartbreak House* and Chekhov's four major plays, particularly *The Cherry Orchard*, is obvious: the society is a decadent one, facing extinction because it cannot come to terms with modern social realities; the setting is a country house; the characters are upper middle class, sophisticated but aimless, listless, and frustrated; the dialogue is disconnected, dissonant, self-centered; the atmosphere is one of pathos, dreaming, heartbreak, and disillusionment; the technique is one of seeming plotlessness, small incident, and minor tones; the philosophic attitude is fatalistic; and the genre is tragicomedy, the wry comedy of life's minutiae being caught in multifold ironies and tragic ramifications. In both playwrights these microcosmic elements suggest macrocosmic counterparts,

3. Among the prominent critics who consider *Heartbreak House* Shaw's best, or one of his best, plays are Emil Strauss, *Bernard Shaw: Art and Socialism* (London, 1942), p. 76; Frederick P. W. McDowell, "Technique, Symbol, and Theme in *Heartbreak House*," PMLA, 68 (1953), 335, 356; Robert Brustein, *The Theatre of Revolt* (Boston, 1964), p. 227; and Louis Crompton, *Shaw the Dramatist* (Lincoln, Nebr., 1969), p. 168. Thomas Mann described it as "a play of which neither Aristophanes nor Molière nor Ibsen need have been ashamed" ("He Was Mankind's Friend," in *George Bernard Shaw: A Critical Survey*, ed. Louis Kronenberger [Cleveland, 1953], p. 254). Most negative about the play is Stark Young, "Heartbreak Houses," in Kronenberger, ed., *George Bernard Shaw: A Critical Survey*, pp. 233–35, followed by the less vehement qualifications of S. C. Sen Gupta, *The Art of Bernard Shaw* (Oxford, 1936), pp. 106–7; Louis Kronenberger, *The Thread of Laughter* (New York, 1952), p. 270; J. I. M. Stewart, *Eight Modern Writers* (Oxford, 1963), pp. 169–74; and Homer E. Woodbridge, *George Bernard Shaw: Creative Artist* (Carbondale, 1963), pp. 106–7.

4. The comparison is common, but most extensive are Charles W. Meister, "Comparative Drama: Chekhov, Shaw, Odets," *Poet Lore*, 55 (1950), 249–57; and Michael J. Mendelsohn, "The Heartbreak Houses of Shaw and Chekhov," *Shaw Review*, 6 (1963), 89–95.

the poetry of detail evoking an epic awareness of ineptitude, waste, and futility. The greater world lurks as an all-too-real ghost just offstage and in the fringes of consciousness.

As obvious as these similarities, however, are basic differences between Chekhov and Shaw, and it is largely in terms of these differences that certain critics have found Shaw wanting. Chekhov's idiom of understatement, subtle implication, and deep inner emotions appears to be at odds with the Shavian mode. The surge of Shaw's mind, the flow of his rhetoric, and the assertiveness of his ego would seem to be inimical to quiet effects. The fact that they are not, and that he maintains many of Chekhov's qualities in spite of his more vigorous artistry, speaks for the versatility and flexibility of his talents. As one might expect, his pace is more rapid, his tone more robust, his characters more abstract and self-conscious, his intellect more didactic, and his presence more overt. However, these are qualities which impinge his particular genius on Chekhov's, giving *Heartbreak House* distinction more through uniqueness than imitation. The aesthetic direction in Shaw is away from a sad tone poem of nostalgia toward a cacophonous fantasia which forebodes apocalypse. Shaw's adoption of many of the Chekhovian qualities assures that a sense of the tone poem survives poignantly in *Heartbreak House*, but he counterpoints Chekhov's muted cadences with a toccata of doom which is distinctly Shavian, and which rises in a crescendo as the play evolves.

This counterpoint shifts the entire emphasis of *Heartbreak House*, evoking a dramatic idiom more complex, as dark, and nearly as subtle as Chekhov's. A sense of dreams, frustration, and illusions prevails in both, but while Chekhov represents a dreamy society through the distractions, traditions, obsessions, and impracticality of his characters, Shaw compounds illusion by placing this society in the context of an all-encompassing dream.[5] Only in a limited aspect is his play about cultured, leisured Europe. Far more profoundly it is about the anguish and despair of a sensitive

5. A few critics have briefly mentioned the dream quality of the play, notably McDowell, "Technique, Symbol, and Theme," p. 339; Woodbridge, *Shaw: Creative Artist*, pp. 104–5; and Brustein, *The Theatre of Revolt*, p. 222.

consciousness facing the vanity, stupidity, vileness, and insanity of social and historical realities. As the microcosm of the situation in *Heartbreak House* symbolically represents the macrocosm of Europe, the microcosm of the heartbroken impresses us as a fragmented, frustrated outpouring of a macrocosmic despair. This despair gains primary, almost tangible reality through the numerous individual disillusionments, misanthropies, and traumas which coalesce aesthetically with the pervasive disenchanted, nihilistic movement of the entire play. The surface farce and trivia sustain the action, but in the end their amusement wanes, transmuted into the grim fascination of a dreamlike, apocalyptic harlequinade.

The basic mode of *Heartbreak House*, consequently, is as much Strindbergian as Chekhovian. The subtle reproduction of detail through which Chekhov raises his theater of modern realism to poetic heights is complemented by the consciousness of a single agonizing oversoul, through which arises the poetry of expressionism. While the power of Chekhov lies in the keen fidelity and typicality of his portrayals of individuals, the greatest power of *Heartbreak House* lies in a central, inner psychology which evokes a tension of reference between fact, symbol, and self. The differing bases of reality in realism and expressionism clarify the distinction. In Chekhov the characters, though highly foibled, are the fulcrum of reality, and their emotional attachments, depths, capacities, and incapacities are the realities which on one hand give them meaning and on another set them helplessly adrift on society and life. In Shaw, the fulcrum of reality is implicit in the oversoul or dreamer, and against this consciousness the characters are set. The characters manifest fragments of this consciousness in their un-Chekhovian self-awareness, the tearing away of masks; the oversoul manifests itself as it sits in judgment. The mindlessness of many is thus coalesced and reacted upon in the mind of one, and while the many are subject to a determinism as relentless as that in Chekhov, the one has an independence which provides a hopeful element of free will. Most important aesthetically, the emotional base which in Chekhov resides in the individuals moves in Shaw toward the oversoul. In either case it is profound, but the former stresses variety while the latter produces concentration. The dream atmosphere of *Heartbreak House* prevails from beginning to end through dreamlike structuring, cumulative references to sleep, fanciful images and connotations, a strongly subjective point of view, and the probing spirit which constantly seeks realities beneath masks. Although this atmosphere is less obvious than in Act III of *Man and Superman*, where abstraction reigns supreme, it is more natural through being far less overtly dialectical. In a conversation with Henderson, Shaw remarked that *Heartbreak House* "began with an atmosphere and does not contain a word that was foreseen before it was written."[6] Indeed, its development is impressively episodic, following as it were the wandering progress of a dream. Entrances and exits, wanderings back and forth and in and out, recurrent references to forgetfulness in Act I, bizarre coincidences, movements, and surprises provide a sense of disconnected impressions drifting in and out of the mind of a dreamer.[7] The episodes are tied together as much by common associations as by a string of plot, and they seem to develop more by accretion than by logic. The relative focus of the total action furthers the mood of drifting in and out of a dream by being far more fragmentary in Acts I and III than in Act II. Characters and situations accumulate and fluctuate rapidly in Act I, with an air of hectic intrusion, while in Act II they stabilize in terms of more prolonged and developed encounters, with characterization becoming deepened as differing levels of reality become apparent. Act III returns to fluctuation, but this time in

6. Quoted in Henderson, *Shaw: Man of the Century*, p. 625.

7. This sort of movement led Harold Clurman to present *Heartbreak House* as "rapid, hectic, almost 'wild,'" with "an element of 'ballet-extravaganza'" and *opéra bouffe* ("Notes for a Production of *Heartbreak House*," *Tulane Drama Review*, 5 [1961], 59–60). Such action is hardly an end in itself, and Clurman's notes reveal that he caught the surface but not the soul of the play—a limitation which Paul Kozelka observes in his review of the production ("*Heartbreak House* Reviewed," *Shaw Review*, 3, no. 1 [1960], 38–39). *Heartbreak House*, like so much of Chekhov, has a subtlety which makes high demands on the director. Desmond MacCarthy remarks that *when it is well performed* "it is one of the most excitingly amusing and interesting of Shaw's plays" (*Shaw's Plays in Review* [New York, 1951], p. 149).

greater serenity, with a modulation toward the grimness of fatalism. Two acts begin with characters sleeping, and all three have a
ceremonial, unrealistic conclusion, with a ritualistic chant at the
end of the first and nihilistic invocations at the ends of the second
and third.

These dreamlike actions and structuring are reinforced by the
nearly thematic recurrence of sleeping and dreaming throughout
the play. The sleeping and dreaming are of many varieties, furthering an otherworldly atmosphere and suggesting an indolent
society, while in their shades of consciousness bringing into question the very nature of reality. On the most mundane level Ellie
dozes onstage as Hesione dozes offstage. Their sleep and drows-
iness set the tone of the play in the first act. Slightly more complex
are the conscious illusions of daydreaming, engaged in by Ellie
regarding Othello and by Hector in his pantomime heroics. In
Ellie's case the daydreaming results from youthful naïveté. For
Hector daydreams seem to be the compensation of a man who
finds himself at a dead end, one which Captain Shotover makes
explicit: "[Hesione] has used you up, and left you nothing but
dreams" (p. 527). On another plane is Shotover's forgetfulness,
which may or may not be real, but perhaps is half so, and at any
rate serves him as a great convenience. If it is not real, it is ironically a manifestation more of mind than of senility, as is his sleep
in Act III, which he turns on and off at will. More complex is the
matter of Mangan's hypnotic trance, a curious and authentic
combination of consciousness and sleep. In the trance Mangan
can hear reality but not participate in it, and as those present assume he is not conscious, he hears the truth. For once he can align
his personal reality with an objective view—this latter being so
disillusioning, so improper, so inconvenient that Hesione insists
he is obliged to forget all he heard as though he were asleep: "You
dreamt it all, Mr. Mangan" (p. 550). Thus social, factual, and
personal views are set at odds. Dreams functioning in this manner
float all life on illusion. Ellie's dreams of Othello and Marcus
Darnley, which unfit her for reality, are matched by Hector's
dream of heroism, Hesione's dream of culture and femininity,

Ariadne's dream of homecoming, Mangan's dream of dignity, Mazzini's dream of Mangan's beneficence, and Randall's dream of Ariadne—all social, cultural, and bogus. Insofar as the characters act upon them, however, their dreams attain deformed, paradoxical reality.

The urge to disrupt and penetrate such fraudulent reality is behind the unmasking theme of the play. Being so rudely antisocial and recurrent, the game of unmasking in itself furthers the total dreamlike impression, as though it were the obsession of a single consciousness. As Hummel in Strindberg's *Ghost Sonata* peels away the social image of the Colonel, the characters in Heartbreak House peel away at one another with a singular compulsion to discover the man beneath the image, and, more deeply, the subconscious beneath the conscious. The fact that the characters are ultimately ineffectual in dealing with the fundamental realities of survival produces the irony that their very sense of honesty and civilization is in substance a dream, inadequate to save them. Mangan's dignity and wealth may be fraudulent, but his bombs are real. Ellie's search for a spiritual direction, Hesione's sense of fair play, and Hector's iconoclastic cynicism are thrusts toward truth, but they prove to be romantic and ineffectual because they are devoid of objective power.

The dream atmosphere, engendered in part by the unmasking games, shortcuts prolonged psychological probes in favor of symbolic truths, and it is the *pattern* of these truths unfolding which suggests the psyche of the play. Realistically, certain portrayals may be faulted for inconsistency: Ellie suddenly shifts from the romance of Marcus to pragmatism and then to spirituality. Hector turns from pet lapdog into bitter misanthrope. Mangan falls from Napoleonic self-assurance to infantile tears. Randall degenerates from man-about-town to a pettishly jealous small boy. The mutations of these characters are consistent with the mode of the action, which is not realism, but an intuitive penetration of fraud in search for the essential factors of life and survival. Thus Ellie's transformation, the most sudden and startling of all, is executed through a psychological shorthand. It could well be logical and natural in an extended context, but here it is highly condensed in a manner of the prevailing patterns of a dream.[8] Her change, and that of the others, is toward a greater sense of reality, a symbolic movement toward truth which serves the function of the dream. By contrast, the characters who have the greatest normal consistency—Hesione and Ariadne—are the ones who are not severely shaken in their delusions and who consequently show the least growth. As education through heartbreak is the central motif of the play, Hesione and Ariadne are not truly schooled, and to be "normal" is to be uneducated. Consistency may be a fault if one is attached to dreams which impose false images on the flux of life.

Once heartbreak shatters the most romantic illusions, each character finds a portion of a new reality. Ellie finds that materialistic motives are more prudent than romantic ones, but both are ignominious when compared to spiritual aspiration. Hector finds that he has wasted himself in romance and domesticity, and that only in danger and daring can he realize true life. Mazzini recalls that in the past he had joined socialist societies, but that the societies, long on talk and short on action, brought about no change. All three express aspects of a disillusionment which should enable them to move in a new, more purposeful direction. But Ellie and Hector's resolutions that the world is vile, and Mazzini's resolution that there must be a Providence, while partially true, are sterile, and the insights the characters achieve through disillusionment are fragmentary. As individuals they contribute substantially to the ethos of the play. Their cumulative self-discovery and despair takes on intellectual and emotional power which fuses, and aesthetically they become agonizing aspects of a greater consciousness. But the individuals in themselves are futile; their means are naïve, and their ends point toward nihilism. A focal point aiming toward a genuine resolution is needed.

The ostensible focal point of moral vision in the play is in Shotover. As a focal point he is deliberately flawed, a grotesque exaggeration whose "madness" furthers both the atmosphere of the

8. MacCarthy (*Shaw's Plays in Review*, p. 151), Stewart (*Eight Modern Writers*, p. 172), and others, dealing with the play on a realistic level, have found Ellie's transformation implausible.

dream and its sense, the meaning of the play being caught in both. Through him the dreamer's intellectual presence is best sensed and defined, since in all of the mask-stripping he is nearest to the crux of reality, most clearly perceiving the inefficacy and power-lessness of the others' dreams, and in his despair he concentrates emotionally the frustrations of the others. Obviously, with beard and manner, here is an aged counterpart of Shaw.[9] Ironically, this is another mask, but one which achieves lively, poignant dimen-sion through being recognized as a mask and not being torn off. In the sense of conventional characterization Shotover attains re-markable life, but as a projection of Shaw he has an extra magne-tism which provides a kinetic effect. Regarding Shotover, Mazzini comments: "He is so fearfully magnetic: I feel vibrations when-ever he comes close to me" (p. 539). This is bizarre, but poetically appropriate to the mythical associations of a man who is seeking the seventh degree of concentration, and dramatically appropriate to a character *sui generis*. Dramatically, Mazzini expresses what is dramaturgically a tour de force: as Shotover exists both in his own right and as a projection of Shaw, he takes on a double reality—that of fiction and that of authorial self-caricature, a character whose capriciousness is matched by earnestness and whose "mad-ness" becomes a testament. In this sense he is, among the other players, quite supernatural, with a powerful symbolic presence which tends to confirm the sense of a dream and to make the dream Shaw's.

In this world where life is founded on illusions, Shotover, with his steady vision, ironically feels that he is dreaming. However, his particular "madness" is akin to Shaw's professed madness of see-ing life with 20–20 vision while all others suffer ocular defects. This vision becomes the touchstone of the play as Shotover curses "the happiness of yielding and dreaming instead of resisting and doing, the sweetness of the fruit that is going rotten" (p. 568).[10]

9. The likeness of Shaw and Shotover has received attention from Francis Fer-gusson, *The Idea of a Theater*, Anchor Books ed. (New York, 1953), p. 197; Hen-derson, *Shaw: Man of the Century*, p. 628; and Julian B. Kaye, *Bernard Shaw and the Nineteenth-Century Tradition* (Norman, Okla., 1958), pp. 16–17.

10. The Shavian spirit of this quotation is reflected in Shaw's later comment: "Happiness is never my aim. Like Einstein I am not happy and do not want to be

His inner conflict is between the slothful dreams which flesh is heir to, especially in age, and the dynamic ethic of action with a moral purpose—which itself becomes a dream when set in a world of immorality and inaction. In all life, dreams of escape are repeatedly in conflict with the dreams of creative imagination, since the latter complement action rather than avoid it. Shotover's particular, prolonged heartbreak lies in the frustration of one type of dream debilitating the other, partially in himself but especially in his society.

A lively network of fantasy reinforces Shaw's Strindbergian mode, contributing to the effect of the action being dreamed, as distinct from the Chekhovian mode in which the action is dreamy. As the play progresses, the audience becomes conditioned more to the unusual, à la Strindberg, than to the usual, à la Chekhov. Physically, the country house is like a ship; metaphorically, the ship is a country. In either case the setting is incongruous—a ship on land or a country at sea—and the people in it dislocated. These people are strange, to say the very least. The captain, who is no longer truly a captain of this ship that is not a ship, is "a wild-looking old gentleman," the "Ancient Mariner," emitting "vibrations" and seeking supernatural powers. He was formerly married to a "black witch," reputedly sold his soul to the devil, and his mystical progeny are two "demon daughters," Hesione and Ariadne. One has so much heart that she emasculates men; the other has so little heart that she enslaves them. Emasculated husband Hector has a T. E. Lawrence complex, dressing like an Arab sheik, a true hero who is a liar pretending he is a hero. Absent husband Hastings is a numskull, appropriately resembling a ship's figurehead with a skull which is presumably wooden. The industrial Napoleon, Mangan, is more bossed than boss; the Italian revolutionary Mazzini has reincarnated as an apologist of the status quo. Even burglars cannot behave naturally. Billy Dunn, by

happy: I have neither time nor taste for such comas, attainable at the price of a pipeful of opium or a glass of whiskey, though I have experienced a very superior quality of it two or three times in dreams" (*Sixteen Self Sketches* [New York, 1949], p. 72). Shaw's reference to whiskey suggests his attitude toward Shotover's rum, which is ambiguous in the play. The Captain's addiction indicates his desperation and decline.

230

chance a former husband of the housekeeper, distant cousin to Mazzini, pirate in China, and boatswain to the Captain—possessing a confusion of relationships which Strindberg would glory in —feigns burglary so that he can be caught to extort money and avoid prison by finding religion and pleading for imprisonment. He preys at the same time on social consciousness and the lack of it, both of which come to the same conclusion. Classical names add a mythical flavor to this fantasia, but, similar to Milton's Latinisms in *Paradise Lost*, they are more for mood than matter. Hesione and Ariadne are hardly even ironic reflections of their mythical counterparts, and Hector is just remotely the hero of another Troy.[11] More apropos to this topsy-turvy world is an allusion to *Alice in Wonderland*, whose spirit is caught especially in Act I. Ellie falls asleep over her book and awakens to a grotesque tea conducted by a strange old man who is "as mad as a hatter" (p. 501). The adventures of Ellie in this dreamlike wonderland could hardly have a more appropriate connotation and commencement. Madness is the order of the day, and one might guess that sanity lies only in the Captain's rum.

The deciphering of this madness and the implicit search for sanity introduces still another dimension into *Heartbreak House*. The intuitive sensibilities of Strindberg and Chekhov are counterpointed by the impression of a highly active mind which is seeking a direction out of the morass, though it is profoundly thwarted by clouds of illusion. Most obviously, this is the Shavian intellect asserting itself in the semi-tangibles of this elusive, seemingly spontaneous dramatic medium. But more profoundly, the intellect takes on the caste of the medium itself by probing away at infinite layers of masks, reminiscent of the complex mode of Pirandello. The bizarre setting, functioning in part as a psychological state made visible, and presided over by a sane old man who is thought to be mad, is a haunting precursor of Pirandello's *Henry IV*, and the concern about levels of reality, with the authorial presence being one of those levels, anticipates *Six Charac-*

---

11. McDowell's effort to make the mythological associations of Hesione and Ariadne specifically meaningful ("Technique, Symbol, and Theme," pp. 343–45) is valiant but unsuccessful.

ters in Search of an Author.[12] The sacrosanctness of objective fact is severely shaken, since so few characters appear to have a true grasp of it, and those who are most confident that they do are also most suspect. As fact is interpreted through the subjective consciousness, it is frequently so transmuted that the subjective consciousness may be said to create fact, which then takes on reality only in terms of consensus and may or may not have an objective correlative. Since the nature of genius is to run at cross purposes or to reach beyond consensus, geniuses may therefore be admired as transcendent or derided as mad. Frequently, of course, they are a little of both, and it is difficult for mundane standards to properly discriminate between transcendence and madness. Such is the case regarding Captain Shotover.

The greatest subjective consciousness of *Heartbreak House* is clearly that of the dreamer, whose presence is sensed most forcefully in Shotover but also less purely in Hector and Ellie, and finally in fragments of insight, emotion, and tone throughout the play. As this consciousness moves both mode and mood, its sense of reality is pervasive, even in madness. The incoherence of the action reflects that of a dream and depicts the aimlessness of society, providing a psychological complement to the erratic behavior of Shotover. More hauntingly, it reflects a feeling of frustration in the play's oversoul as the oversoul seeks to inform intransigent materials. In terms of this greater consciousness the most influential reality of facts exists more in their symbolic significance than in their objective details. Most revealing about *Heartbreak House*, therefore, are not the grim fragments of political and social incompetence which historically led up to World War I but the interpretation of those fragments via individual characters who serve as vital indicators of man's nature, a nature whose limitations portend man's future. These characters have a treble reality, personal, social, and symbolic. Aesthetically, their personal realities, flawed and diverse, contribute to a more complete sense of the symbolic reality of the play, since through their microcosmic

12. McDowell has revealed the greatest sensitivity to this reality/illusion element, discussing it in terms of Shotover, Mangan, Hastings, and the relativity of truth, sanity, and reality (ibid., pp. 341, 348–51).

world of pettiness and delusions the macrocosm of society, normally an inaccessible abstraction but a powerful reality in its own right, is laid bare in its all-too-human weaknesses. The tragedy of the situation thus revealed is that a myriad of mores, conceits, and illusions take on a social reality as these finite minds project themselves onto society in terms which are tangible and influential. The dynamics of assertion tend to create the realities—or illusions —by which men live. The despair of *Heartbreak House* lies in the fear that those of noble and cultured sensibilities have lost their dynamism, and that the vacuum has been filled by ignoble, self-centered, materialistic seekers of power or by guardians of a mindless status quo. Reality itself has shifted in a dangerous direction, because, in Yeats's words: "The best lack all conviction, while the worst/Are full of passionate intensity."[13]

This is starkly objectified in the play by Ariadne's pungent oversimplification: "There are only two classes in good society in England: the equestrian classes and the neurotic classes" (p. 579). The comment is an example of symbolic assertion which gains strength in the irony that, though it is outrageous, it approximates truth graphically and becomes definitive through being memorable. Limited to "good society," the two classes represent the sophisticated, educated pool from which leadership should arise. In this lies a crux of the play: Heartbreak House has no stables because its inhabitants appreciate personal values over horsey ones. Blessed with imagination, culture, and leisure, the Shotover demesne has indeed incorporated as its highest values the cultivation, charm, advancement, humanity, democracy, and free thought which are praised by Mazzini in the last act. By all signs its bohemianism is the outgrowth of a sensitive touch with the greatest realities of life, those involving individual freedom and conscience which abhor fraud, cant, and hypocrisy. From these ranks one might expect the most benevolent, open-minded, qualified leadership.

Juxtaposed to Heartbreak House is the horsey set, dubbed "Horseback Hall" in the preface. This group, concerned more

13. "The Second Coming," *The Collected Poems of W. B. Yeats* (New York, 1956), p. 185.

with animals and sport than with humans and ideas, gravitates toward answers which make life simple and accommodating.[14] Its realities involve order, ceremony, authority, and rules which lift the complexities of life from the shoulders of the individual. Thus Ariadne at the beginning of Act I recalls her early dislike of the "disorder in ideas, in talk, in feeling" of Heartbreak House, and her desire "to be respectable, to be a lady, to live as others did, not to have to think of everything for myself" (p. 495). And near the end of Act III she reemphasizes this in a reference to Mazzini's pyjamas—life is *simplified* by rules of propriety. In a similar vein, far more pathetic and telling, is Mangan's desperate question: "How are we to have any self-respect if we dont keep it up that we're better than we really are?" (p. 584). A life of well-regulated appearance leaves time for a life of easy escape in well-regulated pleasure. Life with such order is life with balance; life without it is, naturally, neurotic.

What Shaw has symbolically and sharply (albeit oversimply) defined is archetypal: his distinction is as old as the one between the ideals of Athens and the ideals of Rome, and as modern as that between college intellectuals and college athletes, humanists and scientists, or professors and businessmen. He has given the distinction a new idiom and place, but, more important, he has attached to it the question of the world's physical and spiritual survival. As such, idiom and locale symbolically transcend the characters, England, and even the play's dreamer in terms of a universal schism confronting a universal imperative.[15] As might

14. Shaw's attitude toward Horseback Hall is apparent in his recollection of a great aunt who thought nothing of mounting him on a frisky pony, but who hid *The Arabian Nights* from him, considering it improper: "This way of producing hardy bodies and timid souls is so common in country-houses that you may spend hours in them listening to stories of broken collar-bones, broken backs, and broken necks, without coming upon a single spiritual adventure or daring thought." In Hesketh Pearson, *George Bernard Shaw: His Life and Personality*, Atheneum ed. (New York, 1963), p. 35; derived from preface to *Misalliance, Complete Plays*, IV, 42.

15. Thus Fergusson feels that in *Heartbreak House* Shaw has achieved a broader perspective, transcending the Victorian parlor: "We feel around it and behind it the outer darkness, the unmapped forces of the changing modern world" (*The Idea of Theater*, p. 195).

be expected, the outward simplicity of the problem is belied by myriad complexities, complexities involving not only values but basic, contradictory assumptions regarding reality. The realities of Heartbreak House are illusions to Horseback Hall, and vice versa. The contradictory assumptions of the two houses are dramatized in conflicting views of man and society, order and disorder, social masks and social games. In prizing human values and culture, Heartbreak House assumes that society must above all be honest and free, allowing each man's genius to express itself openly and without intimidation. The assumption is philosophically romantic, stressing that the greatest reality is in being true to oneself, and that disorder is a healthy reflection of human differences. Social masks and abstractions, consequently, are fair game to the iconoclast, since they conceal and pervert personal reality. Horseback Hall, on the other hand, is philosophically closer to Hobbes, though its inhabitants would probably never bother to read him. From its viewpoint the individual is untrustworthy, and true reality lies in society because society fosters order. The individual realizes himself in terms of social standards, and his greatest reality is tied to his respectability in performing his social role well.

The play is partly structured on the personal reality, disorder, and games of Heartbreak House tearing away at the social illusions, order, and masks of Horseback Hall.[16] We might expect a dramatization of Shaw's distinction regarding the reformer-realist as the great unmasker, which he drew in *The Quintessence of Ibsenism*. But other forces are at work in the play which reveal a vision far more sensitive and complex. The gospels of both houses are apocryphal. While the personal realism of the heartbreakers— Hesione, Hector, and Shotover—enables them to strip away social masks through devastating games, the disorder of their house debilitates them. Instead of moving society, they are playing with it. Their games are ring-around-the-rosy, dizzying but leading nowhere because they do not affect the center of power. These people chastize hypocrisy but do not reform it. Indeed, their

16. In a limited respect Edward Albee's *Who's Afraid of Virginia Woolf?* is a modern analogue. See D. C. Coleman, "Fun and Games: Two Pictures of *Heartbreak House*," *Drama Survey*, 5 (1967), 223–36.

greatest reality is that their bohemianism incapacitates them, setting them adrift from meaningful affairs. Thus their personal reality, lacking pragmatic power, renders them irrelevant, almost illusory, in terms of the great social machine which is grinding toward man's destruction. Conversely, the horsebackers—Ariadne, Hastings, Randall, and their bourgeois cousin Mangan—with all of their illusions of propriety, are nearer to the reality that counts. Their order, though artificial, equips them for action, and their thick-headed insularity removes fear of the consequences. They may be personally humiliated by the heartbreakers, but their creations, their institutions and machinery, will not be. In a curious way their pragmatic skepticism regarding individual human nature has brought about monsters far greater than man, Frankenstein terrors beyond their control. But they dance the social dance nonetheless, insensitive to fate, in an odd sort of romance with their abstractions. Romancing with life is ultimately the failing of both houses. One romances on its own little island of culture, sophistication, and intellectual games; the other, between intervals with horses and social chatter, romances with business, church, politics, and war.

The dichotomy takes on intriguing qualifications in terms of the individual characters. The temporal ruler of Heartbreak House is, notably, neither Shotover, who has faded from vigorous manhood into petulant eccentricity, nor Hector, who is debilitated by frustration between heroic aspirations and ignominious realities. Rather, the real monarch is Hesione, with an infirm daddy and a princeling regent. Appropriately, Hesione remarks, "Oh, I say it matters very little which of you governs the country so long as we govern you. . . . The devil's granddaughters . . . The lovely women" (p. 583). With her beauty, charm, intelligence, and ability to adapt herself admirably to whomever she is speaking to, Hesione is the ideal hostess and the real power of her society. In this fact lies the fatal weakness of Heartbreak House, for the essence of Hesione's capacities is derived from congenial, entrancing feminity. As a delightful portrayal of womanhood, she is superb. With her uncorseted figure naturally asserting her beauty, she exudes a natural frankness with women, an intuitive tact with men, a warm and lucid love for her husband, and even an attractive feminine absentmindedness, revealed in her confusion about introductions. But because of these very qualities Hesione's house is in trouble. Ariadne senses the problem in observing that Heartbreak House is "only a very ill-regulated and rather untidy villa" (p. 590), and Mazzini unwittingly pins it down as he exclaims, "Bless you, dear Mrs Hushabye, what romantic ideas of business you have!" (p. 540). For although Hesione may be practical about money to keep the household going and sensitive to the realities of Ellie's young love, her intuitions above all reflect her womanhood, reacting more than acting, feeling more than thinking. Her obsession with the domestic domain of loves, fancies, and heartbreaks indicates the obliqueness of her touch with the real world outside of Heartbreak House. Thus she at first misappraises Mangan and looks upon Mazzini as the selfish father of a melodrama. Despite all her good intentions, Hesione's house is not in order because of her supremacy in it. Woman's intuition, valuable as it may be at a tea party or a weekend social, is not likely to guide a ship into port, to govern a country well, or to save the world.[17]

Hector's mind, vision, and capacities indicate that he is probably the one who should be the new captain of this ship. Rather, he is its self-conscious, tormented gigolo.[18] Hector's character unfolds in dreamlike fashion as the play progresses, becoming deeper, richer, and more tragic. He gains greater self-awareness and disgust as the full implications of his impotence become apparent. In the face of demands on his psychic virility, he evolves from his position as Hesione's household pet and Ellie's romantic fiction to absurd Byronic escapism ("Let us all go out into the night" [p. 553]), to a despairing sense of unreality ("We do not live in this house: we haunt it" [p. 589]), to the sensational nihilism of tearing down the curtains at the end. Ironically, it is Hector, the

17. The powers that women's intuition *may* have are admirably displayed by Shaw in *Captain Brassbound's Conversion*.

18. Shaw described Hector as a "liar, boaster, hero, stylist, Athos and D'Artagnan rolled into a single passionately sincere humbug" (quoted in Crompton, *Shaw the Dramatist*, p. 158). Crompton describes him as Sergius Saranoff of *Arms and the Man*, after twenty years of marriage (p. 159).

man of masks, daydreams, tall tales, and costumes who objectifies the sport of Heartbreak House: "In this house we know all the poses: our game is to find out the man under the pose" (p. 571). The fact that all the while he has the greatest potential of all suggests his confusion of spirit. He is perhaps more aware than anyone else of the elusiveness of reality and the reality of illusion as he advises Randall, "Never waste jealousy on a real man: it is the imaginary hero that supplants us all in the long run" (p. 571).

Hector's greatest problem is that at one time in his life he surrendered to romance, and ever since he has been unable to extricate himself. The fact that his heroics are more counterparts than surrogates of a genuine heroism indicates his potential, yet at the same time it hints at a psychological incapacity to live up to reality. The particular poignancy of Hector's frustration lies not in a lack of ability, but in a failure to make his ability meaningful. The crux of his problem is Hesione, whose feminine, marital, and maternal powers have prevailed over her husband, destroying his independence and effecting an insidious emasculation. Hesione, well meaning but perverse, has turned their original deep love into a projection of her ideal society, a society which is essentially matriarchal. With cutting disparagement Ellie inveighs against Hesione, "I should have made a man of Marcus, not a household pet" (p. 548), and later Hector rants, "Is there any slavery on earth viler than this slavery of men to women?" (p. 575). His threat to choke Ariadne is but a desperate, pathetic attempt to recover his lost masculinity—an admission, in its violence, of his defeat and despair. The twentieth-century matriarchy prevails. The female principle of the Life Force has asserted itself in a cancerous way, sapping the noble, creative, affirmative impulses of the male by petty romance, social games, and domesticity. The result, naturally, is no sort of superman, but proper, conventional children who are scarcely worth mentioning. And thus we have a Lear-like Hector at the end of Act II exclaiming, "Oh women! women! women! [He lifts his fists in invocation to heaven]. Fall. Fall and crush" (p. 576).

In this light we may see once again in Shaw the type of subtle irony between action and setting which he employs so well in

Arms and the Man, Caesar and Cleopatra, and *Major Barbara.* Except for a small teak table, the setting is strikingly, assertively masculine. But as this ship is displaced in space, it is also displaced in time. Clearly it is an anachronism, a relic and symbol of bygone days when the exploring, adventuresome spirit of men *did* rule the world. As an aesthetic device the setting makes immanent and subtly, quietly pervasive the sense of passing time, of nostalgia, and of social evolution in which entirely new and less dynamic principles of life have come into being. The captain of this ship, Shotover, personifies this sense, giving the impression of a ghost flitting in and out. As the setting is anachronistic and not quite real, neither is he. Similarly, his convictions echo upon the scene as assertions of the past, and, as they are counterpointed with impressions of the present, the tones are those of a weird, nightmarish cacophony. A sense of the universal gap between generations is thus given highly poetic expression. What is vital and real to one age is abstraction and illusion to the next.

Except for Ellie, youthful exuberance plays very little role in *Heartbreak House,* since this is the middle-aged society on whom the country's fate depends. Once again, however, Shaw sets up a youth-age dichotomy, this time primarily between the middle-aged and ancient. And once again, as in *Caesar and Cleopatra* and *Major Barbara,* he inverts usual patterns of vital insight and reveals in age the more dynamic spirit. When Shotover expresses his abhorrence of yielding and dreaming instead of resisting and doing, a yielding which he depicts as his own senility, he is with cutting accuracy describing the mode of Hesione and Hector's bohemian existence. His grip on fatal realities is all too clear, and his senility proves to be more game than fact: his observation that Ariadne is no longer the daughter that left home twenty-three years before reveals a natural sensibility to a reality devoid of sentiment, and his mixing of the two Dunns is proven by Ellie to be conscious play. Similarly, he is lucid on ethical grounds, perceiving the debilitating sterility, disorder, and inaction which are subjecting Heartbreak House to the danger of Horseback Hall's inhumanity. His realistic answer to the problem is twofold: first, he appeals to eternal verities—the kindness and charity of "God's way," which he mentions to Ariadne, and the spiritual quality of selflessness, which he approves of in Ellie. Second, he urges a specific combination of the virtues of both houses—the culture and vital individualism of Heartbreak House must be given relevance to life through the sense of order and action possessed by Horseback Hall. Thus Shotover's reality is a sensitive synthesis which combines eternal values of charity with modern humanism and vitalism. The fact that with these views he is considered "mad" reveals the desperate spiritual plight of his society.

Mazzini Dunn is poised between the two houses. As an employee of Mangan he is physically subservient to the Establishment. But his sense of social propriety, which makes him "safe" with Hesione, is subordinate to an instinctive kindliness and understanding, which make him appreciate the informality and honesty of Heartbreak House over the social façades of Horseback Hall. It is clear whose side he is naturally on when at the first he comments, "The great question is, not who we are, but what we are" (p. 520). The statement, which would be commonplace were it to come from a more sophisticated source, is so typical of the humility and sincerity of Mazzini that it comes through with quiet effectiveness and depth. Mazzini combines naïveté with a sharp sense of reality, both originating from a good heart, and the subtlety of his portrayal results in large part from the humanizing mixture of both. Shaw manages to capture a rounded sense of a truly sweet soul without becoming saccharine—a rather rare feat in literature. With great naturalness Mazzini is engaged by the charms of Hesione, but unlike Mangan he maintains his integrity. He may be deluded about the personal villainy of Mangan toward himself, but his delusion rises from an instinctively charitable and trusting spirit. On the other hand, his vision is amazingly clear regarding Mangan's weaknesses, Ellie's strengths, and the nature of poverty. His suggestion that the burglar become a locksmith is incidental, but it pinpoints his particular coalescence of naïve simplicity, charity, and a practical mind. Obviously, saintly simpletons who work for industrial Napoleons, who admire the humanity, charm, and freedom of the Heartbreak House society and who trust in Providence (like Shotover's drunken skipper), are most unlikely to save the world and are most likely to be taken advantage of. However, with economy and purity of statement, Mazzini's sensitive innocence is poignantly portrayed. He has the unreal reality of an ideal that is seldom realized, prompting Ellie to remark, "There seems to be nothing real in the world except my father and Shakespear" (p. 584).

As Hesione rules over Heartbreak House, Ariadne is the queen of Horseback Hall. It is she who articulates the distinction between the two in terms of the "wrong" people, the neurotic heartbreakers, and her type, the "right" people, the "natural, wholesome, contented, and really nice English people," i.e., the equestrians (p. 579). But before the issue is articulated, Shaw presents it dramatically and thereby achieves an implict dialectical effect. At the very first he juxtaposes Ariadne's sense of social propriety and order to the bohemianism and disorder of her sister's house. Ariadne, as fully corseted as Hesione is not, returns home after twenty-three years expecting a warm and joyous reunion, only to be met by casual indifference. The situation would be shocking to any conventional sensibility, and humor is at first evoked at what seems to be the unconventional response of her sister and father. The base of humor switches very quickly, however, and Ariadne begins to appear foolish as she insists on her prerogatives. The prevailing logic, in short, assumes some of the "madness" of the house as the representation of reality shifts slightly. Obviously, Ariadne is no longer "little Paddy Patkins," and her desire for The Kiss takes on absurdity as it seems more social than familial. She is in one aspect an anachronism, a memory, an illusion the family dismissed long ago, which returns not as the nineteen-year-old girl of memory but as a forty-two-year-old apparition, demanding a better room in proper regard for her age and position. In this respect she is a silly, pompous, sentimental ghost. As an apologist of society, her views are compromised when she admits to Hector that a woman may do as she pleases as long as she is socially respectable, and she becomes ridiculous when she defends social masks in the last act: "I know by experience that men and women are delicate plants and must be cultivated under glass. Our family habit of throwing stones in all directions and letting the air in is not only unbearably rude, but positively dangerous" (p. 585). Such a defense of the façades which seem desirable to Horseback Hall echoes the more epigrammatic observation of Lady Bracknell in *The Importance of Being Earnest*: "Ignorance is like a delicate exotic fruit; touch it and the bloom is gone."[19] The weight of the simile is not likely to be to the advantage of the society which supports it.

The role of Ariadne in Horseback Hall offers a ready gauge with which to compare the two houses. Like Hesione, she is the devil's granddaughter with a beauty and fascination for men, but unlike Hesione, the king is not emasculated—he is merely not present. Ariadne may have an emasculating influence as she leaves lovers strewn about the Empire, but she does not surrender her propriety, nor does she respect weak men. Randall is a rotter because he is lazy, and she cites Napoleon's opinion that "women are the occupation of the idle man" (p. 573). Hector is a handsome diversion, possessing gallantry and a degree of dash, but he is part of a social game akin to the one she is playing with Randall, since she has no intention of paying off. The absent Hastings, on the other hand, is her lord in a very well-regulated world, and the manner in which she cites him reveals that she never forgets it. Randall remarks disparagingly that Hastings "has the gift of being able to work sixteen hours a day at the dullest detail, and actually likes it" (p. 570). Obviously, this is part of what qualifies Hastings as governor and husband, and what disqualifies Randall and Hector. Hastings may be pedantic, he may be a numskull, but he has power not only because he can ride horses, but because he *works*. Thus Ariadne can make her assertion, "The man is worth all of you rolled into one" (p. 583). The dangerous irony is that men of so little imagination have climbed to the top while greater, lazier men play games in their wives' parlors. Hastings could save the country with autocratic power and enough whips, but would a country thus saved be worth living in?[20]

19. *The Complete Works of Oscar Wilde* (New York, 1923), VIII, 41.
20. Shaw is ambivalent, however, commenting in his preface, "From what is called Democracy no corrective to this state of things could be hoped" (p. 452). He is apparently still searching for a benevolent superman.

Mangan may not belong in Horseback Hall in terms of family, but according to position, temperament, and values he does. He overdresses, which a man of good family would consider in poor taste, but he reveals thereby a consciousness of image which is the mystique of Horseback Hall society. In defiance of Mazzini's sententiousness, he asserts that who we are is a fair measure of what we are. He is in many ways a parallel of Hastings—both are pedantic drudges, both are ruthless, and both have power. Sadly, worldly respect and influence come to them on an ascending scale according to these qualities, and as they are not imaginative men they assume that the world is right, and that order, aggressiveness, and power are virtues in themselves. The facts that Mangan is a money-grubber, afraid of his men, unsure of himself, and not personally wealthy are less real to the world than his image.[21] As Mazzini remarks, "People believe in him and are always giving him money, whereas they dont believe in me and never give me any" (p. 588). This well-ordered, rational society thus exists on an irony which inverts reality and illusion: what counts is who we are, not what we are, since belief is more important than fact. As might be expected, society is double-crossed, getting the worst, which it deserves. While Ariadne has her games of love, and Heartbreak House has its games of truth, Mangan has his games of business and government, which naturally reflect his ignoble character: "Achievements? Well, I dont know what you call achievements; but Ive jolly well put a stop to the games of the other fellows in the other departments. Every man of them thought he was going to save the country all by himself, and do me out of the credit and out of my chance of a title. I took good care that if they wouldnt let me do it they shouldnt do it themselves

21. Shotover used similar image-power to control his barbarous sailors. But his diabolical guise was a pragmatic trick, and he did not believe in his own mask as, to a large extent, Mangan does. A comment by Shaw in 1896 is apropos: "Nothing is more significant than the statement that 'all the world's a stage.' The whole world *is* ruled by theatrical illusion. . . . The case is not one of fanciful similitude but of identity. The great critics are those who penetrate and understand the illusion: the great men are those who, as dramatists planning the development of nations, or as actors carrying out the drama, are behind the scenes of the world" (*The Works of Bernard Shaw*, XXIV: *Our Theatres in the Nineties* [London, 1931], II, 280–81).

either. I may not know anything about my own machinery; but I know how to stick a ramrod into the other fellow's" (p. 582). Thus, in a devilish game of one-downmanship, the country is incidentally sabotaged. For anyone acquainted with the civil service, probably of any country at any time, this fearful exaggeration of a certain sort of debased mentality has symbolic power.

Strangely, Mangan is more credible in his mask of an industrial Napoleon than as the psychically stripped man of Act III who desperately feels he may as well be physically stripped also. In his extreme incapacitation he is bizarre, almost surrealistically dreamlike, partaking of and contributing to the undercurrent of despair. But there can be no question that he has gone through a most unnerving wringer: the absolute truth. With irony, humor, and drama Shaw presents the symbolic tableau of two women standing over a prostrate, defenseless, hypnotized man, discussing with complete candor, even ruthlessness, his vices and inadequacies and how they plan to use him for their own ends. Social amenities are discarded; female stars are absolutely in the ascendant; the image is smashed. Doubly poignant is the afterview that all the time the poor male was helplessly conscious, hearing reality, as it were, in a dream. Within minutes the shock treatment of Mangan effects the emasculation that Hesione took years to produce in Hector. As in Ellie's case, psychological evolution is dramatically short-circuited, effecting dreamlike economy and sharp symbolic emphasis.

Similarly symbolic, though also as capricious as a dream, is the burglar incident. The Heartbreak House society may bare the man beneath the monster in Mangan, but on practical grounds it is incapable of controlling the monster, and this incapacity is manifested simply in its reaction to Billy Dunn, a less sophisticated thief and fraud than Mangan. The incident with Billy pointedly objectifies vague abstractions of law and order by thrusting them into the parlor, and the sum of the characters' reactions is a desire for disinvolvement, Hesione on humane grounds, Ariadne on grounds of privacy and inconvenience. In its one chance to assert itself in terms of the greater world, Heartbreak House finds its civic responsibility distasteful or too troublesome.[22] Typically, Mazzini manifests the social-worker consciousness in suggesting that the burglar turn to an honest trade, but, most telling, it is the horsebacker Ariadne who finally loses patience and urges prosecution. While the bohemians allow themselves to be run over, the law-and-order temperament takes initiative by default because it will not be pushed too far. The social analogy is poignant—since Mangan is a gangster boss on the side of law and order, the bohemians are in a sorry plight indeed. Not being able to handle microcosmic realities, they are desperately inadequate regarding macrocosmic ones. Surrounded by their upper-middle-class milieu, they are insulated from the total social environment, and their base of conceptualization is pathetically finite. To some degree they are like the average Yahoo that Shaw describes in the preface, for whom World War I existed not as the giant catastrophe it was, which he could not imagine, but as many little catastrophes of a size befitting his limited sensibilities (p. 467). The immense realities do not exist for these people because they do not have the greatness of consciousness to comprehend them.

Apparently a new order of consciousness is needed, and as Ellie evolves toward this she becomes the play's aesthetic focal point, complementing the moral focal point in Shotover. The degrees of self-knowledge that others achieve through heartbreak are but variants and complementary motifs of her movement toward understanding. She progresses through the major options of the play, each with its particular set of realities, clarifying them through a single vision and frame of reference. Starting in an adolescent dream world of Othello and Marcus Darnley, where reality is bounded only by the limits of her fancy, she is jolted into the world of Heartbreak House as her dream of a hero is contradicted

22. McDowell ("Technique, Symbol, and Theme," p. 336) and others have felt that the burglar is superfluous, but Shaw commented that he "is not a joke; he is a comic dramatization of a process that is going on every day" (quoted in Arthur H. Nethercot, *Men and Supermen* [New York, 1966], p. 45n.). More clearly, Shaw remarked that critics "grin at the burglar as the latest Gilbertism, and never reflect on the fact that every day malefactors exploit the cruelty of our criminal law to blackmail humane people" (quoted in Crompton, *Shaw the Dramatist*, p. 163).

by mundane fact. But the realities of the house—the disorder, inaction, frustration, enjoyment of broken hearts, playing at love, sentiment, and iconoclastic games—are clearly no answer for a poor girl. In her station they offer only the most futile and fruitless of diversions, which would end not just in disillusioned, neurotic old age, but in very real penury. So with cold calculation she turns to the practical, ordered world of Horseback Hall with every indication that she can beat it at its own game. The inversion of a potential melodramatic pattern is striking. Instead of the rich, lecherous old man forcing marriage on a poor, innocent young heroine, the hard-minded, practical young woman measures the old man for his money and presses for marriage, at the same time making it perfectly clear that she intends to pursue a close relationship with a younger man. The change in Ellie from innocent young thing to hardened cynic works as a dreamlike foreshortening of very credible psychological processes. But even more, her change involves a self-assertion well motivated by obvious realities: not being a fool, she will exercise the options she has and fill her role as a woman in the individualistic, free, dominating fashion of Heartbreak House, while reaping the rewards of Horseback Hall's money and respectability. With her romantic illusions well chastized she instinctively seeks the best of both worlds, and in taking Mangan she still plans in some degree to retain her original romance with Hector. Such romance may be second hand, but it will at least be well financed.

Ellie's compromise makes excellent sense, being a prudent extraction of all she can hope for from romance and the two houses. But counterposed to this rational course is her soul, and while her response to reality is at first spirited, it lacks spirituality. Her description of heartbreak reveals her awareness of this latter, indicating that her soul is far nearer to Shotover's than to the others': "It is a curious sensation: the sort of pain that goes mercifully beyond our powers of feeling. When your heart is broken, your boats are burned: nothing matters any more. It is the end of happiness and the beginning of peace" (p. 561). The effect of disillusionment has been to propel her toward age and wisdom, rendering her susceptible to education by Shotover, whose words indicate their spiritual kinship: "Old men are dangerous: it doesnt matter to them what is going to happen to the world. . . . I tell you happiness is no good. You can be happy when you are only half alive" (pp. 566, 587). Heartbreak has great potential if it brings an end to the pursuit of illusion, especially illusion founded on self-interest, because only by reversing the spiritually consuming whirlpool of egocentricity can the soul awaken to the broader consciousness of life and reality. Ellie is on the right path when she remarks: "I feel now as if there was nothing I could not do, because I want nothing," which Shotover approves: "Thats the only real strength. Thats genius" (p. 569). This is the great spiritual leap enabled by heartbreak, far transcending the ignoble materialism which Ellie embraced in the first phase of her disillusionment. Through adopting a materialistic course, she might eat, but she would not truly live. Now, in wanting nothing, there is nothing for her to fear or to sell her soul to, and she can be spiritually honest, for, like an old man, she has nothing to lose. Thus Shotover is her spiritual husband and second father, and Ellie offers the glimmering hope of combining youth with wisdom.

However, while Ellie's evolution explores the deeper implications of heartbreak, traversing the social realities and psychological strata of the play, it reaffirms the social problem. Ellie may take to the Captain, but the fact remains that the Captain has taken to rum, and no one is at the helm. Nothing seems to be real except her father and Shakespeare, both of whom give quality to life but cannot save it. "Life with a blessing" is indeed an admirable goal, signifying the beauties and richness of an existence dedicated to humanistic values, but this is not enough. Even Ellie's spiritual marriage to Shotover, while symbolically hopeful, is a futile gesture in the face of cruel fact. All that is left at the end is a *desire* to feel life fully, and this desire reaches its ultimate form in confronting the most inexorable of realities, death. Earlier, Ariadne remarked that she had never *lived* until she rode a horse, and similarly, Shotover felt life most keenly when confronting the reality of the elements, piloting his ship in a storm. To confront danger and death is to confront life. Thus Ellie urges Hector to set fire to the house, so that they will be a better target for the bombers, hazarding, as it were, a double immolation. At this point the action comes full circle back to romance—with Ellie still calling Hector "Marcus"—but it is a romance of life, not an illusion, since it involves a danger which most meaningfully intertwines life and death. This romance loses its sense, unfortunately, as it is linked to hysteria. The tone is grotesque and macabre, the characters behaving, as Hector observes, like moths flying into a candle. Ellie's hope at the very end that the bombers will come again is an ambivalent reaction to fate. At last these people embrace their humanity, sensing life in true violence and danger, but their exuberant reaction is as practicably futile as was their former indolence. Their desire for life is locked in a death wish, and the play ends in a haunting paradox.

This sensational conclusion climaxes not only the mental flux between reality and illusion in *Heartbreak House*; far more potently, it is the culmination of an apocalyptic spirit of prophecy which grows throughout the play. Surprisingly, critics have concentrated on Shaw's mention of Chekhov in the preface, and have usually neglected the nearly equal space he gives to Tolstoy, whom he mentions first. Aside from the dream play aspect, which is very compatible with the Chekhovian mode, the assertive, highly ethical and messianic voice which rises through the action has a distinct kinship to that of Tolstoy.[23] In distinguishing between the two men, Shaw observes that, as opposed to Chekhov's gentle fatalism, aloofness, and charm, "Tolstoy did not waste any sympathy on [Heartbreak House]: it was to him the house in which Europe was stifling its soul; and he knew that our utter enervation and futilization in that overheated drawing-room atmosphere was delivering the world over to the control of ignorant and soulless cunning and energy, with the frightful consequences which have now overtaken it" (p. 449). One need only to substitute "Shaw" for "Tolstoy" in this quotation to capture an emphatic spirit in

23. Both McDowell ("Technique, Symbol, and Theme," p. 339) and Brustein (*The Theatre of Revolt*, p. 222) note the Tolstoyan element. Observing this same quality, Henderson (*Shaw: Man of the Century*, p. 628), Kaye (*Shaw and the Nineteenth-Century Tradition*, p. 16), and Crompton (*Shaw the Dramatist*, p. 153) draw an analogy to Carlyle. The Carlylian spirit does exist in much of Shaw; I adhere to Tolstoy here, however, as being more apropos to the context.

Heartbreak House which qualifies its Chekhovian tone, energizes its Strindbergian consciousness, and informs the entire context of illusion and reality with a grim sense of underlying moral and spiritual truths. In foreboding the consequences of culture and power being in separate compartments, the play assumes much of that deep seriousness about life which Tolstoy had found wanting in *Man and Superman*: "Dear Mr. Shaw, life is a great and serious affair . . . ." [24]

Judging and judgment are recurrent motifs in the play. The characters judge one another, the authorial presence is constantly judging, and, above all, there is the impression of an eternal, immanent, inescapable Judgment presiding over the whole. The depiction of the characters is in keeping with this severe aspect. With a seeming deliberateness they are not rendered strongly sympathetic, and the audience itself assumes the role of judge through a sense of detachment. Emotional disengagement is the general mode: Ellie neutralizes sympathy, since heartbreak hardens rather than debilitates her; the pathos of Shotover is mitigated by his eccentricity, his rum, and his unwanted happiness; Hector is too much a fraud, too bizarre, and too cutting in his disillusionment; Hesione and Ariadne are too confident and self-controlled; Mangan is too ignoble as a boss and too ridiculous in heartbreak; Randall is absurd in his pettiness and childishness; and the burglar is an amusing grotesque. Most sympathetic is Mazzini, whose heart and charm are strong, but he is a motif secondary to the central action. Since the characters are more fascinating than engaging, the dramatic emphasis falls on the social situation and maintains a degree of aesthetic distance. Yet there is a profound quality of emotion which rises from the play as a whole. This results from the accretion of the many expressions of heartbreak, disillusionment, and despair which shadow the house increasingly toward the end, giving constantly greater weight to Shotover's conviction of the folly of it all. Implicit cries of "folly, folly, folly," and "beware of the day of Judgment," though very old-fashioned, seem apropos.

24. From a letter without date, reproduced in Henderson, *Shaw: Man of the Century*, pp. 582–83.

The moral, almost biblical fervor and sense of judgment arise fragmentarily in Act I, gain focus as Shotover lectures Ellie in Act II, and become prophetic in Act III. They exist in a double sense of allegory, Christian and social. The groundwork is laid in Act I, when all mankind is implicated in the drama, presented as a brotherhood in which none are perfect but each is responsible for the other. Man shares a common lot, and with an awareness of this should face his fellow men and his God. Notably, this assertion comes from the bohemians of Heartbreak House, not from the socially respectable horsebackers. Hesione cuts through abstractions of good and evil which, by making a melodrama of life, create false social attitudes: "People dont have their virtues and vices in sets: they have them anyhow: all mixed" (p. 512). Shotover, through the perspective of age, neutralizes social divisions: "Do you suppose that at my age I make distinctions between one fellowcreature and another?" (p. 516). Mazzini asserts the importance of the personal nature of an individual over his social station: "The great question is, not who we are, but what we are" (p. 520). And Hector links this concept of a common order to his personal perception of a higher order: "We are members one of another. . . . I must believe that my spark, small as it is, is divine" (p. 526).

On this ground of man's equality before God, Shotover later addresses Ellie in terms which are universal, Christian, and as old as the distinction between *cupiditas* and *caritas*: "It's prudent to gain the whole world and lose your own soul. But dont forget that your soul sticks to you if you stick to it; but the world has a way of slipping through your fingers" (p. 564). Old-fashioned this may be, as Ellie observes, but it is nonetheless true and relevant. In the manner of *Major Barbara*, Ellie feels that poverty is damning her by inches, to which Shotover responds in a messianic tone: "Riches will damn you ten times deeper" (p. 565)—because, as riches insulate a man from life, with its hardships and dangers, they insulate him from his intrinsic humanity, which is inextricably bound to his spiritual reality, to the spiritual realities of others, and to God. Thus it is harder for a rich man to get into heaven than for a camel to pass through the eye of a needle. The principles of Undershaft are pitted against spiritual principles and ultimately are found to be deficient. The individual who sells himself is not likely to have a soul worth salvaging.

Act III serves as an exemplum of Shotover's words to Ellie. The act opens in a dreamlike mood—here is the social ship drifting toward disaster on the indolence of its middle-class luxury and attitudes. Its soul, having avoided the realities of the greater world for so long, has been incapacitated by irrelevance. Over all hangs Mangan's presentiment of doom, absurd at first, but poetically reinforced by the strange drumming in the sky. The drumming, though reminiscent of the breaking harp string in *The Cherry Orchard*, is more ominous than nostalgic, and Hector sets the tone of the act by describing it with symbolic accuracy as "Heaven's threatening growl of disgust at us useless futile creatures," to which he adds, "There is no sense in us. We are useless, dangerous, and ought to be abolished" (p. 578). The speech has special poignancy both as an expression of Hector's personal frustration and as a general harbinger of doom which rises out of the prevailing mood of the play. After Ariadne's distinction between the equestrians and the neurotics, an obsessive question floats upon the scene, quite illogically, but with dreamlike pertinence to the underlying moral theme: Who will save the country? Mangan is talented at jamming the other fellow's efforts, Hector will not be listened to, Hastings would rule with a stick, Hesione gives women ultimate power, Ellie seeks life with a blessing, and Mazzini trusts in Providence. Implicitly, they are all judged for foolishness, ineffectuality, tyranny, or blindness. Clearly, in Shotover's prophetic terms, which keynote the strain of cosmic disgust at the end, they have not found "God's way," and the old man transcends his rum with sudden savagery and vehemence, envisioning England as a ship and this society as the drunken skipper, all about to smash on the rocks. His final exhortation, citing "the laws of God," comes like that of an exasperated prophet, or as the voice of the dreamer suddenly breaking through before awakening in a sweat: "Navigation. Learn it and live; or leave it and be damned" (p. 594). And, apocalyptically, the bombs explode. The Tolstoyan, Christian, Shavian judgment is upon Heartbreak House.

Augmenting this element of Christian parable and apocalyptic myth is the allegorical frame. Shaw executes the allegory on several levels, both concrete and suggestive, which give an additional poetic richness to the drama.[25] Most obvious is the ship metaphor, expressing the central theme in terms of setting, characters, and action. As we have observed, the setting indicates England's adventuresome past, when, as Shotover remarks, England experienced true life through danger. The props are those of an England of work, creativity, and action, all also past. The characters, playing against the tradition of England's past, are the idlers or rogues of today, members of the class which would ordinarily be looked to for leadership. One group, the cultured society most fit to govern, is too bohemian and detached; the other group is too mundane, corrupt, or unimaginative. Mangan, the "captain of industry," is the pilot at home; Hastings, the petty tyrant of the colonies, is the vestigial remnant of Empire. In their hands lies the poor, honest confidence of the simple Mazzinis. Shotover, who once navigated as England once ruled the waves, selling his soul to the devil (of imperialist ambition) in Zanzibar (the Far East), is too old for power and can do nothing but despair at the corruption and idleness of the modern sailor.

Various names, in a rather haphazard manner, are puns in accord with the allegory. Shotover has overshot, and his shots are over; Hector Hushabye is the hero of Troy, asleep; Ariadne and Hesione are classically irrelevant; Mazzini Dunn is the revolutionary, done, finished; Hastings Utterword is, by inference, hasty in utterance, without thought of moral complexities, a namesake of the notorious, high-handed, authoritarian governor general of British India (the utter word in colonial assertiveness); and Mangan is a "Boss"-man, metallic, manganic—hard, brittle, not magnetic. As culture in Heartbreak House and power in Mangan are in separate compartments, youth in Ellie and wisdom in Shotover coalesce only spiritually. Their union is a sterile one. More fertile was the union of white and black, of Shotover with the "black witch" of Zanzibar (a half-echo of the *Othello* references), which

25. William Irvine gives the clearest explication of the allegory. See *The Universe of G. B. S.* (New York, 1949), pp. 294–95.

produced the demon daughters and which lends a morality tone to *Heartbreak House*. References to devil, demons, damnation, and hell abound, but, like the punning, they are more suggestive than cohesive. Though Shotover's soul was redeemed by the Negress who presumably educated him in the ambiguities of life through the perspectives of another culture, his demon daughters make the world a hell for their lovers by triumphing over them in an inversion of nature. Heaven growls in disgust because this is not God's way. The old orientation involving salvation through action and understanding has begotten a disorientation involving damnation through sloth and bewilderment. Meanwhile the captain, like Adam (and Voltaire), turns ever more to the innocence of his garden, which becomes his Gethsemane.

The dramatic idiom of *Heartbreak House*, in sum, is far more complex than the realistic mode of Chekhov. It is a fantasia in a very full sense of the term, reaching back into the nineteenth century for religious and political tradition and forward to the twentieth century for dramatic expression. Along with Strindberg it finds most intense reality in inner consciousness, and along with Pirandello it is fascinated with the myriad of illusions and realities in art and life. But mutating all of these mediums is the Shavian puritan consciousness, dealing in metaphor, parable, and morality, nearly as old-fashioned and fundamentally Christian as Tolstoy. This latter gives focus to the free movement of the expressionism, while the expressionism gives richness and artistic scope to the moral consciousness. The total effect results from intense personal conviction combining with the broadest worldly concerns in such a way that each gives life to the other. Thus the broken hearts of individual characters in the play cumulate in terms of common denominators to provide a unitive sense of a much greater heartbreak, partly in the consciousness of the dreamer, which is sensed through them, and, more broadly, in the whole society which they represent.

The quality of this heartbreak gives it profound significance. It is not primarily romantic, but anti-romantic, being destructive of illusions as the realities of life force themselves upon the individual: heartbreak, in short, is life educating man. Ellie finds peace in it, but this is atypical, perhaps a feminine reaction, since indications are that Hesione has also found a sort of peace with herself. Far more typical are Hector, Mangan, Randall, and Shotover, for whom heartbreak apparently begins in indignation and ends in despair. Only Mangan experiences the complete process on stage, but all have clearly gone through the cycle at some time and are manifesting some aspect of it, with heartbreak lingering in the despair. The universal sense of heartbreak rises from many particulars, starting in Act I with Shotover seeking the seventh degree of concentration in order to destroy the enemies of society. His ambition, in its irrationality, seems to involve the desperation of a last step where all else has failed, the pursuit of an ideal unattainable because of ubiquitous folly and corruption. The universals of his problem and his feeling of personal inadequacy are expressed in his question, "What then is to be done? Are we to be kept for ever in the mud by these hogs to whom the universe is nothing but a machine for greasing their bristles and filling their snouts?" (p. 525). He reflects the philosophy of *Major Barbara* as he asserts, "We must win powers of life and death over them . . . I refuse to die until I have invented the means" (p. 526). But the absolute fact of death confronts Shotover's age, feeding his despair and breaking his heart because he knows it will overtake him, and he acknowledges the fact by escaping into rum. He built a house so that his daughters might marry well and produce better children, but one married a numskull and the other married a liar, neither producing progeny fit to inherit the earth.

Very likely Shaw found *Heartbreak House* difficult to discuss not only because of its intuitive nature, but also because its dilemma and heartbreak were so personal to him. As Shotover is Shaw, suspended between caricature and alter ego (an aged version of the Tanner-Juan composite), we see in his age, obsolescence, and impotence the playwright's profound agony at his own insignificance and powerlessness in the face of the brutal realities of World War I.[26] There is a strong sense of Shaw's personal an-

26. Irvine interprets *Heartbreak House* as representing the fourth and most acute stage of Shaw's disillusionment (ibid., p. 236). See also Robert W. Corrigan, "*Heartbreak House*: Shaw's Elegy for Europe," *Shaw Review*, 2, no. 3 (1959), 2–6;

imus in Shotover's frustration and vehemence, especially as the frustration gathers force through being echoed by the other characters. Shaw himself was being educated by the world in a manner which confirmed the doubts he had held at the writing of *Man and Superman*. The power to blow up one's enemy's ammunition by a mind ray and the pursuit of a seventh degree of concentration are bizarre projections of Shaw's desire to effect social change through means primarily mental, and to achieve perfection through the will of the Life Force. All, of course, to no avail—instead, the way of the world was violence, not intellect, and the exploding ammunition was directed by capitalists who, virtually unimpeded, had propelled the world into war, a war wherein the drifting, chauvinistic, stupid masses were applauding the death of Beethoven at the hands of Bill Sikes. And instead of Creative Evolution we see the Life Force vitality being sapped by age, the Life Force woman emasculating her husband, and all optimism for a better future drying up in a sterile union of youth and wisdom, a union whose only reality is symbolic.

The moral assertions in Act II might as well be undercut by rum, for all the good they do, and Shaw, like Shotover, may well have dreaded his dreams as the mental meanderings of one whose life was by all odds nearly over—meanderings such as those of this play. In Act III Shaw appears briefly and pathetically in Mazzini, who "joined societies and made speeches and wrote pamphlets.... Every year I expected a revolution, or some frightful smashup: it seemed impossible that we could blunder and muddle on any longer. But nothing happened, except, of course, the usual poverty and crime and drink that we are used to" (p. 592). More tragically, he appears in Hector: "[*Fiercely*] I tell you, one of two things must happen. Either out of that darkness some new creation will come to supplant us as we have supplanted the animals, or the heavens will fall in thunder and destroy us" (p. 578). The image of England as a ship, a metaphor derived originally from Carlyle, stayed with Shaw for years. Don Juan had asserted that to be in hell was to drift, to be in heaven was to steer. Shotover as-

Stewart, *Eight Modern Writers*, p. 171; and Brustein, *The Theatre of Revolt*, p. 221.

serts navigation. But it is too late, since, in Hector's words, again reminiscent of *Man and Superman,* "We sit here talking, and leave everything to Mangan and to chance and to the devil" (p. 592).

The delineation of psychological and associational patterns in *Heartbreak House* does not depend on a knowledge of Shaw's state of mind, since the patterns have independent power and evoke their own moods. They are factors in a nightmare which by inversion creates its dreamer. But as Shotover slips between eccentricity and prophetic coherence, and as Hector gives voice to the cumulative despair, extra dimension is added by sensing the dreamer as Shaw, confronted with the implacable movement of history and unable to do anything about it. Similarly, the bohemians' stripping away of masks gives them a special Strindbergian expressionistic quality, but also makes them more distinctly characteristic of Shaw than of "cultured, leisured Europe." Whether the despair rises through Shaw or an anonymous dreamer, however, it expands beyond finite consciousness toward a foreboding of general dissolution, a result of the spiritual nature of man being too weak to control his material powers. The dramatic poetry is again evocative of Yeats: "Things fall apart; the centre cannot hold; / Mere anarchy is loosed upon the world, / The blood-dimmed tide is loosed . . . ."[27]

The ending comes with a convergence of nightmare and reality. By the time of the bombing, the play has moved sufficiently into a dreamlike atmosphere, with a basic frustration so well conveyed and a psychological pattern so well developed that the characters' abnormal, enthusiastic reception of impending catastrophe is grotesquely appropriate to the situation.[28] The themes of the drama

27. Yeats, "The Second Coming," *Collected Poems,* p. 184.
28. In an ironic contribution to art, a German Zeppelin flew over Ayot St. Lawrence in October 1916, when Shaw was working on *Heartbreak House.* When the craft was shot down, he went to see the wreck. Shaw describes the incident in a letter to the Webbs and reveals a source for Ellie's concluding enthusiasm: "What is hardly credible, but true, is that the sound of the Zepp's engines was so fine, and its voyage through the stars so enchanting, that I positively caught myself hoping next night that there would be another raid" (quoted in Henderson, *Shaw: Man of the Century,* pp. 378–79). See also Arthur H. Nethercot, "Zeppelins over Heart-

are met by a Beethovenesque climax, German and bombastic. In a striking physical objectification of the earlier games Hector tears down the curtains as if he were tearing off masks. Now the reality is death, the one inexorable reality of the play; with metaphorical irony, turning on the lights of the house manifests a desire to turn on the light of the soul in a confrontation with dangers which are the essence of life. Appropriately, the Life Force people want light, while the horsebackers hide or tremble. Aesthetically it takes Beethoven to revitalize the psyche and to destroy the mundane forces, such as Mangan and the Church, which plague the world. The fact that World War I did *not* destroy civilization allows Shaw's sense of anticlimax to save Heartbreak House. But the danger, clearly, is still there, for the bombers will probably come tomorrow, and unless Heartbreak House's frenzy of nihilism can be converted to energy which will steer the ship out of the storm, the ship will no doubt end up on the rocks.

Poetically, the end speaks for itself, but in his preface Shaw strikes a significant note in accord with the ending's hollowness and lack of resolution: "Heartbreak House, in short, did not know how to live, at which point all that was left to it was the boast that at least it knew how to die: a melancholy accomplishment" (p. 457). Lest some nobility other than that born of madness and desperation be attached to such suicidal bravery, he observes: "In truth, it is, as Byron said, 'not difficult to die,' and enormously difficult to live. . . . Does it not seem as if, after all, the glory of death were cheaper than the glory of life?" (p. 474). Looking ahead, Shaw speaks of the vindictiveness of England in demanding stringent reparations after the war, and he prophesies that "this thoughtless savagery will recoil on the heads of the Allies" (p. 473). He refers to "the next war" (p. 475) and remarks that, "with the usual irony of war, it remains doubtful whether Germany and Russia, the defeated, will not be the gainers" (p. 476). His remarks are strikingly apropos, reminding us how Shaw, though occasionally wrong, could so frequently be penetratingly right. In fruitlessly urging charity and humanity, Shaw is once

break House," *Shaw Review*, 9 (1966), 46–51. In the play this impulsive response is far better founded.

again Shotover: "Alas! Hegel was right when he said that we learn from history that men never learn anything from history. . . . If men will not learn until their lessons are written in blood, why, blood they must have, their own for preference" (p. 485). The stage was being set for a repeat performance.

CHAPTER TEN

SAINT JOAN

Spiritual Epic as Tragicomedy

The unique power of *Saint Joan* arises from its stress on factors which would seem to conflict with the legend of a saint, yet which undergird the legend through giving it a fresh, contentious, and broad context. Shaw subjects mysticism to rationalism, heroism to skepticism, villainy to understanding, and sanctity to humor, piercing traditional stereotypes with an irreverent, unrelenting scrutiny. The myth, far from being destroyed, is tested, and as it ultimately triumphs it emerges with a new energy and strength, having been rendered both credible and poignant on grounds which appeal to the modern imagination. The tale of Joan is vividly presented, but more intriguing is Shaw's penetrating conceptualization of the intrinsic nature of Joan, of the complex society in which she lived, and of their nearly epic interrelationship. While qualifying the supernatural with the human, Shaw links the human to great abstractions. He thereby vitalizes both myth and history with a twofold thrust, rendering them movingly alive through convincing human denominators and memorably significant through timeless social and spiritual implications. His undertaking, combining the immediacy of drama with a sensitive view of myth and a broad philosophical perspective of history, is a heroic attempt at a heroic totality. It incorporates both tragedy and comedy, which ultimately fuse in terms of compassionate understanding. To isolate the tragedy, the comedy, the myth, or the history, as have so many critics, is to distort his total achievement by partitioning it or by overemphasizing one aspect of a subtle complex. Responding to this complex, Luigi Pirandello was most apt when he described *Saint Joan* as "a work of poetry from beginning to end."[1] Indeed, in its language, scope, cohesion, and inner dynamics the play involves poetry of a very bold and impressive sort.

Shaw's preface to *Saint Joan*, while extensively ramified by the play, is well worth a brief examination since it helps clarify germinal elements of his approach. Most notably, Shaw discusses the uniqueness of Joan, his particular artistic-historical viewpoint, and the "medievalism" or sense of allegory which distinguishes his dramatic method. His distinction of Joan as both genius and saint objectifies her nature on multiple levels. Joan as a personal figure takes on life as a "hardy managing type . . . a born boss . . . [a] combination of inept youth and academic ignorance with great natural capacity, push, courage, devotion, originality and oddity."[2] When these qualities are combined, Joan's genius also becomes credible, with its "different set of ethical valuations" (p.

1. In the *New York Times Magazine*, 13 Jan. 1924; reprinted in *The Shavian*, 2, no. 8 (1964), 11. More than any other Shaw play, *Saint Joan* has been cited for its poetry. See John Mason Brown, "The Prophet and the Maid," *Saturday Review*, 27 Oct. 1951, p. 29; Thomas Mann, "He Was Mankind's Friend," in *George Bernard Shaw: A Critical Survey*, ed. Louis Kronenberger (Cleveland, 1953), p. 254; H. Lüdeke, "Some Remarks on Shaw's History Plays," *English Studies*, 36 (1955), 245; and Arthur Mizener, "Poetic Drama and the Well-Made Play," in *English Institute Essays: 1949* (New York, 1965), pp. 33–54. Mizener's analysis is particularly apt: "Shaw's work has—again like the work of all great poets—the inexhaustible fascination of thought and feeling dramatically suspended in a controlled medium. . . . Every great moment in the play echoes the whole play, exactly as do the great moments in a poem" (pp. 48–49). While a few critics have objected to isolated lapses in Shaw's prose poetry (i.e., Joan's speech in Scene V about the bells; her expression in Scene VI of a love for rural life), and some have found the play too wordy, more have sensed the greater qualities which I shall deal with here, and a number would agree with J. I. M. Stewart that this is conceivably the finest English drama since Shakespeare (*Eight Modern Writers* [Oxford, 1963], p. 179).

2. *Bernard Shaw: Complete Plays with Prefaces* (New York, 1963), II, 270, 284, 285. All citations and quotations from the preface and the play are from this volume.

269) from the norm, valuations which contribute to her spectacular destiny. But most significant, and most haunting, is a sense
that rationalists "will never catch Joan's likeness" (p. 270), because in her coalescence of drive, insight, personality, circumstance, and power there was "something more mystic," which
Shaw describes as "forces at work which use individuals" for transcendent purposes—an "appetite for evolution, and therefore a
superpersonal need" (pp. 275–76).

We may not grant Shaw his specific terms, but as Joan emerges
through his play we are likely to grant her an extra power which
qualifies rational explanations with at least a covert sense of the
supernatural. Thus he may call Joan's visions and voices illusory
and describe her as a Galtonic visualizer, with "nothing peculiar
about her except the vigor and scope of her mind and character,
and the intensity of her vital energy" (pp. 279–83), but in the
accretion of her manifest capacities lies a hint of something transcendent which gives her a quality beyond genius. Shaw's ambivalence regarding this quality is suggested in the preface and grows
in the play. Ironically, he creates a sense of Joan's mystical nature
through his rational examination of the multiplicity of her genius.
Her visions and voices may be only the result of a hyperactive
imagination, but the inspiration she derives from them, and her
stunning achievements, suggest forces at work which far transcend mundane humanity.[3]

According to any conventional view of history, Shaw is certainly
being blatantly anachronistic when in both the preface and the
play he points up Protestantism, nationalism, and Napoleonic
realism in Joan. These elements were obviously not articulated in

3. In a speech to the Heretics Society of Cambridge on 29 May 1911 Shaw remarked: "As for my own position, I am, and always have been, a mystic" (reproduced in *The Religious Speeches of Bernard Shaw*, ed. Warren S. Smith [Univer-
sity Park, Pa., 1963], p. 33). By and large, critics have felt that the miraculous over-
powers the rational in *Saint Joan*. See J. Kooistra, "*Saint Joan*," *English Studies*, 7
(1925), 14; Patrick Braybrooke, *The Subtlety of Bernard Shaw* (London, 1930),
p. 205; S. C. Sen Gupta, *The Art of Bernard Shaw* (London, 1936), p. 139; Stanley J. Solomon, "*Saint Joan* as Epic Tragedy," *Modern Drama*, 6 (1964), 441–43;
and Louis Crompton, *Shaw the Dramatist* (Lincoln, Nebr., 1969), p. 194. Solomon and Crompton perceptively indicate the play's ambiguity regarding the natural
and the supernatural, skepticism and faith.

any such manner in the early fifteenth century. However, as they symbolize elements in Joan's spirit and help objectify her actual influence on her environment, they serve as touchstones of understanding, touchstones which render Joan's medieval world more real by making it accessible and relevant to the modern mind. Critics who have objected to Shaw's lack of historicity have misappraised his method and missed the point of his drama.[4] Shaw is striving for poetic truth rather than specific accuracy of fact—for a balanced, philosophical (and inevitably somewhat Shavian) comprehension of the times rather than for detailed verisimilitude. He acknowledges that Joan was a pious Catholic (p. 265), but with the instinct of an artist he points up those unique elements in her which had implications far beyond the Catholic mold.

On his most vulnerable historical point—his assertion of Cauchon's fairness—Shaw remarks in his preface that "the writer of *high tragedy and comedy*, aiming at *the innermost attainable truth*, must needs *flatter* Cauchon nearly as much as the melodramatist vilifies him" (p. 313; my italics). The purist may object, with good cause, that this is not truth, but the purist may be missing greater truths, since involvement in detail can so frequently obscure underlying principles. While Cauchon may have indeed played the role of a villain, such a category distorts him because it is no doubt at odds with his estimate of himself and because it stereotypes him in a pattern which emotionally obscures his historical position as a defender of the Church. For balance, both the personal and religious realities must be clearly presented and not melodramatized. Congruent to this vein, Shaw continues: "But it is *the business of the stage* to make its figures

4. See M. C. D'Arcy, "Bernard Shaw's St. Joan," *Month*, August 1924, pp. 97–105; J. van Kan, "Bernard Shaw's *Saint Joan*: An Historical Point of View," *Fortnightly Review*, July 1925, pp. 37–45; J. M. Robertson, *Mr. Shaw and "The Maid"* (London, 1925); Charles Sarolea, "Has Mr. Shaw Understood Joan of Arc?" *English Review*, 43 (1926), 175–82; J. L. Cardozo, "*Saint Joan* Once More," *English Studies*, 9 (1927), 177–84. Robertson's book-length study, an interesting broadside on Shaw's historical inaccuracies, curiously qualifies itself by doubting that *Saint Joan* will be discussed thirty years hence (p. 98). The historical critics have two major objections: (1) Joan's saints were *not* imaginary to her, and she was in no conscious way a revolutionary; (2) her trial was a partisan one and by its very nature could not be fair.

more intelligible to themselves than they would be in real life; for *by no other means can they be made intelligible to the audience.* . . . The play would be unintelligible if I had not endowed them with enough of this consciousness to enable them *to explain their attitude to the twentieth century* [with an] *inevitable sacrifice of verisimilitude"* (pp. 313–14; my italics). History is thus given meaning through art. In heightened self-awareness both individual characters and great abstract movements take on memorability through a poetic discipline involving concentration, selection, and dramatic patterning. Joan is subjected to rationalism and her age is subjected to anachronistic terms, with both Joan and her age becoming all the clearer as they transcend rationalism and anachronism on grounds which appeal to enduring levels of spiritual and temporal understanding.[5]

Shaw's medievalism, a quality which influences the philosophy and structure of many of his dramas, is a central element in *Saint Joan.* In comparing his play with those of Shakespeare, Shaw comments, "There is not a breath of medieval atmosphere in Shakespear's histories," whereas "I have taken care to let the medieval

---

5. Shaw wrote to Sarolea: "Read the trial and nothing else, and you will see that it turned, with insistent laborious explicitness, on the Protestant point. . . . I have no theory about Joan, and understand her no more than I understand myself. . . . None of us *know.* . . . I have deliberately abstained from learning in this matter so that I might the easier get into Joan's skin, and not into that of her historians" (Sarolea, "Has Shaw Understood," p. 182). Earlier he had remarked to Walter Tittle: "But this play of mine is simply a dramatisation of the facts as chronicled" ("Mr. Bernard Shaw Talks about *Saint Joan,*" *Bookman,* 67 [1924], 144). Shaw's apparent inconsistency is analyzed by Ludwig Lewisohn as "an extraordinary blending of actuality and interpretation. . . . Joan, like the inquisitor, knows too much. But it is precisely this too much of knowledge which, brought home to the imagination and the heart with touches of sublimity, differentiates Shaw's *Saint Joan* at once and permanently from all other plays and books on this mere subject" (*Nation,* 23 Jan. 1924; quoted in Irving McKee, "Shaw's *Saint Joan* and the American Critics," *Shavian,* 2, no. 8 [1964], 15). This view, with which I concur, has also been expressed by Kooistra ("*Saint Joan,*" pp. 12–13), and J. H. Buckland, "*Saint Joan,*" *History,* 9, no. 36 (1925), 273–87. Louis Martz points out that Joan's most Shavian remarks are usually her own, taken closely from T. Douglas Murray's 1902 translation of the official trial records, which were published by Jules Quicherat in 1841–49. See "The Saint as Tragic Hero: *Saint Joan* and *Murder in the Cathedral,*" in *Tragic Themes in Western Literature,* ed. Cleanth Brooks (New Haven, 1956), pp. 163–64.

atmosphere blow through my play freely" (pp. 311–12). Though he is indulging in overstatement, his distinction between Shakespeare's Renaissance spirit and his own is a key one. In *Richard II* Shakespeare typically explores the depths of humanity in a king, while in *Saint Joan* Joan's efforts are to make a king out of a flawed human being. While Shakespeare stresses the reality of the individual, Shaw stresses the reality of abstractions, commenting that "a novice can read [Shakespeare's] plays from one end to the other without learning that the world is finally governed by forces expressing themselves in religions and laws which make epochs rather than by vulgarly ambitious individuals who make rows" (p. 311). The case is surely not this simple, since the problems of power are very much a concern of Shakespeare, just as the problems of the vital individual are a concern of Shaw. But there can be no doubt that the social-religious-political context prevails in Shaw while the psychological context prevails in Shakespeare. As Shaw perceptively delineates those great abstractions which impinge upon the individual, his focus is less on a string of specialized human encounters than on the great forces and patterns which bring about life's recurrent tragedies and comedies. Insofar as the germ of man's moral disease lies not just in the heart of the individual, but in the individual as influenced, mutated, or corrupted by the complexities of his society, Shaw's emphasis is in this aspect more ambitious and far-reaching. Ultimately he is both old fashioned and modern, caught in the abstractions of the Middle Ages and the abstractions of the twentieth century, imaginatively relating one to the other in hopes of illuminating both.

Shaw's most Shakespearean character is Joan herself, who from the very first distinctively thinks of people as individuals, an outlook evidenced in her calling most men by their first names. One of Shaw's alterations of history is to have Joan refer to the Dauphin as "Charlie," whereas in fact she generally referred to him as "gentil Dauphin." The dramatic objective is clear: to use given names is to equalize, to place all on a common human footing. The effect is to elevate Joan and to project her spiritual egalitarianism on the play, since as humans we are all children of God. Such an attitude in part accounts for Joan's direct power, but it is her fatal weakness as well, since she falters through failing to appreciate the grim reality of the abstractions behind individuals. The aesthetics of the play are in large part involved with the strength of her simplicity moving in counterpoint and contest with the stifling complexity of her society. As she ignores the latter, she rises meteorically, but as she does not understand it, it at last crushes her. In terms of spirit she is the stronger, but in terms of mankind which exists in spite of spirit, the social, religious, and political realities which surround her impose their mundane will. Joan, with her individualistic viewpoint, dramatically reveals both the power and the limitations of that viewpoint.

Joan's nature and status may be clarified by comparing her to Shaw's Caesar. Each represents a highly evolved manifestation of the Life Force, and the two have kinship as impressive historical phenomena whose genius serves as a context against which their respective worlds may be defined. Both are superhuman in a Nietzschean sense, since they create their own ethics, but while Joan is instinctive, unselfconscious, naïve, and spiritual, Caesar is rational, introspective, sophisticated, and transcendently moral. Their roles are similar in their great spiritual superiority, in their sense of spiritual isolation, and in their attempt to educate royalty to its responsibility. Caesar's power is both temporal and inspirational, but Joan's is mainly inspirational, and her tragedy has a different aspect from his. Caesar thoroughly understands his world, and his problem involves being caught in its schemes of sociopolitical vengeance despite his better instincts. Joan, on the other hand, is largely ignorant of the corrupt society which opposes her and is beaten by her ignorance as well as by her spirituality. Her tragedy is less internal than Caesar's, since she has not compromised herself in the world's terms. Hence the center of tragedy lies less in her personally than in the world which martyrs her. Powerful social, political, and religious abstractions bear the burden of guilt in proportion to the innocence of their victim, and in affairs of spirit the guilty are the most deeply tragic.

Shaw's method of dealing with these abstractions is as medieval as his subject matter—he fully exploits the potential shorthand, dramatic force, moral concern, and timeless emphasis of allegory.

The aesthetic result is that his method fuses with his matter, augmenting the play's medieval atmosphere while providing it with a symbolic view of Joan, her world, and the ramifications of their interrelationship. Through this medium Shaw discerns basic, commonly neglected patterns in fragmentary historical events, patterns which reorient simplistic preconceptions regarding the Joan legend. The allegory ultimately gives a medieval mood to the play and a wide view of the age, besides giving an epic dimension to the characters, a poetic frame to the action, a point of reference clarifying historic and poetic ambiguities, and a context transcending time. On the other hand, the dramatic action vitalizes the allegory, making it memorable, especially through characters whose personalities are sharply individualized. Thus Joan has vibrant reality in a double sense: first, the romantic young victim of legend is personalized with a focus on her weaknesses as well as on her strengths; second, she is portrayed as a very real power in a historical situation which has symbolic permanence. Similarly, all of the characters have dramatic immediacy as contentious individuals with a mixture of personal virtues and vices, a mixture which upsets conventional stereotypes of them, while in a symbolic sense they represent great abstractions in an almost one-to-one relationship.[6] In accordance with the issues of his allegory Shaw seeks to play up the spiritual drama while playing down the spectacle. In contrast to his directions regarding elaborate sets for *Caesar and Cleopatra* he urged that the settings for the original production of *Saint Joan* be austerely simple.[7] Against a neutral background the universal and timeless implications of Joan are allowed a simpler, purer expression.

6. I agree with Mizener that "we feel each speech first as a recognizable product of the speaker's character and only after that as a general idea" ("Poetic Drama," p. 46). E. J. West effectively extends this observation, speaking of "realized human figures whose ideologies are fascinating because of the warmth and vitality of their holders" ("*Saint Joan*: A Modern Classic Reconsidered," *Quarterly Journal of Speech*, 40 [1954], 253).

7. Regarding the Theatre Guild production, Shaw wrote to Lawrence Langner: "The scenes in *Joan* can all be reduced to extreme simplicity. A single pillar of the Gordon Craig type will make the cathedral. All the Loire needs is a horizon and a few of Simonson's lanterns" (quoted in Langner, G. B. S. *and the Lunatic* [London, 1964], p. 58).

The double vision which Shaw propounds in his preface, a vision sensitively perceiving both historical and allegorical reality, is carefully developed in terms of the insights and perspectives of the play. Through this vision Shaw evokes ambivalent sensibilities, qualifying material usually considered almost exclusively tragic. The conventional melodrama regarding Joan's fate is bypassed according to a deeper understanding which reorients fundamental assumptions regarding the mundane and the spiritual, the tragic and the comic. In this light Shaw's vision compounds itself, finally, into a six-fold view—historical, allegorical, mundane, spiritual, tragic, and comic. All interlock in many illuminating and ironic relationships, but most notably the historical perspective is subject to allegory, the mundane perspective is primarily tragic, and the spiritual perspective is primarily comic. The play is structured to bring out the full implications of each of these elements, as they tend to develop in parallel, mutually relevant patterns. To trace the allegorical, tragic, and comic patterns and to be aware of their coalescence is to arrive at the heart of the play. As each pattern evolves through the nature of Joan, the nature of her opponents, the conflict between Joan and her opponents, and the outcome, the end result is a clear, compassionate comprehension of the Joan myth, a comprehension which is distinctive in combining a rational balance and dramatic power. Fictional renditions of Joan have traditionally suppressed the rational in pursuit of the dramatic, and, in the process, have achieved neither so successfully as has Shaw.

Allegorically and historically, the sainthood of Joan is tied to her genius, with the credibility of her mystical role linked to the precocity and power of her natural talents. Joan's genius has two main aspects: first is her undoubted ability, but equally important is her absolute commitment, integrity, and self-confidence regarding her cause, a cause she therefore asserts irrepressibly, despite awesome social obstacles. Her relentlessly directed singleness of purpose attracts a mystique of simplicity and moral strength which artfully complements the depth of her natural talents. Possessing this combination, her genius is kinetic and accumulates power as it meets resistance. In addition, Joan's genius involves what she believes she is, as well as what she represents. Appearing in the right place at the right time, her goals and her person do indeed promote and undergird a nationalistic spirit, as Cauchon observes in Scene IV, just as her insistence on the divinity of her visions and on her personal right to determine their divinity forebodes Protestantism, as Warwick observes. Thus genius, moving through an indomitable will and a deceptive simplicity, forces its own terms on the world and accrues symbolic meaning and influence beyond its intention.

The issue of Joan's sainthood is developed through an impressive dramatic ambivalence in which skepticism complements conviction. Shaw builds the aesthetics of Joan's mystery by a subtle use of counterstatement. In Scene I he has Joan herself interpret her voices as coming from her imagination, and in every successive scene he qualifies mysticism by offering a commonsense explanation through one character or another. Rationalism beats in constant counterpoint to mysticism. Ironically, the real mystery, through ultimately triumphing over rationalism, is thereby given a firmer, more convincing foundation. Despite the rational refrain, Joan's miracles accumulate throughout the play, numerically shattering coincidence and qualitatively confounding detraction. Frequently they are magical and fly in the face of their detractors, but the most significant miracles are usually those of Joan's supernal character as it triumphs repeatedly and most improbably against immense odds. When she wins over not only Poulengey and de Baudricourt, but also the rough Captain La Hire, the subtle Archbishop, the snivelling Dauphin, and the tough-minded Dunois, her other miracles seem almost inconsequential—but they are all definitely, hauntingly there, and the accretion overwhelms rationalism. The aesthetic effect of the rationalism is that of an argument which strengthens the case it opposes by being too insistently repeated in the face of impressive contrary evidence. Part of the grim humor of Stogumber, Courcelles, and D'Estivet in the trial scene is less that their attribution of petty magic to Joan seems so improbable, than that it is so trivial and insignificant when compared to her real powers, which impress us emotionally, if not logically, as supernatural and transcendent. Joan's genius and sainthood tend to fuse, informed most dynamically by the power of faith—her own faith in her cause, and her countrymen's faith in her divine inspiration. The miracle of her popular image and the poetry of her conviction coalesce with the fact of her accomplishments, routing skepticism. The old spiritual myth regarding Joan gains new life.

Confronting the spiritual force of Joan is the social, political, and religious world surrounding her, which Shaw objectifies through allegory. Shaw's allegorical scheme of the institutions of medieval society is impressive in scope and equally striking in its artistic condensation of so much complex material. The idea of the monarchy, with its powers, privileges, and weaknesses, he represents in the Dauphin. The aristocracy, corrupt, shallow, dull, and pompous, he represents in La Trémouille, Bluebeard, and the court. The petty aristocracy is present in de Baudricourt and Poulengey. The military, in its best, most pragmatic sense, finds voice in Dunois, while the army as a whole, simple, direct, superstitious, rough-speaking, is personified in La Hire. Warwick represents the feudal system; Stogumber represents British nationalism. The Archbishop of Rheims is a political prelate, representing the Church's combination of spiritual and temporal power; Cauchon represents the Church Militant, confronted by threats to its prerogatives; Ladvenu is the quiet spirit of compassion and altruism in the Church. The Inquisitor is the Inquisition at its theoretical best, while Courcelles and D'Estivet are the Inquisition at its ignorant, barbaric worst. The common people, being without organized influence, are off-stage. Shaw thus carefully and economically portrays a wide strata of powers in the medieval world and, by testing them against so unusual and dynamic a phenomenon as Joan, probes the substance as well as the surface of the entire society.

The remarkable history of Joan's conflict with most of these forces is nearly allegorical in itself, and Shaw's achievement involves a pointing up of universals within the conflict. While each character has vital dramatic force on a personal level, sustaining the surface vigor and credibility of the drama, each has also to a large degree sold his soul to an abstraction. The institutions have codified vital thoughts, social desires, and spiritual aspirations into laws, mores, class distinctions, and a religious hierarchy. Free will is encompassed by numerous tyrannies, monsters largely of its own making, to which habit or self-interest has effected a slavish obeisance. When Joan's genius and saintliness confront this morass—with the impact of an irresistible force meeting an immovable obstacle—the struggle, like so many in Shaw, is bound to be archetypal and epic. The conflict involves a myriad of fundamental antagonisms: the young and the old, the vital and the stagnant, the spiritual and the mundane, the individual will and the collective ethic, the upstart and the social elite, the new faith and the old Church. As the conflict exposes the ossification and corruption of the institutions, Joan is in a very significant spiritual sense the winner. But when her spiritual victory is linked to her personal destruction at their hands, the result is grimly ironic. How is one to assess the ultimate historical and spiritual significance of geniuses and saints when their power is more spiritual than temporal and they are cruelly martyred by a race which is persistently, institutionally, barbaric? The influence of such as Joan echoes more in the inner consciousness of a few who truly understand, and only faintly if at all in the collective consciousness of the multitude. Time and the limits of the imagination transmute the great spiritual examples of sainthood into puerile superstitions, fairy tales, or, even worse, into new institutions. Historically and allegorically man ignores the meaning of his saints.

The tragic and comic patterns which grow out of Shaw's allegorical-historical view reveal a tight linkage of genres wherein the tragedy of man's blindness and folly frequently becomes indistinguishable from the comedy of that same blindness and folly. As these patterns reflect upon the allegory, the result is a tragicomic perception which transcends alternate emotions. In his preface Shaw hints at basic elements of his approach, and incidentally acknowledges the artistic gap between preface and play which has plagued so much Shaw criticism: "This, I think, is all that we can now pretend to say about the prose of Joan's career. The romance of her rise, the tragedy of her execution, and the comedy of the attempts of posterity to make amends for that execution, belong to my play and not to my preface" (p. 307). Thus, according to Shaw, the play involves a poetry which rises above prefacing, and romance, tragedy, and comedy are all a part of that poetry. Later Shaw focuses more specifically on the martyrdom: "The tragedy of such murders is that they are not committed by murderers. They are judicial murders, pious murders; and this contradiction at once brings an element of comedy into the tragedy: the angels may weep at the murder, but the gods laugh at the murderers" (p. 313). In both quotations Shaw emphasizes the tragedy of the martyrdom and the comedy of man's relationship to it. In so doing he is touching on ambiguities of the play which go even deeper than he indicates. Several times he includes comedy and tragedy in the same phrase, finally asserting his "classical manner" in both genres (p. 317). While it seems hardly likely that he can in one play have both classical comedy and classical tragedy, he does most remarkably cross-fertilize laughter, irony, and high seriousness according to patterns which suggest classical antecedents.

Historically and classically it would appear that tragedy prevails. Particularly in her role as a genius Joan's case suggests the pattern of Aristotelian tragedy, her fall resulting in part from hubris, in part from inexorable fate.[8] It certainly arouses pity and terror and is to a great extent cathartic of these elements. In Scene V the Archbishop specifically cites her hubris with reference to Greek tragedy; while his comment may result from personal animus, Shaw substantiates it throughout the play with a strong subtheme regarding Joan's pride. From Scene I onward, Joan's scarcely modest identification with the will of God gives her both boldness and influence. When at the end of Scene II she asks, "Who is for God and his Maid?" (p. 349), the question rings rhetorically, for who is against God? Such language is the property not only of saints, but also of bigots, fanatics, U.S. presidents, and tyrants. In the name of God and in a spirit which seems inextricably bound to an element of ego, Joan ascends in power. Shaw illustrates her grow-

8. The case for *Saint Joan* as a classical tragedy is argued by John Fielden, "Shaw's *Saint Joan* as Tragedy," *Twentieth Century Literature*, 3, no. 2 (1957), 59–67.

ing hubris by opposing her awestruck humility before the Archbishop in Scene II—"[*She falls on both knees before him, with bowed head, not daring to look up*]"—to her insolent bluntness toward him in Scene V: "Then speak, you; and tell him that it is not God's will" (p. 375). As Joan's pride in wearing a gold surcoat brings about her capture, so her pride in defying the court hastens her martyrdom. Aristotelian tragedy moves like a ghost behind the action.

While a pattern of Aristotelian tragedy grows out of Joan's genius, a Promethean tragedy grows out of her saintliness.[9] In asserting direct communion with divine forces, Joan threatens man's institutional gods by stealing their spiritual fire, fronting their self-assumed sanctity, and offering the dangerous ember of independent spiritual inspiration to all mankind. Her spark of divinity forebodes a blaze of insurgency, and forces of tradition and the status quo naturally feel it imperative both for their image and for their self-preservation that Joan's threat to them be adjudged heresy. The heretic is especially dangerous, since so much spiritual justice (and perhaps even God) is on her side. In the very strength of her virtue Joan is a challenge to society's estimate of itself, an estimate all the more tenacious and pompous because it is fundamentally petty. So, appropriate to Promethean legend, the vultures attack the saint, but the vital organ (in this case, Joan's heart) cannot be destroyed. Joan's foes, as fundamentally pagan as the avenging Zeus and his myopic vultures, cannot see that in destroying Joan physically they are immortalizing her spiritually. The unburnable heart is a phoenix symbol portending the renewal of Joan's spirit, purged and pure, from the ashes of her body.

The Promethean tragedy and the Aristotelian tragedy develop

9. Counter to Fielden, Crompton finds *Saint Joan* anti-Aristotelian, anti-classical, and anti-Shakespearean; he describes it as Hegelian, neo-Gothic, and Promethean—a tragedy of faith rather than a tragedy of despair (*Shaw the Dramatist*, p. 206). To Archibald Henderson, Shaw commented: "What more do you want for a tragedy as great as that of Prometheus? All the forces that bring about the catastrophe are on the grandest scale; and the individual soul on which they press is of the most indomitable force and temper" (quoted in *George Bernard Shaw: Man of the Century* [New York, 1956], p. 603).

as diverse implications of a common set of facts, most simply being two ways of looking at the same event, but most profoundly representing two philosophical views—the optimistic, aspirational, and spiritual as opposed to the pessimistic, static, and mundane. The fact that the Promethean tragedy prevails, especially in light of the Epilogue, means not that the Aristotelian tragedy is erased, but that it comprises a minor theme or counterpoint which renders Shaw's total statement more richly comprehensive. We have a sounder vision if we can acknowledge Joan's flaws while recognizing her inspiring spiritual example to her society. But as the conflict is Promethean, the focus of tragedy shifts away from Joan's person onto all mankind, past and present, represented by her self-centered, pragmatic, schismatic, doctrinal foes. Society, in judiciously murdering her, and in its conviction of the prudence and propriety of the murder, reveals its true decadence. And as the modern "monkey gland" mind finds itself superior to such inspiration as that provided by Joan, modern man partakes of the guilt of the murder. In Shaw's words, "For us to set up our condition as a standard of sanity, and declare Joan mad because she never condescended to it, is to prove that we are not only lost but irredeemable" (p. 279). Shaw indicates that a central problem of Joan's society and of our own is persistent mundanity, in which "rationalism" is an excuse for base vision and social conformity a haven from personal morality.

The conflict of repressive conventionalism and exuberant individualism is replete with tragic ironies. From a Christian as well as an Aristotelian point of view, the would-be saint's hubris and potential for tyranny have disturbing implications. How is one to be sufficiently selfless in the service of God so that he is sure his incentive is altruistic and divine, rather than egocentric and expressive of covert personal drives and ambitions? This is the dilemma which confronts Thomas Becket in T. S. Eliot's *Murder in the Cathedral*[10] and which Eliot finally glosses over, answering symbolically in a manner which imposes only on the most gullible

10. Arthur H. Nethercot observes this briefly in *Men and Supermen* (New York, 1966), p. 126. For a sensitive comparison of Shaw and Eliot, see Martz's essay, "The Saint as Tragic Hero."

and blindly faithful. Symbolically, Becket surrenders his personal will to the greater will of God, but dramatically and dialectically he seems to be merely rationalizing a grotesque death wish, and the play's resolution, a supposed affirmation of faith, falls into rhetorical and poetic camouflage, concealing a spiritual evasion. Shaw's answer is more direct and satisfactory: the saint does not forgo personal will, but expresses God through it—as Joan's will is refined and noble, it is a natural outpouring of the divinity which informs all life. Hence there is little conflict, since hubris in the saint is at most a venial flaw, a by-product of ego, a secondary aspect of genius. Indeed, if hubris helps the saint's cause, it may well be a virtue.[11] The problem of potential tyranny is far more serious, but it is only hinted at in the play. As Joan gains great power through her identification with God, she is implicitly subject to the corruption that feeds on power. The cruelest of leaders have claimed divine sanction, and the most incredible barbarities, such as those of the Crusades and the Inquisition, have justified themselves in the name of God. By assuming too much, Joan is vulnerable. Hence Dunois's speech in Scene V, that "God is no man's daily drudge, and no maid's either" (p. 377). Joan's tragedy, which is closely tied to her virtue, lies partly in her inability to understand Dunois. In her accumulation of worldly power she is subject to the vanities and hazards of power politics, while in her naïveté she cannot deal with them effectively.

Even more strikingly, the conflict reveals manifold tragic ironies among those surrounding Joan. As her vigorous, assertive, independent presence places stress on timeworn institutions, the fallibilities of such institutions become starkly apparent. Were they unchallenged, the Church, the Inquisition, the feudal system, the court, and the king would each complacently presume to have its secure niche as a part of God's plan, its predestined link in His Great Chain of Being. Joan threatens these presumptions, tran-

11. Hans Stoppel thus delineates Shaw's Joan as a modern mystic, a Life Force heroine, combining imagination and rationalism. See his "Shaw and Sainthood," *English Studies*, 36 (1955), 49–63. Stoppel's explanation is qualified and spiritually deepened by Joan's statement to Dunois in Scene V: "Well, I have to find reasons for you, because you do not believe in my voices. But the voices come first; and I find the reasons after: whatever you may choose to believe" (p. 373).

scending them according to her own system of values, and as these institutions are so profoundly affected by her in the temporal realm, they must account for her in the spiritual realm as well. The spiritual issue at stake is their own implicit or explicit claim to divine sanction, and the temporal issue involves their relative worldly influence. The fact that they are all rendered terribly uncomfortable by her, as she tends to level all men and to disorient tradition, reveals their intrinsic, very human weakness. Their repute is clearly less divine than man-made, and it rests upon a god made in man's image, congenial to man's systems, and generally more corrupt according to the degree of veneration he exacts. This god (or, in his fragmented form, these gods) are a central element in man's tragedy as they deflect man from a true spiritual awareness. Institutions have become a substitute for the spirit they claim to represent, and man, for the most part unconsciously, is damned by the baseness of his self-created false idols. As he serves them he becomes a wretched automaton, having surrendered his soul to a worldly power. Quite naturally, when a true saint comes along, the institutional man cannot recognize her, since his most fervent convictions are committed to what are in fact diabolical interests. Most simply we see this in Stogumber, who has apotheosized nationalism and whose sense of spirit is caught in narrow chauvinism and petty superstition. Most complexly it is manifest in the subtle Inquisitor, whose uttermost charity is cruelty and whose doctrinal wisdom leads him to condemn as a heretic a young woman whom his church will later glorify as a saint. Institutional tragedy is thus fragmented into millions of little personal tragedies, all manifesting man's great hunger for respectability, a hunger which gnaws at his already finite spiritual sensibilities.

The power and scope of the tragedy, thus interpreted from historical record, is impressive. But the tragedy is primarily social, with a focus on the mundane, and there is a deeply founded comic refrain in the play which offsets its dark tones. Joan's Promethean nature tends to defy pessimism and to overwhelm the tragic pattern with a counterassertion rising forcefully from individual will and divine inspiration. Spiritually, there is a strong comic rhythm which both counterpoints and frequently coexists with the worldly tragedy, not entirely overwhelming it but profoundly transmuting its nature. Thus the genius of Joan, which develops on one level as hubris, leading her to her doom, develops on another level as spirited comedy, the humor of the nonconformist, filled with *élan vital*, opposed to convention, surprising, dismaying, and even at times overwhelming staid institutions and ossified modes of thought. Joan's spontaneity and pertness are irrepressible, prevailing from Scene I through the horrors of the trial scene and bursting forth in the Epilogue. They may be partly born of naïveté, but they are also born of a vital, optimistic principle underlying her nature; as she combines them with decisive action, they emerge as an aspect of her genius. With hubris evolving as pertness, the whole notion of Joan's Greek tragedy is qualified most quixotically by keen delight.[12]

Concerning Joan's saintliness, the range of humor is even broader. In the first three scenes not even her miracles are allowed an exalted aura. From hens that will not lay and cows that hold back milk, to the drowning of Foul Mouthed Frank, to the obedient pennon, God seems to be guiding his saint with an earthy laughter. This strain is taken up once again as a leitmotiv in the dark moments of Scene VI with the piddling questions about magic spells, her voices' native tongue, and the Archangel Michael's attire—or lack of it. But more subliminal and basic is the intrinsic Christian consolation of spiritual rebirth, echoing the Resurrection, which transmutes Joan's Promethean tragedy into a Christian triumph. A spirit of transcendent comedy develops in a triple sense. First, as a Christian context accompanies the tragic pattern, the play's Greek pessimism cannot seem truly central, and its Promethean defiance takes on spiritual power. Second,

12. This comic overtone, combined with Joan's Promethean power, characterized Sybil Thorndike's performance of the role. In contrast, Ludmilla Pitoëff created a major success in France through portraying Joan as slight, mystical, and childlike, with a glowing inner light. On Pitoëff's interpretation, Shaw remarked: "What! That frail, delicate woman is your idea of Joan of Arc? NO. Joan of Arc was a strong peasant who could take a soldier by the scruff of the neck and throw him out the window. Your Mme Pitoëff is charming, touching, but she would never have driven a single Englishman out of France." See Daniel C. Gerould, "*Saint Joan* in Paris," *Shaw Review*, 7 (1964), 11–23; quotation, p. 17.

Joan fulfills the classically comic role of youth confronting age, with youth ultimately prevailing. Third, in a strictly temporal sense, Joan's cause is won, as the English are driven out of France in the aftermath of her inspiration, and as her image in the popular memory obliterates her foes and immortalizes her as the true victor, an enduring ideal. Joan's final transcendence is a fundamental joke on her contemporaries and on all such deluded men, as it moves ironically in a timeless pattern, mocking conformity and institutionalism.[13]

While the institutionalized men who desert or convict Joan are in their blindness and guilt actually more tragic than she, Shaw takes care to mitigate even their tragedy. The characters, being both distinctively allegorical and convincingly human, dramatically humanize the allegory. Thus Shaw has at the same time the significance and epic quality of the abstractions and the idiosyncrasy and triviality of their human representatives, with the space between the allegorical and personal providing special insights regarding both, setting a dramatic tone which incorporates the ponderous implications of the one and the vital dynamics of the other. The dichotomy destroys shallow notions of villainy by discriminating between abstractions that people follow, which may in effect be villainous, and the people themselves, who, like most human beings, feel honorable, kindly, and fundamentally well-intentioned. Shaw aptly remarks in his preface that a villain is a *diabolus ex machina*, two-dimensional, unreal—he is usually a confusion of a man with the role he plays. By discriminating between the man and the role while emphasizing the fact of both, Shaw's art combines a level of realistic drama with the consciousness of a morality. Thus some of his characters in the abstract may

13. While most critics have focused on the tragedy of the play, a few have emphasized various aspects of comedy. Martz, observing tragedy's double vision, involving both doubt and affirmation, comments that Shaw is "hanging on by his hands to the very rim of tragedy" ("The Saint as Tragic Hero," p. 177). Sylvan Barnet posits that Shaw's teleology is fundamentally opposed to tragedy ("Bernard Shaw on Tragedy," *PMLA*, 71 [1956], 888–99). Don Austin, with reference to Greek comedy, explores Shaw's youth-age dichotomy ("Comedy through Tragedy: Dramatic Structure in *Saint Joan*," *Shaw Review*, 8 [1965], 52–62). Too few critics have been sensitively in touch with the play as tragicomedy.

be villainous, menacing, and tragic, while concurrently as persons they are heroic, kindly, or even comic.

This double aspect is especially notable in Stogumber, Warwick, Cauchon, and the Inquisitor. Politically, Stogumber is a fervent nationalist, nearly as mad a bull as Sir John Talbot, a relentless, petty, cruel advocate of Joan's immolation; personally, he is a short-sighted, simple, rather comic man who would not harm a fly. Politically, Warwick is a ruthless and capable defender of the feudal system; personally, he is a cultured, sensitive gentleman with a suave, wry sense of humor. In an exceptional reversal of the pattern, Cauchon seems less admirable personally than officially. Ecclesiastically, he is a staunch, hard-line, but fair defender of the faith; personally, his cleverness is offset by a hint of pomposity, and his sincerity is qualified by a tone of vengeful animus, possibly the result of his having been removed from his diocese by Joan's faction. More typically, the Inquisitor is a subtle, exacting, well-meaning but ironically cruel persecutor of saintly simpletons, while personally he is a type of kindly old uncle. Similar disparities between official capacity and personal nature exist in most of the other characters, being strikingly comic in de Baudricourt and the Dauphin. When the characters are not outrightly comic, the disparity in each of them renders them subtly so, on a level of deeply ingrained incongruity. The disparity suggests that each has compromised his personal instincts in terms of an abstract standard; while this involves a tragic loss of soul, it concurrently suggests the implicit comic element of automatism, the humor of man as machine. In this latter sense the institutions themselves provoke a grim humor, being caught in rules, patterns, and laws which inaccurately apply to life, which time has rendered irrelevant, or which have virtue only in a mad inner consistency.

The very structure of Saint Joan serves as a vehicle for Shaw's tragicomic vision, graphically setting forth the archetypal, classically comic conflict between youth and age. In Scenes I through III the spirit of youth, with its optimism, iconoclasm, innocence, and determination, is in the ascendency. The vital characters are all young—Joan is seventeen, the Dauphin and Dunois are both twenty-six. In these three scenes Joan rises through tests of increasing toughness. Each scene develops with society's skepticism, rational and cynical, being confronted and dazzled by Joan's assertiveness, and each scene ends with the skeptics at last won over to Joan's cause, enthusiastically concurring in the divinity of her mission. Through skepticism thus being dramatically overcome, Joan's miraculous nature is rendered all the more convincing and her cause all the more triumphant. Scene III, undergirded by parallel elements in Scenes I and II, ends as a minor climax, the peak of the dramatic romance of Joan's ascendency.[14] Following this the tone shifts drastically, suddenly moving away from spiritual exuberance and comedy toward mundane prudence and tragedy. Aesthetically the movement is from lightness to darkness, from youth to age. Warwick, Cauchon, and Stogumber are all middle-aged, and it is their institutionalized world which takes over in Scene IV, impressing its will upon Joan for the remainder of the play. The conflict evolves tragically toward the martyrdom of youth at the end of Scene VI. But the Epilogue at last shifts the entire tone as it brings together the vital spirituality of Scenes I through III and the repressive mundanity of Scenes IV through VI. It is comic in the transcendence of Joan and in her reconciliation with society, since man retrospectively admires saints. But the reconciliation is ambiguous—negatively so, as society shies away from the idea of Joan's possible rebirth; positively so, in the very fact that saints will continue to appear in the world despite all odds against them.[15]

While the structural pattern thus complements the allegorical, comic, and tragic patterns of the play, the individual scenes offer a constant accretion of details which energize the pattern with vary-

14. Regarding the material preceding Scene IV, Shaw remarked to Sybil Thorndike: "That's all flapdoodle up to there—just 'theatre' to get you interested—now the play begins" (quoted in Martin Meisel, *Shaw and the Nineteenth-Century Theater* [Princeton, 1963], p. 51). Structurally and aesthetically, Shaw's comment is a gross oversimplification, refuted by his own repeated insistence that he had cut the play to the bone (Henderson, *Shaw: Man of the Century*, p. 601; Langner, *G. B. S. and the Lunatic*, pp. 67–72).

15. Eric Bentley, following Shaw's suggestion in the preface (quoted earlier in this chapter), structures the play according to Romance (Scenes I, II, III), Tragedy (Scenes IV, V, VI), and Comedy (the Epilogue). See *Bernard Shaw*, amended ed. (New York, 1957), p. 172.

ing levels of consciousness. As these levels coexist and interact, they produce richly ambivalent drama. Most striking about the play's opening is that this rendition of a tale so frequently romanticized and sentimentalized begins on a tone of farce, the key joke of which is a miracle—hens which will not lay. The effect is cunning, first as the romantic tradition of the legend is at the outset countered by an irreverent tone, and, further, as one laughs at the inexplicable while one's laughter in no way removes an awareness that the event *is* inexplicable. A minor miracle is presented as fact, but the fact is conveyed in a mood of complete unpretentiousness. The simplicity of Shaw's description of Joan is in keeping with this double awareness, for through her seeming simplicity and naïveté arises a sense of profound strength. Joan's directness and audacity, flowing from a combination of absolute conviction and steadfastness, and covertly suggesting a suprarational ability, keep de Baudricourt off balance. He tries to categorize her—as a camp follower, as mad, as a victim of Poulengey's immoral intentions—but since she does not fit his categories she easily disorients him, deflating his defenses and rendering him putty, especially with her incredible ambition to raise the siege at Orleans and to crown the Dauphin. The real miracle of the scene is that Joan wins her way, but even this is carefully prepared for by the portrayal of de Baudricourt as having *"no will of his own"* (p. 321), and Poulengey as *"dreamily absent-minded"* (p. 324)—they are easy prey. Epitomizing the scene's double vision, Joan (quite unhistorically) admits that her voices come from her imagination, but nonetheless represent God's intention. Doubt plays in counterpoint with wonder most convincingly as Poulengey points up the miraculous essence of Joan: "I think the girl herself is a bit of a miracle. . . . We want a few mad people now. See where the sane ones have landed us!" (p. 327). The halo which Joan sees around the head of de Baudricourt, causing him to look up apprehensively, catches the tension between humor and the miraculous which lends weight to his final exclamation: "She d i d come from God" (p. 332).[16]

16. Stewart notes this incident as fusing laughter and deep emotion, typifying Shaw's "new tact in the use of laughter" (*Eight Modern Writers*, p. 179).

Joan's power, having moved the weak-willed and dreamy men of Scene I, faces a test far more severe in the Dauphin's court, which, though it is ripe for her in its irresolution and contentiousness, offers a much greater obstacle in the person of the clever, worldly Archbishop of Rheims. The likes of La Hire, a direct and earthy captain, and of the Dauphin, who delights in her as a new toy, may be easily impressed, but the Archbishop establishes a counterrefrain by rationally undercutting Joan's famous discovery of the Dauphin. His description of a miracle as "an event which creates faith," a nourishing of faith by poetry (pp. 340–41), subtly defines the tension between fact and imagination, rationalism and religion which comprises an aspect of Joan's mystery. On a pragmatic level he senses her usefulness. His admiration of Pythagoras, who believed in a round earth revolving around the sun, indicates his sensitivity to very natural realities which seem incredible to less imaginative men. La Trémouille's response—"What an utter fool! Couldnt he use his eyes?" (p. 342)—typifies the rationalism of lesser men, a rationalism confined by the finite limits of their imagination. La Trémouille is the type to whom science is superstition and superstition is science. As such he is a precursor of modern man, inclined either to debunk Joan's voices as entirely impossible or to apotheosize them as strictly divine, unaware that there is a middle ground more impressive than either alternative. For once again Joan's ostensible miracles are overshadowed by her character, so direct, pure, and dedicated as to make the sophisticated Archbishop blush, and so stirring as to cause the ineffectual Dauphin to assert himself. With instinctive sharpness Joan realizes that the miracle of making the Dauphin into a king will be less one of crowning him than of changing his personality. As in *Caesar and Cleopatra* the prospect of such mundane sorcery borders on the supernatural, and, like Cleopatra, Charles's character changes less than his position. In a cutting observation of human nature Shaw later notes that Charles's true self-realization ultimately derives more from inspiration of the flesh than from inspiration of the spirit—Agnes Sorel, not Joan, makes him Charles the Victorious, much as Antony, not Caesar, brings forth Cleopatra the Queen.

Scene III is the climax of the spiritual-comic half of the play. Early themes culminate here, and rationalism is at this point shaken with a dramatic turn toward the miraculous. Dunois is more spontaneous and sensitive than the leaders Joan has previously encountered. He is a combination of pragmatist, poet, and believer, a man with *"no foolish illusions,"* but one who can appreciate the poetry of a kingfisher and the mystery of a saint. Like the Archbishop, his poetry complements his pragmatism, and, similar to Poulengey and La Hire before him, he recognizes Joan's inspirational importance, whether her voices be divine or not. He comments that Joan is in love with war, as the Archbishop had observed that she is in love with religion: Joan's dual loves render her a sort of latter-day Crusader,[17] but Dunois wants a saint, not a daredevil. The fact that he has in Joan precisely what he is looking for is objectified by a poignant theatrical effect—that of the wind-swept pennon. Achieving in three dimensions the combination of simplicity and power which renders Joan's character so remarkable, the pennon is a device both dramaturgically audacious and psychologically forceful, serving to alter the entire supernatural emphasis of the play. Mounted on Dunois's lance, it stands out starkly on top of the single vertical prop on a horizontal landscape. The simplicity of the setting, a necessary aspect of so short a scene, and Dunois's vehement curse at the wind, which he emphasizes by shaking his fist at the pennon, doubly enforce the pennon's dramatic importance. It flutters in an east wind, almost possessing a personality, mute but assertive. After Dunois's opening speech the characters forget about it, but the audience obviously cannot, and when it droops suddenly at Joan's blazing entry it provides a stark, ironic comment on the ensuing dialogue. Once again a mi-

17. As Joan combines the adventurous and imaginative with the ascetic and contemplative, Stanley Weintraub suggests parallels between her and T. E. Lawrence. Shaw was reading Lawrence's *Seven Pillars of Wisdom* while he was writing *Saint Joan.* (See "Bernard Shaw's Other Saint Joan," *South Atlantic Quarterly,* 64 [1965], 195–98.) St. John Ervine cites Mary Hankinson, a Fabian worker, as Shaw's most immediate source for Joan. Shaw gave her a copy of the play, inscribed: "To Mary Hankinson, the only woman I know who does not believe that she is the model for Joan and the only woman who actually was" (quoted in *Bernard Shaw: His Life, Work and Friends* [London, 1956], p. 497).

raculous effect combines humor with wonder, but this time it is reinforced by being impressively visual, and by providing the audience with the dramatic and psychological relish of secret knowledge. As Joan and Dunois speak rationally about the logistics of warfare, they echo the chorus of rationalism which has offset the miraculous up to this point—and all the while the pennon flutters in defiance of reason, in affirmation of faith, turning at last with a west wind. Dramatically and emotionally, if not logically, rationalism is at this point severely compromised, and when Dunois crosses himself, saying, "God has spoken" (p. 355), he echoes far more dynamically the conversion of de Baudricourt and the Archbishop in Scenes I and II. The issue has come to a tripartite conclusion, and, most movingly, the whole weight of this climax shifts conviction toward the supernatural.[18]

While the characters of Scene III are a boy, a seventeen-year-old, and a twenty-six-year-old, the characters of Scene IV are forty-six, fifty, and sixty. The reaction of age is juxtaposed to the action of youth; prudence and policy set themselves against optimism and exuberance. The scene's distinction lies in the fine economy, beauty, and forcefulness with which it conveys a great amount of complex material. Once again, reminiscent of the hell scene of *Man and Superman*, Shaw transmutes talk and a flux of ideas into highly energized, almost musical theater. He does this by scoring both the allegorical and personal levels according to emotional, rhetorical, and symbolic values which are nearly tonal. Thus Warwick, being suave, sophisticated, and imperturbable, with a voice which bridges the contentiousness of the other two men, suggests the quality of a lyric tenor, promoting feudalism with the social grace and subtlety of a consummate gentleman. Cauchon, by contrast, is pompous, dogmatic, and bombastic, with a voice ponderous and staid, suggesting the quality of a basso, defending the

18. Thus Brown refers to the scene as a touching affirmation of faith ("The Prophet and the Maid," p. 29), and Burns Mantell cites it as "a spark of genius" (*News*, 10 March 1936; quoted by McKee, "Shaw's *Saint Joan*," p. 16). Both are in marked disagreement with Stark Young, who calls it "the worst in the play" (*New Republic*, 16 Jan. 1924; quoted by McKee, "Shaw's *Saint Joan*," p. 15). Young, not appreciating the play's rational-mystical tension, objects that the mystical themes lack beauty.

Church in a tone appropriate to its dignity, tradition, and divine pretensions. Stogumber, finally, is excitable, bouncy, and impulsive, with an intrusive and vehement voice, suggesting the quality of a comic baritone, asserting the cause of English nationalism in a manner exuding the fervor, narrowness, and self-righteousness of chauvinism. As these personalities, emotions, voices, ideas, and allegorical forces develop in counterpoint, the aesthetics of drama, music, and philosophy are brought into a stirring interrelationship.[19] Neither Warwick nor Cauchon can brook Joan because she bypasses both feudal system and Church in terms of king and God, and her instinctive nationalism advances an institution which could severely diminish the power of peer and priest. As a royalist, Protestant, and nationalist, she is a harbinger of the end of their systems. So while they are by nature rivals, they join forces in a resolve to remove the threat. Their contrapuntal interaction throughout the scene, personally and allegorically contentious yet aimed at a common goal, develops with the immediate dramatic life of their characters, the tonal values of their interaction, and the epic overtones of the great abstractions which they so fervently represent. Thus the dialectic takes on the effectiveness of refined and powerful poetry.[20]

19. My discussion here is in close agreement with Martin Meisel, who speaks of the scene as a "concerted trio" and quotes Shaw: "Opera taught me to shape my plays into recitatives, arias, duets, trios, ensemble finales, and bravura pieces to display the technical accomplishments of the executants" (from "The Play of Ideas," *New Statesman and Nation*, NS 39 [1950], 511). On hearing Shaw read *Saint Joan*, Sybil Thorndike was struck by his musical sense of the lines and characters. See Meisel, *Shaw and the Nineteenth-Century Theater*, pp. 50–52.

20. Pirandello thought Scene IV the best in the play ("Shaw's *Saint Joan*," p. 7); Mann objected to its didacticism and anachronism ("He Was Mankind's Friend," pp. 253–54). The didacticism is sufficiently pointed to have provoked a Roman Catholic objection which killed an early proposal to film *Saint Joan* (Henderson, *Shaw: Man of the Century*, p. 601), and the script for the 1957 film version was written by Graham Greene, who cut Shaw's Protestant argument (see Harry W. Rudman, "Shaw's *Saint Joan* and Motion Picture Censorship," *Shaw Bulletin*, 2, no. 3 [1958], 1–14). Under the circumstances, the film could scarcely be expected to catch the play's central spirit. Reflecting Shaw's comment that the trial turned insistently on the Protestant point (Sarolea, "Has Shaw Understood," p. 182), Desmond MacCarthy remarks: "In a sense the play can be described as an exceedingly powerful Protestant pamphlet" (*Shaw's Plays in Review* [New York, 1951], p. 166). Countering all of this, and revealing Shaw's deceptive mixture of art and

The tragic pattern continues to unfold in Scene V, with a classical sense of fate inexorably closing in upon Joan. As Scene IV represented Joan's foes uniting in opposition to her, this scene reveals her "friends" deserting her. Ironically, the tragic situation has been largely of her own making and is inextricably bound to her success. Dunois touches upon a key cause in his question, "Do you expect stupid people to love you for shewing them up?" (p. 372). He attributes the court's hatred of Joan to jealousy, but even deeper than jealousy, no doubt, is the Establishment's humiliation at owing so much to a person so lowly. Sincere gratitude is hard on pride and is not the commonest of human emotions; human nature instinctively seeks to cancel it out, either by reciprocity or by finding fault in the benefactor. Being both small in charity and so very deeply in debt to Joan, her contemporaries naturally choose the latter course. Joan's essential spiritual nature has not greatly changed, but through her efforts the society around her has been materially rejuvenated. Hence that society denies her gratitude by condemning in victory those same qualities in her which it had found admirable during darker days—her voices, her love of war, her hubris. Joan's virtues are critically examined, and her divine inspiration is subjected to increasing rational doubts. Now that the miracle has been accomplished—the Dauphin crowned and the French reestablished—the saint who did it is an embarrassment and a nuisance. Almost inevitably, at the moment of her greatest triumph, Joan is symbolically deserted by King, Church, and Army. The effect is purgatorial, awakening Joan at last to an awareness of her true spiritual isolation, but as this isolation identifies her with Christ, she is all the more pure and transcendent. The ironies are multifold: Joan's temporal success brings temporal isolation which in turn objectifies her spiritual triumph, though it portends her physical destruction. The tragedy of the world is implicit in the ignoble role it plays in making such ironies possible.

propaganda, several critics have specifically observed that in *Saint Joan* art totally eclipses didacticism. See C. E. M. Joad, *Shaw* (London, 1949), pp. 96–97; Maurice Colbourne, *The Real Bernard Shaw* (New York, 1949), p. 199; William Irvine, *The Universe of G. B. S.* (New York, 1949), p. 324.

Scene VI owes much of its effectiveness to the intrinsic human-ness of its horror. Man's greatest tragedy has already been depicted in Scenes IV and V, when he isolates Joan, rejecting her spirit and her God in the name of all of his personal, traditional, self-glorify-ing little gods. Now, in playing out his convictions, in justifying himself through tediously prosecuting one who is spiritually su-perior, man reveals the pathetic comedy which lies at the heart of his tragedy. The scene is especially distinctive as it brings together and clarifies at length the tragicomic disparity between man's highest spiritual achievement—his Church—and Joan's well-tested convictions. A spectrum of medieval Catholicism is represented—its subtlety, dignity, litigiousness, narrowness, foolishness, and compassion are manifest respectively in the Inquisitor, Cauchon, D'Estivet, Courcelles, Stogumber, and Ladvenu. The institution, divine as it may profess to be, is laid bare as primarily a composite of those who make up its ranks; though it may have great power as an abstraction, that power is inextricably bound to the strengths, weaknesses, wisdom, and ignorance of its adherents. Shaw points up the tragic absurdity of the court's pretense by observing the foibles of its priestly constituency. In such a light the trial may be comprehended in more realistic terms—terrible as a conglomerate but pathetic in piecemeal and tragicomic in toto. The time-worn melodramatic stereotype of Joan's persecutors is destroyed. In-deed, melodramatic stereotyping is revealed to be one of the pri-mary flaws of the persecutors themselves, as they subject life to their version of religion, religion which is a spiritual melodrama.

Thus despite its inherent tragedy Scene VI ranges from farce to irony. The pertness of Warwick's page at the opening sets an irreverent tone as he calls Cauchon "Pious Peter." This boy, pro-viding a minor resurgence of the voice of youth, reflects the page of Scene II, who thumps assertively on the floor to gain the atten-tion of the court, and Dunois's lively young page in Scene III, who is so naturally informal with his master. Warwick's fatherly toler-ance toward the boy is but one of many strokes by which Shaw briefly but sharply gives dimension to character,[21] and as Warwick

21. A. C. Ward perceptively notes the "larger-than-stage life" which Shaw gives his characters by such details as Warwick's appreciation of the illuminated man-

addresses Cauchon and the Inquisitor, the mood of his boy's mockery is subtilized and extended in the nobleman's droll, pragmatic irony. The context of Warwick, who is present at the opening and closing of the scene, indicates that the court may play its games, but that they are really only games, in which the religious body is serving the ends of secular interests. Thus contextually circumscribed, the court's presumption of self-importance and seriousness is given a touch of Lilliputian absurdity, a touch which it fully lives up to as it goes into session. While Cauchon seeks to maintain fairness and dignity, Stogumber pops up and down in his fanaticism, Courcelles promotes his petty sixty-four-count indictment, and D'Estivet urges a litigious formality. The air is filled with the farce of English-speaking Latin saints, a bishop's stolen horse, fairy trees, haunted wells, a rhetorically growing tower, and a naked archangel. Even threats of torture and cries of treason fall into a foolish pattern, putting Cauchon beside himself in irritation as the court's solemnity collapses. Joan does not help the situation, since she refuses to be impressed by tradition-bound dignity and follows the dictates both of divine voices and personal reason in a spontaneous defiance of her persecutors' sanctity. To the extent that she shocks the court, as she does most deeply, it appears all the more ridiculous.

But the farce is leavened by tragic irony, since these ridiculous men have the power to send Joan to the stake. With his usual sensitivity to visual effect Shaw dramatizes this fact in the person of the Executioner, who enters with Joan and stands like a shadow of death throughout her trial. Ladvenu brings about her temporary recantation by pointing out his presence. It is only at this point that Joan may be said to "fall"—in despair, ironically the one sin which was in fact regarded by the Middle Ages as truly unforgivable. Most impressive is the sophisticated, mild, kindly, treacherously benevolent Inquisitor, who, understanding Joan both in her innocence and in the terrible threat of that innocence to the

uscript at the opening of Scene IV (*Bernard Shaw* [London, 1951], p. 159). Similar examples are the Archbishop's admiration of Pythagoras, and Dunois's fascination with the kingfisher. By such means Shaw in large part compensates for the verisimilitude which he sacrifices in making some of his characters supraknowledgeable.

Church, gently but firmly deprecates the foolishness of the others. One charge—heresy—is enough to burn her; while pleading compassion, righteousness, and mercy in terms of a greater cause—the cause of the Church, which is to him the cause of God—this man urges the inexorable point of ecclesiastical law and doctrinal common sense.[22]

As the Inquisitor has the clearest sense of the religious factors, and as he follows them with a pure will, his personal irony is finally the deepest. He is the ultimate statement of spiritual authoritarianism, as opposed to Joan, the spiritual individualist. When Joan contends that "God must be served first. . . . What other judgment can I judge by but my own?" (p. 400), his response is implicit: the Church was created by God as His vehicle on earth; as the Church's judgment is derived from Him, you must abide by it. Both views are actually based on personal judgment, for it is, finally, the individual who always makes the choice in such matters. In the face of such an impasse one can only reasonably question whether it is indeed compassionate, righteous, and merciful to burn *anyone* for your own fervently held convictions. The weakness of the Inquisitor's case is suggested at the end when he and Cauchon seek "perfect order" in Joan's conviction, and when he admits that she is an "innocent creature crushed between these mighty forces, The Church and the Law" (p. 409). He has attached his spirit to a system and is willing to impose that system on others to the point of their death, despite his awareness of their personal innocence. Compassion is perverted into its opposite, and God's supposed cause must cruelly compromise itself in its very fulfillment. The ultimate conviction is the ultimate absurdity.

While irony is subtle and implicit in the Inquisitor, it is starkly dramatic and explicit in Stogumber. Throughout Acts IV and VI Stogumber is chafing to burn Joan, to the point of impatiently calling his superiors traitors for their compunctions. It is he who at last cues the Executioner—"Light your fire, man"—and helps push Joan out, exclaiming, "Into the fire with the witch" (pp.

22. Shaw compared the Inquisitor to Torquemada—saintly, but "a most infernal old scoundrel" (Archibald Henderson, *Bernard Shaw: Playboy and Prophet* [New York, 1932], p. 556).

408–9). Humor is thus at its grimmest when he stumbles back after the burning, throws himself with a symbolic appropriateness on the prisoner's stool, and declares his soul guilty and damned. The terrible sight, smell, and emotion of the martyrdom have at last brought the reality of his barbaric impulses home to him. With emotional simplicity, again clearly symbolic, and providing a hint of the cyclic nature of such events, he identifies Joan with Jesus and himself with Judas. In his simple way Stogumber has been shocked into compassion and understanding. He has borne graphic witness and has experienced a spiritual purgation in Joan's fire, a purgation which the Inquisitor cannot feel, being numbed by habit, and which Warwick avoids by staying away from the burning. The fact that the latter have greater sensibilities which they thus suppress implies that their state of mind, as well as their guilt, is even more damnable than Stogumber's. They have the capacity to *know* what they are doing, but they do it anyway and insulate themselves from the consequences. The dark comedy, so clearly linked to tragedy and the macabre, rises in poignant gro-tesqueness as Stogumber, with a singular consistency of character, thanks God that the man who gave Joan a cross at the end was an Englishman, and as he is desperately convinced that those who laughed were French.

Stogumber's hysteria serves as a choric despair, but for deep tragic resolution a subtler tone is called for. Shaw stabilizes the concluding moments with the reentry of Ladvenu, who provides a sane, composed aesthetic balance. Ladvenu does not contradict the hysteria; rather, he affirms its cause and carries its implications a step further: "This is not the end for her, but the beginning" (p. 412). Ladvenu hopes the laughter was English. Humor and optimism are thus further entwined with the moment of tragedy and despair, serving to reduce the melodrama, to increase the human reality, and to give a philosophical perspective. The heart that would not burn serves as a final symbol of Joan's spiritual transcendence, the most haunting of the unexplained miracles, and a grim joke on her persecutors, one which Warwick appreci-ates *"with a wry smile"* as he echoes Ladvenu's words: "The last of her? Hmm! I wonder!" (p. 413). With comedy and tragedy joined, with the question of the miracles left dramatically ambiguous, and with Joan paralleled to Christ, the ending evokes a spiritual power and poetic ambivalence which reverberate beyond the fallen curtain.

Were *Saint Joan* only a historical account, the play might well end at this point. Shaw, however, claimed that the Epilogue was necessary to show that Joan's history did not end with her martyrdom, but truly began with it.[23] While this sounds simplistic, its ramifications are not. Aesthetically, the Epilogue is a pastiche, primarily comic, serving to offset the grim clouds of the preceding scenes with a more dispassionate perspective. Beneath its levity is a fulfillment of a spiritual rhythm through a ghostly resurrection in which a divine force reasserts itself on mankind, producing a timeless spiritual lesson. As the play's concern is primarily with the interrelationship of the mundane and the spiritual, reflected in the tragicomic nature of man and the supernal nature of Joan, Shaw develops an allegorical pattern which calls for a broad symbolic resolution. The Epilogue effects this resolution, immortalizing the nature of Joan's relationship to man, forcing out its inner meaning and thereby propelling the modern audience into the center of the play's spiritual implications.

Most notably, the Epilogue dramatically refutes any comfortable notion that *now* man is spiritually more enlightened than were Joan's contemporaries. Man by nature is wisest in hindsight, lording over history in retrospect. The fact that now we make Joan a saint and put statues of her in cathedrals and in our city streets seems to speak for the superiority of our civilization. But the Epilogue graphically points up the persistence of mankind's mundanity. By canonizing and by erecting statues man sterilizes and crystallizes his saints, complimenting himself that in freezing them as symbols he is both paying proper homage and revealing his own state of grace. To the contrary, he thus by and large puts his saints out of the way through converting them to his own

23. See *Complete Plays*, II, preface, p. 315; "Program Note," pp. 430–31. Many critics have disagreed with Shaw. Reaction to the Epilogue has been sharply and almost evenly divided, from Kooistra and Irvine, who call it incongruous and unnecessary, to MacCarthy and Bentley, who call it congruous and integral.

terms. Joan was removed by her contemporaries through being immolated at the stake; she and her type are commonly removed by successive generations through being abstracted and revered, transformed into a spiritual concept and example, and consequently set in ice. Modern man, like medieval man, glories in his dead Joans who, were they living, might well upset his self-esteem, contradict his values, and endanger the status quo. In this light Shaw opens and closes the Epilogue with the rhetorical proposition of Joan's actual resurrection, a proposition followed by man's inevitable response. Charles comments: "If you could bring her back to life, they would burn her again within six months, for all their present adoration of her" (p. 416). This assertion states the central theme of the Epilogue, a theme which lurks ironically behind the universal praise of Joan—when all of the characters in turn kneel to her—and which emerges with pointed dramatic power, when, in response to the praise, Joan asks, "Shall I rise from the dead, and come back to you a living woman?" (p. 428). The notion is dramatically, psychologically, and spiritually overwhelming, and the answer, of course, is that man wants his Joans in *spirit*, where he can pay lip service to them as an ideal, where they will serve as a noble example both of and to humanity and as a hopeful indication of God, but where, thank God, man will not have to *live* with them. Thus the characters slink away muttering apologies, and Joan is left as isolated as she was at the end of Scene V— a symbol of the glory of God, tragically, sheepishly, repeatedly avoided by mundane man.

The distinction between theoretical and actual spirituality is drawn most poignantly in Stogumber. As a simple, direct exemplum revealing man's state, his significance rises above his limited nationalistic role to that of an Everyman. In the Epilogue he emerges as an aged, senile version of the broken man who provided the real climax of the play itself. Now a beloved rector who is able to do a little good, a kind man who would not harm a fly, Stogumber is portrayed touchingly and memorably through his drastic change from his former self. Unlike most of the others, his spiritual rejuvenation seems complete—not through Christ, who remains an abstraction, but through Joan, whose martyrdom was so intensely real: "Well, you see, I did a very cruel thing once because I did not know what cruelty was like. I had not seen it, you know. That is the great thing: you must see it. And then you are redeemed and saved." Cauchon's response touches the key of man's perennial spiritual tragedy, as it is represented in Stogumber: "Must then a Christ perish in torment in every age to save those that have no imagination?" (p. 423). The answer lies in the nature of man and in his potential to draw perceptively and creatively upon his own spiritual resources. In the interim, Joan's question, "How long, O Lord," is open-ended.

Were man to possess any great degree of imagination, Shaw's Epilogue would be unnecessary. But if Shaw had excluded it, his point would probably have been missed, since the total pattern would have been less clear. Shaw's contemporaries, no less than Joan's, had amply revealed their appalling lack of imagination. Modern man, tenaciously dense and worldly, by nature equally slow to think and quick to enshrine thoughtlessness, posed much the same problem for Shaw that medieval man did for Joan. The artist-reformer felt a certain kinship to the mystic-crusader in seeking to stimulate man's embryonic imagination to a deeper, braver, more spiritual understanding. The major difficulty was age-old: how to vitalize abstract spirit, how to render it meaningful so that it might provide both a new conscience for man and a new base for decisive action. The answer in both cases was similar: to objectify by symbols, to wed artistry to theory, concretion to abstraction, poetry to inspiration, since to truly understand is to truly see, and ideas take on most poignant reality as they are tested, strained, and mutated by life. Not unlike a crusading saint, the great dramatic artist seeks to move men by being spiritually memorable, and to be spiritually memorable is to be both transcendent in insight and accessible in parable: "That is the great thing: you must see it. And then you are redeemed and saved."

CHAPTER ELEVEN

AFTERWORD

Defining Shaw's Art

The skeptic who predicted that *Saint Joan* would not survive more than thirty years is himself outdated. The critics who at the turn of the century complained that Shaw could not write plays look curiously myopic and obsolete. After nearly eighty years Shaw's early works still play a major role in the popular and classical repertory. Clearly, Shaw will survive as a vital force on the stage for many years to come.

What accounts for this enduring popularity? And, more important, what qualities inform this popularity with an aesthetic depth and strength which are likely to confirm Shaw as a dramatist of classical standing? Answers to the first question emerge in abundance; answers to the second are more elusive and have been the primary concern of this study. There is a surface brilliance to Shaw's works which reflects a splendid, vigorous art. One can quickly cite the astonishing energy, wit, paradox, rhetoric, the great array and vitality of characters, the enduring relevance of issues which have *not* died with the Victorian age. The combination of such elements alone places Shaw among the great playwrights. But all these factors, distinguished as they are, are only obvious aspects of deeper aesthetic qualities which give Shaw his greatest stature and which can only fully be grasped by focusing on the plays as separate works of art.

Most simply stated, Shaw's best plays have a classical quality as they achieve the depth, complexity, economy, and coherence of fine dramatic poetry. In each there is a coalescence of many aesthetic factors which are not only individually evocative, but which, as they interact and fuse, give the particular work an impressively rich, vitally reverberating aesthetic soundness. Such factors, possessing the intrinsic power lying within most great art, expand as they are scrutinized and gain clarity and force as they are defined in specific contexts. It is important to study the plays individually, therefore, for many of the same obvious reasons that it is important to study poems individually. A considerable diversity in matter and method separate them. Each develops in a distinctive context and idiom, from domestic comedy and romance to social drama and epic tragicomedy, from farce and parody to irony and allegory. As there is a great range of subject matter, there is a great artistic flexibility responding to and projecting that matter, and in the interrelation of matter and manner lies the subtlest dimensions of Shaw's achievement. This can be defined in many ways; for convenience, one may approach it in terms of dramatic action, characterization, and a pervasive, cohesive poetic spirit.

Dramatic action in Shaw has been greatly underrated, usually on grounds that his plays frequently suspend incident for talk. Such criticism simplistically regards "things happening" on a physical level, consisting of a goodly number of occurrences which provide changing contexts and viewpoints. By fixating on Shaw's discursive passages it overlooks the more general truth that, with a few notable exceptions, Shaw's plays are packed with incident, especially if incident is defined as changing contexts, and that the most vibrant and profound action of Shavian drama exists in terms of multifold evolving tensions—tensions involving frame of reference, meaning, and character.

Frame of reference and meaning in the plays partake of dramatic action in several ways. First, they are vital in themselves, being informed not by a rigid context or attitude but by a highly energetic consciousness which is strongly concerned and vibrantly individualistic yet which moves and evolves, being more fluidly artistic and relativistic than fixed or static. Second, they are artistically keyed to grow naturally and vigorously out of contentious characters, thus wedding a sense of spontaneity to conceptual control. And third, as they gain life from characters, they in turn give the characters fuller dimension by challenging them with a substantive, vitally charged environment.)

Frame of reference, meaning, and action thus intertwine through structures in which individualistic and determined authorial control coalesces with vital, relativistic aesthetic factors. Structure is there, but working, complementary, supple, and viable. Behind the structure is the playwright, but in a far subtler role than the crude one which "Shavian mouthpiece" critics have allowed. Philosophical order is subordinate to poetically oriented development, existing in such structural devices as antithetical stances, crossing tensions, frequent anticlimaxes, and movements toward synthesis. These devices reveal the playwright's disposition through his artistic control, but they take on life primarily through intrinsic dramatic relationships and only secondarily through extrinsic authorial energy. Similarly, the force of these devices is augmented by an internal and external virtuosity of cross-reference, tightness of context, and economy of detail. Characters are unfolded, opposed, contrasted, paralleled, parodied, mythologized, and developed in criss-crossing evolutions in such a way as to form patterns, patterns with sufficient substance to provide a subliminal harmony and aesthetic balance—an evidence of the conceptualizing artist—while through their stress-filled components furthering, not compromising, the image of spontaneous life.

(This combination of individualistic authorial control and artistic, lifelike spontaneity comprises Shaw's personal mutation of the well-made play. Subliminal but intrinsic both to the meaning and the life of *Arms and the Man*, for instance, are the crossing evolutions of romance and reality in Raina and Bluntschli, with the central theme counterpointed, paralleled, and reinforced by the roles of Sergius, Nicola, and Louka. Similarly intrinsic to *Caesar and Cleopatra* is the juxtaposition of civilization and barbarism vigorously realized in the two principal characters, complemented by minor characters and by the contest of their societies. The vengeance theme informs the action, while the action reciprocally gives life to the theme. And in *Pygmalion* as the image of Eliza unfolds, the image of Higgins contracts, spiritual growth overwhelming spiritual stasis in a vital pattern which defines character and illuminates humanistic realities. Even *Heartbreak House*, with its expressionistic, associative progression, develops according to the opposition in the values of Heartbreak House and Horseback Hall, with Shotover serving as the moral focal point and Ellie as the aesthetic focal point. As a function of the theme, Ellie moves through the dialectical options of the play, illuminating them; as a human being, she grows in the process, illuminating herself. Such designs, woven with inevitable, mutually compromising, interlacing tensions, provide fabrics of aesthetic beauty, intellectual integrity, and dramatic power.

The tightness of context and economy of detail which typify these dramatic patterns are aspects which have been generally overlooked by critics of Shaw. Frequently, indeed, he has been detracted as verbose and redundant by those who choose to focus on such passages as the hell scene of *Man and Superman*, Scene IV of *Saint Joan*, or on the minor disquisitory plays. This criticism overlooks the special aesthetic qualities of these specific passages —a combination of orchestration, vital dialectic, and relevance to dramatic action elsewhere—and misses a close dramatic integration of details which is far more typical of Shaw. Hardly a speech, incident, or character in *Candida*, for instance, is wasted in the full development of the ambiguous triangle. And such characters as Burgess, Britannus, Straker, Doolittle, and Billy Dunn, as quirky as they might at first appear in their respective plays, offer eccentric relief and are all integral to major concerns of dramatic or thematic development. A pointed example of Shaw's economy and aesthetic discipline is his elimination (in the pre-cinema text) of what might be the triumphal climax of *Pygmalion*—the Ambassador's party scene. In terms of his exposition and character development such a scene is superfluous. As it is, each act, speech, and character in the play is functional in rounding out his portrayal of Eliza's growth, with its full social and spiritual meaning. In sum, to miss the relevance of a passage in one of Shaw's greater plays is frequently to miss an element which renders the whole aesthetic scheme richer and more complete.

Another aspect of Shaw's aesthetics which many critics have neglected is his sensitivity to visual effects, especially those involving irony when they are reflected against the action. From *Arms and the Man*'s prosaicism by starlight and high romance in the prosaic backyard, to *Saint Joan*'s knowledgeable and mocking pennon, settings, props, and lighting in the plays are frequently employed for unique effects. They are used not merely for atmosphere or background; they also partake, as it were, of the dramatic action. A director who fails to clearly represent Titian's "Virgin of the Assumption" in *Candida*, the cannon and dummy soldiers in *Major Barbara*, or the ship setting of *Heartbreak House* is missing a central aesthetic point. Less easy to avoid are the subtle, metaphoric uses of light and darkness in *Caesar and Cleopatra* and *Pygmalion*, the first evoking a distinction between civilizations, the second complementing mythical and spiritual patterns.

Also contributing to the action, influencing its organization, movement, and aesthetic conveyance, are tonal effects. Since Shaw himself called special attention to this element in his work, critics have been more responsive to it. Most obviously, they have noticed the scoring of certain scenes according to voices and ensemble groups. However, less attention has been paid to the music of his rhetoric, with its cadences, balances, and counterpoint, and few have caught the full musical subtlety of contrapuntal and antiphonal characters and themes in which allegory complements characterization in resonant orchestral effects. On the simplest level one can imagine a prosy *Candida*, but ideal direction would bring out the music of the play, casting a bass Burgess, baritone Morell, tenor Marchbanks, contralto Candida, and soprano Proserpine, with Lexy's tenor serving when Marchbanks is not present. On a far more complex level are the voices of Act IV in *Saint Joan*, where tonality is linked to personality and allegory, the simple trio of personalities being haunted by the concurrent orchestration of epic forces. In such contexts tonality becomes a matter not merely of sound but of aesthetic resonance, perspective, and meaning.

Another element of Shaw's dramatic action, one closely related to his complex structural tensions and his theatrical effects of setting and music, is his imaginative use of multiple genres or dramatic idioms. Striking first of all is the sheer number and variety of genres in his works, but most admirable is his ingenious employment of them, the manner in which he cross-circulates one with another in a fluid, generative process of compromise, qualification, definition, and mutual aesthetic enrichment. His combination of comedy and tragedy, farce and epic, problem play and romance, suggests but the beginning of a vast array of integrated contrarieties. Specific nineteenth-century dramatic genres there are aplenty. Deeper than these are more generic and universal aspects and qualities, widely disparate, skillfully melded. As these provide shifts in viewpoint, contrasts, or concurrent levels of awareness, they vitally influence the very assumptions and direction of the action.

Beyond a doubt, the most basic genre in Shaw is the morality play, with allegory and parable serving as attendant qualities or sometimes existing independently as sub-genres. The conventional description of Shaw as the author of "plays of ideas" tends to conceal this more traditional designation and to imply a largely new form and content. Rather, in the major plays discussed here, Shaw's allegorical form and moral content are at heart primally Christian, modified for the Darwinian death-of-God era. Shaw's innovation arises less from new spiritual impetuses and technical devices than from aesthetic and social sensibilities which are more complex than those of the old moralities. Vivie Warren, Don Juan, Barbara Undershaft, Eliza Doolittle, and Ellie Dunn are all morality characters as they struggle for their spiritual salvation, being set upon by devils of one sort or another. When one considers the devils, however—from Praed and Mendoza to Undershaft, Higgins, and Mangan—the aesthetic and social inventiveness of Shaw's use of the genre becomes clear. Contrary to the old moralities, abstractions usually do not flatten Shaw's characters but are an integral element of their roundness, and absolutes are not allowed to stand without a thorough qualification through personal and social ambiguities.

Diverging from the morality pattern, parable and allegory can by themselves be flexible tools in his hands. Androcles and Saint Joan, for example, combine allegorical characters, economy of statement, and an implicit search for spiritual realities, all of which are morality qualities. But these plays reach beyond the morality in special contexts. In Androcles a simple beast fable is transmuted into a parable of Christianity individual and collective, past and present. In Saint Joan a heroic legend is crafted into a many-sided, dramatically personalized, allegorical revelation of medieval institutions. In both plays allegory gives symbolic timelessness to history, Christian method fuses with Christian matter, and epic dimension accrues around details. Spiritual realities and history are thus linked, becoming mutually informative.

Shaw's spiritual proclivity for the morality play, intellectual proclivity for dialectic, dramatic proclivity for contention, and aesthetic proclivity for ambiguity lead him unabashed into numerous paradoxes which have caused some critics to be confused by an ostensible conflict in his genres. Just as he is a modernist with strong traditional roots, he is an aristocratic socialist, a pessimistic optimist, and a romantic realist. Such paradoxes may be clarified (though not resolved) by appreciating in Shaw an old-fashioned distinction between spirit and matter, the same distinction drawn by the moralities. Clearly in this context there are two realities in life—the spiritual or aspirational, and the mundane or humanly factual. To truly represent life, one must represent both—the spiritual compromised by the mundane, the mundane given hope and direction by the spiritual. Thus, as medieval moralities combined farce and earthy matter with their spiritual message, contrasting the profane and sublime while anchoring noble abstractions in a lifelike, down-to-earth dramatic idiom, Shaw juxtaposes and counterpoints heroic ideals with the mundane facts of life. Each can only be fully realized as it comes to terms with the other.

An essential Shavian genre, consequently, is realism. Even in his most socially and spiritually ambitious plays Shaw closely observes the fallibility of human nature, the absurdities of life, and the inevitability of anticlimax. Such observations are naturally consistent with a man who regarded himself, à la Ibsen, as a realist in a world of philistines and idealists, and who confidently referred to his 20–20 moral vision. To be credible, one's spiritual vision must not float free of life. Rather, it must engage life, and in the engagement be tested, chastised, and proven. Thus the austere morality of Vivie Warren is confronted with the human dynamics of her mother, the conflict rendering *Mrs Warren's Profession* an ambiguous, vital, and convincing play. And in kindred veins Bluntschli's efficacy and character are revealed against the hard facts of war, Caesar's great image is subjected to a close focus on his human fallibility, Don Juan the transcendent realist derives from Tanner the frustrated idealist, Tanner the idealist is mocked by society as Tanner the clown, and even Undershaft, the Prince of Darkness, needs a wife to straighten his tie. On a broader scale the anticlimaxes of *Pygmalion, Heartbreak House*, and *Saint Joan*, so essential to those plays, reveal that Shaw possesses no small degree of Chekhovian realism, finding some of the most interesting and significant moments of life after or between climaxes, when existence assumes a minor key.

A further Chekhovian, almost Brechtian, quality in Shavian realism moves it from the personal and spiritual realm to the social sphere, wherein vitally conceived individuals become ultimately less significant than the great social abstractions which move them. This holds true not just in the socially didactic *Mrs Warren's Profession*, but in nearly all the plays, comprising a central aspect of *Major Barbara, Pygmalion, Heartbreak House*, and *Saint Joan.* Personal fortune involves a limited realism, significant largely as it is representative and dramatically demonstrable, or as a single motif, sometimes major, sometimes minor, occasionally off-key, in a symphony. The harmony of the dramatic symphony depends on the fidelity of its parts; but if the second flutist drops dead, he is rapidly replaced. So it is, Shaw indicates, with life.

To complicate matters further, this personal and social realism, effective as it may be in linking Shaw's moral and spiritual vision to life, is caught in a fundamentally romantic aspect of his vision. In fact romance, paradoxically, could be called a major Shavian genre. Shaw ostensibly attacks it. Its insubstantiality is exposed in play after play. The romantic illusions of Raina, Sergius, March-banks, Octavius, Eliza, and Ellie Dunn are revealed as incapaci-tating them for life in the real world. They must grow out of such illusions or fade into irrelevance. But there is a romanticism which is relevant, even transcendent in Shaw: Mrs. Warren, Bluntschli, Caesar, Undershaft, Shotover, and Joan are all romantic figures, as the Life Force theory which informs them is a romancing with philosophy. The uniqueness of these characters is that in most cases their romance grows initially out of its antithesis—each is portrayed as possessing very human frailties, and each, except Joan, is firmly in touch with prosaic social realities. Such earthly perspective gains distinction through conjunction with a personal inner light which is joined to a vital, persistent motive power. It is this conjunction—a frankly acknowledged personal humanity, penetrating social realism, and independent, forceful idealism—which produces the strongest Shavian individualists and renders them especially fascinating dramatic portrayals. Their assertion of their inner light, reinforced by a personal credibility and realistic social view, is all part of a tough yet transcendently romantic rationale.

Complementing Shaw's romanticism is a quality of fantasy and myth which he employs so frequently that it almost could be de-fined as another major genre. It adds to his dramas overtones of fanciful universals, playful in the use of names, haunting in arche-typal images and patterns. Fantasy joins with allegory in such simple corollaries as candid for Candida, moral for Morell, bour-geois for Burgess, becoming more complex in the variously allusive meanings of Shotover, Mazzini Dunn, Mangan, and Hastings Utterwood, and yet more subtle in the implicit references lying within the name of Undershaft and the Emperor's designation in *Androcles* as "Defender of the Faith." It is evoked through animal imagery, where it serves as a poignant poetic shorthand, ranging from the tagging of Sir George Crofts as a bulldog and Mrs. War-ren as a sparrow, to the mythologizing of Ann Whitefield as a predatory beast (cat, lioness, grizzly bear, boa constrictor), and, further, ranging from a cultural distinction between the feline Egyptians and canine Romans in *Caesar and Cleopatra*, to the tour de force of *Androcles'* pantomime lion, which affects the whole aesthetic tone of that play. Beyond names and animal imagery, fantasy moves into myth, humorous in the fable of *Androcles*, wry in that perversion of Horatio Alger legend, Mrs. Warren, complexly evocative and functional in the converging myths of *Pygmalion*, Blakean in the diabolism of *Major Barbara*, magical in the Caesar-sphinx kinship, and sublimely ironic in the dramatic resurrection of Joan. As allegory broadens the context of so many of the plays, fantasy and myth enrich them, imparting delight and the fascination of familiar patterns newly molded, patterns transmuted in the furtherance of aesthetic distinctions.

Underlying Shaw's spectrum of genres is an authorial presence which is manifest more as a consciousness than as a voice, and which may best be described generically as expressionistic. Expressionism in Shaw exists most notably in ostensible dreams and dreamlike action, and in the occasional surfacing of a coherent consciousness or oversoul. The dreamlike idiom appears as early as *Caesar and Cleopatra*, becomes a major vehicle in *Man and Superman*, and virtually controls the action, characters, setting, allusions, and symbolic values of *Heartbreak House*. Beyond this, one might well argue that the drifting, associational, dreamlike patterns which are a success in *Heartbreak House* are a harbinger of less dramatically disciplined patterns in Shaw's later dramas. The authorial consciousness in the major plays is generally far more implicit than explicit, dwelling behind the action as a sharp quality of mind and opinion, a sensitive and probing disposition unfolding itself according to psychological, social, and symbolic values. As this disposition is deeply enmeshed in the dramatic medium, vitalizing and sharpening it in terms of many-faceted dramatic contexts, it is dispersed through a great diversity of characters and perspectives as more spirit than body, more mode than identity.

The authorial oversoul is most baldly present in Tanner, Juan, and Shotover, but even these characters function in such disparate roles as self-caricature, alter ego, and a combination of the two. Dramatically all three stand on their own as individual, sharply developed entities—indeed, their dramatic richness results in part from the coalescence of their double identity as bizarre Shavian counterparts and knocked-about fictional protagonists. Elsewhere the oversoul is far more obscure, more deeply integrated with drama, in such elements as structural patterning and the very diversity and contentiousness of characters which make for vital, thoughtful drama. For example, an authorial message no doubt surfaces in the Epilogue of *Saint Joan*, but it does so only in context, and only after it is made convincing by a severely disciplined dramatic development and the contention of realistic but carefully selected representative characters. Those who favor an absolutely neutral author may desire even less oversoul than this, but Shaw's intrusiveness has generally been oversimply attacked through being oversimply misrepresented. His presence lies more in an implicit energy than in an explicit voice; when it does express itself, it usually does so with a dramatic integration, vigor, and brilliance uniquely his. In its extreme it provides at times an expressionistic Strindbergian dimension to his plays, giving them a deeply personal sense of verisimilitude in which the dramatic medium experiences the subliminal excitement of a sensitive soul unwinding itself in art.

As dramatic action in Shaw takes on its special vitality via subtly evolving structural tensions, contentious characters, and elements of setting, lighting, and sound, it is subjected also to an implicit spectrum of viewpoints via a wide assortment of genres, various beams whose brightness and focus are in flux, each revealing a different sort of reality. Action in this latter sense is psychic action involving the dynamics of multiple, flexible shafts of illumination, providing a myriad of apperceptions regarding a given set of facts. Morality, allegory, and parable inform a twentieth-century realism which brings to mind at times Ibsen, at times Chekhov, a realism which frequently moves into or is overcast by a social view reminiscent of Brecht, but which interacts with a sense of delight in fantasy, a sense of mystery or archetype in myth, and a sense of dreamlike movement or subconscious control reminiscent of Strindberg. This multiplicity of perspectives might evoke a Pirandello-like quality—there is indeed some of that author's cerebral crispness—but it is generally less self-conscious than in Pirandello, less forced, arising intuitively more from a dramatic ethos than from intellectual preconception. Critics have tended to interpret Shaw's dramatic action narrowly because all too frequently they have viewed him in the abstract, through the lenses of his prefaces, pronouncements, and essays. His plays themselves contradict this narrow view, functioning as they do in such a wide, complex, sensitive, and vital range of action.

Informing this impressive range of action is an equally impressive range of characters, manifesting not only the greatest variety in one writer since those of Dickens, but the greatest psychic energy as well. One has but to touch on Shaw's gallery of remarkable women—Mrs. Warren, Candida, Cleopatra, Ann Whitefield, Barbara Undershaft, Eliza, Hesione, Joan—to exemplify the life, depth, and individuality, as well as the vibrant charisma, of his portrayals. And a brief selection of his minor characters (such as Sir George Crofts, Louka, Proserpine, Burgess, Britannus, Violet, Straker, Lady Britomart, Ferrovius, Doolittle, Mrs. Higgins, Mazzini Dunn, and the Dauphin) points up Shaw's imaginative fertility in characterization. Even his nonentities (such as Ptolemy, Mrs. Whitefield, and Charles Lomax) have poignant, convincing reality, revealing how effective Shaw can be with quick, suggestive strokes. Many of the characters may serve partly as voices for a dialectic, but this is usually turned to dramatic advantage, sharpening and vitalizing them as individuals. They seldom function primarily as living ideas; rather, living ideas within them make for distinctive personalities, and if a dialectic is furthered, it is generally furthered via personality in a most lifelike, ambiguous manner. A searching survey of Shaw's Life Force men and women, for instance, will more quickly point up their differences than their similarities. They may all be vital, but in significantly different ways. One must observe that certain Shavian characters move into the realm of the grotesque, though in fewer numbers than those of Dickens. Grotesqueness in Shaw usually bears marks of a heightening of reality, a dramatic step beyond verisimilitude serving to sharply etch a memorable character and to significantly qualify the action or to capture generic human truths lying behind surface mundanities. Such is the case, for example, with Sergius, Marchbanks, Britannus, and Doolittle.

A distinguishing aspect of the vitality of Shaw's characters lies in his sensitive projection of the multiple characteristics—or persons—which can exist within one human being. In each major character and most of the minor ones Shaw offers a distinctively clear, many-leveled study of the complexity of the individual psyche, showing it to exist somewhere in a tension between numerous roles, masks, personal games, identities, and personalities. Unless one approaches superhuman status where self has a mystic coherence, the idea of unitary man is a fiction, frequently a dangerous, dehumanizing one insofar as it categorizes life into melodramatic niches. Comically, Shaw defines this complexity most clearly in such cases as Sergius's absurd torment over his multiple images of himself, Ferrovius's struggle between Christian conviction and heathen impulse, and Mangan's despair at the unmasking games of Heartbreak House. Candida is perhaps most effective in this regard since its major characters so clearly unfold as a bundle of contradictions, each true in its light, and Saint Joan is most far-reaching because it focuses on the tragic monstrosity of those who surrender personal integrity for social or religious roles.

Shaw's sensitivity to such ambiguities of temperament and image in individual characters moves from a private to a public realm as the stresses of role-playing within the individual interact with the stresses of role-playing in society. The self is realized only as one's many personal images and masks contend with the diverse images fixed upon one by society, as well as with the images society fixes upon itself. Layers of subterfuge are mixed with layers of reality as the various characters function on numerous levels at the same time—personal, social, religious, political, archetypal. Most simply, parallel roles of the various characters develop on these levels according to parallel modes of action. For example, on a personal level Tanner is pursued by his childhood sweetheart, and romance is fulfilled when he is eventually captured. More complexly, on the other hand, various roles of the various characters are in infinite, subtle interaction. In this light Tanner is pursued not simply by Ann, but by an archetypal Life Force woman who exploits personal ties as well as social obligation and cosmic purpose. Against her machinations he employs personal, political, philosophical, and even cosmic defenses, but to no avail. In a similar way throughout all the plays private roles become enmeshed with public roles, both effecting mutual illuminations. This takes on clearest form in a fundamental problem which Shaw frequently poses—the failure of the individual to distinguish between an integrated individual consciousness, presumably a tension of viable roles, and certain static abstractions, usually a straitjacket of illusory but enduring conventions and images.

Shaw's complex art of character thus complements his complex art of action. Dramatically, characterization approached in this way is less likely to be didactic than profoundly human in foibles, contradictions, and qualifications. Conceptually, however, it has intriguing ramifications. On a primal level it is many-layered, according to multiple personal values, senses of self, and senses of other people. On a secondary level it is infinitely relative to the numerous levels of consciousness in the action and to the images which society seeks to impose upon it. Accordingly, character is constantly being judged in all the plays, its value or integrity being examined and illumined by a constant flux in point of view. Even the greatest Life Force figures—Caesar, Undershaft, and Joan—are first subject to their human fallibilities, and, upon sublimating these to a higher moral vision, are then subject to the incompatibility of their vision with the ubiquitous ignoble viewpoints of the world. Only as he is diabolical, grounding his ethic in ignoble realities, does Undershaft come off best. Clearly the real life of thought in Shaw derives predominantly from the variety, vitality, and many-faceted aspects of his characters thus revealed, set in an action of artistically thorough stresses and imaginatively diverse perspectives.

Finally, Shaw's plays achieve a poetic integration through a cohering factor which lies behind this vitally complex dramatic action and characterization. A unitive drive, which may be de-

scribed as a prevailing thrust for expansion of consciousness, constantly informs the motives, means, and ends of his works. This
drive has been oversimply interpreted by the consensus which
refers to Shaw's "plays of ideas." It is in fact tripartite. First and
foremost it is aesthetic; second, it is social; third, it is spiritual. On
all these levels it seeks ever greater understanding—a heightened
poetic sensitivity, a more penetrating social perspective, a firmly
founded aspiration of spirit. It is the common denominator of the
artist, social revolutionary, and mystic in Shaw and serves partly
to synthesize in him these three roles. Consciousness expands as
social realities are pierced by spiritual insights and as both are
ordered by an ultimate sense of poetic dissection, discretion, and
justice.

Shaw's primary idiom in his drive toward an expansion of consciousness is comedy. Comedy may be classified as another Shavian
genre, but in Shaw's hands its use is so basic, its spectrum so wide
and its ends so closely aligned with his intellectual and aesthetic
instincts that it underlies the other genres, serving a seminal function. Ironically, comedy is fundamental to the very seriousness of
Shaw, to the artist seeking to communicate an inner vision of
truth, a quintessential way of looking at the world. It is an element
which helps render Shaw the teacher-socialist-mystic primarily
poetic, dramatic, and intuitive, and only secondarily prosaic, didactic, and rational. For inner vision, noble as it may be, is irrelevant to life unless it is tested, and a true expansion of consciousness
can only be achieved when the poetic has been thoroughly subjected to the prosaic—when the two have, in fact, intermingled in
a mutual contest of essences which more frequently than not involves the deeper reaches of comedy. As Shaw's action partakes of
stress and his characters of contention, his underlying aesthetic-
social-spiritual vision partakes of contradiction, incongruity, and
paradox, thereby gaining perspective. Sometimes his optimism is
qualified by brutal and pessimistic human realities, as in *Caesar
and Cleopatra* and *Heartbreak House*, but more frequently its
soundness is subjected to humor in the disparity between noble
principle and ignoble life.

The special values of comedy for Shaw over other idioms, particularly over tragedy, are apparent in his specific uses of it. In his hands and for his purposes comedy offers the greatest flexibility and latitude. It most efficiently exposes humanity's foibles; it can also purge the pompousness which frequently obfuscates doctrine —the author's as well as the world's—and hence allow for a great freedom of mind, emotion, and perception. In Shaw comedy is a vehicle both for heightened intellectual awareness and for a sensitive, artistic immersion in the ambiguities of life. It is multidirectional, radiating (frequently all at once) toward the sweet, the bitter, the tender, the scathing, the saintly, the sardonic. In contrast, the somber vision of tragedy is less congenial to him insofar as it tends to be more emotional and obsessive, on the one hand elevating man with a dignity and stature which belie life's ubiquitous absurdities, while on the other hand dashing man down with a despair which belies life's hope. Further, tragic tradition tends to throw the blame for man's misery onto some nebulous Fate or fates (except, perhaps, as it posits a limited personal failing), to the relative neglect of multiple human and social flaws which Shaw finds more relevant to life. Tragedy's reputed purgations seem to Shaw more vague and less universal than purgation through laughter which stimulates understanding; its potential for self-knowledge and regeneration seem to him more accessible through comedy; and the tragic vision seems more apt as a prelude to suicide than a precursor to living life more abundantly—an abundant life, on as many levels as possible, being for Shaw the only tenable rationale for existence. In short, tragedy tends to inflate humanity and turn it toward dead ends, while comedy deflates humanity and in the process leaves room for new, more fertile growth. Shaw by no means avoids tragedy—it lurks profoundly within the seriousness from which his comedy springs. But tragedy in itself is no aesthetic end for him, since deformity and illusion can so easily develop in its darkness, and Shaw is seeking, with a nearly mystical fervor, a healthy reality manifesting hope.

Shaw's great comic spectrum results in large part from his conviction that comedy is the most efficient key for the unlocking of consciousness, comedy's irreverence and iconoclasm pricking bloated abstractions and emotion, opening the senses to greater perspectives and higher levels of awareness. The breadth and depth of his comic focus is testimony to this conviction. His plays and portions of them vary from high to low comedy, romantic comedy to social comedy, comedy of manners to comedy of humors. From farce and Bergsonian laughter to irony and tragicomedy, his control is firm, imaginative, and brilliant. On the broadest level of farce, for example, is Ann's pursuit of Tanner, a pursuit whose comic effect lies not merely in the classical inversion of sexual and social roles but in its spectacular objectification, materially as Ann commandeers a twentieth-century machine for the chase, metaphysically as she is a vital integer in a cosmic speculation, fulfilling her Life Force function. Farce vibrates here on multiple planes of delight—sexual, social, mechanical, historical, and metaphysical.

More sophisticated is Shaw's varied use of Bergsonian man-as-machine humor. In ascending degrees of complexity are Ptolemy, who is wound up by his mentors like a miniature talking robot; Eliza, who as Higgins's Cinderella doll can barely suppress her curbstone idiom; Sergius and Tanner, both victims of biological drives and mental fixations; and Vivie, Bluntschli, and Higgins, described respectively, with considerable metaphoric aptness, as a steam-roller, machine, and motorbus. Most profound aspects of Bergsonian humor are evidenced by those characters in whom the individual has become an automaton through surrendering his soul to an abstraction. Ominous cases are those of Mangan, Stogumber, Undershaft, and the Inquisitor, the first two nudging a farcical black humor, the latter two caught in most subtle ironies as they appreciate humane reality but coldly violate it under the aegis of dehumanizing institutions. Such examples point up a fundamental qualification of Bergson which Shaw's sense of humor makes. Bergson wrote with Molière as his model, and consequently found the comic laugh to be directed at the errant individual who mechanically pursued his unsocial ways into eccentricity and estrangement from the norm: laughter in this context supports the social consensus. Shaw most typically does exactly the opposite. He supports the individual in all his lack of sociability, occasionally enjoying his falls, as in Tanner's *faux pas*, but in the long run extolling as marks of genius the insights and courage of the nonconformist. In people such as Caesar and Joan the hope of the world resides. Conversely, the social norm and its slaves are truly the mechanical factors of life, fit for derision and possibly not a little compassion, since their comic automatism is the result of myopia and cowardice and accounts for so many of the world's tragedies.

Complementing Shaw's spectrum of Bergsonian humor, and employed with an equally great range, is his much celebrated, vibrant element of wit. To Shaw's credit, his wit exists less in devices, tricks, and epigrams of the Oscar Wilde variety than in character and dramatic structure. Witty detail abounds, such as in the inversions of words, concepts, and characters in Act III of *Man and Superman*—a cleverness so abundant that it can conceal the weakness of the total argument. But more interesting is the wit of caricatures such as Britannus, originals such as Doolittle, and the very conception of character which pokes, shakes, and shatters stereotypes. In character Shavian wit runs the gamut from the simplicity of Androcles to the complexity of Caesar, including the flaccid, the assertive, the gentle, the ferocious, the normal, the grotesque—so rich a variety that it beggars brief listing. And wit of character joins that of structure as parody moves both inside and outside the plays, in such debased internal parallels as those Violet and Hector offer of Ann and Tanner, or as Lucius Septimius offers of Caesar, and in such external references as Shaw to Tanner and Shotover, or religious melodrama to *Androcles*. Structurally, wit prevails in sudden shifts of context which so poignantly reveal the characters, in the enjambment of incident and allusion and in the juxtaposition of various levels of meaning, from the sexual puns and *double-entendres* of *Candida* to the orchestral wit of *Saint Joan*. Finally, there is an overviewing wit, a wit of total conception, such as in *Pygmalion*, where the comedy evolves step by step from a humor of confusion in Act I to a humor in Act V which seeks order and understanding, and in *Saint Joan*, where the comic spirit of Scenes I through III is leavened by the sober countermovement of Scenes IV through VI, with the

Epilogue tenuously managing a compromise. Most bizarre is the wit of *Androcles*, in which an aesthetic tautness between the absurdity of the clown lion and the grim realities of Christian martyrdom suspends horror in laughter. The fact that tragedy is just around the corner makes the laughter more boisterous, because at heart it is a trifle frantic.

Frantic laughter is haunted laughter and is but one mode of Shaw's most ambiguous comic sensibility, tragicomedy. When the ironies of life take on the bitterness of self-deception, cruelty to others, or disastrous moral directions, Shaw moves toward tragedy, but generally his tragedy is qualified by the fundamental absurdity or multiple tiny absurdities which are involved in anything inimical to the welfare of man. Tragedy and absurdity in Shaw go hand in hand as they reflect life caught in the emotional and mundane. Conversely, comedy and seriousness go hand in hand as they seek intellectual and spiritual direction. Tragedy's intense seriousness can be comical when it is too self-conscious or too densely obsessive and somber regarding the importance of worldly things, while comedy's humor can be serious when its perspective encompasses both the ignobility of the flesh and the nobility of man's spiritual potential. As the broad view must encompass the narrow, as spirit encompasses flesh, a tragic sub-strain is by definition an integral part of the whole. And while this substrain may have less reality for Shaw, there are times, especially if flesh constrains spirit, when its ascendancy can be deeply troubling.

To each side of the well-lighted stage there is darkness in the wings, and after the show the lights go out. Shaw's comedy, so sensitive to space and time, incorporates an awareness of such realities at some of the moments when it is having the most fun. At the comic climax of truth in *Arms and the Man*, for example, Bluntschli tells about his wounded friend being burned alive in a woodyard; in a kindred vein, Caesar, after playing with Cleopatra at the lighthouse, stops her short with the admonition that her head is not worth the hand of one of his soldiers, and though the play ends with Caesar's triumph, it is haunted by the somber ghost of his forthcoming assassination. In the very laughter of

Heartbreak House lies despair, and in the very comedy of Joan's rise lies the tragedy of her end, just as in the ridiculousness of her petty persecutors and in the comedy of their automatism lies the tragedy of their emptiness of soul. In such instances comedy and tragedy coalesce, becoming part of a compassionate overview. Salvation may lie in values personal, Promethean, and spiritual, while damnation results from values socially mindless, traditional, and mundane. One is the way of saints, the other the way of the world. But in such terms the temporal tragedy of saints is their spiritual comedy, while the temporal comedy of man is his spiritual tragedy. At its finest, Shaw's tragicomic perception encompasses the alternate implications.

Shaw's plays thus qualify the criticism that his total vision is restricted because his comic propensities prevail over seriously dramatic or tragic insight. There can be no doubt that wit, vigor, and optimism are fundamental to Shaw, and one may choose to find such factors delimiting if one sympathizes with Yeats's dream of him: "Presently I had a nightmare that I was haunted by a sewing-machine that clicked and shone, but the incredible thing was that the machine smiled, smiled perpetually."[1] Certainly in Shavian drama there is more mind than viscera, more energetic verbalizing than understatement, more of the civilized drawing-room than the sensate, emotional reaches of the human psyche. But such qualities are virtues, vices, or limitations depending on how one looks at them. In many ways Shaw's virtues are his vices —or his vices are his virtues—in a paradox appropriate to his talents. Basically, he is a playwright who vigorously seeks the values of true civilization, and though his search engages barbarism, it chooses not to focus on the animal side of man. To Shaw, fascination with such subject matter involves a degradation of spirit, a negation of what is worthwhile in humanity, and is worse than a waste of time. He aims, rather, at elevation of spirit, fine discriminations as to what is humanly admirable, time well spent. This aspirational spirit informs the drive for an expansion of consciousness which underlies each of his works, unifying and

1. W. B. Yeats, *Autobiographies* (London, 1955), p. 283.

ennobling them. It is a spirit which Yeats fails to appreciate, perhaps because he fails to see the poet in Shaw.

The aesthetics of Shaw's plays apparently need to be closely defined in order to counter facile misappraisals as well as critical neglect. These aesthetics involve the power of a distinctive dramatic poetry which emerges from a coherence of strongly realized elements, most basic of which are the following. First, the plays have a structural soundness, life, and beauty in multifold tensions which are woven in stress and cohere in patterns. Second, they have a visual subtlety in effects which contribute to action and meaning via a discrete use of settings, props, tableaux, and lighting. Third, they partake of a musical idiom in tonal qualities ranging from fine rhetoric, to ensembles of varied voices, to symphonic allegory. Fourth, they employ the psychic action of disparate genres operating concurrently, offering differing views of reality. Fifth, they benefit from the dramatic complexity and depth of a great variety of characters wrought on multiple personal, social, religious, political, and archetypal levels. These levels are sharply dramatized and intersect with the multiple generic views of the action, producing an interaction which offers a great spectrum of perspectives. And sixth, the plays reveal an impressively fertile, sensitively probing breadth and depth of comic perception, ranging from farce to tragedy, interpenetrating all levels of character, structure, and concept. The heart of Shaw's dramatic poetry lies in the coalescence of these factors, effected with economy, tightness, ambiguity, and basically stimulated and integrated by his constant impetus toward an expansion of consciousness.

Although there is nothing new in the observation that Shaw is primarily an artist, there is much yet to be said about the art of Shaw's drama. As this art involves a coherence of so many subtle and complex aesthetic factors, clearly a primary way to approach it is through its own specific contexts, the individual plays. Each major play is an aesthetic unit significant both for its uniqueness, which indicates the flexibility and scope of the Shavian idiom, and for its particular artistic resonance, which sounds forth the depth of the Shavian talent. Considered cumulatively, the plays reveal Shaw most deeply as an aesthetician whose artistic, social, and philosophical goals merge in a prevailing desire for poetic proportion, poetic justice, and poetic aspiration. Like his Caesar, he approached life as an art, to be explored on as many planes and from as many viewpoints as possible. He scorned art for its own sake but found its greater qualities central to civilization, and thus he wrote with unflagging vigor. For if, as Caesar remarks, civilization is an art, one who seeks to civilize is pursuing the highest aesthetic ends.

BIBLIOGRAPHY

Adams, Elsie B. "Bernard Shaw's Pre-Raphaelite Drama." *PMLA*, 81 (1966), 428–38.

Adler, Jacob H. "Ibsen, Shaw, and *Candida*." *Journal of English and Germanic Philology*, 59 (1960), 50–58.

Albert, Sidney P. "Bernard Shaw: The Artist as Philosopher." *Journal of Aesthetics and Art Criticism*, 14 (1956), 419–38.

———. " 'In More Ways Than One': *Major Barbara's* Debt to Gilbert Murray." *Educational Theatre Journal*, 20 (1968), 123–40.

———. " 'Letters of Fire against the Sky': Bodger's Soul and Shaw's Pub." *Shaw Review*, 11 (1968), 82–98.

———. "More Shaw Advice to the Players of *Major Barbara*." *Theatre Survey*, 11 (1970), 66–85.

———. "The Price of Salvation: Moral Economics in *Major Barbara*." *Modern Drama*, 14 (1971), 307–23.

———. "Shaw's Advice to the Players of *Major Barbara*." *Theatre Survey*, 10 (1969), 1–17.

Archer, William. *The Theatrical "World" of 1893–1897*. 5 vols. London: Scott, 1894–98.

Auden, W. H. "The Fabian Figaro." *George Bernard Shaw: A Critical Survey*. Ed. Louis Kronenberger. Cleveland: World, 1953, pp. 153–57.

Austin, Don. "Comedy through Tragedy: Dramatic Structure in *Saint Joan.*" *Shaw Review,* 8 (1965), 52–62.

―――. "Dramatic Structure in *Caesar and Cleopatra.*" *California Shavian,* 3 (Sept.–Oct. 1962), no pagination.

Bab, Julius. *Bernard Shaw.* Berlin: Fischer, 1926.

Barnet, Sylvan. "Bernard Shaw on Tragedy." PMLA, 71 (1956), 888–99.

Barnett, Gene A. "Don Juan's Hell." *Ball State University Forum,* 11, no. 2 (1970), 47–52.

Beerbohm, Max. "A Cursory Conspectus of G. B. S." *George Bernard Shaw: A Critical Survey.* Ed. Louis Kronenberger. Cleveland: World, 1953, pp. 3–6.

Bentley, Eric. *Bernard Shaw 1856–1950.* Amended ed. New York: Laughlin, 1957.

―――. "My Fair Lady." *Shavian,* 1, no. 13 (1958), 3.

―――. *The Playwright as Thinker: A Study of Drama in Modern Times.* New York: Meridian, 1955.

Bergson, Henri. *Creative Evolution.* Trans. Arthur Mitchell. New York: Holt, 1911.

―――. *An Introduction to Metaphysics.* Trans. T. E. Hulme. New York: Putnam's, 1912.

―――. "Laughter." *Comedy.* Ed. Wylie Sypher. New York: Doubleday, 1956, pp. 59–190.

―――. *Time and Free Will.* Trans. F. L. Pogson. London: Allen, 1910.

Blanch, Robert J. "The Myth of Don Juan in *Man and Superman.*" *Revue des Langues Vivantes,* 33 (1967), 158–63.

Blankenagel, John C. "Shaw's *Saint Joan* and Schiller's *Jungfrau von Orleans.*" *Journal of English and Germanic Philology,* 25 (1926), 379–92.

Boas, Frederick S. "Joan of Arc in Shakespeare, Schiller, and Shaw." *Shakespeare Quarterly,* 2 (1951), 35–45.

Bowman, David H. "Shaw, Stead and the Undershaft Tradition." *Shaw Review,* 14 (1971), 29–32.

Braybrooke, Patrick. *The Genius of Bernard Shaw.* Philadelphia: Lippincott, 1925.

―――. *The Subtlety of Bernard Shaw.* London: Palmer, 1930.

Brodeur, Arthur. "Androcles and the Lion." *Gayley Anniversary Papers* (1922), 195–213.

Brower, Reuben A. *Major British Writers II.* New York: Harcourt, 1959.

Brown, Ivor. *Shaw in His Time.* London: Nelson, 1965.

Brown, John Mason. "The Prophet and the Maid." *Saturday Review,* 27 Oct. 1951, pp. 27–29.

————. "Straight from the Lion's Mouth." *Saturday Review,* 11 Jan. 1947, pp. 24–27.

Brustein, Robert. *The Theatre of Revolt: An Approach to the Modern Drama.* Boston: Little, 1964.

Buckland, J. H. "Saint Joan." *History,* 9, no. 36 (1925), 273–87.

Bullough, Geoffrey. "Literary Relations of Shaw's Mrs. Warren." *Philological Quarterly,* 41 (1962), 339–58.

Burton, Richard. *Bernard Shaw: The Man and the Mask.* New York: Holt, 1916.

Cardozo, J. L. "Saint Joan Once More." *English Studies,* 9 (1927), 177–84.

Carpenter, Charles A. *Bernard Shaw & the Art of Destroying Ideals: The Early Plays.* Madison: University of Wisconsin Press, 1969.

————. "Notes on Some Obscurities in 'The Revolutionist's Handbook.'" *Shaw Review,* 13 (1970), 59–64.

Chesterton, G. K. *George Bernard Shaw.* Dramabook ed. New York: Hill, 1956.

Clurman, Harold. "Notes for a Production of *Heartbreak House*." *Tulane Drama Review,* 5 (1961), 58–67.

Colbourne, Maurice. *The Real Bernard Shaw.* New York: Philosophical Library, 1949.

Coleman, D. C. "Fun and Games: Two Pictures of *Heartbreak House*." *Drama Survey,* 5 (1967), 223–36.

Collis, John Stewart. *Shaw.* London: Cape, 1925.

Corrigan, Robert W. "*Heartbreak House*: Shaw's Elegy for Europe." *Shaw Review,* 2, no. 3 (1959), 2–6.

Costello, Donald P. *The Serpent's Eye: Shaw and the Cinema.* Notre Dame: Notre Dame University Press, 1960.

Couchman, Gordon W. "*Antony and Cleopatra* and the Subjective Convention." *PMLA,* 76 (1961), 420–25.

————. "Comic Catharsis in *Caesar and Cleopatra.*" *Shaw Review*, 3, no. 1 (1960), 11–14.

————. "The First Playbill of *Caesar*: Shaw's List of Authorities." *Shaw Review*, 13 (1970), 79–82.

————. "Here Was a Caesar: Shaw's Comedy Today." *PMLA*, 62 (1957), 272–85.

————. "Shaw, *Caesar*, and the Critics." *Speech Monographs*, 23 (1956), 262–71.

Crane, Milton. "*Pygmalion*: Bernard Shaw's Dramatic Theory and Practice." *PMLA*, 66 (1951), 879–85.

Crompton, Louis. *Shaw the Dramatist.* Lincoln: University of Nebraska Press, 1969.

D'Arcy, M. C. "Bernard Shaw's St. Joan." *Month*, August 1926, pp. 97–105.

Demaray, John G. "Bernard Shaw and C. E. M. Joad: The Adventures of Two Puritans in Their Search for God." *PMLA*, 78 (1963), 262–70.

Drew, Arnold. "*Pygmalion* and *Pickwick*." *Notes and Queries*, 200 (1955), 221–22.

Dickson, Ronald J. "The Diabolonian Characters in Shaw's Plays." *University of Kansas City Review*, 26 (1959), 145–51.

Duerkson, Roland A. "Shelley and Shaw." *PMLA*, 78 (1963), 114–27.

Duffin, Henry C. *The Quintessence of Bernard Shaw.* London: Allen, 1920.

Dukore, Bernard F. *Bernard Shaw, Director.* Seattle: University of Washington Press, 1971.

————. "The Fabian and the Freudian." *Shavian*, 2, no. 4 (1961), 8–11.

————. " 'The Middleaged Bully and the Girl of Eighteen': The Ending They *Didn't* Film." *Shaw Review*, 14 (1971), 102–6.

————. "The Undershaft Maxims." *Modern Drama*, 9 (1966), 90–100.

Elliott, Robert C. "Shaw's Captain Bluntschli: A Latter-Day Falstaff." *Modern Language Notes*, 67 (1952), 461–64.

Ervine, St. John. *Bernard Shaw: His Life, Work and Friends.* New York: Morrow, 1956.

Fergusson, Francis. *The Idea of a Theater.* Anchor Books ed. New York: Doubleday, 1953.

Fielden, John. "Shaw's *Saint Joan* as Tragedy." *Twentieth Century Literature,* 3, no. 2 (1957), 59–67.

Frank, Joseph. "*Major Barbara*—Shaw's 'Divine Comedy.'" *PMLA,* 71 (1956), 61–74.

———. "Take It Off! Take It Off!" (*Heartbreak House*). *Shaw Review,* 13 (1970), 10–13.

Frankel, Charles. "Efficient Power and Inefficient Virtue (Bernard Shaw: *Major Barbara*)." *Great Moral Dilemmas in Literature Past and Present.* Ed. Robert M. MacIver. New York: Harper, 1956, pp. 15–23.

Fuller, Edmund. *G. B. S.: Critic of Western Morale.* New York: Scribner's, 1950.

Furlong, William B. *Shaw and Chesterton: The Metaphysical Jesters.* University Park: Pennsylvania State University Press, 1970.

Ganz, Arthur. "The Ascent to Heaven: A Shavian Pattern (Early Plays, 1894–1898)." *Modern Drama,* 14 (1971), 253–63.

Gatch, Katherine Haynes. "The Last Plays of Bernard Shaw: Dialectic and Despair." *English Stage Comedy.* Ed. W. K. Wimsatt. New York: Columbia University Press, 1955, pp. 126–47.

Gerould, Daniel C. "*Saint Joan* in Paris." *Shaw Review,* 7 (1964), 11–23.

Gilkes, A. N. "Candour about Candida." *Fortnightly,* NS 171 (1952), 122–27.

Golding, Henry J. "Bernard Shaw and His Saint Joan." *Standard,* November 1924, pp. 83–87.

Grecco, Stephen. "Vivie Warren's Profession: A New Look at *Mrs Warren's Profession.*" *Shaw Review,* 10 (1967), 93–99.

Green, Paul. *Dramatic Heritage.* New York: French, 1953.

Griffin, Alice. "The New York Critics and *Saint Joan.*" *Shaw Bulletin,* 1, no. 1 (1955), 10–15.

Hamon, Augustin. *The Twentieth Century Molière: Bernard Shaw.* Trans. Eden and Cedar Paul. New York: Stokes, 1916.

Harrison, G. B., ed. *Julius Caesar in Shakespeare, Shaw and the Ancients.* New York: Harcourt, 1960.

Harvey, Robert C. "How Shavian Is the *Pygmalion* We Teach?" *English Journal*, 59 (1970), 1234–38.

Hausler, Franz. "*Androcles*: Shaw's Fable Play." Trans. Felix F. Strauss. *Shaw Bulletin*, 1, no. 2 (1954), 8–9.

Henderson, Archibald. *Bernard Shaw: Playboy and Prophet*. New York: Appleton, 1932.

———. *George Bernard Shaw: His Life and Works*. Cincinnati: Steward, 1911.

———. *George Bernard Shaw: Man of the Century*. New York: Appleton, 1956.

Holt, Charles L. "*Candida*: The Music of Ideas." *Shaw Review*, 9 (1966), 2–14.

———. "Mozart, Shaw and *Man and Superman*." *Shaw Review*, 9 (1966), 102–16.

Hornby, Richard. "The Symbolic Action of *Heartbreak House*." *Drama Survey*, 7 (1968–69), 5–24.

Howe, Percival P. *Bernard Shaw: A Critical Study*. London: Seeker, 1914.

Hoy, Cyrus. "Shaw's Tragicomic Irony." *Virginia Quarterly Review*, 47 (1971), 56–78.

Huggett, Richard. *The First Night of "Pygmalion."* London: Faber, 1970.

Hugo, Leon. *Bernard Shaw: Playwright and Preacher*. London: Methuen, 1971.

Huneker, James. "The Quintessence of Shaw." *George Bernard Shaw: A Critical Survey*. Ed. Louis Kronenberger. Cleveland: World, 1953, pp. 7–25.

Irvine, William. "*Man and Superman*, a Step in Shavian Disillusionment." *Huntington Library Quarterly*, 10 (1947), 209–24.

———. *The Universe of G. B. S.* New York: Whittlesey, 1949.

Jacobson, Sol. "Androcles in Hollywood." *Theatre Arts*, December 1952, pp. 66–69.

Joad, C. E. M. *Shaw*. London: Gollancz, 1949.

———. "Shaw the Philosopher." *Shaw and Society: An Anthology and a Symposium*. Ed. C. E. M. Joad. London: Odhams, 1951.

Johnston, Sir Harry. *Mrs. Warren's Daughter: A Story of the Women's Movement*. New York: Macmillan, 1920.

Jones, Doris Arthur. *Taking the Curtain Call: The Life and Letters of Henry Arthur Jones.* New York: Macmillan, 1930.

Jordan, Robert J. "Theme and Character in *Major Barbara.*" *Texas Studies in Language and Literature,* 12 (1970), 471–80.

Kaufman, Michael W. "The Dissonance of Dialectic: Shaw's *Heartbreak House.*" *Shaw Review,* 13 (1970), 2–9.

Kaye, Julian B. *Bernard Shaw and the Nineteenth-Century Tradition.* Norman: University of Oklahoma Press, 1958.

King, Walter N. "The Rhetoric of *Candida.*" *Modern Drama,* 2 (1959), 71–83.

Kooistra, J. "*Saint Joan.*" *English Studies,* 7 (1925), 11–18.

Kozelka, Paul. "*Heartbreak House* Reviewed." *Shaw Review,* 3, no. 1 (1960), 38–39.

Kronenberger, Louis, ed. *George Bernard Shaw: A Critical Survey.* Cleveland: World, 1953.

———. *The Thread of Laughter.* New York: Knopf, 1952.

Krutch, Joseph Wood. "A Review of *Candida.*" *A Casebook on "Candida."* Ed. Stephen S. Stanton. New York: Crowell, 1962, pp. 212–14.

Langner, Lawrence. *G. B. S. and the Lunatic.* London: Hutchinson, 1964.

Larson, Gale K. "*Caesar and Cleopatra*: The Making of a History Play." *Shaw Review,* 14 (1971), 73–89.

Lauter, Paul. "*Candida* and *Pygmalion*: Shaw's Subversion of Stereotypes." *Shaw Review,* 3, no. 3 (1960), 14–19.

Leary, Daniel J. "Dialectical Action in *Major Barbara.*" *Shaw Review,* 12 (1969), 46–58.

———. "The Moral Dialectic in *Caesar and Cleopatra.*" *Shaw Review,* 5 (1962), 42–53.

———. "Shaw's Use of Stylized Characters and Speech in *Man and Superman.*" *Modern Drama,* 5 (1963), 477–90.

Lerner, Alan Jay. "*Pygmalion* and *My Fair Lady.*" *Shaw Bulletin,* 1, no. 10 (1956), 4–7.

Levi, Albert William. *Philosophy and the Modern World.* Bloomington: Indiana University Press, 1959.

Levy, Benn W. "Shaw the Dramatist." *Shaw and Society: An An-*

thology and a Symposium. Ed. C. E. M. Joad. London: Odhams, 1951.

Lüdeke, H. "Some Remarks on Shaw's History Plays." *English Studies,* 36 (1955), 239–46.

MacCarthy, Desmond. *The Court Theatre, 1904–1907: A Commentary and Criticism.* London: Bullen, 1907.

———. *Shaw's Plays in Review.* New York: Thames, 1951.

McCabe, Joseph. *George Bernard Shaw: A Critical Study.* London: Paul, 1914.

McCollom, William G. *The Divine Average: A View of Comedy.* Cleveland: Press of Case Western Reserve University, 1971.

McDowell, Frederick P. W. "Heaven, Hell, and Turn-of-the-Century London: Reflections upon Shaw's *Man and Superman.*" *Drama Survey,* 2 (1963), 245–68.

———. "Technique, Symbol, and Theme in *Heartbreak House.*" *PMLA,* 68 (1953), 335–56.

McKee, Irving. "Shaw's *Saint Joan* and the American Critics." *Shavian,* 2, no. 8 (1964), 13–16.

Macksoud, S. John, and Altman, Ross. "Voices in Opposition: A Burkeian Rhetoric of *Saint Joan.*" *Quarterly Journal of Speech,* 57 (1971), 140–46.

Manchester, William. *The Arms of Krupp 1587–1968.* Boston: Little, 1968.

Mander, Raymond, and Mitchenson, Joe. *Theatrical Companion to Shaw.* London: Rockliff, 1954.

Mann, Thomas. " 'He Was Mankind's Friend.' " *George Bernard Shaw: A Critical Survey.* Ed. Louis Kronenberger. Cleveland: World, 1953, pp. 250–57.

Martz, Louis. "The Saint as Tragic Hero: *Saint Joan* and *Murder in the Cathedral.*" *Tragic Themes in Western Literature.* Ed. Cleanth Brooks. New Haven: Yale University Press, 1956, pp. 150–78.

Matlaw, Myron. "The Dénouement of *Pygmalion.*" *Modern Drama,* 1 (1958), 29–34.

———. "Will Higgins Marry Eliza?" *Shavian,* 1, no. 12 (1958), 14–19. Repeats material of preceding entry.

Mayne, Fred. *The Wit and Satire of Bernard Shaw.* New York: St. Martin's, 1967.

Meisel, Martin. *Shaw and the Nineteenth-Century Theater.* Princeton: Princeton University Press, 1963.

Meister, Charles W. "Comparative Drama: Chekhov, Shaw, Odets." *Poet Lore,* 55 (1950), 249–57.

Mencken, Henry L. *George Bernard Shaw: His Plays.* Boston: Luce, 1905.

Mendelsohn, Michael J. "The Heartbreak Houses of Shaw and Chekhov." *Shaw Review,* 6 (1963), 89–95.

Meredith, George. "An Essay on Comedy." *Comedy.* Ed. Wylie Sypher. New York: Doubleday, 1956, pp. 1–57.

Mills, Carl Henry. "*Man and Superman* and the Don Juan Legend." *Comparative Literature,* 19 (1967), 216–25.

———. "Shaw's Debt to Lester Ward in *Man and Superman.*" *Shaw Review,* 14 (1971), 2–13.

———. "Shaw's Superman: A Re-examination." *Shaw Review,* 13 (1970), 48–58.

Mills, John A. *Language and Laughter: Comic Diction in the Plays of Bernard Shaw.* Tucson: University of Arizona Press, 1969.

Mizener, Arthur. "Poetic Drama and the Well-Made Play." *English Institute Essays: 1949.* New York: AMS Press, 1965, pp. 33–54.

Morgan, Margery M. *The Shavian Playground: An Exploration of the Art of George Bernard Shaw.* London: Methuen, 1972.

Nethercot, Arthur H. *Men and Supermen: The Shavian Portrait Gallery.* 2nd ed., corrected. New York, Blom, 1966. 1st ed. Cambridge: Harvard University Press, 1954.

———. "*Mrs Warren's Profession* and *The Second Mrs. Tanqueray.*" *Shaw Review,* 13 (1970), 26–28.

———. "The Truth about *Candida.*" *PMLA,* 64 (1949), 639–47. Included, revised, in *Men and Supermen.*

———. "Zeppelins over *Heartbreak House.*" *Shaw Review,* 9 (1966), 46–51.

Nietzsche, Friedrich. *The Works of Friedrich Nietzsche.* Ed. Alexander Tille. Vol. X: *A Genealogy of Morals.* Trans. William A. Haussmann. New York: Macmillan, 1924.

Noyes, E. S. "A Note on *Peregrine Pickle* and *Pygmalion.*" *Modern Language Notes,* 41 (1926), 327–30.

O'Donnell, Norbert F. "The Conflict of Wills in Shaw's Tragicomedy." *Modern Drama*, 4 (1962), 413–25.

———. "On the 'Unpleasantness' of *Pygmalion*." *Shaw Bulletin*, 1, no. 2 (1955), 7–10.

Ohmann, Richard M. *Shaw: The Style and the Man*. Middletown, Conn.: Wesleyan University Press, 1962.

Ovid. *The Metamorphoses of Ovid*. Trans. A. E. Watts. Berkeley: University of California Press, 1954.

Ozy. "The Dramatist's Dilemma. An Interpretation of *Major Barbara*." *Shaw Bulletin*, 2, no. 1 (1958), 18–24.

Pearson, Hesketh. *G. B. S.: A Full Length Portrait*. New York: Harper, 1942. Reprinted as *George Bernard Shaw: His Life and Personality*. New York: Atheneum, 1963.

———. "The Origin of *Androcles and the Lion*." *Listener*, 48 (1952), 803–4.

——— ."A Shavian Musical." *Shavian*, 1, no. 13 (1958), 4–6.

Perrault, Charles. *The Authentic Mother Goose Fairy Tales and Nursery Rhymes*. Eds. Jacques Barchilon and Henry Pettit. Denver: Swallow, 1960.

Pirandello, Luigi. "Bernard Shaw's *Saint Joan*." *Shavian*, 2, no. 8 (1964), 6–12. Reprinted from the *New York Times Magazine*, 13 January 1924.

Purdom, C. B. *A Guide to the Plays of Bernard Shaw*. New York: Crowell, 1963.

Quinn, Michael. "Form and Intention: A Negative View of *Arms and the Man*." *Critical Quarterly*, 5 (1963), 148–54.

Rattray, Robert F. *Bernard Shaw: A Chronicle*. London: Leagrave, 1951.

———. "The Subconscious and Shaw." *Quarterly Review*, 291 (1953), 210–22.

Reardon, Joan. "*Caesar and Cleopatra* and the Commedia dell'Arte." *Shaw Review*, 14 (1971), 120–36.

Reed, Robert R. "Boss Mangan, Peer Gynt, and *Heartbreak House*." *Shaw Review*, 2, no. 1 (1959), 6–12.

Reinert, Otto. "Old History and New: Anachronism in *Caesar and Cleopatra*." *Modern Drama*, 3 (1961), 37–41.

Richardson, Henry B. "The Pygmalion Reaction." *Psychoanalytic Review*, 43 (1956), 458–60.

Riding, George A. "The *Candida* Secret." *A Casebook on "Candida."* Ed. Stephen S. Stanton. New York: Crowell, 1962, pp. 166–69.

Robertson, J. M. *Mr. Shaw and "The Maid."* London: Cobden-Sanderson, 1925.

Rosenblood, Norman, ed. *Shaw: Seven Critical Essays.* Toronto: University of Toronto Press, 1971.

Roy, Emil. "*Pygmalion* Revisited." *Ball State University Forum*, 11, no. 2 (1970), 38–46.

Rudman, Harry W. "Shaw's *Saint Joan* and Motion Picture Censorship." *Shaw Bulletin*, 2, no. 3 (1958), 1–14.

Sarolea, Charles. "Has Mr. Shaw Understood Joan of Arc?" *English Review*, 43 (1926), 175–82.

Schuchter, J. D. "Shaw's *Major Barbara*." *Explicator*, 28, no. 9 (1970), item 74.

Scott, Dixon. "The Innocence of Bernard Shaw." *George Bernard Shaw: A Critical Survey.* Ed. Louis Kronenberger. Cleveland: World, 1953, pp. 72–104.

Sen Gupta, S. C. *The Art of Bernard Shaw.* London: Oxford University Press, 1936.

Shaw, George Bernard. *Advice to a Young Critic and Other Letters.* Ed. E. J. West. New York: Capricorn, 1963.

———. *Arms and the Man.* Ed. Louis Crompton. New York: Bobbs-Merrill, 1969.

———. *Collected Letters 1874–1897.* Ed. Dan H. Laurence. New York: Dodd, 1965.

———. *Complete Plays with Prefaces.* New York: Dodd, 1963.

———. *Ellen Terry and Bernard Shaw: A Correspondence.* Ed. Christopher St. John. New York: Putnam's, 1932.

———. *Florence Farr, Bernard Shaw, W. B. Yeats: Letters.* Ed. Clifford Bax. New York: Dodd, 1942.

———. *The Intelligent Woman's Guide to Socialism and Capitalism.* New York: Brentano's, 1928.

———. "Letter to James Huneker." (April 1904). Reprinted in *A Casebook on "Candida."* Ed. Stephen S. Stanton. New York: Crowell, 1962, pp. 165–66.

————. *The Perfect Wagnerite: A Commentary on the Niblung's Ring.* New York: Brentano's, 1916.

————. "The Play of Ideas." *New Statesman and Nation,* NS 39 (1950), 510–11.

————. *The Religious Speeches of Bernard Shaw.* Ed. Warren S. Smith. University Park: Pennsylvania State University Press, 1963.

————. *Saint Joan.* Ed. Stanley Weintraub. New York: Bobbs-Merrill, 1971.

————. *Shaw on Theatre.* Ed. E. J. West. Dramabook ed. New York: Hill, 1959.

————. *Sixteen Self Sketches.* New York: Dodd, 1949.

————. *Standard Edition of the Works of Bernard Shaw.* 37 vols. London: Constable, 1930–1950.

Solomon, Stanley J. "The Ending of *Pygmalion*: A Structural View." *Educational Theatre Journal,* 16 (1964), 59–63.

————. "*Saint Joan* as Epic Tragedy." *Modern Drama,* 6 (1964), 437–49.

Spender, Stephen. "The Riddle of Shaw." *George Bernard Shaw: A Critical Survey.* Ed. Louis Kronenberger. Cleveland: World, 1953, pp. 236–39.

Spink, Judith B. "The Image of the Artist in the Plays of Bernard Shaw." *Shaw Review,* 6 (1963), 82–88.

Stamm, Julian L. "Shaw's *Man and Superman*: His Struggle for Sublimation." *American Imago,* 22 (1965), 250–54.

Stanton, Stephen. *A Casebook on "Candida."* New York: Crowell, 1962.

————. "Shaw's Debt to Scribe." *PMLA,* 76 (1961), 575–85.

Stewart, J. I. M. *Eight Modern Writers.* Oxford: Oxford University Press, 1963.

Stockholder, Fred E. "Shaw's Drawing-Room Hell: A Reading of *Man and Superman*." *Shaw Review,* 11 (1968), 42–51.

Stoppel, Hans. "Shaw and Sainthood." *English Studies,* 36 (1955), 49–63.

Strauss, Emil. *Bernard Shaw: Art and Socialism.* London: Gollancz, 1942.

Thompson, Alan R. *The Dry Mock: A Study of Irony in Drama.* Berkeley: University of California Press, 1948.

Tittle, Walter. "Mr. Bernard Shaw Talks about *Saint Joan.*" *Bookman*, 67 (1924), 143–44.

Tyson, Brian F. "Shaw among the Actors: Theatrical Additions to *Plays Unpleasant.*" *Modern Drama*, 14 (1971), 264–75.

Underhill, Evelyn. *Mysticism.* New York: Noonday, 1955. Original ed., London: Methuen, 1912.

Ure, Peter. "Master and Pupil in Bernard Shaw." *Essays in Criticism*, 19 (1969), 119–39.

Ussher, Arland. *Three Great Irishmen: Shaw, Yeats, Joyce.* New York: Devin-Adair, 1953.

van Kan, J. "Bernard Shaw's *Saint Joan*: An Historical Point of View." *Fortnightly Review*, July 1925, pp. 37–45.

Wainger, Bertrand M. "Henry Sweet—Shaw's *Pygmalion.*" *Studies in Philology*, 27 (1930), 558–72.

Walkley, Arthur Bingham. Review of *Arms and the Man*. *Speaker*, 9 (1894), 471–72.

Ward, A. C. *Bernard Shaw.* London: Longmans, 1951.

Watson, Barbara Bellow. "Sainthood for Millionaires: *Major Barbara.*" *Modern Drama*, 11 (1968), 227–44.

————. *A Shavian Guide to the Intelligent Woman.* London: Chatto, 1964.

Webster, Grant. "Smollett and Shaw: A Note on a Source for *Heartbreak House.*" *Shaw Review*, 4, no. 3 (1961), 16–17.

Weintraub, Stanley. "Bernard Shaw's Other Saint Joan." *South Atlantic Quarterly*, 64 (1965), 194–205.

————. " 'Shaw's Divine Comedy': Addendum." *Shaw Bulletin*, 2, no. 2 (1958), 21–22.

————. "Shaw's Lear" (*Heartbreak House*). *Ariel*, 1, no. 3 (1970), 59–68.

————. "Shaw's Mommsenite Caesar." *Anglo-German and American-German Crosscurrents*, II. Eds. Philip A. Shelley and Arthur O. Lewis, Jr. Chapel Hill: University of North Carolina Press, 1962, pp. 257–72.

Wellwarth, George E. "Mrs. Warren Comes to America; or, the Blue-Noses, the Politicians and the Procurers." *Shaw Review*, 2, no. 2 (1959), 8–16.

West, Alick. "A Good Man Fallen among Fabians." London: Lawrence, 1950.

West, E. J. " 'Arma Virumque' Shaw Did Not Sing." Colorado Quarterly, 1 (1953), 267–80.

―――. "Hollywood and Mr. Shaw: Some Reflections on Shavian Drama-into-Cinema." Educational Theatre Journal, 5 (1953), 220–32.

―――. "Saint Joan: A Modern Classic Reconsidered." Quarterly Journal of Speech, 40 (1954), 249–59.

Whitehead, George. Bernard Shaw Explained: A Critical Exposition of the Shavian Religion. London: Watts, 1925.

Williamson, Audrey. Bernard Shaw: Man and Writer. New York: Crowell, 1963.

Wilson, Edmund. "Bernard Shaw at Eighty." George Bernard Shaw: A Critical Survey. Ed. Louis Kronenberger. Cleveland: World, 1953, pp. 126–52.

Wisenthal, J. L. "The Cosmology of Man and Superman." Modern Drama, 14 (1971), 298–306.

Woodbridge, Homer E. George Bernard Shaw: Creative Artist. Carbondale: Southern Illinois University Press, 1963.

Yeats, William Butler. Autobiographies. London: Macmillan, 1955.

Young, Stark. "Heartbreak Houses." George Bernard Shaw: A Critical Survey. Ed. Louis Kronenberger. Cleveland: World, 1953, pp. 232–35.

―――. Immortal Shadows: A Book of Dramatic Criticism. New York: Scribner's, 1948.

Zimbardo, Rose A., ed. Twentieth Century Interpretations of "Major Barbara": A Collection of Critical Essays. Englewood Cliffs, N.J.: Prentice-Hall, 1970.

INDEX

Acting: seriousness in *Arms and the Man*, 23; importance to *Candida*, 43–44, 47n; in *Heartbreak House*, 225n; role of Joan, 276n

Action: dreamlike in *Caesar and Cleopatra*, 82–83; enveloping sense of, in *Caesar and Cleopatra*, 90; of social contentions in *Man and Superman*, 120–21; via Ann's instinct, 125; dreamlike in *Heartbreak House*, 225–26; and setting in *Heartbreak House*, 238–39; vitalizes allegory in *Saint Joan*, 266; multiple levels of, 294–304; art of, 306; stress in, 307

Actors: and reality, 243n

Adler, Jacob H., 66n

Age of Reason, 203

Age-youth dichotomy. *See* Youth-age dichotomy

Albee, Edward: *Who's Afraid of Virginia Woolf?*, 235n

Albert, Sidney P., 103n, 160n, 168n

Alger, Horatio, 212, 302

Allegory: complements characterization, 12, 297; versus realistic level in *Mrs Warren's Profession*, 13, 15; power of Undershaft as, 167; in *Androcles*, 182; in *Pygmalion*, 204; in *Heartbreak House*, 250–51, 252–53; in *Saint Joan*, 260, 265–67, 269; hu-manized by characters, 277; music of, 283–84; of medieval Catholicism, 286; as sub-genre, 298, 299; in names and images, 301–2; broadens context of the plays, 302; mentioned, 294, 303, 313. *See also* Morality play; Parable

Anachronism: of god Ra, 87; of Britannus, 89–90; validity of, 94; in *Caesar and Cleopatra*, 95; revealing Christian mentality, 194; of setting in *Heartbreak House*, 239; in *Saint Joan*, 261–62, 263

Analogy. *See* Christ

Andrew Undershaft's Profession, 159

Androcles and the Lion: genres in, 175–77, 193–95; fable of, 177–78; parody of Christian melodrama, 179–80; parable of Christianity, 180–93; types of Christians in, 181–86; nature of orthodoxy, 186–89; modern relevance, 189–93; mentioned, 299, 301, 302, 304, 305, 310

Animal imagery: humans represented via, 13, 18, 110, 114, 119, 123; function in *Caesar and Cleopatra*, 89; cross-reference of, 120; cartoon effect in *Androcles*, 177–78, 180; as poetic shorthand, 301–2; ambiguous humor in *Androcles*, 311

"*This book is clearly the product of an original and penetrating critical mind. It is written with verve, incisiveness, and often with wit.*" — Arthur H. Nethercot, Northwestern University.

BERNARD SHAW AND THE ART OF DRAMA

Charles A. Berst

The poet in Shaw, holds Charles A. Berst, reaches beyond the philosopher. Yet there have been few critical studies of Shaw as a dramatic poet whose individual plays are distinctive works of art. The bulk of scholarly writing on Shaw has been of a biographical, philosophical, or generalized nature, and his plays are most often seen as "plays of ideas," despite Shaw's observation that "people's ideas are not the true stuff of drama, which is always the naïve feeling underlying the ideas." Shaw described his dramas as "plays of life, character, and human destiny like those of Shakespear or Euripides."

In a critical analysis of ten of Shaw's most important plays, Berst emphasizes the artistic talents that make Shaw the greatest English playwright since Shakespeare. By exploring Shaw's ideas in the framework of his art, Berst demonstrates that Shaw is a greater dramatic artist than philosopher or social theorist. He examines *Mrs Warren's Profession, Arms and the Man, Candida, Caesar and Cleopatra, Man and Superman, Major Barbara, Androcles and the Lion, Pygmalion, Heartbreak House,* and *Saint*

continued back flap